Table of Contents

Part I

Part II

Contributions by academic, business and other professionals about the causes of the clash between Globalism and Populism and ideas to allay its effects and close the Digital Divide. The 24 contributors are distinguished professionals from 21 countries, including one each from most of the top twenty economies in the world by volume of GDP. They provide both a global perspective and with regards to the country where they are from and/or where they have developed their careers.

Acknowledgements

When I began to question my unwavering support for unfettered free markets as a result of the beginning of the global financial crisis in 2007-2008, I reached out to Bernat Montagut, a former student at Pompeu Fabra University, with the idea of a brief chronology of the XXth century and a deeper description and analysis of the 2007-2010 period conducted through a conversation with a resurrected Karl Marx. Given capitalism's apparent crisis as venerable banks went bankrupt (Lehman Brothers and others) or were nationalized in 2007-08, I submitted the idea in a brief conversation to Timothy Garton Ash, one of the world's foremost historians and political scientists. He liked it. I used Karl Marx as a sparring partner. Despite Communism's utter failure, the resurrected Karl Marx failed again to understand that restricting freedoms can never be accepted in the pursuit to empower the weaker and poorer. As Albert Camus told Jean-Paul Sartre when they fell out, we must strive for social justice. It is an open question as to whether we may someday achieve it or not. But Camus warned Sartre -- and all of us -- that any attempt to attain social justice at the expense of basic freedoms is doomed to fail. Hence, in my *Conversations with Marx*, the resurrected Karl Marx teamed up with Hugo Chávez and Vladimir Putin, while I presented my proposals on how to improve and reform capitalism by making it more ethical, social and environmentally sustainable.

Àngels, Lluís, Bernat and I worked feverishly in the middle of 2010 and managed to publish "Conversations with Marx: Dialogues about a more ethical capitalism" without having a single meeting while I served as speechwriter and assistant (working 15-hour days) to the president of the World Bank and lived in Washington, D.C. I took my first five days off as speechwriter to the president of the World Bank in October of 2010 to fly to Barcelona. I met Àngels and Lluís at the presentation of the book. It was presented at the prestigious SEBAP institution in Barcelona by Miquel Roca Junyent, one of the founders of the Spanish Constitution and a leading reformist politician in Catalonia and Spain who now heads an international law firm.

Aresta subsequently published my *Ethical Capitalism: What it can do for you*, an updated (to March 2011) English version of *Conversations with Marx*. The presentation took place at the Spanish Embassy in Washington, D.C. in June of 2011. Aresta again accepted my proposal to describe and analyze the economy's recovery from the Great Recession (2011 to 2015), on this occasion through a conversation with a resurrected John Maynard Keynes. Almost all governments (even the Germans!) and international institutions embraced Keynesian policies to some degree to spur the economic recovery after the financial crisis and the Great Recession. I had the thankless task in my sixth book, titled *Of Bureaucrats, Politicians and Statesmen: How to Right-Size the American Dream* of questioning Keynes' refusal to entertain the notion that stimulus must be coupled with austerity and structural reforms in the wake of the mountains of debt incurred by governments, businesses and families.

I have deep gratitude for Professor Horst Teltschik, one of the most decisive officials who negotiated German unification, for authoring the foreword to this book, as he did for my previous one. I also am very grateful to all of the professionals and distinguished professionals from over twenty countries who have taken time to provide input for the second part of the book.

I would be remiss in not thanking the many people who work for or live in the Brookside Community in Oxon Hill, Maryland, where I have been living since November of 2013. The

Bonangelino family has stood by me in good times and bad, and they are the closest thing I have to a family in Washington, D.C. Honeybelle Torres has been a source of support since June of 2018.

In the many hours I have spent by myself in the condominium at the Brookside Community in the past five years, CNN has continued to be the closest things to a roommate. Its fearless and idealistic international correspondents (Nic Robertson, Karl Penhaul, Diana Magnay, Arwa Damon, among many) risk their lives to bring us live reporting from conflict- and disease-ridden countries. I am sometimes tempted to switch to MSNBC or Fox most of the time to get an alternative point of view. But I quickly realize that the former has a left-wing bias, whereas the latter represents a very conservative ideology. I eventually return to CNN, comfortably reassured that its anchors and senior analysts – Chris Cuomo, Brooke Baldwin, Wolf Blitzer, Erin Burnett, Anderson Cooper, Don Lemon, Richard Quest, Fareed Zakharia, Jake Tapper, John King, Jim Sciutto, Dana Bash, Jeff Toobin -- are not only outstanding journalists and professionals who ask tough questions and ensure fairness in the coverage of any story. They are also individuals who passionately search for the truth, influence events and highlight the plight of the weakest and those who cannot speak out for themselves. It may seem odd that I have devoted an entire paragraph lavishing praise on CNN (US and International), but in the past years I have spent more hours with CNN turned on while I work and do other things in my condo than with any individual.

I want to also pay tribute and express my deepest gratitude to the women and men of the armed forces of the United States and all democracies. Open societies, as Karl Popper warned, have many enemies and can be vulnerable to scheming and ruthless dictators who seek to divide and conquer us. It is worth highlighting that there is no example in history of two democracies that have waged a war with one another. The Cod Wars between the UK and Iceland (the only possible exception) over fishing rights featured some shooting and ramming of vessels but did not claim a single life. We must therefore be vigilant and strengthen the institutions that underpin democracy, foster civil society, combat populism and demagogues and manage to lure the disenchanted back into the fold.

I am not giving up on my quest to join the US Army or the National Guard as a linguist and thus serve the United States in this capacity. The United States is still the Shining City on a Hill that president Ronald Reagan so eloquently and optimistically spoke about. I am in no way a militarist and hope that there will never be another war in Europe in my lifetime. But Russian President Vladmir Putin's hostile activities since 2014 must be monitored and checked. He has ordered the annexation of Crimea, armed and funded separatist rebels in eastern Ukraine, ordered the killings of prominent anti-Putin voices (Boris Nemtsov) and former Russian spies (Alexander Litvinenko), and almost assassinated Segei Skripol and his daughter in the UK with a nerve agent only manufactured in Russia. Putin has also jailed hundreds of members of the opposition and the press, and routinely orders his security forces to arrest some of the thousands who still dare to take to the streets to protest his crony dictatorship. Putin is extremely smart and tough and is regarded as one of the richest and most powerful men in the world. And his disinformation and election-meddling in Western democracies is unacceptable. Several FSB officers have been indicted in the US for their interference in the US's 2016 presidential election.

I have traveled to and stayed in Russia on many occasions since my first visit in 1993, and even delivered conferences in Moscow, St. Petersburg and Saratov. I speak reasonably good Russian. I would not feel safe entering Russia today as a civilian and speaking my mind.

Unfortunately, I did cover as a journalist the wars spawned by the violent break-up of Yugoslavia in the 1990s. They killed approximately 133,000 people, displaced millions and reduced thriving and harmonious societies and cities to war-ravaged and ethnically separated communities. But at least NATO and the United States managed to stop the ethnic cleansing, and the post-Yugoslav states are either already in the European Union (Slovenia, Croatia), negotiating their accession (Montenegro, Serbia), ready to begin negotiations (Former Yugoslav Republic of Macedonia) or stabilized candidates that someday will join the EU (Bosnia-Herzegovina and Kosovo).

In my view, the presidents of the US from the XXth century who embodied idealism, strength and intelligence and changed America and the world for the better are Theodore Roosevelt, Woodrow Wilson, Franklin D. Roosevelt, Dwight Eisenhower, John F. Kennedy, Lyndon B. Johnson, Ronald Reagan, George H.W. Bush (whose is very frail and whose wife passed away in April of 2018) and Bill Clinton. President Obama heads the list of such presidents in the XXIst century. I lived in the US during six of his eight years in office and very much miss his intelligence, acumen, steady stewardship of the world's greatest power, motivation to empower the weaker and inspiring oratory.

I would include Harry Truman in this list if he had not fired one of the US's most brilliant, courageous and intelligent generals, Douglas MacArthur, who obviously could have finished off the Chinese in 1950 if Truman had not dismissed him. MacArthur was not allowed to engage in hot pursuit of Chinese planes in Korea that flew back into Manchuria. The Joint Chiefs of Staff also rejected his request to bomb the airfields in Manchuria. And they even gave him the absurd order that he could only bomb the southern part of the bridges spanning the Yalu river, the border between North Korea and China. History has vindicated MacArthur, one of only five five-star generals in US Army history to have attained the rank of General of the Army.

When Truman, the Joint Chiefs of Staff (JCS) and other members (UK) of the UN multinational force commanded by MacArthur panicked over the prospect of World War III, neither North Korea nor China had nuclear weapons. The Soviet Union had a rudimentary nuclear arsenal. The Soviet Union would not have set off a nuclear bomb in western Europe in 1950 or early 1951 if MacArthur had been granted his very logical and targeted requests. US nuclear superiority over the USSR was overwhelming in 1950. MacArthur was not trying to conquer China, rather project force so its forces would leave the Korean peninsula. Truman and the JCS were considering using tactical nuclear weapons while tying MacArthur's hands behind his back with these ridiculous rules of engagement. And MacArthur opposed the dropping of nuclear bombs in Hiroshima and Nagasaki.

Sixty-eight years later, the US West Coast has to shudder at the thought that North Korea will be able to launch an ICBM with nuclear warheads within a couple of years, and Japan and South Korea are within easy range of Kim Jong Un's nuclear arsenal. China and Russia continue to not only tolerate North Korea's attempts to reunify the island under Communism, but actually support them. There are many other US generals from the second half of the XXth century who have passed away whom I greatly admire. In my view, a ranking that combines military and political achievements should be the following: George Marshall, FDR's military right hand and driving force behind the plan that bears his name that helped rebuild Western Europe after World War II; Dwight Eisenhower, the brilliant and balanced supreme allied commander for the Normandy landings and the rest of the war in Europe. Omar Bradley, the GI General and first Chairman of the Joint Chiefs of Staff. Admiral Chester Nimitz, whose military prowess allowed the Navy to team up with the Army and US Air Force to liberate the Pacific and Asia from Imperial

Japanese barbarism. General Lucian Truscott, the neglected and self-effacing man rated by Eisenhower as his second-best commander after Patton. General George Patton, the pioneer of mobile warfare and the best tank commander in history. Among the living, I need to at least list General Colin Powell, who also served as Chairman of the Joint Chiefs of Staff and Secretary of State, and Wesley Clark, supreme Allied Commander of NATO, and others whose names I do not have enough space to mention.

But the real heroes in any war the US has waged are the young soldiers who have died or die or are injured fighting in the front lines to defend democracy, defeat fascism, abolish slavery or assure independence from the United Kingdom. As Eisenhower told his Chief of Staff, General Bedell Smith, the real heroes were the 416,800 US soldiers and officers who died to defeat fascism, ensure the survival of democracy and deal an almost fatal blow to racialism. Few people who are not military historians know that the US was the third country among the Allies with the highest number of military fatalities in World War II (416,800), barely edged out by Yugoslavia and obviously paling in comparison to the eight to ten million Soviet military fatalities. But the cause of the much higher Soviet figure can partly be attributed to Stalin's pact with Hitler in 1939 and his disregard for repeated warnings from British intelligence that Hitler would turn on him and attack the Soviet Union in the summer of 1941.

There are generals, admirals or lower-ranking officers from the US and other Western countries I also admire. They are Australian General Thomas Blamey, RAF Air Chief Marshall Sir Trafford Leigh-Mallory (UK), Major General Roy Urquhart (UK), Lieutenant General Brian Horrocks (UK), Lt. Colonel John Frost (UK), Brigadier General John Gavin (US), Major General Maxwell Taylor (minus his role in the Cuban missile crisis), Major Julian Cook (US) and General Stanislaw Sosabowski (Poland). It is obvious that I am going a bridge too far. The epic and star-studded Hollywood movie that depicts the ill-conceived Operation Market Garden (General Montgomery's idea) is a reminder that wars or any kind of undertaking must carefully ponder the risks against possible benefits involved when putting civilian and military lives or assets in harm's way.

The 1977 film A *Bridge Too Far* starred, employed or had cameo appearances by many officers and soldiers from both sides who were involved in Operation Market Garden, as well as thousands of Dutch civilians. It is impossible to run into a Dutch person who does not have some friend or relative that was cast as an extra in the movie, or at least knows about the brave but ultimately failed attempt to capture the bridge at Arnhem. The famous phrase -- A bridge too far -- is attributed to British Lieutenant General Frederick Browning, who supposedly told General Bernard Montgomery that trying to seize the bridge at Arnhem in addition to those at Eindhoven and Nijmegen on the Rhine was going a bridge too far.

Bernard Montgomery is one of the most overrated generals of the XXth century, whose greatest achievement was holding his own in northern Africa against Erwin Rommel's Afrika Corps until the US forces under Patton delivered the final blow that expelled the Nazis from northern Africa. Montgomery was a megalomaniac and obsessive Methodist who was always more worried about his own glory than boldly attacking the enemy. And his relentless pressure on Eisenhower to authorize a dagger thrust into the heart of Germany (the Ruhr) during the months that preceded the Normandy landings was compounded by his inability to seize Caen until six days after D-Day. Montgomery unfortunately managed to convince Churchill and FDR to execute the very poorly planned Operation Market Garden. It dropped 35,000 Allied troops behind German enemy lines against intelligence reports that proved that the Nazis had crack SS units and not just old men and Hitler Youth in the Netherlands in the fall of 1944. The British lost 8,000 troops when Market

Garden failed. And a *bridge too far* has become an English expression that warns against the dangers of trying to bite off more than you can chew.

In case I am going a bridge too far with this book, it is something I hope will be forgiven! I seek solutions, along with the 22 distinguished professionals who have written contributions in the second part of the book, to the clash between globalism and nativism. Finding and applying measures that close the economic and digital divide may help to slow populism and bring people together in an era when many forces are generating deeper chasms. Above all, I hope this book is regarded as an attempt to describe specific policies and ways to strengthen the bonds among the constituencies of free and open societies, thus also setting an example for those that are not. I hope the reader will deem this pursuit a worthy and noble endeavor.

Oxon Hill, Maryland. September 29, 2018

About the Author

Alexandre Muns Rubiol is a Professor at OBS Business School and EAE Business School, writer, consultant, editor, and regular contributor to media, specifically to the Spanish newspapers Cinco Días, El Periódico, Economía Digital and La Razón, as well as to Spanish radio stations and TV channels. He has served as Speechwriter and Assistant to three presidents of multilateral development banks: to the President of the European Bank for Reconstruction and Development in London (1998-99), and to the President of the World Bank Group and to the President of the Inter-American Development Bank in Washington, D.C. (2009-2011).

Alexandre has also served as Head of the CIDOB Foundation's (Spain's second think-tank) Europe Program, Director of Studies of the American Chamber of Commerce in Spain and Director of International Relations at Barcelona-Catalonia Logistics Center.

Alexandre has been a professor at several Spanish universities since 1997. He has taught or teaches courses on European Integration, International Economic Institutions, International Economics, European Economics, Culture & Business, Integration and International Economic Environment, Regional Economic Environment and International Trade Management in Europe at the undergraduate and graduate level at Pompeu Fabra University (1997-98, 1999-2009, 2011-2013), International University of Catalonia (2008-2009), Rovira i Virgili University (2004), ESADE Business School (2008-2009) and at OBS Business School since February of 2017.

Alexandre has authored books on the break-up of the USSR (in Spanish, "De la perestroika a la CEI"), the post 9/11 world order and U.S. Foreign Policy (in Spanish, ¿USA, Quo Vadis?), German reunification (*The End of the Cold War: German Reunification*), the global economic crisis ("Conversaciones con Marx: Diálogos en torno a un liberalismo ético" and *Ethical Capitalism: What it can do for you)* and the post-BRICS challenges of Technological Competitiveness, Inequality, Ageing of the Population and Energy Security (*Of Bureaucrats, Politicians and Statesmen: How to Right-Size the American Dream*). Since 1992, he has also published about 300 articles in the main Spanish and Catalan newspapers and newsmagazines on international and national economic, political and security topics, as well as several academic articles. He is a frequent analyst on international, European, U.S. and transatlantic affairs on Spanish and Catalan radio and TV.

He has been a consultant for the Spanish bank Bankpyme, to the Catalan government (in 2000-01 and 2012), and for the Spanish government in a development project in Equatorial Guinea and another related to Spain's presidency of the European Union in the first half of 2010.

Alexandre holds a degree in Geography and History and a PhD in Contemporary History from the University of Barcelona. His doctoral thesis versed on the international negotiations that enabled German reunification in 1989-90.

Foreword by Professor Horst Teltschik

Born in 1940, Horst Teltschik studied Political Science, History and International Law at Berlin's Free University from 1962 to 1967. In 1972, the then President of the German Land of Rhineland-Palatinate, Helmut Kohl, chose Teltschik as his chief of staff. He was promoted to head the office of the president of the CDU/CSU parliamentary group in Rhineland-Palatinate's Parliament in 1977. When Helmut Kohl became Chancellor of Germany in 1982, he appointed Teltschik to the position of deputy director of the federal chancellery. For eight years, Teltschik was one of Chancellor Kohl's closest advisers, effectively serving as his national-security adviser. In 1989-90, he played a key role in successfully and swiftly negotiating the conditions for Germany's reunification with the four wartime allies that still held rights over Germany (US, USSR, United Kingdom and France). His discreet diplomacy enabled him to win the trust of both the George H.W. Bush administration as well as that of Mikhail Gorbachev and his top aides. Other than Helmut Kohl himself, Teltschik was probably the German politician that exerted the most influence and displayed more skill during the 2+4 negotiations that secured German reunification.

Teltschik turned to the business world and served from 1993 until 2000 as a member of the board of BMW. From 1993 until 2003 he was president of the Herbert Quandt Foundation, and from 2002 to 2010 held a senior position on the board of Roche. He combined these activities with teaching at the Technical University of Munich, where he became a professor in 2003.

Teltschik headed the renowned Munich Security Conference from 1999 until 2008, and also served as President of Boeing for Germany. Teltschik is a member of the International Advisory Board of the Council on Foreign Relations and holds similar positions at the Atlantic Initiative in Berlin and the Eugen Biser Foundation.

Those of us who played a leading role in bringing about the end of the Cold War have witnessed many momentous changes since the collapse of the Soviet Union, the transition to democracy of most Communist regimes and the peaceful reunification of Germany in less than one year. At the time, it appeared that most countries in eastern Europe, the former Soviet Union, but also Latin America, Asia and some parts of Africa were embracing liberal democracy and a social market economy.

It may have been the giddy optimism spawned by the Year of Miracles (1989) or the presence on the world stage of statesmen -- Helmut Kohl, George H.W. Bush, Mikhail Gorbachev, Lech Walesa, Miklós Németh -- who at great risk to themselves brought about historic transformations in their countries and the world. At any rate, we did not expect the end of history, but a gradual yet irreversible spread of democracy and free markets around the world, as well as increasing standards of living in emerging as well as developed countries. Democracy and prosperity have indeed spread, and hundreds of millions have been lifted out of poverty. But new challenges threaten this progress.

Twenty-nine years later, it is disheartening and to some degree unbelievable that the bedrock of multilateral institutions and values that shaped our world for the better is being challenged and undermined by the forces of military aggression, economic populism, protectionism, nativism, xenophobia and a rejection of open and multicultural societies. In 2017, we celebrated the sixtieth anniversary of the Treaty of Rome and the seventieth anniversary of Secretary George Marshall's speech announcing the plan for European reconstruction that provided $103 billion in aid and technical assistance to the ravaged countries of Western Europe that were allowed to embrace it. In fact, the Marshall plan was a catalyst for the founding of the European Coal and Steel Community in 1951 and the European Economic Community (EEC) in 1957 because it made delivery of the assistance contingent on the integration of Western Europe's economies. From the Bretton Woods conference in 1944 to the Treaty of Rome in 1957, a network of effective multilateral institutions came into being, and they in turn promoted regional economic integration, the spread of democracy, social market economies and free trade. Sixty years after Germany, France, Italy, Belgium, the Netherlands and Luxembourg founded the EEC, their project has become the most successful economic integration scheme in history. With a total population of 500 million, the 28-member states of the European Union share the largest common market in the world. Moreover, they have transferred full or partial sovereignty of many policies -- agriculture, fishing, trade, competition, transportation, research, energy -- to strong European institutions. Nineteen of those countries with a combined population of 338 million share the world's second reserve currency and allow the European Central Bank to determine monetary policy. And most of the EU's 28 members are committed to deepening integration with regards to fiscal and banking matters, foreign and security policy and possibly a new European military alliance.

This is unquestionably the enduring legacy of Chancellor Helmut Kohl. He not only masterfully achieved German reunification in less than a year, but also anchored Germany even more deeply in the EU by pushing through Economic and Monetary Union and convincing Germans to exchange their beloved Deutsche Mark for the Euro. Since 2015, great German statesmen have left us: Chancellor Helmut Schmidt, Egon Bahr (the architect of Germany's *Ostpolitik* under Chancellors Willy Brandt and Schmidt) and former Foreign Minister Hans-Dietrich Genscher. Now the world and Europe mourn the passing of the longest-serving Chancellor in Germany's democratic history. Even his bitter political adversaries recognize that Helmut Kohl acted decisively, boldly and intelligently before and after the fall of the Berlin Wall, and in 329 days pulled of the reunification of West and East Germany. He forged strong relationships with foreign leaders, thus paving the way for the signing of the Treaty of Maastricht and the adoption of the single currency. Chancellor Kohl will undoubtedly go down as one of the greatest statesmen of the XXth century. Europe will always owe him a great debt of gratitude.

He probably would have wanted that, after paying our respects to his life and achievements, we continue to carry the not always easy burden of fostering European integration. At a critical time in Europe's history, we can best honor his legacy by redoubling our efforts to deepen European integration and the transatlantic alliance.

European integration is often derided as a top-down process driven by elites that yields insufficient benefits to Europe's citizens. Nothing could be further from the truth. Despite a pitifully small budget, the EU has brought about the liberalization of air, road and sea transportation and thus offers citizens a much broader range of routes at lower prices. The single market has enabled companies to manufacture to harmonized European standards, achieve economies of scale and therefore deliver a much wider array of consumer goods at lower prices. Millions of scientists, professors and students have benefited from the EU's education, training and research programs. And since the fifteenth of June of 2017, Europeans are able to make unlimited phone calls and transmit data on their cell phones without paying any roaming charges.

Despite these tangible benefits, the EU's successes are at best competing with an alternative narrative. Accustomed to peace and a relatively high standard of living, many demographic groups are turning inwards and rejecting free trade, globalization and the EU. Two years ago, Europe's radical right- and left-wing parties were anticipating victories in Austria, the Netherlands and France that would have come only months after the United Kingdom's decision to withdraw from the EU. The Anglo-Saxon press and many analysts predicted and hoped that *Nexit* (Dutch exit from the EU) and *Frexit* would in due course lead to the break-up of the European Union and the eurozone. The Brexit-Nexit-Frexit narrative has been stopped in its tracks by the decisive victory of moderate parties in the Netherland's elections in March of 2017 and Emmanuel Macron's spectacular 30-point defeat of Marine Le Pen in May of 2017, as well as his party's absolute majority in Parliament. In fact, most of the EU's 28-member states are governed by center-right, left-of-center or grand coalitions. Both the CDU and the SPD have rejected any cooperation with the anti-immigration *Alternative für Deutschland* and in late 2017 again formed a grand coalition. Moreover, the UK election result can be interpreted as a desire by both moderate supporters of the Conservative Party and the Labor Party to negotiate a soft Brexit. A little over two years after 52% of Britons opted to leave the EU after a flood of xenophobic lies, populism and demagoguery have been dealt severe setbacks across Europe.

In fact, in light of Prime Minister Theresa May's loss of an absolute majority on June 8th, 2017 many in the EU's institutions and member states are delighted -- and feel vindicated -- to witness the tough stance taken by their leaders with London at summits in April and May of 2017. At one of them, Ms. May's attempts to try to negotiate a post-Brexit deal with the EU were brushed aside in four minutes by the 27 member states' unanimous demand that the UK first ensure the rights of its nationals in the UK, pay the 60 billion "divorce" bill *in euros* and design a soft border between the republic of Ireland and Northern Ireland. It is now the EU Commission which exudes a sense of confidence about the Brexit negotiations. In fact, the UK's political establishment has had to accept that the UK will remain in the EU until 2020, May's government and the Tories openly spar over a hard Brexit or a slow phase-out of EU law and there is not idea in sight to design the soft border both Ireland and Northern Ireland demand. Moreover, the British Parliament will have a right to vote on any EU-UK Brexit deal, and submitting it to a popular vote -- which could reject the Brexit agreement -- is no longer an unrealistic proposition.

The EU can and should press ahead with an ambitious agenda to deepen economic, political and military integration. The harmonization of indirect taxes, full implementation of the banking union and its deposit guarantee, supervision of member states' budgets by the Commission and other elements of the fiscal and banking union should be finalized in the coming months. The fact that we overcame the eurozone debt crisis and Spain and Italy are paying less than the United States to place their ten-year bonds should not lead to complacency. The need to recapitalize or sell some of Italy's troubled banks and Greece's insurmountable debt level are reminders that the EU and eurozone's institutional instruments need to be nimbler and anticipate crises. The IMF's repeated calls for a partial write-off of Greece's crushing debt should be heeded, as austerity has been overdone in its case.

The ECB's quantitative easing, the bail-outs of Greece, Portugal and Ireland, the structural reforms and austerity applied by the debt-stricken countries jointly enabled us to overcome the eurozone's sovereign-debt crisis. Northern Europeans would be unfair in thinking that their emphasis on austerity was the only reason for the turnaround. And southern European countries need to apply additional structural reforms that increase productivity and competition in key markets.

Member states and EU institutions need to push ahead to develop a common energy policy that will allow us to reduce our energy dependence and proceed with the transition to a cleaner energy model -- the *Energiewende* Germany has pioneered. After Germany's elections in September of 2017, none of the major EU powers (with the exception of Italy) will hold general elections for almost three years. This is a window of opportunity that European leaders need to seize. A first tangible step to strengthen the EU would be to allocate the UK's divorce bill to the

EU's budget, instead of its 27 members wrangling over the spoils of Brexit. We will not have transeuropean infrastructure and energy networks until member states properly fund the EU budget and begin negotiating the financial perspectives for 2021-2027.

EU institutions will have their hands full with the Brexit negotiations and the aforementioned deepening of economic, financial and political integration. But they also need to address the disruptions around the world that are feeding populism, nativism and violence. Their task would seem manageable if the current bout of protectionism could be attributed to the middle classes' painful recovery from the Great Recession and the desperation of those left behind by globalization. To be sure, free-trade treaties have outsourced many well-paying jobs. Estimates put the job losses resulting from the liberalization of trade between the United States and China between 1999 and 2011 at two million. But opposition to globalization runs deeper than hostility to free trade.

There is a growing digital divide between the young and well-educated professionals who live in cities and the rural and small-town inhabitants who lack the skills to secure a decent job. Whether it is the blue-collar workers of Ohio or the former coal miners of Alsace or the Ruhr, governments need to recognize that those -- predominantly older -- citizens who feel left behind by globalization are not a passing phenomenon. As life expectancy grows, new policies need to be crafted to bring globalization's discontents (the title of Joseph Stiglitz's prescient book in 2000) back into the fold. Life-long training, a greater role for foundations, charities and other NGOs, a permanent income for the poorest and neediest, and taxes on the use of robots are some of the remedies that should be discussed. Europe has done a reasonable job of containing the rise of inequality. But in order to continue to fund the welfare state's benefits, many who have left the labor force need to be assisted in order to grow the tax base.

Our societies need to urgently engage in a deeper debate about the acceleration of technological progress, automation, artificial intelligence and robots. The International Federation of Robots defines an industrial robot as a machine that can be controlled automatically, and which can be reprogrammed. There are currently 2 million robots worldwide, and 2 robots for every 1000 employees in the US. A recent study concluded that robots have eliminated between 360,000 and 670,000 jobs in the United States. Some suggest that companies using robots should pay a contribution to the pension and health-care system as if they were employees.

It is not just industrial robots that have been replacing humans at factories. There are now 4.9 billion devices of all kinds connected to the Internet of Things, and by 2020 the number is projected to rise to 50 billion. Many workers in the services sector will soon be replaced by software that executes perfect translations, drives vehicles, steers the delivery of packages and teaches languages. Proponents of the acceleration of technology argue that life will be easier, and we can focus on more added-value jobs. But not everybody has the mental or financial capacity to become an engineer, physicist or IT expert. We therefore run the risk of developing a labor market where well-trained scientists and engineers will reap the rewards of programming machines and tasks that the poorer and less-educated will not be able to perform.

It would be fabulous if technology, artificial intelligence and robots could produce the goods and services we need, and everybody could work fewer hours. But this is wishful thinking. In a free society, individuals, societies and countries will never agree on *which* resources should be employed to design and construct *which* goods and services. Even if they somehow could, the proliferation of cyberattacks, hacking, terrorism and technological malfunction means that humans will always have to remain in the loop.

Nobody has a magic formula to resolve these matters. But Europe can lead the way in crafting sensible measures that employ technology to reduce inequality and prevent the ageing of our societies. On the one hand, as developed and even emerging countries' populations continue to age, the need for skilled immigrants will remain high. According to UN estimates, by 2050 forty percent of Germany's population will be over 60 and the country's population will have declined from 82 to 75 million. Since the 1970s, deaths have outpaced births. The German economic miracle was partly fueled by immigration from southern Europe. But many of the 1.2 million immigrants and refugees allowed into Germany since 2015 are having trouble adapting to Western society, let alone finding a job. If non-European immigration has to be curbed because natives resent their competition, ageing developed countries will have to come up with creative ideas. Fees on the use of robots and technology can be allocated to training the un- or underemployed. Unemployed German youths could teach German to Syrian immigrants with advanced software. A machine can train a human in order to provide social care, and the person in turn can use that knowledge to obtain a better job. Executives at technological companies should put aside some of their profits to train the native un- or underemployed. If they are not willing to do so voluntarily, governments might have to impose a tax to obtain the necessary revenue.

Europe needs to engineer its transition to a digital economy at a particularly difficult time. Until the US reverts to its leading role on global issues, Europe will have to fill the void. Despite the manifold challenges, it can do so. The EU is the world's first provider of development assistance and first exporter. It accounts for 25% of the world's GDP and is the world's leading importer and exporter. It needs to continue to craft advanced trade agreements that open up markets to not just goods, but also foreign investment, bidding, services and protect intellectual property. The recently ratified deal with Canada is a perfect example. The EU has trade or association agreements with 50 countries, and is the main trading partner of 59 economies, surpassing both China (32) and the United States (23). External trade accounts for 34% of the EU's GDP. But we are nonetheless negotiating with other powers from a position of strength, as 63% of our trade takes place within the EU.

Western leaders have a long list of pressing security issues: the rise of China as a military power and its actions in the South China Sea; the continuing provocations by North Korea; Russia's aggressive posture in eastern Europe and around the world; the Syrian civil war; the instability of failed states like Libya, Yemen and Somalia; and the threat posed by both jihadist terrorist groups as well as self-radicalized individuals. It is precisely the EU's soft power as an economic and trade powerhouse that enables it to engage other powers on climate change, immigration, tax havens and corruption. The agreements it has and the ones it is negotiating with other countries or groups (China, India, ASEAN, the Gulf Cooperation Council) should continue to demand high environmental and labor standards and zero tolerance for corruption.

The radicalism in the Arab and Muslim world is partly fueled by the lack of job opportunities for young people. Under the German presidency of the G20, the EU should call for the development of a Marshall plan for the Arab and Muslim world. A contribution of 10 billion dollars by each member of the G20 would create a pool of 200 billion dollars, an amount that can finance projects in renewable energy, transportation infrastructure, education and R+D for the well-educated labor force of countries in northern Africa and the Middle East.

The XXIst century is a daunting time. Emerging and developing powers now generate 45% of the world's GDP. The relative calm and predictability of the Cold War era, with its rival hegemons, has given way to a multipolar world where ideologies are in a flux and old norms and values are disappearing. Many of those disenchanted with globalization know what they reject – free trade, immigration, multinationals, elites and rising inequality. But they have not figured out what they want. The main challenge is to forge a coalition of countries whose societies have a positive vision of the course they wish to pursue and the objectives they want to attain. Protectionism, nativism, economic populism and xenophobia will only stoke the world's problems. The EU can and should lead the way in offering a model that others will want to emulate. It has done so since the early 1950s, overcoming many crises along the way. Global governance is a daunting task. But just as the US helped 18 European countries get back on their feet after the massive destruction of World War II with the Marshall Plan, Europe can point the way for the emerging and developing countries struggling to find a template for our complicated world.

Professor Dr. Horst Teltschik
Munich, June 17th, 2017

Introduction

This book follows in the footsteps of *Ethical Capitalism: What it can do for you* and *Of Bureaucrats, Politicians and Statesmen: How to Right-Size the American Dream*. The former, my fifth book, was presented at the Spanish Embassy in Washington, D.C. at the behest of the Spanish ambassador in the United States in June of 2011 and at several institutions in Spain, including at the prestigious Ateneu of Barcelona (founded in 1860) and the INCIPE think-tank in Madrid. The Spanish-language version of *Ethical Capitalism* (*Conversaciones con Marx: Diálogos en torno a un liberalismo ético*) was published in October of 2010 and presented at the illustrious SEBAP institution (founded in 1822) in Barcelona by Miquel Roca Junyent, one of the founders of Spain's 1978 Constitution and long-time parliamentary leader of *Convergència i Unió*, a moderate free-market nationalist party that ruled Catalonia between 1980 and 2003.

In *Ethical Capitalism*, I argued for a more ethical, social and sustainable capitalism in a multi-country four-year (2007-2011) conversation with Karl Marx, which enabled me to summarize some of the XXth century's most relevant political, economic, financial, business, scientific, technological and social developments. Karl Marx died in 1883, and I resurrected him as the financial crisis broke in 2007 as a literary construct. He obviously needed an update on what had happened in the world between his death and his return to life. While I brought him up to speed, I made the case for a reform of capitalism while he misinterpreted the financial crisis and Great Recession and again resorted to actions -- such as working with Hugo Chávez and Vladimir Putin -- and a strategy that eliminated basic freedoms in a doomed attempt to achieve equality and social justice. I also hope and feel that the update for Karl Marx was useful for readers.

Some may criticize the format of this book and the two preceding ones in terms of conversations with three of the most distinguished economists of all time. The idea of bringing Karl Mark back to life as a literary construct in order to debate the causes and remedies of capitalism's recurrent crises in general and the financial crisis of 2007 and Great Recession of 2007-2009 in particular was mine. But Timothy Garton Ash, one of the world's most prestigious historians and political scientists, endorsed and lauded my idea in a brief conversation I held with him in Berlin.

I feel that reviewing political, economic, business and financial developments in an accurate and appealing way is a tall order, especially because it involves analyzing complicated trends the average reader might not find too exciting. Doing so in a conversation with resurrected VIPs attempts to make the subject matter more light-hearted.

In *Of Bureaucrats, Politicians and Statesmen*, I used the same format in the first half of the book. Published in 2015 and presented at the Catalan Association of Economists, on this occasion the review of world events an analysis of the international economy was conducted with John Maynard Keynes. I brought Keynes back to literary life in 2011 to witness the absolute triumph of his theories as governments around the world and international institutions employed Keynesian economics – higher debts and deficits, public-works programs, very low interest rates, transfers to spur demand – to overcome the financial crisis and recession and later on to foster a stronger recovery.

In *Globalization versus Nativism: How to Bridge the Digital Divide*, I complete the trilogy by engaging in a conversation with Milton Friedman, the forceful advocate of rolling back Keynesianism. Friedman convinced many political and business leaders, among them Ronald

Reagan and Margaret Thatcher, about the virtues of liberalization, privatizations of state-owned enterprises, deregulation, as small a role for government as possible, and slashing or eliminating taxes. Friedman was instrumental in creating an ideological and theoretical framework for the deregulation of the economy, business and financial sectors in the United States, United Kingdom and other countries beginning in the 1980s. This development arguably brought about or magnified the build-up and bursting of speculative bubbles such as the S&L one in the 1980s, as well as the .com technology and real-estate ones since the year 2000.

In the context of the strong growth and full employment bequeathed by the Obama administration to president Donald Trump in 2017, I can again play devil's advocate by pushing back on *laissez-faire* economics. This time the context is synchronized international economic growth and the nine-year expansion of a US economy with full employment which did not need a regressive and unfunded tax cut at the end of 2017 which will favor the rich and big corporations. This book, however, is not a diatribe against the Trump administration and its policies. Although there are many criticisms of the current US administration, they are grounded in logic and facts. Moreover, I have endeavored to understand the frustrations and anger (some of which I share) that prompted many Americans to elect Donald J. Trump president in 2016. Indeed, since 2014 I have driven over 52,000 miles around the United States, visited many small towns and rural areas. Part of my travel (only 3000 miles) was as a volunteer for the 2016 presidential campaign of Senator Marco Rubio, a positive and principled politician who finished third in the number of delegates among a field of seventeen contenders for the GOP presidential nomination. In addition, for decades I have visited and sought to understand the challenges facing small towns and rural communities across the United States.

I have chosen Karl Marx, John Maynard Keynes and Milton Friedman, among other reasons, because they have been consistently ranked by the BBC and fellow economists as the most influential economists and thinkers of the XXth century. Marx, for better or worse, is regarded as one of the most influential philosophers, writers and economists of all time in general and of the XXth century in particular. Keynes is unanimously acknowledged as the father of modern macroeconomics and the most influential economist of the XXth century. Friedman, for his part, is considered the most influential economist of the second half of the XXth century.

In *Of Bureaucrats, Politicians and Statesmen*, I sparred with John M. Keynes and warned about the dangers of accumulating excessive deficits and debt in the name of reviving the economy in the short term. The sovereign-debt crisis in the eurozone and other public-debt fueled crises in developed and emerging economies alike have proven that my warnings and those of others were prescient. In the second half of the book, thirty VIPs from twenty-three countries provided contributions regarding what I labeled the post-BRICS TIDE challenges: (T)echnological Competitiveness, (I)nequality, the impact of ageing populations (Demographics) and (E)nergy Security. These prominent academics, business leaders, heads of business associations, members of think-tanks and other professionals analyzed how countries in general (or specific ones) are coping with these four challenges. It is my belief that all economies will have to address these four issues in the coming years, and some are already successfully doing so. I made it a point to include a respected professional from each of the world's top twenty economies by volume of nominal GDP among the contributors.

The second half of this book draws on the knowledge, experience and ideas of some of the contributors of my previous book and new ones to describe and analyze the rise of populism in many countries around the world. The prestigious academics, heads of business associations, executives, members of think-tanks and other professionals also furnish ideas on how to address populism in general and specifically on how to bridge the economic and digital divides between the winners of globalization and those who feel that free trade, immigration and technological progress are marginalizing them and threatening their way of life. The purpose of these contributions is, among others, to provide policymakers with specific policy prescriptions. These measures can be adopted to narrow this chasm between the winners of globalization and those who are retreating to nativist, populist and nationalist attitudes.

I have endeavored through the aforementioned formats to prevent my books from being excessively technical. However, some of these topics are inevitably complex.

I have written my last two books during a time when I have waited for and applied first for Legal Permanent Residence and now for US citizenship. America has always been an inspiration for me. I now have no family. I fulfil all of the criteria to become a US citizen. But the process has become longer. Sometimes I am tempted to return to an easier life in Barcelona, Spain, but I continue to believe that the American dream is possible in the US. Tom Hanks as a person and his fantastic roles as James Donovan (Bridge of Spies), Ben Bradlee (The Post) a fictional US Army Captain in Normandy (Saving Private Ryan), Professor Robert Langdon (The Da Vinci Code, Angels and Demons, Inferno), Captain Phillips is a source of great inspiration.

If I manage to attain the great honor of becoming a US citizen before the second half of 2019, it will be in part because during the past six years I have extensively read about certain individuals, political and military leaders whose idealism, commitment to a higher cause and accomplishments inspired me. We must all put up with many frustrations in our everyday lives. I therefore list quotes from politicians, writers, philosophers and military leaders in the first chapter of the book. It is my sincere hope that these quotes -- as well as the book itself -- inform and inspire readers.

Oxon Hill, September 19, 2018

<u>**Inspiring Quotes**</u>

"Make no little plans. They have no magic to stir men's blood." Winston Churchill

"Attitude and not aptitude determines altitude." Anonymous

"Our problems are manmade -- therefore, they can be solved by man. And man can be as big as he wants. No problem of human destiny is beyond human beings." John F. Kennedy

"In life you have to decide whether you want to soar with the eagles or hang out with the turkeys." Joel Osteen

"Only the dead have seen the end of war." Plato

"If you cry because the sun has gone out of your life, your tears will prevent you from seeing the stars." Rabindranath Tagore

"If you can take it, you can make it." Louis Zamperini. Olympic athlete, Word War II US Air Force officer and hero who was savagely tortured in Japanese prison camps and became a Christian evangelist in 1952.

"It is my destiny to defeat Communism, and only God or those politicians in Washington will keep me from doing it." General Douglas MacArthur (five-star General)

"*L'audace, toujours l'audace*" (Audacity, always audacity)." Frederick the Great and General George Patton Jr.

"Country, honor, duty." General Douglas MacArthur

"Wisdom is knowing the right path to take, integrity is taking it." M.H. McKee

"An Army marches on its stomach." Napoleon and Frederick the Great

"Change is the law of life. And those who look only to the past or the present are certain to miss the future." John F. Kennedy

"God grant me the serenity to accept the things I cannot change, the courage to change the things I can, and the wisdom to know the difference." Reinhold Niebuhr (theologian)

"Look at these thousands of men (in our regiment). Many of them not much more than boys. Each one of them is some mother's son, some sister's brother, some daughter's father. Each one of them a whole person, loved and cherished in some home far away. Many of them will never return.

An army is power. Its entire purpose is to coerce others. Now, this kind of power cannot be used carelessly or recklessly. This kind of power can do great harm. We have seen more suffering than any man should ever see. If there is going to be an end to it, it must be an end that justifies the cost. Now, somewhere out there is the Confederate army. They claim that they are fighting for their independence, for their freedom. I cannot question their integrity. I believe they are wrong. But I cannot question it. But I can question a system that defends its freedom while it denies it to others, to an entire race of men.

I will admit it, Tom. War is a scourge, but so is slavery. It is the systematic coercion of one group of men over another. It has been around since the book of Genesis. It exists in every corner of the world. But that is not an excuse for us to tolerate it here when we find it right before our very eyes in our own country. As God is my witness, there is nobody I hold in my heart dearer than you. But if your life, or mine, is part of the price to end this curse and free the negro, then let God's will be done."

Colonel Joshua Lawrence Chamberlain (also a professor of rhetoric and oratory at Bowdoin College) to his brother, Lieutenant Thomas Chamberlain, to convince him about the need to end slavery in the wake of Lincoln's Emancipation Declaration.

"Winners do not quit. Quitters do not win." Anonymous

"If you complain you will remain. If you praise, you shall be raised." Joel Osteen

"Like anybody, I would like to life a long life…But I am not concerned with that now. I just want to do God's will. And he's allowed me to go up to the Mountain. And I've looked over. And I've seen the promised land. I may not get there with you. But I want you to know tonight, that we, as a people, will get to the promised land." Martin Luther King Jr., addressing an African-American church in Memphis, a day before he was assassinated[1].

"Ask not what your country can do for you, but what you can do for your country." John F. Kennedy

"George, the difference between you and I is that I do this job because I was trained to do it. You do it because you love it!" General Omar Bradley to General George Patton Jr.

"I came through -- and I shall return." General Douglas MacArthur

"With a good conscience our only sure reward, with history the final judge of our deeds, let us go forth to lead this land we love, asking His blessing and His help, but knowing that here on earth God's work must truly be our own." President John F. Kennedy (1961 inaugural address)

"A general's wife is a general's general." Caesar

"There is nothing stronger than the heart of a volunteer." Colonel James Doolittle

"An old soldier never dies. He just fades away." US Army ballad

"It's the economy, stupid." James Carville

"Never underestimate the strength of a martyr's cause or the size of a Texan's balls!" Lyndon B. Johnson, after his advisors cautioned against trying to enact and have Congress approve too much of John F. Kennedy's domestic legislative agenda in the wake of his assassination (the Civil Rights Act and Voting Rights Act).

---

[1] Quoted in "MLK, 50 years on. Like a mighty stream". The Economist. March 31st, 2018, page 81

"Now the trumpet summons us again -- not as a call to bear arms, though arms we need; not as a call to battle, though embattled we are -- but as a call to bear the burden of a long twilight struggle, year in and year out, rejoicing in hope, patient in tribulation -- a struggle against the common enemies of man: tyranny, poverty, disease, and war itself." President John F. Kennedy (1961 inaugural address)

"In the long run we are all dead." John Maynard Keynes

"Underlying most arguments against the free market is a lack of belief in freedom itself." Milton Friedman

"*Governments never learn. Only people learn.*" Milton Friedman

"You are the light of the world. A city that is set on a hill cannot be hidden." Parable of Salt and Light in Jesus's Sermon on the Mount.

"I have quoted John Winthrop's words more than once on the campaign trail this year -- for I believe that Americans in 1980 are every bit as committed to that vision of a shining 'city on a hill' as were those settlers long ago. These visitors to that city on the Potomac do not come as white or black, red or yellow; they are not Jews or Christians; conservatives or liberals; or Democrats or Republicans. They are Americans awed by what has gone before, proud of what for them is still…a shining city on a hill." Ronald Reagan on the eve of his inauguration

"Give me liberty or give me death." Patrick Henry

"There is nothing quite as permanent as a temporary government program." Milton Friedman

"Government of the people, by the people, for the people, shall not perish from the Earth." Abraham Lincoln

"The only thing we have to fear is fear itself." Franklin D. Roosevelt (1932 inaugural address)

"Nearly all men can stand adversity, but if you want to test a man's character, give him power." Abraham Lincoln

"I am a slow walker, but I never walk back." Abraham Lincoln

"Keep this movement going. Keep this movement rolling. If you can't fly, run. If you can't run, walk. If you can't walk, crawl. But by all means keep moving." Martin Luther King Jr.[2]

"In life what counts is not whether you fall down, but whether you get up again." Joseph Biden

"America will never be destroyed from the outside. If we falter and lose our freedoms, it will be because we destroyed ourselves." Abraham Lincoln

"There is no such thing as a free lunch." Milton Friedman

"You can fool some of the people all of the time, and all of the people some of the time, but you cannot fool all of the people all of the time." Abraham Lincoln

"Work hard, study, and keep out of politics!" The title of James A. Baker III's memoirs.

"Power is where power goes". Lyndon B. Johnson

"If a free society cannot help the many who are poor, it cannot protect the few who are rich". John F. Kennedy (1961 inaugural address).

---

[2] Quoted in "MLK, 50 years on. The mighty stream". *The Economist*. March 31st, 2018, page 82.

"George, your worst enemy is your big mouth!" General Walter Bedell Smith to General George Patton Jr. (in the movie "Patton")

"We choose to go to the moon in this decade and do the other things, not because they are easy, but because they are hard." John F. Kennedy speech in 1962 at Rice University.

"A moment of pain can mean a lifetime of greatness." Pete Zamperini to his brother, Louis.

<u>Some dumb expressions</u>

1)"I understand where you are coming from."

This expression is often used by customer service representatives (people who answer the phone after you have to wait for minutes, sometimes an hour) from big companies when an exasperated client complains about an unexplained high charge on a bill or a deficient or lack of service -- cable, cell telephony, car insurance, etc. The agent is trying to show empathy with the customer with the aforementioned expression, which roughly translates as "I understand the source of your frustration". If the agent were to say something like "I understand why you are upset", it would be more to the point. But this "I know where you are coming from" does not make any sense. The person has no clue where you have been, where you are coming from, whether back home from work, or driving to work. Or maybe you have not moved during the day and have been at home all day. In this case, you are not coming from anywhere. You are not moving.

I become especially irate when I am driving around the US for whatever reason and I attempt to solve issues with my service providers. After a long day of driving, as I approach my destination on an interstate, I finally get through to a Comcast agent after being on hold for 30 minutes, and the person says: "I know where you are coming from!". I shoot back, "No you don't, you have no clue where I am coming from. Maybe I am coming from St. Louis to Lexington, Kentucky, or from NY to Washington, D.C., but that is beside the point. What matters is your lousy service!"

 2)"You are fine". Let us imagine you are at an electronics store and are touching some gadgets which are displayed in a case. You are not sure that this is allowed. You establish eye contact with the closest employee to ascertain whether such behavior is allowed or not. The employee answers: "You are fine". This means that there is no problem in touching the gadget on display. Years ago, people would use more precise and logical phrases in such circumstances, such as "It is all right" or "It is OK". The "You are fine" is absurd. Little pebbles of sand can be fine. A person can have fine skin. One may be a fine person, as in a person with notable qualities. But a person being fine in a situation is an inappropriate way to express the idea. Just say "It is ok". It is clear, succinct and to the point.

3) "To be honest with you": The Latin expression "Justification non petita acusato manifiesta"

4) "I got you": This expression has gradually become part of the vernacular in the US in the past few years. The expression is voiced usually as a result of someone asking for help, or for the provision or complaint regarding a service offered by a company. For example, I complained to Comcast that they overcharge me because the wi-fi was so slow I could barely work. And I am paying at least 250 dollars per month for three boxes and wi-fi. Two of the boxes have the On-Demand function that allows me to purchase or rent a movie, as well as to replay the movies I have already purchased.

People think that by saying "I got you", the person will take care of you or whatever matter you brought up, when the person who utters this phrase has no clue as to whether they will be able to deliver.

Chapter 1: Milton Friedman reappears during the 2016 US presidential election

Most people think that Milton Friedman passed away on November 16th, 2006 in San Francisco at age 94 of heart failure. That is what the newspapers reported. Friedman was still writing op-eds and performing serious economic research in the weeks before he supposedly passed away. In fact, the Wall Street Journal published an op-ed he authored the day after he officially died.

Friedman is universally regarded as one of the three most influential economists of the XXth century (alongside Karl Marx and John Maynard Keynes), and the most influential one in the second half of the XXth century. During decades as a professor, writer, and consultant he managed to roll back Keynesianism and was instrumental in convincing President Ronald Reagan and British Prime Minister Margaret Thatcher about the virtues of unfettered free markets, deregulation, tax cuts, privatizations and unleashing the animal spirits of financial markets.

But Milton Friedman did not die on November 16th, 2006, as the media reported at the time and the world believes. It is not a case of "fake news". In fact, Friedman was kidnapped at his home in San Francisco by mercenaries hired by the late Venezuelan dictator Hugo Chávez. If this sounds far-fetched, consider that Venezuela assisted Hezbollah in the execution of terrorist attacks in Buenos Aires in 1992 and 1994 against the Israeli Embassy and a Jewish center that killed over one hundred people and injured thousands. These were the worst terrorist attacks in Argentina's history. The Department of Homeland Security and Mexican officials have also confirmed the presence of Hezbollah terrorists in Mexico. The Chávez regime also engaged in drug trafficking and an array of illegal activities since Chávez became president in 1999 and continues to do so under president Nicolás Maduro. Chávez was spreading the Bolivarian revolution to other countries in Latin America such as Bolivia, Ecuador, Argentina, countries in the Caribbean and Central America, and bankrolling like-minded presidents like Evo Morales in Bolivia and Cristina Kirchner in Argentina.

In this context, Chávez wanted to silence Milton Friedman, a leading champion of free markets, and he was egged on by the Castro brothers. Milton was held in a remote and sparsely populated location in the region in southern Venezuela near the Yapacana National Park. He was treated very well and allowed to read, write, watch TV, exercise and perform other everyday activities within the confines of a compound guarded by Venezuelan security forces. He lived in a nice house with a garden but was not allowed to leave without an escort of security men.

Milton's health was frail in 2006, but the years spent in Venezuela were less stressful. He was away from the limelight and his wife was by his side. He eventually accepted his captivity, and spent many hours writing, performing research and strolling in the countryside in the company of his wife and ubiquitous guards.

Milton Friedman was unable to escape from the compound. It was too much to ask a 94-year-old to outrun well-built security guards and jump over a high fence. Chávez dispatched ministers, professors and close aides who attempted to ingratiate themselves with Friedman. The regime promised him a life of luxury in Venezuela on the Caribbean coast, which he could share with his wife Rose. But the offer was conditional upon Friedman stopping publication of books, articles and other documents in defense of free markets. Milton stuck to his guns and refused the offer. He was eventually liberated after a high-ranking Venezuelan official defected to the United States and alerted the US government about Friedman's captivity, as well as the location of the compound. US special operations soldiers flew from neighboring Colombia and, in a spectacular night raid, took out all of the security men at the compound and rescued Friedman in April of 2016.

After his release from captivity and return to the United States, Milton was more eager than ever to make up for the lost time. A workaholic, he decided to launch a campaign to preach the virtues of free markets to governments around the world. We met at a conference he delivered in Washington, D.C, in September of 2016. I had just returned to Washington, D.C., from Spain and was looking forward to the final two months of the presidential election pitting Donald J. Trump against Hillary Rodham Clinton.

Friedman was interested in my books and accepted a deal whereby I would keep him informed about political, economic, financial, business and security developments in the US and Europe in exchange for having the right to meet with him regularly and ask him questions for my seventh book. Milton received dozens of invitations to deliver conferences at universities and summits of multilateral institutions around the world, as well as to provide consulting to many governments. He was too busy. He needed a professor and informed news junkie like me to stay abreast of the news.

I flew back to the United States in late September of 2016. I was looking forward to the final stretch of the presidential campaign, with its debates, advertisements and town hall meetings. I was convinced that Hillary Clinton would defeat Donald Trump. Most analysts also predicted that the former Secretary of State would be America's 45th president. All polls gave her a lead over Trump. Milton Friedman was too busy delivering conferences and advising governments to keep track of day-to-day developments. Our first meeting took place at the Spanish restaurant Jaleo, in downtown Bethesda. Milton peppered me with questions right away.

Milton Friedman (MF): So, what is the latest regarding the U.S. presidential election?

Alexandre Muns (AM): Well, Hillary Clinton almost fainted at a campaign event commemorating the 15th anniversary of 9/11. Milton, you were alive in 2001. You remember the cowardly and barbaric use of jetliners as suicide missiles against both of the World Trade Center's towers and the Pentagon in Arlington, Virginia.

Hillary felt dizzy and briefly lost her balance. She was rushed to her daughter's apartment in New York City. Her campaign later disclosed that she had been diagnosed with bacterial pneumonia two days earlier. A virus had also been wreaking havoc among many of Hillary's campaign staffers at their headquarters in New York. The former Secretary of State had to cancel all events as her doctors ordered her to rest. Trump immediately pounced on the news to drive home the point that Hillary does not have enough energy (a return to his low-energy taunt) or is not healthy enough to be the leader of the free world. Moreover, Trump vowed to immediately release his medical records to prove his great health.

MF: Will this development hurt Hillary?

AM: The pneumonia does not seem serious. She was diagnosed by her doctors with viral or "walking pneumonia", which does not require a stay in the hospital nor serious treatment. Unlike viral pneumonia, it is not infectious, so she did not put anyone at risk. She is taking antibiotics and will rest for about a week. But Hillary admitted she should have followed her doctor's advice and rested for five days after the initial diagnosis. Clinton's communications director also acknowledged that the matter had not been handled well. Hillary only informed her family and closest aides about the diagnosis but kept the rest of her staff in the dark until the near-collapse on September 11th, 2016.

Everyone with common sense understands that more than a year of non-stop campaigning and fund-raisers across the U.S., numerous debates against her rivals for the Democratic presidential nomination (especially senator Bernie Sanders), the constant travel and the Democratic Party convention in Philadelphia would exhaust anyone. The problem with Hillary, as is sometimes the case, is that she was not forthcoming at first in disclosing her pneumonia until it became obvious when she almost fainted. I sympathize with her. She has had a remarkable career in public service and running for president is exhausting. But those who think the Clintons have a penchant for secrecy and play according to their own rules were given more ammunition to criticize her and her campaign. While Hillary got some rest, president Barack Obama filled the void by campaigning on her behalf.

If Hillary recovers quickly and has no more health issues, I doubt this episode will cost her any votes among her base. Her campaign subsequently disclosed a full medical report from her physicians. It indicated that Hillary Clinton takes a vitamin supplement and a blood thinner due to her collapse a few years ago and a blood clot in her head. Hillary also takes medication for an underactive thyroid. The former Secretary of State's health ailments and the inept cover-up could drive some undecided middle- and lower-income blue-collar white men (a demographic she is struggling with) into Trump's arms. These are men who distrust the Clintons, and like and want a "tough" leader.

Trump, for his part, did wish Hillary a speedy recovery, but his surrogates were quick to point out that Hillary's pneumonia confirmed she was not "mentally or physically fit" (words used in the past by Trump) to be commander-in-chief. The Donald himself is a bit older (he is 70) than Hillary. But he has displayed no weakness during the campaign, nor been ill at any time. In fact, he is full of energy. Nonetheless, he might have to tread carefully regarding age. Trump announced he would be providing extensive medical records. His physician has stated that the real-estate tycoon should lose weight. His body-mass index makes him technically overweight. Tim Kaine is the only one of the four candidates (2 for president, 2 for vice president) whose health is excellent.

What was much more damaging to Hillary was her remark at another event a few days before the 9/11 commemoration to the effect that half of Trump's supporters are "deplorables" who are "racist, xenophobic, and homophobic." Insulting half of your opponent's supporters is not a smart idea. In fact, it is a very dumb idea. Hillary apologized a few days later, but the damage was done. Many Trump supporters subsequently showed up at rallies proudly wearing caps, hats or T-shirts emblazoned with the "deplorable" label. Trump likened Clinton's *faux pas* to GOP presidential candidate Mitt Romney's assertion during the 2012 campaign that 47% of the US electorate would always vote Democrat because they pay no income taxes and have become dependent on help from the government – food stamps, unemployment benefits, Medicaid. Romney's words to a private meeting of donors (which were leaked) did indeed hurt him. It remains to be seen whether some independents and undecided voters might be swayed to vote for Trump because Hillary's remarks personally offended them.

MF: What do the polls look like?

AM: The latest polls do indeed show that Trump has drawn even with Hillary, who had been consistently leading the Republican candidate by about six points since the end of the conventions in July. And Trump has also made up ground in key battleground states such as Ohio, Pennsylvania and Florida. Trump had been catching up with Hillary even before the "deplorable" comment and the pneumonia diagnosis. The next batch of polls will reveal whether the election has become a dead heat.

Milton, you achieved everything in life. You were awarded the Nobel Memorial Prize in Economic Sciences in 1976 for your research on consumption analysis, monetary history and theory, and the complexity of stabilization policy. You taught for decades at the University of Chicago, as well as Cambridge University, the University of Wisconsin at Madison and the Hoover Institution. You also served on the National Resources Planning Board (1935–37), National Bureau of Economic Research (1937–40) and the US Treasury Department during World War II (1941-43).

You mentored people who went on to become very prestigious professors and Nobel Prize recipients in their own right. Your unwavering support for free markets had a profound influence on the administrations of Ronald Reagan and the UK government led by Margaret Thatcher in the 1980s. They privatized state-owned companies, cut taxes, and removed regulations as you advised them. You taught at the most prestigious universities in the US and advised governments around the world. A survey of economists determined that you were the second most influential economist of the XXth century. The Economist newsmagazine considers you the most influential economist of the second half of the XXth century.

MF: Who came in first in the survey of my fellow peers?

AM: John Maynard Keynes.

MF: Not him again! I spent years debunking his flawed theories. How could other economists do this to me?

AM: You do not have to take things so seriously. You know that many countries implemented Keynesian economics in the two decades after the end of World War II. Keynes is regarded as the father of modern macroeconomics.

MF: Why? Keynes is so overrated!

AM: Come on! You know that you actually drew from his work in order to later criticize it! And you are aware that the ideas of neoclassical economics needed to be challenged, as Keynes did. Keynes argued against the idea that free markets would, in the short to medium term, automatically provide full employment as long as workers were flexible in their wage demands. Keynes instead advocated that aggregate demand determined the overall level of economic activity and that insufficient aggregate demand could result in prolonged periods of high unemployment. Keynes lobbied for the use of fiscal and monetary policies to allay the negative consequences of economic recessions and depressions.

MF: Yes, I guess Keynes was an important and influential economist. But he got very lucky. His challenge of neoclassical economics coincided with the Great Depression. The stage was set for politicians to implement his ideas.

AM: Well, some could argue that stagflation in the 1970s facilitated your efforts to overturn Keynesianism. *The Economist* did rank you as the most influential economist of the *second* half of the XXth century. But you do have to admit that Keynes influenced governments' economic policies beginning in the 1930s, as US president Franklin D. Roosevelt used his ideas to craft the New Deal and pull the US out of the Great Depression. And president Ronald Reagan awarded you the Presidential Medal of Freedom in 1988, a distinction Keynes did not receive.

MF: It sure took them a while to get the US economy back to the 1929 baseline! Anyway, I appreciate your kind words. And I predicted that stagflation (high inflation and high unemployment) would happen in the 1970s. What is your dream?

AM: Before I tell you my dream, I must tell you that I admire your marriage.

MF: Thank you.

AM: I want to highlight your extremely successful marriage to Rose. You were both economists. She graduated from Reed College and the University of Chicago after emigrating to the US from the Volhynian Governorate, then in Russia but in present-day Ukraine. It must have been hard for her, working with such distinguished professors.

MF: What do you mean? My parents were also from humble origins. My father, Jenő Saul Friedman, and my mother, Sára Ethel, were Jewish immigrants from Beregszász in Carpathian Ruthenia,then in the kingdom of Hungary (now in Ukraine). Both of my parents worked as dry goods merchants in Brooklyn. Shortly after my birth in July of 1912, they moved the family to Rahway, New Jersey. I did not therefore have a privileged upbringing. Not by any extent of the imagination. I received very good grades in high school, and during my formative years was always offered scholarships by leading US universities.

AM: Yes, of course, I understand. You are extremely intelligent and hard-working. But your wife immigrated to the US from eastern Europe as well. And women had a very hard time competing with men in those times. Her brother, Aaron Director (1901–2004) was a well-known professor at the University of Chicago Law School and one of the founders of the economic analysis of law.

MF: Yes, Rose was great. Her support helped me a lot. We co-wrote two books on economics and public policy, *Free to Choose* and *Tyranny of the Status Quo*. We also jointly authored our memoirs, *Milton and Rose D. Friedman, Two Lucky People*, which were published in 1998.

AM: Yes, both of you were very smart and hard-working, but also lucky in finding each other. You also worked together to fund Educational Choice (formerly the Milton and Rose D. Friedman Foundation), in order to foster the use of school vouchers and freedom of choice in education. You obviously know that both policies are championed passionately by the Republican Party, and even some Democrats who want to reform public schools. You and Rose had the best partnership by two economists of all time.

Look, as you know, Keynes never married and was gay. In terms of having a family, Keynes was a dismal failure. That is probably why he famously said that in the long run we are all dead. As he had no children, it was hard for him to link the long term to something personal. On the other hand, you and Rose achieved everything professionally and had a son, David.

After Donald Trump defeated Hillary Clinton in the presidential election of November 8, 2016. Friedman and I met up at a steak restaurant in Alexandria. He would always pick up the tab, an additional benefit of our agreement.

AM: Milton, the new US administration of Donald Trump will have to continue to contain Russian president Vladimir Putin, who purposely undermined Hillary Clinton's campaign. Julian Assange worked with the US military traitor (Snowden) and was offered asylum by Russia.

I wrongly predicted that Hillary Clinton would be the US's 45th president, and have gone on the record in Spain, Europe and the US as describing Donald Trump's trade policies as irresponsible. My denunciations of him were strong, even when the latest revelations in the Access Hollywood tape had not surfaced and he was trailing in the polls two weeks before the election. Despite Trump's victory, I will not give up Legal Permanent Residency and will pursue US citizenship. I can apply for US citizenship in February of 2018, in four months.

Today it dawned on me that no analyst in the context of the presidential campaign pointed out that the Violence Against Women Act was passed (with bipartisan support) under president Bill Clinton in 1994. As Trump spent the last 27 days of the campaign blasting Bill and Hillary Clinton, I re-tweeted about Clinton and VAWA to some analysts who are on TV. Vice president Joe Biden headed congressional (Senate) efforts to draft and approve VAWA. It provided $1.6 billion in funding for victims of sexual violence. VAWA was re-authorized in 2000, 2005 (under George W. Bush) and in March of 2013. The bipartisan support of the nineties for VAWA gave way to Republican (conservative) opposition to VAWA funding for LGBT, for undocumented immigrants subject to domestic violence (U visa) and to same-sex marriage provisions.

I think the Democratic Party is complacent. There is visceral hatred for Hillary and Bill Clinton. Its intensity is irrational. Unfortunately, people alienated by globalization are turning against the elites in many countries. I am very saddened by what Philippine president Rodrigo Duterte is doing in the Philippines, and in most European countries there are radical right-wing parties (but not Spain, I can say proudly). Extreme right-wing parties are attracting votes by unfairly denouncing immigrants as competitors who drive down wages, take natives' jobs, bring in their entire families, are criminals, and are a security threat if they are Muslims. This assertion is completely untrue and can be proven so using statistics. But it is politically appealing and resonates with many voters, especially those who are not well-off and resent the subsidies given to non-European immigrants.

Chapter 2: Volunteering for Marco Rubio and wishing Joe Biden had run

In this chapter I will interrupt my conversation with Milton Friedman in order to describe and explain the very interesting experience of volunteering for Senator Marco Rubio during the 2016 presidential campaign. I drove over 3000 miles and spent $2000 in hotel and gas bills to assist his team in the primaries in New Hampshire, South Carolina and Florida. This chapter also analyzes the Rubio campaign, the GOP and Democratic Party nomination processes and pays tribute to the Obama administration, president Barack Obama himself and vice president Joseph Biden.

In this and previous books, articles and conferences I have praised many of the accomplishments – domestic and foreign – of the Obama presidency. I firmly believe that, with the passage of time, it will go down as one of the most successful and transformative in US history. The current administration is obviously trying to reverse many of president Obama's signature treaties, agreements and regulations (Paris climate change, Iran nuclear agreement, Trans-Pacific Partnership, opening up to Cuba). But I firmly believe they will stand the test of time. The Iran agreement, however, could have been improved on. And Cuba's government has apparently poisoned US diplomats while keeping a tight grip on political power and slowing economic reform to a crawl. But in the latter two treaties Barack Obama achieved realistic goals which should be improved on, not torn up.

In addition to its specific accomplishments, one of the Obama administration's great successes was in avoiding any major scandal for eight years. No member of his cabinets was reasonably accused of wrongdoing. In fact, president Barack Obama, vice president Joe Biden and the members of their cabinets did not face a single serious accusation of having broken any law.

Apart from the Benghazi affair, there were no investigative committees set up by Congress into purposeful political wrongdoing. And, despite months of testimony by Secretary Hillary Clinton and numerous witnesses before many committees, no evidence was found to prove that Benghazi was anything other than an unfortunate – although predictable – result of a chaotic revolution and lack of funding for security at the US Consulate in Libya. The handling of the fall-out from the deaths of Ambassador J. Christopher Stevens, US Foreign Service officer Sean Smith and CIA contractors Tyrone Smith and Glen Doherty was botched, but there was no willful intent to not protect them, let alone a conspiracy to have them die as millions of dollars of taxpayer money failed to prove.

Hillary Clinton is undoubtedly a divisive figure in American politics. She has been in public life and service for decades. I do not agree with some of her policies, but overall, she has been a force for good and achieved many specific improvements in the lives of many, especially the less advantaged and poor, whether in the United States or around the world. Her otherwise successful tenure as Secretary of State was marred by her use of a private server and email, an unfortunate and irresponsible practice that undoubtedly cost her a lot of votes in the 2016 presidential elections but which the FBI and the Justice Department concluded did not break the law.

Leaving aside these two unfortunate but not illegal episodes, the Obama administration was arguably one of the least corrupt in US history. Trump Republicans and the media can try very hard. But they simply will not find wrongdoing. The best they can do is point to a failed scheme by the Bureau of Alcohol, Tobacco, Firearms and Explosives (ATF) to sell guns to criminals in order to track Mexican cartels, an operation that had also been carried out under President George W. Bush[3]. Moreover, Barack Obama, Joseph Biden and all of the cabinet secretaries in their personal lives behaved themselves beyond any possible reproach. There were simply no professional or personal scandals. The no-drama Obama presidency was already appreciated by many when the first African-American president was in the White House. It is sorely missed now, regardless of party affiliation or policy preferences, as mainstream Republicans would privately concede.

It is important to highlight the moral and ethical dimension of the Obama presidency. Not just because it is a fact. But also, because in the context of populism, terrorism, climate change, technological transformations and many other wrenching changes and disasters in the US and around the world, the conduct of the president and cabinet of the world's lone economic and military superpower sets an example. It is not a matter of trying to patronize others. But the behavior of the leader of the free world and his (or her) cabinet is followed around the globe. As in many other regards, the United States is the place where many around the world look to for leadership.

It is impossible and unfair to single out individual cabinet secretaries from the two Obama terms. However, I would include John Kerry (State), Jack Lew (Treasury), Ash Carter (Defense), Arne Duncan (Education), Tom Vilsack (Agriculture), Shaun Donovan (Housing and Urban Development and Office of Management and Budget), Ken Salazar (Interior), Thomas Perez (Labor), Julian Castro (Housing and Urban Development), Ernest Moniz (Energy), Sylvia Burwell (Health and Human Services) and US Trade Representative Michael Froman on the list of the ones I most respect. Bob Gates (a Republican) was a good Secretary of Defense and former CIA director, but his tasteless memoirs disappointed me.

I spent almost the entire eight years of the two Obama terms in Washington, D.C. Barack Obama's leadership, charisma, oratory, acumen, willingness to accept mistakes, political courage and grasp of policy were exemplary. In this regard, he set the tone for those who served for and next to him. I continue to enjoy the insights, fairness and decency of some of his non-cabinet advisers, such as David Axelrod, Van Jones and Dennis McDonough (his last chief of staff). Obama undoubtedly chose men and women of high integrity with a deep commitment to public service. In the course of eight years they obviously committed mistakes. But I have no doubt that they were all guided by the mission to improve the lives of all Americans. They also enhanced America's role in the world as well as defended and advanced democracy, freedom and the rights enshrined in the Constitution around the world.

It is true that in some regards president Obama believed and publicly said that he wanted the United States to be more like certain northern European countries. This in no way undermines the notion of American exceptionalism.

All countries learn from others. Globalization has many positive effects, but it undoubtedly leaves some behind. The thread that bound the Obama administration's policies -- as well as his behavior and speeches -- was the desire to empower the middle class and the less fortunate in the face of a plethora of global trends and challenges. Some of these challenges are the ageing of population, the fourth industrial revolution and its extraordinary technological progress, climate change, massive capital flows, thinly-regulated financial markets that can both generate and

---

[3] During investigation of the Fast and Furious program, it was revealed that nearly 2,000 firearms were illegally purchased for $1.5 million, according to a DOJ inspector General report. Hundreds of guns were later recovered in the US and Mexico. Fast and Furious was one of the operations under Project Gunrunner, part of the Department of Justice's broader National Southwest Border Counternarcotic Strategy. Fast and Furious was not the ATF's first "gun walking" investigation, which allowed illegally purchased firearms to "walk" out of gun shops. It was preceded by Operation Wide Receiver, which began in 2006 under a Republican administration. *Operation Fast and Furious Fast Facts*, CNN. September 2017.

destroy great amounts of wealth, a global labor market that demands more skills, competition from emerging markets, and threats and challenges to Western liberal democracy.

Measured by almost any metric, the Obama administration was extremely successful. It inherited an economy in January of 2009 with 10% unemployment, mired in the worst financial crisis in peacetime since the 1930s and battling a recession. The economy was shedding hundreds of thousands of jobs every month and many big corporations were on the edge of bankruptcy. When Donald Trump was sworn into office in January of 2017, the US was registering the third-longest period of economic growth in its history. In January of 2017, unemployment stood at 4.7%, fourteen million jobs had been created during the Obama years, wages were rising among working-class Americans, inflation was contained, and the United States had become the world's top producer of both oil and natural gas. Twenty million Americans who were previously uninsured had affordable access to health-care. The economic expansion that began in the summer of 2009 may not have been as strong in terms of GDP growth as in previous decades, but it was certainly not anemic. And the XXIst century features a multipolar global economy with much tougher competition from emerging and developing countries, which generate 45% of the world's GDP.

Republicans obviously were eager to regain the White House after eight years of a Democratic president. But the notion they advanced of American decline is untrue. US nominal GDP according to the IMF figure for 2017 is approximately 19.3 trillion dollars, with China in second place but quite a bit of ground to cover, as its nominal GDP is 11.9 trillion dollars. And in per capita GDP and income, China is still an emerging country, with hundreds of millions in relative poverty in the interior of the country. Those predicting for years that China will soon overtake the US in nominal GDP are wrong -- especially with China's GDP now growing at little more than 6% and the US's having accelerated to close to 3%.

President Obama's administration also negotiated the Trans-Pacific Partnership (TPP), a new-generation trade agreement that strengthened the US's role in global governance. The TPP and other trade agreements signed during the Obama administration (US-Colombia and US-Peru Free-Trade Agreements) were not just about cutting tariffs. They also opened up other countries' markets to US exports of services and public-sector bidding, included mechanisms to enforce intellectual-property rights, ensure resolution of investment disputes and force emerging and developing countries to adopt and enforce higher environmental and labor standards.

Some will ask how it was possible for Donald Trump to defeat Hillary Clinton in 2016 in such a favorable context. Trump did not win the electoral vote, and his triumph in the electoral college was not big by historical standards. But setting aside these Democratic talking points, the 2016 presidential election was the first one since 1952 (with the exception of 2008) in which neither a sitting president was running for reelection or a sitting vice president from either the Republican or Democratic Party was running for the presidency. In this regard, it was a wide-open contest in which nobody in either party benefited from the power of incumbency or had high name recognition. There are of course two notable exceptions regarding name recognition. Almost everybody in America knew who Hillary Clinton and Donald Trump were. The real-estate magnate was very skillful in employing his communications skills honed during years of hosting "The Apprentice" to persuade those still struggling to get back to pre-2008 income levels – or simply conservatives – that he was the businessman-strongman that a complicated world requires.

Hillary Clinton, for her part, evinced many flaws as a presidential candidate: a sense of entitlement about the nomination, a long track record in public life vulnerable to criticisms, a level of oratory and charisma inferior to that of Barack Obama or her husband, a certain detachment from everyday life, and difficulty connecting with working-class white voters. Hillary Clinton's strengths were what many voters in 2016 did not want: experience in public life, personal ties to national and international political and business leaders, knowledge, amazing grasp of policy, continuity and detailed policy proposals.

As I had the chance to witness on the campaign trail, neither Republican, independent nor many Democratic voters were in the mood for these qualities. They wanted simple solutions to a complex world. They sought a disruptor who would shake up the political establishment and the dreaded and unfairly maligned federal government. Many wanted a Molotov cocktail they could hurl at the political, business and economic elites – and Donald Trump recognized, tapped into, channeled and amplified these feelings. In a more dignified way, Bernie Sanders in the Democratic primary proved the accuracy of this diagnosis. He is a former self-styled Socialist senator from liberal and lily-white Vermont with decades of experience in the Senate. Yet he promised millennials free health care and university education without a feasible plan to accomplish these goals and fanned the flames of conflict by pitting the poor and young against the wealthy and the elites.

I initially tried to volunteer for Hillary Clinton in New Hampshire in February of 2016. But even mid-level staffers were out of reach. It was impossible to even come close to catching a glimpse of Bill and Hillary Clinton, and I am a pretty perseverant person. I disliked Donald Trump's message intensely. I felt it was my obligation and duty to volunteer for a candidate who could defeat him.

In February of 2016, I stood in line for more than two hours, like everyone else, outside of an auditorium in Nashua, New Hampshire, and cleared the metal detectors. I kindly reached out to many of Hillary's staffers and volunteers while I waited in line, gave them my card, and indicated my desire to volunteer. After we finally entered the auditorium, many of us were placed in the bleachers. It was difficult to even see Bill and Hillary Clinton during the event. I nonetheless left a copy of my fifth book, which praises them both, just as many left copies of Hillary's book for the candidate to sign. Needless to say, my book was never signed, and the only feedback I received after eight hours of the Nashua event (including taxi cab from Concord, two hours in line, the event itself, the cab back to Concord) was a request for a donation, which a Legal Permanent Resident in the US is allowed to make.

In contrast, at the end of a Marco Rubio town hall the next day in Bow, New Hampshire, I approached the senator himself and had a nice conversation with him. He was very kind and graceful when I offered to volunteer for him. I only introduced myself as a professor from Spain, yet he was sincerely grateful, and we were in the middle of a crowd of adoring supporters. I subsequently attended many of his upbeat town halls in New Hampshire (in the Manchester and Nashua area) during the next days, and even had the opportunity to have meaningful short conversations with him. I handed him a copy of my sixth book and other documents, which he sincerely appreciated.

Marco Rubio was swamped by supporters at every event in New Hampshire. Yet I admired how he waited patiently for more than an hour until every single participant at his town hall (there were hundreds, if not thousands) who wished could greet him and have a picture taken with him. In a campaign that wanted anger, Marco Rubio finished a very distinguished third in number of delegates behind Donald Trump and Texas Senator Ted Cruz in a field of seventeen. Trump obtained 13.3 million votes during the primaries and caucuses, but Rubio's 3.4 million vote total was a noteworthy result for a first presidential run.

Rubio of course did criticize president Obama, Hillary and their policies at his events. But his stump speech was much more focused in content and time on spelling out how he wanted to ensure that the next generation of Americans enjoyed and inherited a better America. With a mix of charisma, wit, solid grasp of policy detail, specific proposals, uplifting oratory, an infectious optimism and a strenuous commitment to talk to every voter, Rubio finished second in the Iowa caucus.

In New Hampshire, he had been the object of blistering attacks from Donald Trump and others in the GOP field, and unfortunately was singled out in a critical TV debate in New Hampshire by then New Jersey Governor Chris Christie. Marco Rubio's campaign staff was enthusiastic, but as even insiders later acknowledged, relied excessively on the candidate's appeal and charisma. There were serious shortcomings which I witnessed first-hand in New Hampshire that could not be blamed on Rubio: no yard signs, lack of organization at town halls held in auditoriums whose maximum capacity was exceeded, and an unwillingness or inability to help Rubio after hours of campaigning to prepare for TV debates. Rubio's campaign was mostly made up of second-rate staffers from Mitt Romney's 2012 run. They were good people but simply not experienced enough.

Rubio was nonetheless on track to finish second in New Hampshire after Donald Trump and was gathering momentum. But at the debate among the still-crowded GOP field, Rubio froze under Christie's unrelenting questioning as to why he was repeating that Barack Obama wanted to change the United States. The junior senator from Florida himself admitted that he had performed poorly at the debate. Despite finishing fifth in New Hampshire, Rubio praised Christie, who dropped out. After disappointing results in secondary primaries, I drove to South Carolina and followed Rubio. The former speaker of the Florida House of Representatives had received the endorsement of popular South Carolina governor Nikki Haley and one of the Republican senators from the state, Tim Scott. The African-American senator is very affable, eloquent and intelligent. I had the chance to speak to him and he sincerely complimented my dedication of my sixth book for CNN's John King. South Carolina's other Republican senator, Lindsey Graham, was running for president himself.

As the field narrowed in South Carolina and with Haley, Scott and other popular Republicans (Trey Gowdy) campaigning with him, the son of Cuban-Americans finished second in the Palmetto state, garnering 22% of the vote. But Trump had pulled ahead of the field and was amassing many more victories and delegates than even his closest followers combined.

After the withdrawal of Christie, Jeb Bush and other sitting or former governors (Wisconsin's Scott Walker, Louisiana's Bobby Jindall, Texas' Rick Perry, Arkansas' Mike Huckabee, New York's George Pataki, Virginia's James Gilmore) and sitting or former senators Rand Paul of Kentucky and Rick Santorum from Pennsylvania, it was a four-man race between Trump, Cruz, Rubio and Kasich. By this time, former Hewlett-Packard CEO Carly Fiorina and retired neurosurgeon Ben Carson had also dropped out of the race.

If Ohio Governor John Kasich, Ted Cruz and Rubio had teamed up after the Nevada primary, they could have defeated Trump. But this was an unrealistic proposition. Cruz's ego is way too big. Kasich was the sitting governor of a key battleground state. Although Kasich ran a positive campaign and stayed away from personal attacks, he would not have formed a coalition even if the Rubio campaign had asked him to. Indeed, it is very likely that Kasich will challenge president Trump in 2020, although he will no longer be Ohio's governor due to term limits.

The vulnerabilities of the junior senator from Florida as a presidential candidate had been exposed. Some were unavoidable. He was a young (43) junior senator with a track record as representative, Majority Leader and Speaker of the Florida legislature. But some of this track record involved compromise and bipartisanship, something more conservative GOP voters disliked. He had invested political capital in an unfortunately failed attempt at immigration reform as a senator. As a member of the Senate Foreign Relations Committee, he could claim to have more foreign-policy experience than Trump, Kasich and Cruz. But on immigration and climate change he was too liberal for 2016 GOP voters, forcing him to disown immigration reform and uncomfortably fudge climate change. Another Achilles heel was his relative lack of a legislative record as a federal senator. Although the matter was never openly discussed and is probably not very relevant today, Rubio would have been (and could be if he runs again) only the United States' second Catholic president. John F. Kennedy's powerful and rich family had to invest all of its political capital to neuter this issue. Choosing Lyndon B. Johnson as his vice-presidential running mate was a clever decision that Joseph Kennedy Sr. forcefully recommended, and JFK made over the strenuous objections of Bobby Kennedy and many of his advisers.

Many analysts had warned Rubio that it was too soon for him to run for president, as he was completing his first term in the Senate. The four-term member of the Florida legislature countered with a pledge not to run for re-election in the Senate. He would either win the presidency or become a private citizen and return to academia at Florida International University or law practice. The Cuban-American senator also ran a dynamic and optimistic campaign, whose slogan was a New American Century. His adorable family traveled with him in Iowa and New Hampshire and enabled him to underscore his family values.

After a subpar performance on Super Tuesday, Rubio staked the continuity of his campaign on his state's primary. Kasich probably knew that he could not win, but Ohio's governor did not suspend his campaign. Cruz was running in second place in the delegate count and continued to launch attacks against Rubio. At one of the numerous GOP primary TV debates, Cruz and Rubio had Trump on the ropes, but were unable to deliver the knockout blow. In hindsight, it may have been impossible to stop Trump, who played the media like a fiddle. Television networks shamelessly allowed his antics in the name of higher ratings. In light of president Trump's conduct and his surprising 42% approval rating in the summer of 2018, it may indeed be true that he could shoot someone on Fifth Avenue and not lose his base's support.

I drove non-stop from Washington, D.C. to Miami in order to continue to volunteer for Rubio in the Florida primary. After leaving the nation's capital at 9 in the morning, I drove by myself for twenty-seven hours without any sleep and arrived in Miami at 1 PM of the following day. I even managed to make phone calls during the drive and check my cell phone. As my hotel room in Little Haiti was not ready, I still managed to make it to the Rubio campaign headquarters, where I volunteered working the phone banks. I made several acquaintances during my stay in Miami, and met Mia Love, the African-American who represents Utah's 4th congressional district. Marco Rubio's wife was also very pleasant. Unfortunately, Trump won the Florida primary in a landslide and Rubio promptly suspended his campaign after finishing in second place.

Rubio's withdrawal was a big disappointment. In addition to the politicians and journalists, I met many interesting and nice people during the campaign, such as Ed Adams from Indiana. I had many telephone conversations discussing strategy with Frank Edelblut, a businessman and New Hampshire state representative who lost the race for the GOP nomination for governor of New Hampshire to Chris Sununu by less than 1000 votes and less than one percentage point. Sununu, the son of former governor John Sununu, went on to defeat Democrat Colin Van Ostern in the general election. I spoke to Van Ostern while standing in line outside of the auditorium for Hillary's event in Nashua. He was kind, but I came away with the feeling that he was very confident of his victory and that he would be New Hampshire's next governor[4]. Edelblut, for his part, was appointed Commissioner of the New Hampshire Department of Education in 2017.

After the Florida primary, many of his supporters wanted Rubio to stay in the race, as he was trailing only Trump and Cruz in delegates. But not winning his home state was also a symbolic defeat. With hindsight, Rubio made the right choice. Had he stayed in the race, he would have struggled to raise money to campaign effectively and would have appeared desperate. After keeping a low profile for a few months, he decided to run for reelection in the Senate after all. Had he remained in the presidential primary after Florida, he probably would not be serving his second term as Florida's junior senator.

I continued to dislike Cruz and respect Kasich, who stayed in the race. On the Democratic side, I wanted Hillary to clinch the nomination and the Sanders camp to rally around the former Senator from New York. Although Trump was on his way to clinching the GOP nomination, I refused to believe that he could defeat Obama's former Secretary of State.

During the primaries I was well aware of the fact that Vice President Joe Biden could have run for president, as most sitting vice presidents in American history have done. I am extremely fond of the former long-time Senator from Delaware whose decades of experience on the Senate Foreign Relations Committee (and many years as its chairman or ranking member) were a great asset to Barack Obama's 2008 campaign and two terms as president. Between 2000 and 2008, the Obamas and Bidens became very close. Biden himself candidly and movingly explained on national television how the president and himself had forged a close friendship that transcended politics. They had become family.

During the beginning of the electoral campaign, Biden was again struck by family tragedy. His eldest son Beau passed away after a two-year battle with brain cancer. He was widely expected to run for the governorship of Delaware. He was Joe Biden's eldest son, had served in Irak with valor, in the Delaware National Guard and as Attorney General of Delaware. Beau had survived the tragic car accident on December 18th of 1972 that claimed the life of Biden's first wife Neilia and daughter Naomi.

The 1972 car accident was one of the biggest blows a person can endure. While driving during the Christmas shopping season, Joseph Biden's wife Neilia suffered a car accident that claimed not only her life, but that of her daughter Naomi, and left Joe's two sons Beau and Hunter with injuries. The driver of a tractor-trailer drove into Neilia's station wagon as she was backing up the car.

Joseph Biden, who had been elected to the Senate a few weeks earlier in November of 1972, was too devastated to contemplate serving in Congress. He was the sixth-youngest senator-elect in US history. Yet tending to his sons was all that mattered to him. In one of Richard Nixon's noble acts, the then president made a famous phone call to the grieving senator-elect to urge him to take the oath of office. Senate Majority Leader Mike Mansfield (D) is credited with convincing Biden to take the oath of office and not resign.

Joseph Biden was sworn in as Senator from Delaware in January of 1973. But for years he focused on raising his two sons, and often contemplated leaving the Senate to exclusively devote himself to Beau and Hunter. Fortunately for the world, he did not step down. He commuted from

---

[4] Sitting Governor Maggie Wood Hassan (D) could have run for reelection but opted to challenge Republican Senator Kelly Ayotte. Hassan beat Ayotte. Chris Sununu (R) defeated Van Ostern in the general election and is now New Hampshire's governor. Both New Hampshire senators – Jeanne Shaheen and Wood Hassan – are Democrats.

Delaware to Washington, D.C. on Amtrak trains for decades. His grief was so deep that even his sons, years later, urged him to remarry. His aides had orders to interrupt him in the Senate should either of his sons call or need anything.

During his battle with cancer, Beau urged his father to run for the presidency in 2016. The vice president agonized for some weeks with the difficult decision. Hillary Clinton's campaign was extremely well-funded and she was the undisputed candidate of the party's superdelegates and officials. If Biden had launched his own campaign, it would have split the moderate Democratic vote and possibly caused a rift in the party. But it is very conceivable that he could have beaten Hillary and Bernie Sanders. He did after all connect with the working-class white voters whom Hillary failed to attract in two presidential runs. When Barack Obama awarded Biden the Presidential Medal of Freedom with distinction in an emotional ceremony during the transition, I could not hold back my tears, as practically everyone at the event.

I have often been moved to tears when Joseph Biden describes in interviews his friendship with president Obama, how their children play together, conversations with president Obama about selling his home when his late son was ill, his exceptional nature, and his extremely difficult decision not to run for the presidency in October 2015. I always learn and appreciate what Joseph Biden has done for millions of Americans when I watch or read one of his interviews. If he runs in 2020, he will elevate the contest.

In early November of 2016, Milton Friedman and I arranged to meet in New York City. He was delivering conferences in the Big Apple. On November 9th, I had to travel to New York on an Amtrak train a few hours after Donald Trump defeated Hillary Clinton in the presidential election to take part in an evaluation of EAE Business School MBA students. I am an Adjunct Professor at EAE Business School. EAE Business School MBA students were spending a week in New Jersey and New York and making presentations at Kean University in New Jersey. I listened and provided input to all of their presentations, continued to do interviews for Spanish radio stations on the US election and wrote an op-ed for La Razón. I was stunned that Trump had won, but too busy to dwell on it. I doubt I slept more than 6 hours in the entire week I spent in New Jersey. Milton invited me to dinner in Manhattan. He was eager to know about the election.

MF: What do you think about Russia's role in the US elections?

AM: Despite massive leaks in State Department communications, DNC servers and emails and those of John Podesta (Hillary's campaign chairman) by Wikileaks and its founder Julian Assange during the summer and fall of 2016, most analysts thought that Hillary Clinton would be the 45th president of the United States.

Let us not forget that Julian Assange, the founder of Wikileaks, cannot leave the Ecuadorian embassy in London. If he did, the United Kingdom would have to extradite him to Sweden because the Scandinavian country's justice wants to question him in connection with his alleged sexual harassment of a former Wikileaks employee. It is obvious that Vladimir Putin orchestrated a campaign of interference in the US electoral process. In addition to being proven that hackers from Russian companies have worked with Wikileaks, Putin gave immunity in Russia to Eduard Snowden, a former consultant to the National Security Agency who also betrayed his agency, his country, and caused much damage to the West by disseminating thousands of secret communications between the US and foreign officials -- in many cases allies.

Russian president Vladimir Putin hates Hillary Clinton because, like John Kerry, she served as Obama's Secretary of State. Kerry oversaw the effort to coordinate with US allies the sanctions applied on Russia by the US and the EU following the annexation of Crimea and Russian financial, military, and logistical support for the occupation of the territory of the Donbas in eastern Ukraine, a conflict that caused thousands of deaths. Former Secretary of State Clinton also harshly criticized Putin's crackdown of peaceful demonstrations in December 2012 in several Russian cities against the Kremlin's rigging of the results of the Duma (parliamentary) elections. The Russian government is replacing Microsoft software with a Russian version on all state enterprise computers or any branch of public administration in Russia -- from the central government to municipalities, through its nearly 100 regions. The headquarters of Amnesty International in Moscow has been closed. It is clear that relations between the United States and Russia will deteriorate, and Russian people will be most affected.

Russian GDP contracted by more than 4% in 2015 and 2016, especially as oil and metal prices plummeted in 2014 and Putin did not diversify his country's economy. Russia's population is also ageing at a rapid pace. Microsoft can afford to lose a customer, namely the Russian state. China also censors Western television networks and restricts Internet access for its citizens and bloggers. The old economic alliance between Russia and China is resurfacing. Russian giant Rosneft will sell 20% of its subsidiary Verkhnechonskneftegaz to Beijing Enterprises Group Company Limited. As the great chess player he is, Putin moves pieces and waits for the West's reaction. Putin threatens more military adventures and has sent nuclear-capable Iskander missiles to the Russian border with Lithuania. Free and democratic societies must maintain a united front. Some Western companies will be harmed and lose business in Russia. Unfortunately, denying that we are facing a new cold war is naive.

The Kremlin has violated and abandoned two decisive treaties from the end of the Cold War: the treaty limiting conventional weapons in Europe (CFE, 1987) and the one eliminating plutonium. Moreover, it routinely launches cyberattacks and violates the airspace of the Baltic republics and Poland. The Russian people are generous and welcoming. I have visited Russia on numerous occasions, delivered conferences in Moscow, Saint Petersburg and Saratov, and even lived there for months. But their president is a ruthless dictator.

MF: Are you not exaggerating a little bit? It would be in both US and Russian interests (and those of the rest of the world) if their respective governments could cooperate in the war to destroy ISIS and begin the very long road to the reconstruction of a semblance of a state and services for Syria's citizens.

AM: That is the kind of argument advanced by Trump and many of his advisers. Putin's cooperation is always self-serving. We were very unlucky when former Russian president Boris Yeltsin named Vladimir Putin as his successor in 2000. His former pro-western finance minister, Boris Nemtsov, was another of his protégés, and Yeltsin tried to marry him to a Swedish princess. Nemtsov had also served as mayor of the city of Nizhny Novgorod (Gorky under the USSR). He often gave interviews to Western television media such as CNN and was well-known outside of Russia. He died riddled by bullets next to the Kremlin walls in 2014 when he was walking with his Ukrainian girlfriend. Curiously, the Kremlin cameras were not recording that night. Nemtsov planned to head a demonstration against the invasion of Ukraine the next day. His apartment was registered, and Chechen-paid assassins allegedly confessed to the murder after they were arrested. But many suspect that it was a hit job ordered by the Kremlin, who resorted to the Chechens to do the actual killing.

For most of its history Russia has been ruled by powerful tsars more or less efficiently. Putin floods television screens with news that appeal to the nationalism of its population -- its rearmament, its external successes -- to divert attention from the country's deteriorating economy.

After my return to Washington, D.C. in March of 2017, Milton and I met in a restaurant in Vienna, Virginia. I also brought him up to speed on the news at a subsequent meeting at the McDonald's near my condo on April 7th. I then set out on another half-marathon run. After reaching 81 degrees Fahrenheit a few days earlier, temperatures had again dropped dramatically. It was in the low 50s when I left my apartment. Janet advised me that it was cold when I jogged past her office. She requested I fill out a form to delegate my vote for an upcoming Brookside association meeting. It was indeed windy and chilly. But I still completed my half-marathon wearing a short-sleeved T-shirt. As I was well-rested, I managed to run my route in two hours ten minutes, close to my lowest time ever.

Afterwards, I continued to watch the coverage and analysis of President Trump's decision to launch 59 Tomahawk missiles against a Syrian air force base whence Syrian president Bashar Al-Assad's jets had bombed the civilian population with sarin gas. Early in the week, both Trump and Secretary of State Rex Tillerson had remarked that they would not get the US involved in the Syrian civil war. Trump had repeatedly vowed as a candidate to stay away from Syria and expressed the hope that Russia and the US could work together to destroy ISIS in Syria. Trump was thus signaling that the US no longer sought to remove Assad from power, whereas the Obama administration rejected any role for Assad in post-war Syria.

Tillerson had literally said early in the week that it was up to the Syrians to determine their future. Regime change was thus completely off the table. Lulled by such talk, Bashar al-Assad blatantly miscalculated. He authorized his air force to attack civilians with sarin gas. Over one hundred civilians were killed by the chemical attack. The footage of children suffocating after being targeted with sarin shocked even those used to the devastation of the Syrian armed forces' brutal bombings of hospitals in the cities of Homs and Aleppo. Ordering the missile attack against the Syrian military base also allowed Trump to shift attention away from the ongoing investigation of his associates' ties with Russian officials and the House's rejection of his health-care plan to repeal Obamacare. But he was sincere when he expressed outrage at the killing of innocent civilians with chemical weapons. The citizens of Idlib in Syria may now face the same fate, in the last opposition-controlled city.

Moreover, several hostile powers had been testing the 45th president of the US. Iran had tested three short-range missiles, deployed a Russian air-defense system and repeatedly harassed US Navy vessels in the Strait of Hormuz. North Korea had fired five medium-range ballistic missiles since Trump's inauguration on January 20th, 2017. Assad's massacre using chemical weapons was one provocation too far, and in this instance killed civilians.

President Trump was hosting Chinese president Xi Jinping at his Florida resort when Assad unleashed the sarin gas against his own people. Members of Congress were flying back home for their spring break. The Chairman of the Joints Chief of Staff, Joseph Dunford, and Secretary of Defense James Mattis presented Trump with several options for retaliating against Syrian military installations. The president opted for the barrage of 59 Tomahawk missiles against the Syrian air force base. I commend Trump for his swift, decisive and measured response.

On the 4th of July in 2017, worrying news from Korea had been reported by the main network channels. North Korea's lunatic dictator, Kim Jong Un, had launched yet another missile. Analysts confirmed that the ICBM had traveled almost 1000 kilometers before splashing into Japan's expanded economic zone, meaning its coastal waters. CNN trotted out the usual array of good military and civilian experts to weigh in on this latest provocation by North Korea's dictator ahead of a G20 Summit in Germany.

A former high-ranking CIA officer who had held talks with North Korean officials a few weeks earlier confirmed that the Hermit Kingdom's leadership was now in no mood to even entertain the thought of negotiating away or even freezing its nuclear program. The North Koreans wanted the US to accept that Pyongyang would remain a nuclear power. As president Trump had stated that a nuclear-armed North Korea was unacceptable, what options could be pursued?

Applying tougher sanctions on countries and companies doing business with North Korea was an obvious starting point. Reinforcing South Korea's and Japan's anti-missile defenses and conducting military drills close to North Korea were also obvious steps. Almost all analysts -- whether military or civilian -- continue to rule out a pre-emptive surgical strike against North Korea's nuclear program sites by the United States as it would probably immediately prompt a barrage of conventional and even nuclear missiles to rain down on South Korea and its capital Seoul, located only 35 miles from the border with North Korea.

A few days later, Milton invited me to dinner at the glitzy Eddy V's restaurant in Tysons Corner, Virginia, in a majestic building opposite from the Hilton hotel. He was very eager to get my take and analyze the results of the UK general election. Theresa May had unnecessarily called the elections despite having an absolute majority. She wanted and requested from voters an even stronger mandate to negotiate Brexit, as the absolute majority had been achieved by her predecessor, Prime Minister David Cameron. May ran a poor campaign and the Tories lost their majority in the House of Commons.

MF: What is your take on Theresa May's devastating defeat in the general elections?

AM: *The Canterbury Tales* is one of the top works of English literature and the most outstanding of the Middle Ages. Written at the end of the fourteenth century by Geoffrey Chaucer, the set of 24 stories in 17,000 lines ironically and critically describes late fourteenth-century England through the experiences of different characters. Chaucer acted as customs comptroller, justice of the peace and scribe of the work of the King. The stories are presented as part of a story-telling competition by a group of pilgrims on a trip from London to Canterbury to visit the shrine of St. Thomas Becket in the cathedral of that town. The contest prize is an agape at a Southward hostel on the way back.

I mention *The Canterbury Tales* because the constituency of Canterbury had been represented for 176 years by a member of the Conservative Party until June's election, when Labor wrested it from the Tories. Theresa May is an arrogant opportunist, in my view. She called unnecessary elections and managed to breathe new life into a deeply divided Labor Party led by a neo-Marxist, Jeremy Corbyn. Labor garnered 40% of the vote, increased its vote total by 10% and its seats by 29. It was only the implosion of the Scottish National Party (SNP) in parts of Scotland that prevented a government coalition between Labor, the Liberal Democrats and the SNP. The Tories have lost their absolute majority and can only govern -- with difficulties -- with the support of the Democratic Unionist Party, a party from Northern Ireland.

Theresa May should go to Canterbury. But she does not have too much time. In twelve days she is scheduled to start the Brexit negotiations. She represents the constituency of Maidenhead, the place where General Dwight D. Eisenhower deployed the brilliant but arrogant General George Patton Jr. with a fictitious army full of plastic tanks and artillery to mislead the Nazis. General Erwin Rommel, in charge of the coastal defenses in occupied Europe, was convinced that Patton would lead the Allied forces that would land in France. The Pas de Calais was the closest and logical point because it is where the Channel is most narrow. The plan worked perfectly. While the Allies landed hundreds of thousands of soldiers on the beaches of Normandy on June 6, 1944, Hitler insisted on maintaining numerous divisions in the area of the Pas de Calais. Although Patton was brave, he slapped two traumatized soldiers and was on a kind of probation before the Normandy landings. To place him as a decoy with a fictional army in Maidenhead was a brilliant move by Eisenhower, who secured Churchill's support for this and many other tough decisions in the lead-up to D-Day.

The Nazi generals never believed reports that the Allies would sacrifice their best tank commander (Patton) because he had slapped two shell-shocked soldiers. They waited in vain for Patton in Calais while their troops in Normandy were vanquished by the Allies despite heavy loss of life both on the beaches and among the paratroopers of the US Army's 82nd and 101st Airborne Divisions. Rommel soon realized the deceit and frantically tried to convince Chief of the Armed Forces High Command Alfred Jodl to call Hitler to obtain permission to transfer the troops stationed at Calais to Normandy. Rommel had been in Germany to attend his wife's birthday on D-Day. But he was soon back in Normandy. Jodl was no fool and also acknowledged that there would be no Allied landings at Calais. But he did not want to wake Hitler up and contradict his instructions. Rommel became exasperated with Jodl's cowardice. Hitler slept for twelve hours, and after he awoke the reinforcements he ordered sent to Normandy were up against successful landings and entrenched Allied positions at the Normandy beaches and nearby towns, as well as Allied command of the skies.

MF: We were talking about the British elections and the Tories' loss of their absolute majority. What does this have to do with the Normandy landings?

AM: Theresa May does not understand that it takes a great team like the one assembled by Eisenhower and Churchill to achieve victory. She is dragging the United Kingdom into complicated negotiations. She still lives in fiction. Negotiating the divorce bill, the rights of EU citizens in the UK, a post-Brexit trade agreement with the EU and replacing the EU legislation that continues to apply in the UK will take much longer than two years. Each member state will claim something from London, from European agencies headquartered in the UK to fishing concessions. And each member state will be able to slow down the negotiations.

European Commission president Jean-Claude Juncker and Council president Donald Tusk say they want to complete negotiations as soon as possible. They fear a reaction from the markets to excessive uncertainty. The shortest route from London to Brussels is through Maidenhead. But Theresa May and her closest advisers do not even live in the *Tales of Canterbury*. Chaucer described through his characters the varied customs of his time. May does not even seem to understand the complexity of her constituency in Maidenhead, let alone the United Kingdom that she and fellow Brexiteers may unwillingly break up.

There has been no break in the ranks among the 27 other member states of the EU in their requirement that the UK pay the so-called divorce deal, recognize the rights of EU citizens in the UK and prevent a 'hard' border from being erected between Ireland and Northern Ireland. Prime Minister May, Brexit Secretary David Davis and Trade Secretary Liam Fox all tried to cajole, persuade or threaten the EU to accept the opening of negotiations on a post-Brexit trade deal between the UK and the EU before the aforementioned three items have been resolved. But the Commission, the Council, the European Parliament and the 27 member states have not budged.

When the UK government warned that there might be no deal before the UK withdraws from the EU in March of 2019, the EU called its bluff. Financial, currency and stock markets obviously do not want uncertainty and turmoil. May was probably expecting that such a scenario might spook EU leaders into beginning the trade talks immediately. She was wrong. May also threatened to withhold important security information that it currently shares with its EU partners.

The Prime Minister is in a difficult bind. The hard 'Brexiteers' prefer a UK with no trade deal with the EU (which would entail reverting to WTO tariffs) to concessions on the divorce bill and the movement of workers. The Chancellor of the Exchequer, Philip Hammond, is a strong proponent of the UK maintaining its access to the EU's single market either through the European Economic Area model (like Norway) or as part of a customs union with the EU. As May realized that the negotiations would not be concluded by March of 2019, she began to backpedal. She delivered a conciliatory speech in Florence. In her remarks she addressed primarily European officials. She dropped her standard "no deal is better than a bad deal" line. For the first time, she unequivocally accepted that the UK would honor the financial commitments it made when the 28 EU member states approved the 2014-2020 financial perspectives for the EU budget. May did not quantify how much London is ready to pay. The EU has insisted that the UK is on the hook for 100 billion euros because, like every other EU member state, it legally committed itself to its contribution to the EU budgets from 2014 to 2020 (the aforementioned 2014-2020 financial perspectives).

MF: So what do you think Theresa May will do?

AM: During her speech in Florence, May also acknowledged that there would have to be a transition period after March of 2019 because the negotiations on the EU's three red lines (divorce bill, rights of EU citizens in the UK and Ireland-Ulster border), other outstanding issues and a post-Brexit trade deal will not have been finalized by then. She hinted that this transition period would last about two years. During the transition period, the UK would continue to honor its contributions to the EU budget, guarantee full rights to EU citizens in the UK, free movement for EU workers and respect the jurisdiction of the European Court of Justice. This is also anathema to Brexiteers, who in May's cabinet are led by Foreign Secretary Boris Johnson[5].

Theresa May again voiced her opposition to the "Norway" model, an arrangement whereby Norway, Iceland and Liechtenstein have access to the EU's single market but are not members of the EU, are not represented in its institutions and have no say over the drafting over directives and other EU legislation. Moreover, Norway makes payments into the EU budget. May also rules out forming a customs union with the EU. She advocates a bespoke agreement tailored to the UK's wishes. It remains to be seen whether the EU will accept setting a dangerous precedent for other possible EU member states by crafting a deal solely to satisfy the UK. Analysts expect EU heads of state and government to conclude in their October 2017 summit that not enough progress has been achieved on the terms of the exit bill and that trade negotiations therefore cannot begin. The EU's commissioner in charge of the Brexit negotiations, Michel Barnier, wants the initial Brexit negotiations (over the exit conditions) to be finalized within the next 12 months.

But the constructive tone used by May in Florence and the concessions she made in her speech are anathema to the hard Brexiteers. May's Foreign Secretary, Boris Johnson, immediately voiced his opposition and insisted there would be no freedom of movement for workers nor observance of EU rules after March of 2019. Johnson and Liam Fox founded a think-tank that will advocate a hard Brexit. The prime minister will find that keeping the hard Brexiteers on board as she negotiates with Brussels will be tough sledding. The only reason the hard Brexiteers are not seeking to oust May though a leadership challenge is their fear that Labor could win if another general election is called so soon after the debacle of June 2017, when the Tories lost their absolute majority. EU officials welcomed May's more conciliatory tone but continued to emphasize they need more specifics on what the UK is offering and cannot negotiate via speeches.

MF: How is French president Emmanuel Macron doing in terms of his economic reforms? Without them, France is doomed to stagnation.

AM: French President Emmanuel Macron should be hard at work pushing the economic reforms he campaigned on. But he could not resist inviting the US president to France. President Trump flew to Paris to take part in the July 14th Bastille Day celebrations. One of president Trump's takeaways from the visit was his idea to have a big military parade in Washington, D.C., which is original, but not something the establishment expected.

I am frankly disappointed that French president Macron is not spending more time pushing much-needed reforms through the French Parliament that his party completely controls. This is a

---

[5] Boris Johnson resigned as Foreign Secretary in July of 2018.

recurring problem with newly elected presidents or prime ministers. Instead of taking care of pressing domestic affairs, they travel overseas or host foreign leaders and thus waste precious political capital and time. The French media and some among public opinion did complain about this unnecessary invitation. After all, Macron had already met and spoken to Trump during the G20 Summit in Hamburg, Germany, only a few weeks earlier. In most democratic countries, it is easier and certainly more glamorous for the head of state or government to engage with foreign leaders or carry out foreign policy endeavors than to get legislation through Parliament.

Milton, as you often come to Washington, D.C. and have friends in very high places, maybe they can fly you into Joint base Andrews as opposed to landing at Dulles International Airport in Virginia or Reagan National Airport, which are further away. I happen to live extremely near to Joint base Andrews (JBAB). It is an Air Force base which is also used by the president of the US, whose Marine One helicopter takes off from the White House lawns and flies him to JBAB, where he can board Air Force One. Just a little tidbit as my condo is located very near to JBAB, in Prince George's County Maryland.

MF: Well, I am well paid and fly business, but getting to fly into Andrews is on another level. I am not the president or vice president. What are you up to?

AM: On the news front, Chuck Todd -- whom I consider a great journalist -- interviewed Corey Lewandowski in the wake of the emails that Donald Trump Jr. was forced to reveal. Lewandowski was pushed aside in a power struggle in 2016 within the Trump campaign. Paul Manafort was already the campaign chairman in charge of financing and policy. Lewandowski himself admitted that he was only in charge of events. On *Meet the Press*, Lewandowski showed off about knowing so many people that he would have to be courteous enough to meet an unknown person (the Kremlin-linked Russian lawyer who met at Trump tower with Paul Manafort and Donald Trump Jr., among others) if one of his multiple friends requested that he do so. Lewandowski knows people and something about politics, but he was a brute who pushed aside journalists during the campaign and therefore wanted the interview to get some revenge on those in the campaign who convinced Trump to fire him.

But I think that this overreporting about the intrigues within the White House by the media is dangerous. President Trump is already obsessed enough with the coverage he gets from the media. He will never get around to reading intelligence briefings and get acquainted with policy matters if the networks spend so much time parsing every comment he makes.

Chapter 5. From Russia with Love: Robert Mueller and his Crack Team

In July of 2017 Milton Friedman paid another visit to Washington, D.C. He was scheduled to deliver conferences at the Peterson Institute for International Economics, the Brookings Institution, the Heritage Foundation and the Center for Strategic and International Studies. I did manage to get Friedman to meet me at the McDonald's on Jefferson Davis Highway in Alexandria, Virginia. Friedman needed to know the developments regarding the Russia investigations by Special Counsel Robert Mueller and the Senate and House Intelligence Committees. Journalists showed up at the end of his conferences and asked him questions. Friedman needed to know what was going on.

MF: Journalists and people at think-tanks ask me about the possible collusion with Russia and Moscow's meddling in the 2016 elections, which has already been proven. What is the latest?

AM: I am disappointed that CNN and MSNBC devote so much time to reporting every small development linked to the ongoing investigation into the Trump campaign. I of course understand that their desire for high ratings is the reason for their wall-to-wall coverage, and they also feel a duty to check the Trump administration's excesses and hold it accountable. But MSNBC, in particular, barely covers international issues, unless they are directly related to the US, the Russia investigation or in the event of a big natural disaster (hurricane, earthquake) or terrorist attacks overseas.

MSNBC and CNN anchors and the analysts on their shows rail against partisanship and the polarization of American society, but they also play a role in fueling it. It helps their ratings. Reporting on the latest character from the Trump campaign who solicited help from Russia or the latest allegation of misconduct by a celebrity or politician is much better for their ratings than informing us, for example, on the size of the Liberal Democratic Party's victory in Japan's legislative elections. I guess they would argue that those kinds of items are listed on their news ticker. I therefore need to spend extra time in order to keep you abreast of international political, economic and business developments, as per our agreement.

At least the combination of CNN and MSNBC (if I am reading the ticker) keeps me somewhat informed about what is happening in the US and around the world. But to get a full picture of political, economic, business and financial events around the world, it is necessary for me to read *The Economist* every week-end and spend quite a few hours reading the Reuters website during the week. MSNBC does not even try to disguise its contempt for president Trump, his behavior, policies and those of his surrogates. Rachel Maddow, Lawrence O'Donnell, Chris Hayes and Brian Williams are all very good journalists, but they are undoubtedly on a quest to get to the bottom of the Russia collusion case and perhaps earn a Pulitzer Prize. It is obvious that MSNBC has an agenda, which is to discredit Trump and his policies. Chris Matthews is the only MSNBC anchor who – while not disguising his contempt for Trump and his policies – does not engage in unabated optimism regarding an eventual Trump downfall. They are certainly entitled to push their agenda, but they cannot claim to be neutral. MSNBC and CNN get most of the scoops on the Russia investigation from the reporting done by journalists from The Washington Post, the New York Times and The Wall Street Journal.

Rachel Maddow is very funny. Although she reads from a teleprompter, she manages to insert witty commentary as she details the latest twists in the Russian investigation, and even her staffers in the studio often cannot contain their laughter.

For example, she reported that President Trump's leading personal attorney, Marc Kasowitz, does not have and would not seek a security clearance. How on Earth could Kasowitz defend Trump if he could not access the documents and information that special Counsel Robert Muller is looking into and might be the basis for an accusation against Trump and others in the White House?

Maddow also reported on July 13th, 2017, that Kasowitz lost his cool when an anonymous person sent him an email pressing him to resign. Kasowitz shot off five emails in less than an hour and a half threatening the anonymous person. The emails were graced with a lot of profanity and clearly showed that Kasowitz was under a lot of stress. Sources in the White House were reporting that he had thought about resigning and that the West Wing was paralyzed by the disclosures. Kasowitz did apologize through a spokesman after a few hours. He attributed his email outburst to the fact that it had been a long day and it was 10 pm when he received the anonymous email. As Rachel Maddow was quick to point out, defending president Trump in the ensuing months would be a tough job requiring many all-nighters. Kasowitz left Trump's legal team a few weeks later.

Jay Sekulow, who is still on Trump's legal team, was officially contradicted after asserting that president Trump had played no role in drafting a statement by his son, Donald Jr, regarding the Trump Tower meeting of June 2016 with the Kremlin-linked lawyer, Natalia Veselnitskaya, who hoped a potential Trump administration would scrap the Magnitsky Act. The White House admitted that the president had weighed in.

Two of Trump's current lead personal attorneys -- Ty Cobb and John Dowd -- are openly sparring over the strategy to defend Trump. Openly is not a word I am using lightly. On September 18th, 2017, both attorneys had lunch on a sidewalk table at a well-known Washington, D.C., restaurant, BLT Steak. The eatery is very close to the White House and located less than 200 feet from the New York Times bureau in the nation's capital. Ken Vogel, a particularly good New York times investigative reporter, overheard much of their conversation, as many others could have. They sat at a table outdoors (it was a nice day) but spoke too loudly and had no sense of their surroundings. For more than an hour they heatedly debated the right strategy to defend the president from further requests for documentation from Special Counsel Robert Mueller's team. One of the attorneys, Ty Cobb, favors furnishing as many documents as necessary. He premises this approach on his conviction that president Trump has done nothing wrong and that maximum transparency is the best way to go.

MF: This is getting complicated! We can eat at the BLT Steak restaurant for our next meeting. Maybe we will overhear an interesting conversation too!

AM: Well, you know I am not a big eater. Moreover, people will recognize you at BLT Steak. The kind of people that eat at this McDonald's – with all due respect – do not know who you are. Anyway, Trump's other attorney, John Dowd, objects and points to the precedent for executive authority that providing many documents and transcripts of conversations between the president and his advisors will set. He believes that the executive authority of future presidents will be weakened if too many documents and witnesses are made available to the Special Counsel. The substance of their argument is very valid. But the two attorneys showed extremely poor judgment by holding this conversation over an outdoor restaurant table within very close earshot of the other people who were also having lunch outdoors. One of the attorneys, Ty Cobb, is very easily recognizable because of his peculiar handlebar moustache. And, to make matters worse, the restaurant is located only 177 feet from the New York Times bureau in Washington, D.C.

The New York Times (as well as the Washington Post, CNN, MSNBC and other media outlets) has dozens of reporters investigating the Russia probe and they all hope they well get great scoops. The fact that Ty Cobb and John Dowd openly and loudly discussed key details of their defense strategy over lunch at a sidewalk table of a popular restaurant shows extremely poor judgment. They are probably very stressed, too. Cobb has already been reprimanded by White House Chief of Staff John Kelly over public comments and tweets. He works at the White House, whereas John Dowd does not. Cobb wants documents locked away by White House Counsel Don McGahn II to be made public, whereas Dowd is wary about such a move. Their conversation also showcased the climate of distrust among Trump's advisors and attorneys.

MF: What is happening to president Trump's legislative agenda? Will Obamacare be repealed?

AM: A significant development in Congress was Senate Majority Leader Mitch McConnell's attempt to garner fifty votes to replace President Obama's Affordable Care Act with a Republican health-care law that would gut Medicaid. Republicans in the Senate had already lost two votes, those of Republican senators Susan Collins of Maine and Rand Paul of Kentucky. If another Republican senator announced that he or she would vote against the Republican plan, the measure would not pass the Senate as the 48 Democratic senators were united in their opposition. This attempt to replace Obamacare was one of the reasons that Congress had not gone on its summer recess as the week of July 9th, 2017, drew to a close. Lawmakers also approved sanctions against Russia in the Senate in an almost unanimous vote. But this measure was being held up in the House of Representatives. Lawmakers also needed to increase the US debt ceiling before going on vacation.

President Trump performed a few more U-turns while in Paris on July 14th, when he declared that his administration might reconsider its position against the Paris climate change agreement and that his infamous wall on the border with Mexico might not need to be so long. These pronouncements were obviously intended to make him less unpopular among foreign leaders. The question was whether his base might hear them, and even care if they did.

MF: What about Donald Trump's first budget? Is he planning to cut the US's budget deficit and begin to slow the acceleration of national debt? Will he cut taxes?

AM: Not at all. His budget proposal included a substantial increase in funding for the US armed forces and a broad range of tax cuts. His attempt to cut the US corporate tax rate, among the highest in the world, should be praised.

MF: Who are his main economic advisors?

AM: Well, his Treasury Secretary is Steven Mnuchin. He had a senior position at Goldman Sachs and was the Trump campaign chairman. He kept a relatively low profile in Trump's first semester in office. He did appear publicly to pitch the administration's tax reform plan. Trump heaped a lot of praise in his first months in office on Gary Cohn, one of his main economic advisors, and respects his intellect. Cohn is actually a Democrat and served as Director of the National Economic Council. But it is hard to tell if Trump's flattering words were just one more instance of his tendency to say glowing things about the latest person who captures his imagination. Cohn might have just been a flavor of the month, or of a few months at most.

The Director of the Office of Budget and Management is Mick Mulvaney. Trump's candidate for the position of Chairman of the Council of Economic Advisors (CEA), Kevin Hassett, was not sworn in until the middle of September of 2017. He has not yet been in the news nor had a high profile. But the note he drafted upon taking up his position is very encouraging. Hassett emphasized the importance and tradition of the Council of Economic Advisors, created in 1946, and even mentioned that his predecessor in the Obama administration (Jason Furman) had left a note in a drawer precisely underscoring the reputation of the office. Hassett also mentioned his task as daunting, and referenced pictures of Alan Greenspan, Janet Yellen, Walter Heller and Martin Feldstein in his office, which is a nod to bipartisanship and the outstanding competence of previous Chairpersons of the CEA. Stephen Miller is another influential White House advisor, but he is focusing on reforming the immigration system and is very conservative.

MF: What about financial deregulation? The Dodd-Frank bill has been a drag on financial institutions.

AM: Well, I beg to differ. If the financial sector had not been deregulated beginning in the 1980s, we would not have suffered the 2007-2009 financial crisis and the Great Recession. Repealing the Glass-Stegall act was a catastrophe. It allowed investment banks to speculate with the deposits of retail banks' customers. The Glass-Steagall act was approved in the wake of the 1929 stock market crash in order to separate investment and retail banking. Alan Greenspan refused to regulate the derivatives markets. You should watch the documentary "Inside Job". After all, you passed away in 2006, right before the financial and real-estate bubble burst.

President Trump has vowed to roll back the financial regulation passed under president Obama. He has nominated Randal Quarles to the position of vice chairman of the Federal Reserve, with the remit of financial supervision. Quarles is an attorney who has represented several financial institutions. He has worked on bank investments at the Carlyle Group, a private-equity firm, as well as at Cynosure, a company that invests on behalf of wealthy families. He has basically worked at places that make rich people even richer. That is not a good omen for financial supervision. Quarles and the new chairman of the Securities and Exchange Commission, Jay Clayton, are proponents of whittling down the stress tests and other reporting requirements banks are subjected to under Dodd-Frank.

MF: Alex, you are much too pessimistic regarding the animal spirits of the financial markets. Tax cuts will lead to higher growth and more jobs with better wages. A rising tide lifts all boats. There is full employment in the US.

AM: Yes, but as companies replace humans with machines, what about people who are not very smart or do not have the means to obtain a degree in engineering, the sciences or IT? How will they make a living ten years from now?

MF: Working in agriculture and low added-value jobs in the services sector.

AM: The problem is that not a lot of people want to toil in the fields, especially when it is very hot or cold, or taking care of elderly or handicapped people is also not something everybody can do. President Trump has indicated that he would like to expand the guest-worker program that precisely enables foreigners to come into the US and work for a few months every year in a sector like agriculture. They are needed, for example, when it is time to harvest a crop. These foreigners are not given any kind of immigration benefit. They do not accumulate time spent in the US towards legal permanent residence.

Everybody knows that not enough Americans are willing to work in agriculture. But even such a straightforward part-time guest-worker program runs into some opposition in Congress from lawmakers in states with higher unemployment. And as technology progresses, the number of manual jobs in agriculture will gradually disappear. Efficient farms are already very mechanized and require very few workers. I can only envision a farm owner or manager making a calculation that paying guest workers a pittance might save money as opposed to operating machinery. The guest workers would probably not want to work for a pittance for a very long time. Therefore, employing low-skilled people in agriculture is at best a part-time short-term solution.

Today president Trump returned from France after his visit on the 14th of July and flew straight to one of his golf courses in New Jersey. He is still hoping that Republicans will muster 51 votes and approve his health care bill this week to repeal and replace Obamacare.

My concern is that the acceleration of technology will foster income inequality. The winners will be the owners, managers, investors and shareholders of companies that are tech-savvy, or which produce technologically-advanced goods or services. The companies that supply these tech-heavy companies will also thrive. But what if you are not an owner, executive, board member, significant shareholder or hold a mid- to high-level position at one of these successful technological companies? There will of course be plenty of winners as the groups I listed are not small.

But inequality has already been increasing in the past decades. In Marxist terminology, those who accumulate the stock, capital and skills of companies that are competitive in the digital era will be well-off. The rest will struggle, and society needs to be ready to deal with their discontent. One of the reasons that demagogues have won elections is that natives who do not have the skills required by today's companies reject immigrants who do have them or are willing to work for a lower wage. In counties in the United States where a majority of the population had more than a high school degree, Hillary Clinton bested Donald Trump by 25 points. But among white working-class males (WWCM) with only a high-school degree, 75% voted for Donald J. Trump.

I will give you another example. This one was reported by *The Economist* in its issue of July 15th, 2017. It analyzed the phenomenon of digital twins. To illustrate the point, the article described a factory owned by Siemens in Bavaria which is 75% automated. It produces industrial computer-control systems which are essential bits of machinery used in a variety of automated systems, which happen to include the Bavarian factory's production line. The Siemens factory is therefore mostly using robots to manufacture industrial robots. This factory in Amberg in Bavaria produces 15 million units a year, a 10-fold increase since 1989. As *The Economist* points out, the factory has decreased its number of employees, and only has 1200 workers. The article goes on to chillingly report that the defect rate at this factory is close to zero. Therefore, in the not-too-distant future there will be factories where robots will manufacture other robots or machinery, with just a few highly-skilled humans (mostly engineers, IT specialists) in supervisory roles.

MF: But there will still be plenty of opportunities to make a living for entertainers, professional athletes, artists and academics, for example. As you know, a society that seeks to eliminate inequality winds up undermining freedom.

AM: Milton, the percentage of the population that can make a good living as an entertainer, artist or in professional sports is relatively small. As for academics, you were of course one of the 20th century's most prominent academics and professors. *The Economist* ranked you as one of the two most influential economists of the 20th century, and the most influential in the second one in the second half of the 20th century.

MF: Who was the other economist I had to share the distinction with regards to the first half of the 20th century?

AM: John Maynard Keynes.

MF: That bastard! I spent decades proving his theories wrong and ushering in decades of economic growth and prosperity by advising governments to ditch Keynesianism.

AM: Well my point is that you have been an extremely illustrious academic. Most academics do not earn much.

MF: Well, I object. I obtained my BA at Rutgers, my Masters' degree at the University of Chicago and my PhD at the University of Columbia. I studied and worked very hard. I taught at the University of Chicago for thirty years.

AM: Yes, Milton. You also received the Nobel Memorial Prize in the Economic Sciences in 1976 for your work on consumption analysis, the theory and history of monetary policy and the complexity of stabilization. Your work influenced Ronald Reagan, Margaret Thatcher, the Cato Institute, and very renown economists and academics such as Thomas Sowell, Gary Becker, Robert Lucas Jr., Robert Fogel, Paul Krugman and many other very distinguished professors. You are in a group of elite academics who have made a good living! You were at the top of your profession at the world level. You did make a good living until you passed away in 2016. And you continue to earn a lot of money now with your conferences and consulting for governments and corporations. But not all academics are superstars.

Speaking of people that you influenced, Senator Rand Paul from Kentucky is one of the two Republican Senators who has announced his opposition to president Trump's health care bill. In Paul's case, his rejection is based on the fact that Trump's plan to replace the Affordable Care Act has some subsidies for low-income Americans. But it was Senator John McCain who delivered the decisive negative vote in the Senate that derailed Trump's plan to replace Obamacare with his administration's plan. McCain felt Trump's plan was not sufficiently debated and lacked detail and necessary provisions.

MF: What about Ron Paul? I remember that he considered himself a disciple of my economic theories.

AM: Ron Paul indeed served in Congress for many years and ran for president on at least two occasions. He and his son Rand Paul consider themselves to be Libertarians. As you know, that means that they are proponents -- like you -- of no government interference in the economy, but more controversially they defend civil liberties and personal freedoms as absolute rights which cannot be limited or curtailed under any circumstance, or perhaps only in extraordinary situations. Unfortunately, in an age marked by terrorist attacks, cyberattacks, hacking and many other threats, authorities need to monitor society in order to keep us safe. Both Ron and Rand Paul also call for the elimination of the Federal Reserve and for the United States to withdraw its military from other countries around the world.

I do not think that you would agree that the Federal Reserve should be abolished. After all, Ben Bernanke and Alan Greenspan were also influenced by your work and writings, and both served as chairmen of the Federal Reserve. The Federal Reserve's reaction to the financial crisis of 2007-2008 is considered by analysts to draw on your work.

MF: Does the Federal Reserve continue to follow my advice?

AM: Well, to be frank, there is a lot of debate surrounding the Federal Reserve's role and specifically its monetary policy. Under its current chairwoman, Janet Yellen, the Fed has kept interest rates at a historically low level despite full employment and low inflation. One of the cornerstones of your economic theory is that unemployment cannot and should not be eliminated and that without a "natural" rate of unemployment inflation inevitably increases. Your theory is being proven wrong. Despite the unemployment rate standing at a little over 4%, inflation is stuck at about 2.1% in 2017 as it was in 2016. Yellen has been very reluctant to increase rates. She and her colleagues at the Fed have only done so on three occasions since late 2015, and the hikes have been of only 25 basis points each time. Despite full employment, why should the Fed hike interest rates if inflation is under control?

MF: Disregarding my theories will have damaging consequences.

AM: Well, Milton, you can get off your high horse for once. Inflation has not increased despite full employment and even a rise in energy prices since the lows reached in 2014. The Fed also has to consider the consequences of a higher dollar. Emerging and developing countries struggled after commodity prices plunged in 2014. In 2016 they registered higher growth, and the projections for 2017 are better. But a rise in interest rates in 2014 and 2015 would have multiplied the flows of capital out of emerging countries and into developed ones. Yellen was wise to not raise them.

In the first six months of the Trump presidency, one million jobs have been created. The unemployment rate has remained around 4.3%. The job market was already doing well under Obama and in the first half of 2017 the economy has benefited from very good weather, especially in the first quarter. Mild weather of course is a boon for the construction sector. The unemployment rate has not dropped more than a couple of decimals because people who had given up are looking for work again and joined the labor market. But the labor participation rate has not recovered to the pre-recession level or even to the post World War II average. The June 2017 jobs report was particularly strong, with 209,000 jobs added.

During the second and third quarters of 2017, the US economy grew at an annual rate of 3%, higher than forecasts had predicted. President Trump boasted he was responsible for the strong growth, job creation numbers and stock market records. President Obama inherited an economy in January 2009 with unemployment at 10% and monthly destruction of 800,000 jobs. By the time he left office, unemployment was below 5% and 14 million new jobs had been added. Moreover, the very mild winter was a major factor behind the unexpectedly higher GDP and job creation numbers, as the construction sector obviously benefits from fewer snowstorms. February was exceptionally warm.

President Trump has little to do with these numbers, with the significant exception of the stock market records, which are the result of the business community believing that the new president will deliver on his campaign pledge to simplify and cut taxes. Investors also believe that Trump's tax reform will manage to get part of the $2 trillion parked by US companies overseas repatriated with a one-time lower tax rate, repeal and replace Obamacare, invest one trillion dollars in modernizing and building new infrastructure, allow for extraction of oil and natural gas in federal lands and coastal waters and eliminate environmental regulations. But six months after his inauguration, Trump has not even come close to achieving any of these goals, with the notable exception of eliminating environmental regulations. In fact, he has made scant progress towards their fulfilment.

MF: Well, why is he not making progress? Republicans have majorities in the House and Senate.

AM: Trump's presidency appears to be unraveling during this summer of 2017. On the 9th of August, two devastating events for Trump took place. The first is that the media reported that on July 26th Paul Manafort's home on Oronoco Street in Arlington, Virginia was raided before dawn (at 3AM) by armed FBI agents. This happened a day after Manafort testified before one of the congressional committees investigating the Russia collusion case. This means that Special Counsel Mueller has so much evidence of criminal activities by Trump's former campaign chairman that he feared that Manafort -- a pro-Russian businessman and political relic from the Nixon administration -- would destroy documents. Manafort had been cooperating with Mueller's investigation and keeping a low profile, meaning not saying anything publicly. Unlike Trump, who cannot control himself, Manafort allowed his lawyers to do the talking and the story did not leak for more than two weeks despite the fact that Manafort was awoken at 3AM by armed FBI agents at his Virginia home. A Washington Post reporter broke the story on August 10th, more than two weeks after the FBI raid. This proves that Mueller runs a tight ship. In fact, he probably felt he had to send Trump and other potential witnesses in the case a powerful message.

Manafort's lawyers stress that he was and would continue to cooperate with both Mueller as well as the two congressional inquiries. He frankly has no choice. He was paid $17 million by a pro-Russian Ukrainian company for lobbying activities. He failed to register and disclose that he lobbied (and was thus paid) by a pro-Russian Ukrainian political party, which violates the law regarding work for foreign entities (the Foreign Agent Registration Act). He might have laundered money and committed bank fraud and laundered millions. His son-in-law is being investigated for his role in a Ponzi scheme. Manafort's alleged criminal offense could land him in jail for dozens of years. It is highly unusual for a pre-dawn raid by the FBI in cases of white-collar crime. This means the evidence gathered by Mueller's team (and the congressional committees) is very incriminating, and that Mueller is now accelerating his prosecutorial process.

I have always believed that many of Trump's advisers wanted to remove sanctions on Russia in exchange for new investments in Russia, which would also cover up the corrupt deals by Trump's pals in Russia, Ukraine and other post-Soviet countries. Manafort was campaign chairman for five months. The removal of sanctions was something that Trump very seriously considered inserting into the GOP Convention platform in the summer of 2016, when Manafort was at the helm. Even Corey Lewandowski -- who was the previous campaign chairman -- has admitted on TV that

Manafort was in charge of policy and he had been relegated to event organization during the Republican Convention.

It appears that Manafort cooperated with Russian companies with whom he did business to rig the election against Hillary Clinton by egging on the release of her emails by Wikileaks and Russian hackers. A pre-dawn raid with a search warrant by the FBI means that a federal judge was convinced by Mueller's team that there was probable cause of criminal behavior by Manafort. Only a federal judge can authorize a search warrant. The US Constitution protects against search without probable cause of criminal activity. Robert Mueller is acting as a prosecutor and building up a case which he will turn over to the Department of Justice. In addition to the fear that Manafort might destroy evidence, Mueller probably wanted to send a message to Trump and his surrogates that the investigation is not a witch hunt as the president's spokesmen repeat ad nauseam.

Mueller is no showboat and goes about his work methodically and without seeking publicity. But he had to push back against the onslaught of lies hurled by team Trump against Mueller and his 16 top-notch investigators. Former National Security Adviser Michael Flynn is of course in terrible trouble and is likely to spill the beans, as he was the first to be thrown under the bus by Trump. Manafort and Flynn can flip and reveal criminal wrongdoing by other people in Trump's inner circle (Jared Kushner, Don Trump Jr, even Jeff Sessions) and even the president himself. As I predicted, Manafort and Flynn are the weakest links. If they face going to jail, they might reveal everything they know about Trump. Flynn and Manafort might be inclined to cooperate without betraying what they know about Trump. But they obviously follow the news. They know that Trump has left the White House for a 17-day working vacation at his golf course in New Jersey after six months of not getting anything passed by Congress. The president continues to engage in his tweeter storms despite the shake-up at the White House and the appointment of General John Kelly as Chief of Staff in an attempt to create more discipline and process around the president. But Manafort and Flynn also know that, even if they are convicted, Trump could pardon them.

MF: This is all very interesting and depressing, but I want to talk about finance and economics!

AM: Me too, Milton. I no longer believe that Trump will have to resign or face impeachment (as his ally Bannon predicted) before the 2018 elections. But two years did transpire between the break-in at the Watergate and Nixon's resignation, which ironically took place 47 years ago, on August 8th, 1974.

MF: But Mueller needs to supply a lot of evidence to the Department of Justice, which in turn needs to analyze it and decide whether it warrants a prosecution by Congress, which is what impeachment is.

AM: Yes, but Trump is unable to just shut up for even one day, even on his ridiculous working vacation. Despite John Kelly trying his hardest to discipline the warring factions within the White House, the backstabbing continues. The Bannon camp continues to undermine National Security Adviser HR McMaster, labelling him an enemy of Israel and attributing other ridiculous policy stances to a very respected general. The alternative right media outlets and Sean Hannity at Fox are on a mission to get Trump to fire McMaster. Tillerson has already hinted that he is getting fed up. Secretary of Defense James Mattis, McMaster, Kelly and Tillerson are the adults trying to discipline the president and his surrogates. As long as these four persons stay in office, Americans and our allies are relatively confident that Trump and Bannon will not actually do anything reckless that compromises national security. But Kelly has not been able to stop the leaks. And nobody will ever stop Trump from tweeting. In fact, his twitter addiction could turn out to be the equivalent to Nixon's tapes.

But Nixon was a former vice president and smart person. He was obsessed with the Kennedys and somewhat paranoid about the press. That led to his downfall, as he stupidly decided to cover up the break-in at the Watergate by crooks who were paid by his reelection funding war chest.

Trump is now boxed in. As long as the aforementioned four respected officials stay on the job, Trump will not dare order a disproportionate measure to stand up to Kim Jong Un. There is a law that allows military officers to refuse to carry out an order from the president that is manifestly illegal or questionable. We therefore do not need to worry that Trump will order the firing of some missile near North Korea. After the Washington Post reported that the Defense Intelligence Agency (DIA) had concluded that North Korea would be able to miniaturize a warhead and deploy it on an ICBM soon, Kim Jong Un threatened the United States. That is nothing new. The North Korean totalitarian dictator routinely threatens to attack the US. The DIA is renowned for its inaccurate predictions, which helped to trigger the Second Gulf War. Before the DIA analysis, the intelligence community consensus was (and remains) that North Korea was at least two years or more away from mastering miniaturization, the capability to launch an ICBM beyond the atmosphere, have it re-enter the atmosphere, and for the missile to accurately reach its target on the US West Coast.

The spectacular shock-and-awe raid by FBI agents of Manafort's home at 3 AM was reported by the Washington Post a day after Trump threatened to unleash hell and fire on North Korea after a reporter shouted out a question about the president's reaction to the DIA statement and Kim Jong Un's threat. The world is used to Kim Jong Un's threats. But a US president had never irresponsibly promised to nuke a country during a meeting of part of his senior aides. Trump's tweet addiction is comical but dangerous. Vacation is supposed to mean that you can tune out. But Trump needs to brag, boast and bluster almost every day.

Kellyanne Conway replaced Manafort during the final stretch of the presidential campaign and managed to reduce Trump's outbursts and have him read from a teleprompter or prepared remarks. That lasted for a few crucial weeks as Hillary Clinton's lead shrunk due to self-inflicted wounds (the deplorables comment, coming close to fainting). The bizarre and unprecedented disclosure only ten days before the presidential election by former FBI Director James Comey that the investigation into Clinton's emails and the Clinton Foundation's pay-for-play methods had been reopened also hurt Hillary.

Chapter 6. Statist France and a reassessment of the Arab Spring

After Trump's threat to attack North Korea with fire and hell shocked the world (because of the language he used) and his senior cabinet officials, Kim Jong Un ratcheted up the tit-for-tat threats by promising to attack the US island of Guam, which is in the western Pacific. There is a military base on Guam. It is not impossible that North Korea could launch a missile that could land close to Guam. But most of the missiles launched by North Korea so far have proven they have little accuracy. They sometimes explode shortly after being launched or fly for a few hundred miles and splash into the Sea of Japan. This does not mean that North Korea is not a threat to Japan, as well as to South Korea. A wise and veteran US general revealed that when president Jimmy Carter considered withdrawing the 50,000 US troops in South Korea in 1974, North Korea secretly planned a possible invasion of South Korea. According to the US general (who was in Korea in 1974), the Kim dynasty and North Korea's elites are determined to reunify Korea under their totalitarian Communist rule. The North's nuclear program -- among other things -- is thus a means to drive a wedge between the United States and South Korea, and not just a formidable tool that ensures Kim Jong Un's grip on power.

The US has been flying B1B bombers over North Korea, and Secretary of State Rex Tillerson flew to Asia to try to allay worries of a potential war. Tillerson has become the firefighter who is often deployed after Trump offends allies or threatens enemies. But the former chairman of Exxon will someday run out of patience. Defense Secretary James Mattis returned from his vacation and -- to my surprise -- also warned North Korea with very tough language, although he did so in a professional manner.

MF: What are the latest developments regarding the Russia investigation?

AM: President Trump obviously knew about the pre-dawn (which means before 6AM in the summer) raid on Paul Manafort's home before the Washington Post broke the story on August 10th. This may explain why he unexpectedly tweeted at the time that after consultation with his generals (which was not true), he would ban transgender individuals from serving in the US armed forces. It was the vintage Donald Trump tactic of trying to distract attention from his troubles by picking a fight with someone else. In this particular case, however, I do share the president's view on transgender service in the armed forces. The problem with this tactic is that Trump has now created so many crises that he has trouble changing the topic. Almost all of the topics the media reports about are related to his mistakes, exaggerations, personal attacks or policy failures: the failure to repeal Obamacare; the raid of Manafort's house; the infighting in the White House; the alternative right's attacks against National Security Adviser H.R. McMaster; the failure six months into Trump's first term to get anything of substance passed by a Republican-controlled Congress; the fact that only 152 political positions have been filled in the federal government; and the provocative threats against North Korea. All of these items have generated wall-to-wall reporting by CNN and MSNBC, among other media outlets.

But it is not only these US media outlets that constantly report about these failures and their potential consequences. The media from the rest of the world is also interested. Japan's government decided to take preventive security measures. Seoul is only fifty miles from the border with North Korea. It is the middle of August and most countries' politicians and elites are enjoying their vacations. This compounds Trump's problem. He does not have targets of opportunity to try to rally his base. Angela Merkel and the president of Mexico are on vacation.

Trump has therefore turned the US political discourse into a reality show. Senator Majority leader Mitch McConnell politely explained in an interview that the president had exaggerated expectations of what the Congress could achieve in six months. McConnell obviously failed to muster 51 votes in favor of repealing and replacing Obamacare in the Senate, which killed the process. But his remarks were not aggressive. Trump and his surrogates described McConnell as being spineless. Bear in mind that McConnell's wife, Elaine Chao, serves as Secretary of Transportation in Trump's cabinet. McConnell might soon join the list of politicians who are routinely criticized by the president.

In the ensuing days, more Republicans will feel comfortable in openly criticizing Trump. The more unhinged Trump behaves, especially in the middle of the summer, the hole he is digging for himself gets deeper. Trump decided to go on the offensive against Manafort by deploying The National Inquirer to report that his former campaign chairman had had an affair with a younger woman. This is not a crime, and makes it more likely that Manafort will flip, especially as Manafort is looking at the real possibility that he could go to jail for many years, maybe for the rest of his life.

I regret to have to report all of this to you. I love the United States. It is the greatest country on Earth. I hope I will become a US citizen in the second half of 2018 or 2019. Although I am not a celebrity, I have published numerous op-eds in Spanish newspapers and been on TV and radio harshly criticizing the president, something I never imagined I would do. I am not afraid. Trump is now reduced to tweeting in the morning after spending hours watching coverage on cable television of his fiascos. He has four White House employees from the communications department compile daily reports of favorable coverage of him. These four employees work full-time gathering these propaganda dossiers which Trump absorbs twice or three times a day. The dossiers are full of favorable pictures.

MF: Frankly, and I am not being flippant, Trump should start searching for a country that does not have a treaty of extradition with the US if he wants to avoid being impeached or having to resign. He would not be able to deliver a dignified resignation speech anyway. He would probably tweet his resignation. But you point out that the economy is doing well. A constitutional crisis and a resignation would harm it.

AM: You are right. A deeper crisis in the presidency would unsettle financial markets and the stock market, at least in the short term. GDP grew at an annualized rate of 3% in the second quarter. But a survey of economists has determined that the expansion cannot last beyond 2019 or, at most, 2020.

MF: They believe a recession or sharp slowdown is inevitable because of the business cycle?

AM: Correct. The current period of economic expansion is one of the longest since World War II. The economy has been growing since the middle of 2009, when it emerged from the recession. Economists can argue until the cows come home whether the current period of growth is weaker or stronger than others. There is full employment. According to your theory, with full employment inflation is bound to increase.

MF: Of course. This has always happened. As an economy reaches full employment, employees can and do exert pressure and wages increase. Employers have no choice other than to raise wages, as they cannot turn to unemployed workers. There is no slack in the labor market.

AM: Yes, you are right. Full employment and healthy GDP growth of about 2.5% to 3% should lead to higher wages. And it usually has happened. But you have to bear in mind that the labor participation rate has dropped. There are people who had left the labor market because they had given up looking for work. As the economy has picked up steam, these people have returned to the labor market. Other factors that explain why inflation is not increasing despite full employment is the rapid acceleration of the use of robots, more technology and artificial intelligence. Employees are now competing with machines as well as other persons and have to accept stagnant wages. There is data, however, that show that wages have been inching up in the past year and a half.

Turning to matters in Europe, I am dismayed that French President Emmanuel Macron has nationalized a shipyard in Saint-Nazaire.

MF: This man is supposedly a liberal who was elected to modernize and liberalize the French economy. What is he up to?

AM: Yes, I am very disappointed too. France places second in Europe in terms of state ownership of companies (only behind Norway). According to the *Cour des Comptes*, an independent public auditor, the French state holds stakes in 1,800 companies with a combined value of 800 billion euros. That is a little bit less than Spain's GDP. These companies employ 800,000 workers. These figures surpass those of most Western economies. We would have to adjust for population. But in the US, 600,000 people work for state-owned companies, in Germany 370,000, in the UK 350,000, in Poland less than 200,000 (and it is a former Communist economy), and in Spain less than 100,000.

French president Macron had promised during the campaign to privatize companies or sell off government stakes in partially privatized companies to the tune of 10 billion euros and promised the revenue would fund innovation by SMEs. But French presidents and prime ministers often find excuses to go back on their promises. They often make the case that the companies are in strategic sectors. But for France almost everything is strategic. On July 27th, Macron stepped in to block the attempt by Italian shipbuilder Fincantieri to buy the Saint-Nazaire shipyard. He will announce in a few weeks whether to nationalize the shipyard or sell a stake to another company. He will also negotiate a possible compromise with Fincantieri.

But it gets worse. The French state owns holdings in companies in a vast array of sectors: defense (Thales, Safran), telecommunications (Orange), energy (EDF, Areva), management of airports (ADP) and vehicle manufacturers (Renault), to name a few.

MF: This is shameful. Public management of companies is always a bad idea. I spent decades advising governments to privatize companies.

AM: And most western economies have heeded your advice. France is the big exception, the outlier. Even French public-sector entities have published reports describing how badly these holdings are managed. First of all, there is not one but three bodies which the French government employs to manage its holdings in companies: l'Agence des Participations de l'Etat, BpiFrance and Caisse des Dépôts et Consignations (CDC). As Economics Minister under President Hollande, Macron increased the state's share in Renault to 20% to ensure that the government has double-voting rights. Areva, where the government held a 92% stake, has collapsed. EDF's share price has tumbled from 86 euros in 2007 to 9 euros today.

MF: I cannot bear to hear this any longer! This sounds like Socialism!

AM: Well, Milton, Macron was a member of the Socialist Party and served as Economics Minister under Socialist President François Hollande. He shrewdly distanced himself from his erstwhile party – which was highly unpopular – and created his new movement and political party, *En*

Marche. You must be realistic. Did you really believe that Macron would follow in the footsteps of Thatcher and Reagan?

MF: I guess we were all too caught up in the Macron hysteria. You know my quote, that the government solution to a problem is usually as bad as the problem. The French had better change their obsession with their public sector, protectionism and government interference in the economy.

AM: I am sure Macron's advisers would argue that he needed to make the decision to block Fincantieri from acquiring the shipyard at Saint-Nazaire in order to get his labor-market reforms through the French Parliament without big demonstrations on the streets of Paris and other French cities. But Macron has the power to pass decrees on labor-market reform without a vote in the Parliament. This is akin to the president of the US issuing an executive order, which does not need approval from Congress. This was supposedly a very confident man. I do not understand why he appears to have lost his nerve.

To make matters worse, Macron has infuriated the Italian government. In addition to blocking the purchase of the Saint-Nazaire shipyard by the Italian company Fincantieri, he did not help authorities in Rome cope with the 200,000 immigrants from Africa and other countries who are in Italy. And to add insult to injury, he convened a summit in Paris between the warring factions in Libya's long-running civil war without notifying Italy in advance. Libya is of course a former Italian colony, and lies across the Mediterranean from southern Italy. Macron was supposed to be a crusader for liberalization, privatization and European integration. I do not care what excuse his defenders can offer. That he needs to tame the labor unions with the Saint-Nazaire decision to give him more leverage to enact the labor-market reforms?

Macron's party, *La République en Marche*, has an absolute majority in both chambers of Parliament. The Socialist Party has practically been wiped out in the French Parliament. In fact, adding the MPs and Senators from Macron's party and the traditional center-right UMP, they almost have a two-thirds majority in both houses of the French Parliament. And the Parliament granted Macron the power to enact some legislation by decree. The hard-left CGT labor union is not as strong as it used to be. The far-right Front Nationale of Marine Le Pen is in disarray. Marine is under investigation for corrupt practices, some leading members may abandon the party and there is even an attempt to rename it. What happened to the analysts – usually skeptics of European integration – who predicted she would become France's president and withdraw France from the eurozone and possibly the EU (Frexit)?

The radical left in France is also licking its wounds. The Communists barely have MPs in Parliament. Jean-Luc Mélenchon can get some radicals to protest on the streets of Paris and other French cities. But these demonstrations are numerically insignificant. The Socialist CFDT labor union has signaled that France's economy needs reforms. The time to act is now. Procrastination is typical of politicians.

Some international crisis could break out, giving Macron yet another reason to put off applying the reforms. It is shameful that spineless énarques for decades have failed to face down weakened labor unions just because they can get a few thousand people on the streets of French cities. In fact, in the month of August most well-to-do Parisians head for their vacations on the coast. August would be the perfect moment to begin implementing the labor-market reforms Macron ran on and promised, such as lowering the cost of dismissals and enabling employers to negotiate working conditions with employees at the company level, therefore avoiding sectorial straitjackets. And even these limited reforms are hardly bold. They are not Thatcherite.

In hindsight, former center-right prime minister François Fillon promised much more radical reforms. And he often publicly stated that he is an avowed admirer of Thatcher and considers himself a liberal (in the European economic connotation), which is toxic for a French politician. But Fillon's candidacy for the presidency was derailed after he clinched the nomination for the center-right UMP by corruption allegations. He paid his wife a lot of money over many years for fake work. Fillon was also an admirer of Vladimir Putin, and the world certainly did not need another head of state or government with such views.

Macron's summit with the Libyan Prime Minister Fayez al-Sarraj and General Khalifa Haftar, who rules over parts of eastern Libya, did produce modest pledges of cooperation between the Tripoli-based al-Sarraj and the Benghazi-based Haftar. But all analysts predict instability in Libya for many years to come. Al-Sarraj hardly controls even all of Tripoli. There is a plethora of militias that occupy cities along Libya's northern coast. An Al-Qaeda affiliate also wreaks havoc in Libya. Most Western politicians have accepted that General Haftar is the best option. He clearly wants to dominate all of Libya. But his forces currently only control parts of the east. Libya's oil production has increased but is still significantly lower than before the popular revolt and ensuing revolution that toppled Muammar Gaddafi in 2011.

MF: But Libya is a sparsely-populated country with huge oil reserves. How is it possible that six years after the overthrow of Gaddafi western powers and the international community have not been able to restore stability?

AM: To be fair, there were many revolts and revolutions in Arab countries in the spring of 2011, beginning in Tunisia, then spreading to Egypt, Syria and even some countries in the Gulf. These were spontaneous uprisings by a population fed up with their authoritarian, corrupt and repressive governments. The revolts also broke out because of high unemployment and lack of economic opportunities, especially among the young.

Only Tunisia has managed a fairly successful transition from repressive one-man rule to a relatively stable free-market democracy where numerous parties (including Islamists) compete at the ballot box. In Egypt, the Muslim Brotherhood tried to take control of the revolution. Although it succeeded, its president Mohammed Morsi was eventually overthrown by anti-Brotherhood opponents financed by Saudi Arabia and other rich Gulf states. General Abdul Fattah el-Sissi had been appointed Minister of Defense by Morsi and was thus commander-in-chief of Egypt's armed forces. El-Sissi capitalized on discontent against the Brotherhood and overthrew Morsi in July of 2013 following widespread protests against Morsi and the Brotherhood. After cracking down very harshly on the Muslim Brotherhood and some secular opposition parties, el-Sissi announced his retirement from the armed forces. He stepped down briefly as head of state, a new Constitution was approved, and el-Sissi ran for and was elected president in 2014.

General el-Sissi trained at the Joint Services Command and Staff College in the UK and in 2006 at the US Army War College in Carlisle, Pennsylvania. President Trump likes him a lot. Western leaders and the Sunni powers – especially Saudi Arabia – voice staunch public and private support for him. He has restored order and the Egyptian economy is growing again. El-Sissi was forced to resort to the IMF, which approved a three-year program that required cutting some subsidies and a devaluation of the Egyptian dinar.

The British and French governments supported the revolt against Gaddafi and provided the opposition with weapons. They also became the opposition's air force. UK, French and ultimately

US military bombers and fighters destroyed Gaddafi's military hardware and decimated his army. Other NATO countries were also involved. You must bear in mind that without such outside support Gaddafi's superior air force and army (tanks, artillery) would have probably crushed the opposition. At a minimum, Western intervention hastened Gaddafi's defeat, and therefore saved lives. President Obama has publicly stated that one of his biggest mistakes was not planning for a post-Gaddafi Libya. He is being too hard on himself. All Arab countries under one-man rule for decades (Gaddafi was in absolute command of Libya since 1969) were simmering cauldrons waiting to explode. Dictatorial rule appeared to provide stability, but underneath this veneer of order the animosity and hatred between clans, ethnic groups and Sunnis and Shias never disappeared. The West cannot send troops to stabilize every country that overthrows a dictator. Several summits were held to raise funding for post-Gaddafi Libya.

The warring factions in Libya shoulder the blame for continuing to fight each other instead of uniting behind a legitimate government that can destroy al-Qaeda and provide stability and ultimately prosperity to its citizens. The Obama administration in fact did not lead the military efforts against Gaddafi. It was the British and the French who took the initiative. At one point, Gaddafi's armed forces were closing in on the city of Benghazi in eastern Libya. Gaddafi vowed to crush and kill all civilians in Benghazi, to hunt them down like "rats". That triggered a more robust US military response. In other words, the US intervened at first to prevent the slaughter of civilians in Benghazi. But finishing off Gaddafi afterwards as opposed to witnessing a long and bloody civil war was a good idea.

People have short memories. President Obama and Secretary of State Hillary Clinton (as well as former French President François Hollande and British Prime Minister David Cameron) did the right thing in Libya. In the US, the debate over post-Gaddafi Libya has become politicized because Islamic extremists from the group Ansar al-Sharia stormed the US consulate in Benghazi in September 2012, killing Ambassador J. Christopher Stevens and three other US citizens, a member of the foreign service and two CIA contractors. Stevens was the first US Ambassador to be killed in the line of duty since 1979.

Republicans charged Clinton and the State Department with negligence. They feel the Consulate should have had more protection, especially given the presence of Islamic extremists, al-Qaeda and the instability in Libya. They are right in this regard. Susan Rice, National Security Adviser under Obama, did blunder in appearing on the Sunday-morning news shows and describing the attack on the Consulate as the work of amateurs who basically had nothing better to do than vent their rage against a US building and its diplomats. That turned out to be false.

The attacks were carried out by Islamist radicals who purposely targeted the US. Hillary Clinton subsequently had to endure months of investigations in Congress over the State Department's insufficient protection of the Consulate in Benghazi, Rice's bungled attempts to mislead the public and Congress about the nature of the attackers and the delay in sending reinforcements to evacuate the Consulate after the attack began. It is obvious that the State Department could have done a better job. But Clinton-haters and radical Republicans who alleged that Clinton purposely allowed US diplomats to be killed know they are lying and used the Benghazi disaster to relentlessly criticize Clinton during the 2016 campaign. Several Congressional committees chaired by Republicans grilled Clinton and obtained copious documents, but all of them ultimately found no evidence willful neglect of the Consulate's security. Hillary Clinton paid a political price for the tragedy at the US Consulate in Benghazi. Susan Rice will probably never hold a high-ranking position in the US government again. Her political career is basically over. The larger point I am making is that a debate about improving the situation in Libya cannot take place in the US because the Benghazi Consulate killings have turned Libya -- like too many issues -- into partisan political tools.

Chapter 7: Revisiting the Great Recession, Financial Greed and its Aftermath

Milton Friedman's political philosophy praises the virtues of free markets with minimal or no government intervention. He once declared that the achievement he was most proud of was his role in eliminating conscription in the United States military. In his 1962 book *Capitalism and Freedom*, he advocated a volunteer military, freely floating exchange rates, the suppression of medical licenses, a negative income tax and school vouchers.

After teaching at the University of Chicago for thirty years, in 1977 Milton retired from his alma mater and he and Rose Friedman moved from Chicago to San Francisco. At age 65, Milton became affiliated with the University of Stanford's Hoover Institution. Milton also became a visiting scholar at the Federal Reserve Bank of San Francisco. Milton and Rose did not slow down because of his statutory retirement. For three years they worked on the project *Free to Choose Network* and produced a television program outlining Milton's economic and social philosophy. In 1980, the ten-part series titled *Free to Choose* was broadcast by PBS, which is the most important public television channel in the US. A companion book to the series co-authored by Milton and Rose with the title *Free to Choose* was the best-selling non-fiction book of 1980 and has been translated into fourteen languages.

In early August of 2017, Milton Friedman was on his way West to attend the Jackson Hole gathering of central bankers, businessmen and politicians in Wyoming. He had been advising governments in Asia and Europe on how to conduct monetary policy. He was in Washington, D.C. for a few days. He summoned me to a mall in Tysons Quarter as his hotel was nearby. We had dinner at a Ponderosa Steakhouse.

AM: Milton, you are extremely influential, through your work as an academic, your consultancy for governments, your books, your television series, and the economists you mentored. By the early 1980s, financial deregulation was undertaken in the US and the UK partly because you advised president Ronald Reagan and British Prime Minister Margaret Thatcher to implement it. I understand your critique that Keynesianism had stifled markets. But don't you think thirty years of total financial deregulation caused the S&L crisis of the 1980s, the Internet dot com bubble of the early 2000s and the financial crisis of 2007?

MF: Not at all. These were not market failures. It was actors making irrational investment decisions that led to the crises you mention.

AM: Yes, Milton, but individual actors make decisions in a context of a regulatory framework which is determined by the government and other institutions. I take exception to your belief that markets are almost perfect and government intervention should only take place in extreme situations. I am of course a capitalist and used to advocate a minimal role for the government. But successive massive crises have changed my mind.

The tech or .com stock market crash of 2000 destroyed $5 billion in market capitalization. Between 1996 and 2016 home prices in the US doubled. It was obvious that a real-estate bubble was developing after the 2000 .com crash. Between 2000 and 2003, the number of mortgages quadrupled every year. Banks knowingly allowed mortgage lenders to persuade NINJAS (people with no income, no jobs, no assets or an insufficient combination of the three) to take out mortgages they would not be able to repay. Banks preferred these loans, known as subprime loans, because borrowers were charged a higher interest.

MF: But everyone should have a shot at the American dream! The economy was growing, job creation was strong and unemployment very low! You know how I feel about government intervention in the economy. As I famously said, governments never learn. Only people learn.

AM: Look, Milton, do not upset me. You worked extremely hard but led a life in the upper class, whereas I am in the middle class, which has been battered by the financial crisis and the Great Recession. Your anti-government views are too extreme for me in the context of the irresponsible deregulation of financial markets in the West which allowed mortgage lenders, retail banks, investment banks, credit-rating agencies and other actors in the financial sector food-chain to design highly-speculative products and gambled recklessly with trillions of dollars of peoples' deposits and mortgages.

I do not share your extreme confidence in markets. I think you did a great service to the US and the world by denouncing the naivete of Keynesian policies beginning in the 1950s. The pendulum had swung too far in the direction of interventionism after the 1929 stock market crash and the Great Depression. But they were preceded by the free-wheeling 1920s, when everyone gambled in the stock market. It is human nature to be greedy, and that causes bubbles. When they burst, governments must step in.

This has been happening since the Middle Ages, and in the XVIIth century there was a bubble in tulips. As Jeremy Iron's character in the movie *Margin Call* brilliantly but cynically puts it: "We cannot help ourselves. There will always be a certain percentage of fat cats and hungry dogs. The percentages have always been the same. Yes, there may be more of them now than before (meaning in absolute numbers), but the percentages remain the same."

MF: What is the context of the scene you are describing from *Margin Call*?

AM: Jeremy Irons plays the part of the CEO of a private (meaning non-listed) investment banking company (Mr. Tuld) who realizes that the amount of mortgage-backed securities on its balance sheet could bankrupt his company given the market instability that is gathering force. Although the company and characters portrayed in *Margin Call* are fictional, the movie is set in the early stages of the financial crisis, in September of 2008. I have watched several movies about the financial crisis. In my view, *Margin Call* is the best. Critics agree. The New Yorker lauded Margin Call as "the best Wall Street movie ever made". Entertainment Weekly praised it as "powerfully capturing the day the money died". Its star-studded cast includes Jeremy Irons, Kevin Spacey, Paul Bettany, Simon Baker, Zachary Quinto, Stanley Tucci and Demi Moore.

Iron's character pressures and convinces everyone at the bank to sell the MBS products, and thus puts other banks out of business. The head of the Risk Management Division, played by Kevin Spacey, desperately tries to persuade Irons and his second-in-command not to go down a course that will cause severe reputational damage to the bank. But Irons feels that his firm has to survive the gathering storm, and that it can only do so by dumping all of its suspect MBS products at fair market value to those who are willing to buy. This strategy damages other banks who will never buy anything from Tuld's bank again. He therefore cajoles and forces Spacey to motivate his traders to liquidate all of the MBS products on the firm's balance-sheet.

MF: And he is right.

AM: Legally, yes, but not ethically.

MF: If the people working at Iron's bank discover the MBS vulnerability first, they are right in legally selling the assets to save their firm.

AM: The movie in a way recreates the environment in September of 2008, two years after you passed away. At that point, Lehman Brothers collapsed under the weight of MBS and other speculative high-risk products, and the US government did not bail it out.

MF: It is great to hear that the US government did not bail out Lehman Brothers. I was advising the US government on how to respond to the crisis in 2006, before the meltdown of 2008. As you know, I feel that underlying most arguments against the free market is a lack of belief in freedom itself.

AM: You did advise the regulators during the months before the financial crisis erupted. And I am sure you did a great job. But your funny but extreme positions against government programs contradict the role you played in advising governments during the years preceding the global financial crisis and Great Recession.

MF: Government intervention is almost always a bad idea. The potential financial meltdown beginning in 2006 was an exception. That is why I advised governments. But generally, I subscribe to the theory that if you were to put the federal government in charge of the Sahara Desert, in five years there would be a shortage of sand.

AM: Your quotes are funny but very unfair and completely exaggerated. FDR got the US out of the Depression with a plethora of government programs. You unfortunately passed away in November of 2006. The developments I am describing transpired during the summer and fall of 2007. By then it was obvious that AIG was in deep trouble. The real-estate and financial bubble in Iceland had already burst, and the Icelandic government decided not to bail out the banks. Icelanders rushed to withdraw money from their accounts. There was a run on a British bank. Panic spread from Wall Street to Main Street of every Western country. In this context, letting Lehman Brothers fail might have been correct, but it was inconsistent with previous and ensuing decisions to bail out big banks and insurance companies.

Jeremy Iron's character in *Margin Call* ponders the situation and tells others. "To be successful in this business, you must be smarter, faster or cheat. I do not cheat. And although I would like to think that we have a lot of very smart people here, it sure is a hell of a lot easier to be first."

I love Jeremy Irons, especially the sophisticated characters he has played in recent movies. His portrayal of a famous Jewish businessman who convinces the US Olympic Committee not to boycott Hitler's 1933 Olympic Games is also brilliant. At any rate, Kevin Spacey's character has to force his traders to sell all the toxic assets. Many of them are fired immediately after their good work (with compensation). Spacey's character confronts Irons. He wants his bonuses and options and wants to leave the bank. Iron gives him the lecture about the inherent greediness of human beings. At one point, he tells him: "Bills, they are just pieces of paper with pictures on them. It is all made up. Money (meaning cash or otherwise) is something necessary, otherwise we would have to kill each other to get something to eat. While delivering his speech to Spacey, Irons is sitting down at a table on the top floor of the bank's building with a stunning view of New York and eating steak. Spacey is exhausted, refuses Iron's offer to sit down and eat with him, and is in no mood for speeches. It is a brilliant scene.

Returning to the events of 2007. Before you cut me off, I was going to remind you that the S&L bubble and crisis of the eighties resulted in $124 billion in losses for those unfortunate enough to have accounts in an S&L. But at least thousands of bankers were convicted of wrongdoing and many went to jail. One of the most notorious bankers in the S&L crisis was Charles Keating. He was a big-time con artist. Keating at one point hired Alan Greenspan and paid him $45,000 to draft a report. These are all established facts and were the consequence of the deregulation of

S&Ls. Your advice to deregulate financial markets was first tried with S&Ls. The outcome was disastrous. Then speculators decided to deregulate investment banking.

Under pressure from Franklin D. Roosevelt, Congress enacted the Glass-Steagall Act in 1933. It created a firewall between commercial and investment banks. The former was not allowed to speculate with depositors' money. But beginning in the early 1980s, and following your advice, the Reagan administration proceeded to tear down the financial regulations that had prevented a financial crisis since the 1930s. For over forty years investment banks were small companies that were owned and managed by several partners. They did not make much money and were very cautious with their operations, because they were investing the partners' money. Investment banks were forbidden from tapping depositors' money in order to speculate with it. Bankers at commercial or investment banks had very modest salaries, and even had to hold down other jobs to make ends meet!

Paul Volcker, who was a successful and ethical Chairman of the Federal Reserve (like Janet Yellen, and in contrast to Greenspan), had an annual salary of $45,000 in 1969 at Chase Manhattan Bank. In 1972, Morgan Stanley, another investment bank, had one office, 110 employees and $12 million in assets. By the time the financial bubble burst in 2007, Morgan Stanley had grown to be a global colossus with 50,000 employees in dozens of offices around the world and billions in assets. Before you start lecturing me, bear in mind that the great financial crisis of 2007-2011 doubled the US national debt, put 30 million people out of work and caused another 50 million in developing countries to drop below the poverty level.

MF: I beg to differ. Aren't you familiar with my analysis of the Great Depression? It was not caused by the markets, but rather by a mismanagement of the crisis by the US government and the Federal Reserve. You should read the book I co-authored with Anna Schwartz, A Monetary History of the United States, 1867-1960. It made the case that the Great Depression was caused by a severe monetary contraction due to the banking crises and poor policy by the Federal Reserve.

AM: Yes, Milton, I agree. The Fed did a poor job after 1929. Instead of increasing the monetary supply, the Federal Reserve did the opposite after the stock market crash of 1929. Fortunately, after the collapse of banks in 2008 policymakers had learned the lesson from 1929 and cut interest rates to 0 and increased the monetary supply. But the millions of Americans who lost their jobs, homes and savings after 1929 were able to get back on their feet thanks to FDR's New Deal. An expansionary monetary policy after Black Friday would have helped and the Depression might have been shorter and less severe. But it would not have magically stopped the stock market crash from unleashing a deep crisis in the real economy. In the 1920s speculation had been rampant on Wall Street.

MF: I beg to differ. Rose and I wrote our memoirs (*Two Lucky People*), which were published in 1998. One of its passages describes the Fed's bungled response to the stock market crash of 1929: "The Fed was largely responsible for converting what might have been a garden-variety recession, although perhaps a fairly severe one, into a major catastrophe. Instead of using its powers to offset the depression, it presided over a decline in the quantity of money by one-third from 1929 to 1933. Far from the depression being a failure of the free-enterprise system, it was a tragic failure of government."

AM: Exactly. You said it yourself in your book. "A fairly severe crisis". That means a deep recession or a depression.

MF: You also have to understand that there is a difference between supporting free markets and backing businesses. If businesses are too powerful, have oligarchic or monopolistic positions and can influence politicians, it is not a failure of free markets. A lack of competition engenders big businesses, which do not have much competition, have no incentive to invest and innovate, and provide poor customer service. I will give you the latest research on the topic.

A new working paper from the National Bureau of Economic Research by Jan De Loecker from Princeton University and Jan Eeckhout of University College, London, furnishes data to confirm that competition in many sectors is diminishing[6]. The authors analyzed data of publicly-traded US companies from 1950 until 2014. The authors conclude that from 1950 until 1980 the average mark-up of US firms (what companies charge customers above their cost of production) was a relatively low 18% over the cost of production. And it did not increase significantly. But since 1980 mark-ups have soared by 67% on average. In some sectors, such as retail banking, telecommunications, mobile telephony and air travel, consolidation has brought about high profits and poor customer service.

AM: Tell me about it. I must deal with Comcast, Sprint, United and others in these sectors. They make it very hard to reach a human being, have outsourced their call centers to Asia, rarely call back in the event the connection drops, rarely admit their mistakes and their credits or compensation are ridiculous. Comcast, for example, charges in advance. But any credits or compensation -- which are always minimal -- are applied to the future. It is hence therefore a lot of work to keep track of billing if you do not have an assistant.

MF: And then we have the technology sector. Giants like Apple, Alphabet (owner of Google), Amazon, Microsoft and Facebook are all very successful and their profits have been increasing at high rates. These giants have accumulated a lot of power in their respective sectors and, arguably, across the economy. Some might argue that consumers have to accept the tech titans' market power and profits as the price for the great innovation achieved by these companies. Patents allow companies to keep a temporary monopoly over their technology, which is a reward for their investment in R+D and new technologies.

In some sectors, dominant companies can cut costs and raise margins without increasing prices. Google, for example, has so much information on customers that it can tailor its advertisements and sell them at high prices[7]. Despite the actions and even fines imposed by regulators both in the US and the EU, Google's dominant market position (65% globally) has strengthened. Its rivals in the search engine sector are relatively puny.

AM: I have heard of and used Bing. But how many people actually know that Google's rivals have names like DuckDuckGo and Quora, let alone use them?

MF: Exactly. And Microsoft also abused its dominant position. Both US and EU regulators levied fines on Microsoft. It forced companies (Dell, HP, Toshiba, etc.) that sell desktop or laptops to include their web browser with its bundle of software and Windows operating system. At one point, 90% of private computers in the world ran on the Windows operating system. This allowed Microsoft to crush some of its rivals. Netscape Navigator was a very good web browser which became a casualty of Microsoft's dominant market position. There are many more examples. The tech giants are expanding into new sectors such as retail and ride-hailing and using their dominant positions and troves of consumer data to pressure suppliers.

---

6 "Free Exchange: An offer we can't refuse", *The Economist*, September 2nd, 2017, p. 66.
7 *Ibidem.*

AM: Yes. I do not like it when I turn on my cell phone and I realize that the most updated stories on topics of interest to me (the US economy, the Russia investigation, the Catalan referendum, how the Packers are doing) are forced onto me. Maybe I am not interested in them anymore. In any case, I want to be able to choose.

MF: The dilemma is whether these dominant positions and behaviors are an unfortunate consequence of the great innovation attained by these companies, which clearly benefits society, or if they amount to unacceptable barriers to competition. But a lack of competition is not the only concern. The Russian government, companies it controls and IT hackers from post-Soviet countries managed to get Facebook to buy thousands of ads in the run-up to the presidential election of November 2016. There are also national-security considerations when determining whether the tech giants' market power should be curtailed.

AM: Back to the 1920s. You believe the free-wheeling 1920s with their lack of financial regulation were not the major cause of the stock market crash of 1929? Joseph Kennedy Sr. and others speculated their way to great wealth. It was Franklin D. Roosevelt who had to create the Securities and Exchange Commission to supervise the stock market. In an ironic twist, FDR appointed Joseph Kennedy Sr. as the first Chairman of the SEC. When he was confronted with the question of how a speculator could lead the SEC, FDR famously replied: "It takes a thief to catch a thief."

MF: Yes, but Herbert Hoover's and the Fed's response turned a stock market crash into a depression. The Fed increased rates, other banks had to sell their assets, there were runs on banks, and soon millions were out of work in addition to having lost all their savings. After graduating from Rutgers University in 1932 -- in the middle of the Great Depression -- with a major in mathematics and economics, I wanted to become an actuary. But two of my economics professors, Arthur F. Burns and Homer Jones, convinced me that modern economics could help end the Great Depression. Therefore, do not blame me for my lifelong quest to overturn Keynesianism! My mentors had a lot to do with it. I accepted a scholarship to proceed my study of Economics at the University of Chicago.

I am sure Noruel Roubini gave you those numbers about the Great Recession of 2007-08! He is always so serious and is never cheerful. Why do you think he has earned the nickname Dr. Doom? And what about the vast amount of wealth, jobs and profits spawned during your so-called bubble years? And the millions of jobs created in the financial sector? You cannot even begin to compare the Great Depression with the Great Recession and the financial crisis.

AM: You are right. But regulators allowed unethical, illegal and surreal practices. They repealed the Glass-Steagall Act of 1933. Investment banks immediately started to expand, and they convinced commercial banks to allow them to speculate with depositors' money. Engineers and mathematicians who had worked for governments or defense companies designing advanced weapons during the Cold War were lured by the better pay offered by banks and designed very complicated financial products with complicated algorithms. George Soros and other very successful businessmen have no qualms admitting in public they did not understand such products.

MF: Give me an example?

AM: In 1999, Citicorp (a commercial bank) and Travelers Group (and investment and insurance bank) were allowed to merge despite the Glass-Steagall Act. The $140 billion merger was the biggest deal in history. It created Citigroup, the largest financial-services company in the world, a colossus with commercial, investment and insurance products in 100 countries and assets of

$698 billion. It had a market capitalization of $135 billion. To put the $698 billion in assets in perspective, it is seven times more than the EU's annual budget, is equivalent to the Department of Defense's annual budget and is roughly one-seventeenth of the United States' total GDP! The Dow Jones celebrated the merger between Citicorp and Travelers by breaching the 9000 level. The deal enabled Travelers to sell its insurance and mutual funds to Citicorp's retail clients and allowed the latter to expand by tapping into Traveler's base of investors and insurance buyers.

You wanted examples. I will give you another one. A year earlier, Morgan Stanley Group, a securities underwriter and asset manager, merged with Dean Witter, a provider of credit cards and retail stockbroker, thus creating another giant in the financial sector.

MF: Well, it was still much smaller than the US economy. And wasn't this better than Communism? Or do you prefer Chinese state-owned banks and financial-services giants?

AM: Of course I prefer American multinationals. But the ensuing financial crisis undermined the credibility of capitalism for the middle and lower classes of many developed countries.

When the Citicorp-Travelers merger was announced, Travelers said it would apply to the Federal Reserve to become a bank holding company and claimed it would sell some of its non-banking operations precisely to comply with the Glass-Steagall Act. A New York Times article in 1998 explained that the merger had to clear regulatory hurdles but also admitted that the separation between commercial and investment banking had already been partially eroded by then.

The highest-ranking economic policymakers at the time (end of Bill Clinton's second term) were: Alan Greenspan, Chairman of the Federal Reserve; Arthur Levitt, Chairman of the Securities and Exchange Commission; Treasury Secretary Larry Summers (whom I once met and was very kind) and Robert Rubin. I believe that Summers and Rubin (who are Democrats) were influenced by the giddy optimism of the late nineties and allowed Greenspan's famous "irrational exuberance" to cloud their good judgment.

Summers was initially the chief economist and vice president of the World Bank, the world's biggest development bank. This position was briefly held by Sir Nicholas Stern, who was also vice president and chief economist of the European Bank for Reconstruction and Development Bank (EBRD) when I was speechwriter to the president of the EBRD. Nick Stern is a brilliant economist and a good person. We stayed in touch after I left the EBRD. When I served as Director of Studies at the American Chamber of Commerce in Spain, we invited the co-author of the famous report on the cost of climate change to a star-studded two-day conference on energy and technology with over forty executives and politicians from the EU, US and other countries.

Larry Summers left the World Bank and served in high-ranking positions at the Treasury Department during the Clinton administration. He succeeded Robert Rubin as Treasury Secretary in 1999. During the Bush 43 administration, Summers served as President of Harvard University. Under president Obama, Summers returned to government and was the Director of the National Economic Council. He is now a professor at Harvard's John F. Kennedy School of Government, alongside very distinguished senior former policymakers such as Ambassador Nicholas Burns (whom I also met and briefly spoke to in 2010 at Harvard) and David Gergen. I feel like I almost know David Gergen because he has been a senior analyst for CNN for many years. Rubin went on to be CEO of Citigroup. Levitt, who was the longest-serving Chairman of the SEC, is a senior advisor to the Carlyle Group and Director of Bloomberg LP, the parent company of Bloomberg News. Levitt, also a Democrat, is 86 years old and lives in New York.

The financial sector lobby convinced the aforementioned big four (Greenspan, Levitt, Summers and Rubin) to get Congress to pass the Gramm-Leach-Bliley Act, which essentially retroactively legalized the merger between Citicorp and Travelers Group. Phil Gramm was a Republican Senator from Texas who made a lot of money after leaving politics in his positions in the financial sector. He was a hawk on defense, and I liked that aspect of him. But the Gramm-Leach-Bliley Act was also known as the Citigroup Relief Act. It removed the wall between retail and investment banking. Some courageous people did try to stop the Gramm-Leach-Bliley Act but ultimately failed. These events are recounted in the 2010 documentary *Inside Job*.

After the egregious mistake of repealing Glass-Steagall, it was off to the races for financial services companies, whether commercial or investment banks, insurance companies or private equity funds. And don't get me started on the damage inflicted by derivatives. As you know, derivatives are financial products whose value is determined by the price of another asset. A law was also enacted by Congress in the year 2000 which prevented the regulation of the derivatives market. By the time the financial crisis started, the derivatives markets were worth $50 trillion, more than double the US GDP of $19 trillion. That is why the big commercial, investment and insurance banks had to be bailed out. They were too big to fail.

MF: You cannot just lump all of these financial products together! Many did a lot of good! Millions of Americans and citizens of other countries were able to purchase a home, cars or other products. This benefited industrial companies and other non-financial firms in other sectors. Moreover, Citicorp/Citibank financed the laying of the first underwater cable between the US and Europe, the construction of the Panama Canal, and was involved in the Marshall Plan. As I famously said, most economic fallacies derive from the tendency to assume that there is a fixed pie, that one party can gain only at the expense of another.

AM: You would expect a bank with more than one hundred years of history to have been involved in some of these US initiatives. And at what cost has it fostered businesses and jobs?

MF: You sound like Kevin Spacey in Margin Call!

AM: Well, you sound like Jeremy Irons in Margin Call. I had an account with Citibank from 2001 until 2017. I am just describing the facts. I do not dispute that the financial sector needed some deregulation by the 1970s. Volcker was making only $45,000 at Chase Manhattan back then. But deregulation clearly went too far, enabling a few banks to gamble with trillions of dollars and cause a crisis that produced a lot of suffering, with millions losing their homes, jobs and savings. I have always pushed back against the Marxists and Socialists who equate the 2007-2009 financial crisis and recession with the Great Depression. Of course, the latter was many magnitudes worse! In fact, many would argue that policymakers prevented even more damage to the real economy beginning in 2007 because they had studied and knew what had happened in 1929 and how long it had taken the US and the world economy to recover from the Great Depression.

MF: As you well know, banks have paid billions of dollars in fines for their unethical operations.

AM: You mean the $486 million fine that Credit Suisse paid for helping clients evade taxes and Iran circumvent sanctions? Or the $780 million fine paid by UBS for also helping their US clients to avoid paying taxes?

MF: Come on, these are Swiss banks!

AM: What about the fact that AIG lied about its profits between 1998 and 2003?

MF: Well, I am not as satisfied with central banks' performance. Under Janet Yellen, the Federal Reserve has consistently not delivered on its 2% inflation target. Inflation needs to be higher. Many -- myself included -- are advocating increases in interest rates, but they have been too slow. They are necessary to stoke inflation, promote savings and get central banks to begin unwinding their massive purchases of assets under quantitative easing. The Federal Reserve has amassed 1.8 trillion dollars of mortgage-backed securities because of quantitative easing.

There are some indications that the Fed wants to proceed with initial sales of these assets. But the pace of this unwinding is too slow. Janet Yellen is very mediocre. She believes in setting interest rates to achieve the lowest unemployment rate possible. You know my feelings about unemployment. It is one of the central tenets of my economic theory. Without a certain level of unemployment, harmful inflation inevitably rises. Unemployment is currently at 4.3% and Yellen still refuses to increase rates! An unemployment rate of 4.3% is full employment. As you know, there is always a certain churn in the labor market as people transition from one job to another. Does unemployment have to go to 3% before the Federal Reserve musters the courage to increase rates?

AM: Well, inflation has not risen despite the Fed interest rate hikes since December of 2015. Despite the recovery in the prices of fossil fuels and commodities, this has not translated into higher inflation. So, why should the Fed increase interest rates again if inflation is contained and approximately 2%?

MF: Well, you know my position on inflation. It is taxation without representation. Companies are not investing enough due to a lack of competition in many sectors. Instead of expanding their operations, they are often resorting to buying back their own shares. They use their profits to execute share buybacks. This would not be happening if interest rates were higher, as all investors would have alternatives to the stock market, which right now is the only place where you can expect decent returns. Higher interest rates would drive up bond yields and provide investors with an alternative to the purchase of stocks. Companies would also have an incentive to invest in new operations as opposed to buying back their shares.

As you know, president Trump is considering who should be the next Fed chairman after Janet Yellen's first term concludes in February of 2018. Gary Cohn is President Trump's senior economic advisor. His formal position is that of Director of the National Economic Council, which under most administrations is a cabinet-level position. A former President and Chief Operating Officer of Goldman Sachs, Cohn is a globalist whom mainstream Republicans are counting on to check the influence of the nativists like Steve Bannon and the senior trade adviser at the White House, Peter Navarro. Both Navarro and Bannon are staunch advocates of protectionism and undermining multilateral economic and financial institutions.

AM: It may therefore be better that Cohn remain in his position as the senior economic advisor to Donald Trump as opposed to heading the Federal Reserve. Cohn has no training in economics. That did not stop Marriner Eccles from being a very successful chairman of the Federal Reserve from 1934 to 1948. He was very successful and close to president Franklin D. Roosevelt. Eccles wholeheartedly undertook stimulus policies as chairman of the Federal Reserve. He began to do so even before Keynes published his general theory.

MF: Eccles was a loser and it is a disgrace that the Federal Reserve building is named after him. How many times do I need to remind you and everybody that Keynesian economics is one of the most overrated concepts of the 20th century? If Keynesian economic measures such as the New Deal were so brilliant, why did it take the United States until World War II to fully recover from the stock market crash of 1929?

AM: Oh, Milton, you are beginning to sound like the Marxists who claim that it was only World War II that rescued the American economy after the 1929 stock market crash and the Great

Depression! You know that GDP was increasing, trade was expanding, and millions of jobs were being created well before the outbreak of World War II and the attack on Pearl Harbor in 1941.

MF: That is arguable. Despite the billions invested by the New Deal in programs such as the Civilian Conservation Corps, building infrastructure, subsidizing mortgages and other stimulus measures, in 1936 the US economy again dipped into a recession. As I once said, nothing is so permanent as a temporary government program.

AM: Maybe it is best if we agree to disagree on the financial crisis. Turning to the situation in Korea, Trump has again repeated his warnings to North Korea, which in turn ratcheted up the pressure by announcing that it is planning to launch missiles against the US territory of Guam, well within the range of the Democratic People's Republic of Korea's missiles. China, as usual, is doing nothing to defuse the crisis other than issuing an appeal to calm and announcing that it would follow a policy of neutrality if North Korea attacked South Korea, Japan or Guam. This raises the question of how China would react if the US, fearing a pre-emptive strike by Kim Jong Un, attacked North Korea first.

The White House has revealed that president Trump is interviewing several people with regards to the chairmanship of the Federal Reserve. It is therefore very possible and even likely that Janet Yellen will not be nominated for a second term when her first one ends in February of 2018. Gary Cohn clearly has the president's ear. General Kelly has been a very positive influence since he became the Chief of Staff in July of 2018. He has restricted access to the president and therefore made the decision-making process more efficient. A recent move attributed to General Kelly was to make Peter Navarro, the protectionist economic adviser, report to Gary Cohn.

In its meeting in late September, the Federal Reserve announced that it would begin the process of unwinding the assets it has accumulated on its balance-sheet as part of its response to the global financial crisis and the Great Recession.

MF: Finally, it is about time! This overdose of Keynesianism that central banks have indulged in is very harmful. It is one of the reasons why growth has been so sluggish.

AM: The US economy grew at an annual rate of over 3% in the second quarter of 2017 and since 2009 has expanded at an average slightly below 2% every year. This is indeed lower than in previous periods of recovery and expansion, but each era has its own challenges. The current period of economic growth is the third-longest in US history. This is certainly something to be proud about. As opposed to most economies in Europe and Japan, the US economy recovered sooner and has been more robust. You predicted that stagflation would strike some economies. The US experienced it in the 1970s, but since 2009 GDP has been expanding a healthy 2% clip and inflation is below 2%. You should give the Obama administration and the Fed more credit. You even advised them before you passed away in 2006!

There are currently $4.2 trillion in assets on the Fed's balance-sheet. In September of 2008, when the financial crisis began, the Fed held only $905 billion in assets. At first the Federal Reserve mainly lent to troubled banks to prevent them from going bankrupt and to forestall credit markets from seizing up. Later it moved into its Quantitative Easing (QE), the program whereby it purchased massive amounts of government debt and mortgages to keep interest rates low and provide a demand-side shock to the economy. It worked, as the US emerged from the recession in June of 2009. There were three massive purchases of bonds under QE. That is why the assets held by the Fed have ballooned to $4.2 trillion, which amounts to more than one-third of GDP. Starting in October, the Fed will begin to not reinvest part of the revenue generated by bonds that mature.

On August 16th, 2017, Milton Friedman flew back to Washington, D.C. He briefly interrupted his conference tour on the West Coast and the Rocky Mountain States. He had attended the Aspen security conference and was going to resume his swing through the West after a few days in the nation's capital. The annual meeting of central bank governors, economists and businesspeople at Jackson Hole, Wyoming, had invited Friedman to deliver a keynote speech. He was understandably very busy and had not had enough time to follow the tragic events that unfolded in Charlottesville, Virginia, on the week-end of August 12th and 13th of 2017. White supremacists and KKK members had obtained a permit to gather in Charlottesville on August 12th. They wanted to protest against the renaming of Robert E. Lee Park, which the city council had decided would henceforth be called Emancipation Park.

But on the evening of August 11th, the white supremacists staged a big rally with Tiki torches, reminiscent of Nazi or KKK marches, and chanted insults against Jews and homosexuals. The following day, Saturday the 14th, the white supremacists staged their sanctioned rally. But counter-protesters also showed up. A street battle soon broke out, with both sides employing bats and clubs to hit each other. The police did their best to break up the battle and protect the peaceful among the crowd who were caught up in the violence. Tragically, after it appeared that the worst had passed and there were no fatalities, a white supremacist rammed a car into the crowd. This was a terrorist attack. A woman was killed and nineteen were injured. Moreover, two Marines on a helicopter who were monitoring the situation were killed when the chopper accidentally crashed. Milton Friedman had been absorbed by the Jackson Hole meetings and needed context on the events in Charlottesville.

MF: Alex, what is going on? The networks have almost stopped reporting on anything else. What happened in Charlottesville?

AM: Well, the tragic events in Charlottesville have enraged many people in America. The nation expected an unconditional denunciation by president Trump of the white supremacists and KKK members. He did criticize their behavior and denounced the bigotry and prejudice. But he also on several occasions controversially spoke about violence "on both sides." The left, the mainstream media and many Republicans were dismayed and upset. They described the president's statement as half-hearted, insufficient and censured him for establishing a so-called "moral equivalency" between the white supremacists and the leftist protesters. On Monday, August 14th, Trump interrupted his working vacation at his golf course in Bedford, New Jersey, flew to Washington, D.C. and issued a stronger statement unequivocally denouncing the white supremacists, KKK members and their bigotry and violence. But he read the statement, so critics claimed it did not come from his heart. Even the US's military leadership felt compelled to issue its own independent denunciation of the white supremacists and their actions, although they did not criticize the president.

Unfortunately, on Tuesday the 15th of August, Trump provoked the outrage of many. A press conference was convened. Trump was supposed to present details and answer questions about his infrastructure plan. During his campaign, he committed to renovating and expanding America's ageing transportation infrastructure. His aides had suggested that $200 billion in private funding be leveraged to come up with the $1 trillion to undertake the massive infrastructure plan.

But Trump was unable to control himself during the press conference. Many reporters asked questions about Charlottesville. Journalists know how to rattle Trump. The president went rogue -- as some of his aides privately described the situation -- and started to improvise. He angrily challenged several journalists to be more neutral and accept that the left-wing protesters were also violent. This is factually true. But he blundered when he claimed that the initial gathering on Friday night was made up of non-supremacists who innocently, peacefully and legally assembled to criticize the renaming of Robert E. Lee park. There was nothing innocent about the marchers with the Tiki torches. Trump insisted that both sides had been violent. He also lambasted the fact that lawless left-wing protesters had taken down a statue of General Stonewall Jackson, the most famous Confederate general after Robert E. Lee. Trump did make a valid point: there is an agenda by the far left to rid the US of any reminder of the Confederacy. George Washington and Thomas Jefferson also owned slaves. General Ulysses S. Grant also owned slaves, and he of course was the Union's best general and served two terms as president after the Civil War. Trump rhetorically asked whether statues of Jefferson and Washington would be next.

MSNBC and most of the mainstream media went ballistic. Even many Republican senators denounced Trump's words. Governor John Kasich of Ohio, Senator Marco Rubio of Florida and Senator John McCain issued particularly strong statements criticizing the president directly. Senate Majority Leader Mitch McConnell and Speaker Paul Ryan strongly rebuked white supremacists, rejected moral equivalency but did not blame the president. Fox News, on the other hand, had pundits (professors, politicians) on its shows who argued that Trump had censured the white supremacists several times, that the left/extreme left has an agenda and is on a quest to destroy anything related to the South's legitimate history, and that, ultimately, they hate America. Social media was completely dominated by this growing intolerance.

The radicals on both the right and left used the tragedy to whip up their supporters into a frenzy and raise money for upcoming elections. Almost nobody reminded viewers that there are elections for governor in Virginia later this year. Virginia used to be a Republican stronghold, then became a swing state. But it has gradually become almost solid Democrat territory -- especially in federal elections -- since 2000. Both its outgoing governor -- Terry McAuliffe -- and its two senators are Democrats, although its delegation in the House has many Republicans, who mostly represent southern and rural parts of the state.

MF: What do you think can be done about the Confederacy names?

AM: Well, Trump is not going to dismiss Steve Bannon and Sebastian Gorka, two senior advisers with a history and strong links to the Alternative Right. If he had common sense, he would empower John Kelly and find a reason to let Bannon and Gorka go. But he is too worried about the backlash that would create from his base. There are reports that Gary Cohn, Trump's Senior Economic Adviser, is pressuring the president to fire Bannon. But Trump is apparently worried about what Bannon would reveal or the public comments he would make if he were let go. Bannon would not be a good soldier and exit gracefully as former chief of staff Reince Priebus did. Even if he did, he would not be able to control the Alternative Right. Trump, in essence, is a prisoner of Breitbart and other extremists he has empowered by appointing them to senior positions in his administration. The current chief of staff, retired Marine general John Kelly, was caught with his head down, staring at the floor with a noticeable look of worry as Trump lectured the media at Trump Tower on their reporting of the Charlottesville violence.

President Trump could create a bipartisan independent commission made up of historians, members of the relevant federal agencies (Department of the Interior, etc.) and other groups that would examine whether and which statues of Confederate Generals should be put in museums. I have traveled extensively in the South and feel the left is exaggerating and needs this issue to fire up its base and raise money for the upcoming 2018 mid-term elections. But if there are too many statues of Robert Lee and Stonewall Jackson, have an independent commission decide how a better balance can be struck between not humiliating Southern whites and offending blacks.

But this tragedy and the outrage must be understood in the bigger context of a decline in the trust that Americans have with regards to several institutions. According to a survey from the University of Chicago, the percentage of Americans who agreed with the statement that "most people can be trusted" dropped from 44% in 1976 to 32% in 2016. Jamie Dimon, JP Morgan Chase's CEO, has described trust as "America's secret sauce" and is concerned that its supply will run very low. He has also asserted that he would defeat president Trump if he ran for president in 2020, despite his disavowal of the intention to actually do so.

MF: So Charlottesville overshadows the US's great economic numbers. You very well know that the stock market continues to break records, GDP is expected to expand by 2.6% in 2017, and there is full employment as the unemployment rate stands at only 4.3%.

AM: You are mostly right. But Trump had promised an undeliverable GDP growth of 4%, the stock market is overvalued, there is substantial underemployment and people who have left the labor market for good. Wage growth has been slow, especially for non-skilled workers. And the labor market participation rate is still low by historical standards.

An OECD report has pointed out that countries with low levels of trust -- such as Mexico and Turkey -- are poorer. According to Gallup, the share of Americans who have "little or no confidence" in big business has increased from 26% in 1976 to 39% now. For banks, the percentage has risen from 10% in 1979 to 28% now. I am sure these numbers -- which are concerning but not alarming -- are much higher in other countries, especially those without a free-market tradition like the US. Despite these feelings, corporations are posting record profits. In some sectors, these record profits are due to insufficient competition. *The Economist* made the point that certain corporations with big public scandals are recording healthy profits because there is insufficient competition and Americans do not have that big of a choice.

Wells Fargo created millions of fake bank accounts and paid huge fines, but its profits surged 5% year-on-year to June 2017. United Airlines had a big fiasco in the spring of 2017 when one of its passengers was assaulted by the airline's security personnel after he refused to give up his seat on an overbooked flight. But its profits have also continued to grow.

All of these matters are currently overshadowed by the fallout from Trump's comments over the white supremacists and bungled and erroneous attempts to justify some of them. The Washington Post headlined "America weeps". The Las Vegas Sun labelled him the first un-American President in history. Even the right-wing New York Post mocked Trump. The heads of the US armed forces' four branches issued unprecedented statements making it clear that they would not tolerate any racism or bigotry in the military. The US president is of course the commander-in-chief. The heads of the four branches of the US armed forces were not challenging their boss. But they explicitly condemned the events in Charlottesville and indirectly criticized the president's attempts to establish moral equivalency between the white supremacists and those who opposed them. The Secretary of Defense, James Mattis, laconically said that "it was very sad". Vice President Mike Pence, who was traveling in South America, stood by the president's statement (unclear which one).

Several CEOs who were members of the Manufacturing Council that Trump had created resigned in the wake of the president's reaction to Charlottesville. According to MSNBC, the Council did not hold a single meeting. Trump also disbanded another body -- the Strategic and Policy Forum -- whose members were quitting. This is very bad news for the president's agenda of economic reforms, from infrastructure to tax reform. Both councils were stacked with CEOs of American companies.

According to Rachel Maddow, one of the top investigators in Robert Mueller's team has left the Special Counsel's team to take up a top position in Human Resources at the FBI. This person was the head of counterintelligence at the FBI during 2016 and until he left to join the Special Counsel's team in the spring of 2017. Unlike the White House and other federal agencies, the Special Counsel's team does not produce leaks. It is therefore impossible to know what prompted this departure. It could be a clash of egos. It might be that this person has a family to take care of and wants a less stressful position. But if other reporting is right and Russia's intelligence service is still infiltrating American institutions, one of the top HR positions at the FBI might be necessary to bolster the US's defenses. The FBI protects America on many fronts, including hostile foreign intelligence services like Russia's FSB, the successor to the KGB.

MSNBC and specifically Rachel Maddow, who is not just brave and brilliant but very funny, reported that Trump's top personal attorney in the Russia case forwarded a tweet equating Robert E. Lee and George Washington and claimed that the movement Black Lives Matter was heavily infiltrated by terrorist groups. As Maddow pointed out, Trump's lead attorney should be very busy preparing the president for the Mueller investigation and not re-tweeting racist emails. This is the same attorney who gave cameras the finger when he was defending another client.

Next week Democrats in Congress will introduce a motion that seeks to censure the President because his remarks after Charlottesville did not properly denounce white supremacists, racists and hate crimes, and even defended the white supremacists. It will be interesting to see whether Republicans will join with Democrats in voting to approve this censure. Even if the censure is approved by Congress (which has Republican majorities in both the Senate and House), it is largely symbolic and has no political or legal consequences.

But a lot of pent-up rage is now going to spill over into real actions. For example, the Alabama state legislature recently passed a law which protects all monuments located on public property that are more than forty years old from being removed. In 1905, a monument to honor the Confederate soldiers was erected in Birmingham, the biggest city in Alabama. Birmingham's mayor, who happens to be black, decided to surround the statue with tarpaulin. He argued that Alabama was not even a part of the Confederacy. But the Attorney General of Alabama has decided to sue him and his city council for tampering with the statue. I envision long legal battles over statues and memorials. Let us hope they remain legal.

The fallout over Trump's remarks defending the white supremacists who gathered in Charlottesville continues. Several senior officials serving in the Trump administration have publicly expressed their outrage at his remarks. Trump had famously said that he could walk down Fifth Avenue in New York, shoot somebody and that his supporters would not abandon him. But his defense of white supremacists and establishing a moral equivalency with the counter-protestors may have crossed a red line in American politics. Upsetting the Jewish community is a career-ender for most people, but probably not for president Trump.

Gary Cohn, the Director of the National Economic Council, is Jewish. David Shulkin, the Secretary of the Department of Veterans Affairs, is also Jewish. They both went on the record to directly criticize Trump. Cohn hinted at the possibility that he might resign. If Cohn goes, Trump can forget about getting his tax reform and infrastructure initiatives enacted by Congress anytime soon. Trump has always praised Cohn and holds him in high esteem. He left a very good position at Goldman Sachs to become Trump's Senior Economic Adviser. His formal position is Director of the National Economic Council. But he clearly has the president's ear on economic and financial matters. There is speculation that Trump could nominate him to succeed Janet Yellen when her first term ends in February of 2018. Cohn will therefore hang on. Resigning would doom his chances of becoming Chairman of the Federal Reserve, as Trump would view his departure as a betrayal. The last three chairmen of the Federal Reserve have all served two terms, and Cohn is a Democrat who would probably be confirmed by the Senate. Republicans would confirm him to strengthen his position vis-à-vis the economic nationalists who exert so much influence over Trump. Steve Bannon boasted that he relishes taking on Cohn every day and remarked that the US is in an economic war with China.

Chapter 9: The terrorist attack in Barcelona, Bannon's departure and Macron's first reforms

August of 2017 had been relatively mild by Washington standards. There were many days in the first half of August when temperatures during the daytime did not surpass the low 80s, and at night they dipped into the low 70s. One could be mistaken for thinking that it was springtime. But on the 17th of August, after delaying my short road trip for several days, I packed my bags and drove west. The weather forecast called for very hot and humid days in the ensuing week for the Washington area. High heat and humidity made it worse. On many nights in the first half of August, I had been able to turn off the AC unit because the temperatures were bearable, although the high humidity persisted even when temperatures dropped at night. Of course, I was also as always trying to save by turning off the AC.

Moreover, most of my professional contacts were away on vacation, not just in Washington DC, but even more so in Europe. After making much progress on my book and during a very brief break in my course, I decided I should undertake a brief road trip to get away from the heat of the Washington, D.C. area and swim in lakes and rivers around the US. I also needed to tune out from all of the worries and uncertainties that I would face during the difficult fall that would ensue. But on the morning of August 18th, Maria Matos from Cinco Días emailed me requesting that I write an op-ed about the hideous terrorist attack carried out by Islamic jihadists against civilians and tourists in the heart of Barcelona's Old Town. Milton Friedman made a brief stop in Washington, D.C. on his way to Asia to deliver more conferences. He was eager to know more. We met at the International House of Pancakes Restaurant at Potomac Yards, which has become my favorite mall in the Washington, D.C. area, commonly referred to as the DMV.

MF: Another suicide attack in a major Western city?

AM: Yes, unfortunately. After Nice, Brussels, Munich, London and Manchester in the past couple of years, another jihadist has used a vehicle to plow into crowds of innocent tourists. This time it happened in Barcelona. A cell of Islamic terrorists had been preparing a more sophisticated attack that would have involved setting off bombs at several locations. They accidentally set off their bombs while preparing them in a flat near Barcelona. Fearful that the detonation would raise suspicion, they proceeded to execute a second plan, their plan B. Twenty-two-year-old Younes Abouyaaqoub boarded a van and drove it to the center of Barcelona, along Pelayo street and to Catalonia square. He then plowed it into a big crowd of tourists on the northern end of the Ramblas and managed to drive down the Ramblas while running over people. Nine hours later, five men from the same cell drove a vehicle into another crowd of pedestrians in nearby Cambrils, killing one woman and injuring six others. The police shot and killed all five attackers in Cambrils.

MF: There have been very similar terrorist attacks involving cars or trucks in Nice, Paris, Berlin, Ansbach and Sweden in the past 13 months. Why didn't the Barcelona authorities cut off access to the city center to private vehicles?

AM: Milton, we have a mayor of Barcelona who does not even have a university degree. She is utterly unqualified to be mayor. She at first wanted to curtail the cruise ships that dock at Barcelona's old harbor and fill the streets with throngs of well-heeled tourists. She then attempted to cancel the International Mobile Congress, the most prestigious in the world. After cooler heads dissuaded her from getting her way on these two matters, she undertook a quest to diminish what leftists label "bourgeois" tourism in Barcelona. She reduced the space on sidewalks that outdoor cafés are entitled to use -- the ones who cater to well-off tourists on the Passeig de Gràcia and other popular avenues. Eager to please her base in a certain district of Barcelona, she obsessively pushed ahead with a plan to link the tram that runs along Avinguda Diagonal with the district of Poble Nou. The Diagonal Avenue does not have enough space for a tram. Buses, cars, pedestrians and bicycles already struggle to fit into its narrow lanes.

MF: Doesn't the opposition to this dim-witted mayor rein her in?

AM: It is very hard. The former right-of-center CiU party of former mayor Xavier Trías (whom I know well) broke up because of former president Artur Mas's determination to pursue Catalan independence. The rest of the city council is mostly made up of Socialists, former Communists and anarchists. Hardly the type to worry about terrorist attacks. They were too busy jostling for power ahead of yet another attempt to hold an illegal Catalan referendum on independence on October 1st.

It is disgraceful that Barcelona's mayor, Ada Colau, and her team did not block access to Barcelona's old town for private vehicles. At a minimum, they could have put up bollards which are deployed to stop vehicles. Many cities have already put them up after the attacks in Nice, Munich and London. I am sure that Colau and the leftists will manage to pin some of the blame for the inability to ward off the attack on the central government in Madrid. But this one is entirely their fault.

By the time the terrorists ran out of time and space, they had killed sixteen innocent persons and injured more than one hundred. Prime minister Mariano Rajoy and the King of Spain immediately traveled to Barcelona. Four of the five members who made up the cell where shot by police. A fifth managed to flee. This was by far the worst terrorist attack in Spain since the barbaric bombing of Madrid's Atocha train station in 2004. That atrocity claimed the lives of 191 persons and injured more than 2,000. In the ensuing years the Spanish police has been very effective in thwarting terrorist plots before they could be carried out. They were sometimes helped by intelligence from our European or NATO allies, but also by Morocco and Algeria. At any rate, the Spanish police arrested dozens of terrorists from 2004 until 2017 in many different parts of Spain. Some were on the verge of executing attacks. Others were recruiting young Muslims in order to send them to the battlegrounds of Irak and Syria.

MF: How sad. What barbarians.

AM: Yes, Milton. This was the worst terrorist attack in my hometown of Barcelona since ETA exploded a massive bomb at the Hipercor mall on the Meridiana avenue on June 19, 1987 that killed 21 and injured 45. The Basque terrorist group murdered 860 persons and injured thousands since the 1960s until declaring a cease-fire a few years ago. Some of the inhabitants of the building where I grew up, including myself, were injured when ETA targeted a French furniture store named Roche Bobois in December of 1987, a few months before the Hipercor massacre. My family and I were getting ready to fly to the US for Christmas. As the building was heavily damaged and everyone was forced to move elsewhere, my father cancelled the trip. My mother had already decided to divorce my father. The bombing of the apartment building precipitated my parents' separation. My mother decided to move in with her parents, while my father moved in with his. My paternal grandfather was in the terminal stage of cancer of the esophagus, which was triggered by a lifetime of smoking.

ETA murdered 860 people and injured thousands from 1968 until it declared a "cessation of hostilities" in 2010. Most of its attacks purposely killed policemen, military officers, soldiers, politicians and ordinary civilians in its ruthless campaign to gain independence for the Basque

Country from Spain. Its attacks were dreadful. But sometimes they did call ahead of time to try to prevent mass casualties. Their aim was to bring the Spanish government to the negotiating table. They therefore mostly assassinated or kidnapped military officers, policemen, politicians and businessmen, much like the Red Army Faction did in Germany, the Red Brigades in Italy and the IRA in Ireland and the UK.

The effectiveness of Spanish police and the will of the Spanish people were stronger than ETA's terror campaign. Supported by French authorities, Spanish police were able to gradually arrest its members and dismantle all of its cells until the group basically begged for a political resolution beginning in 2010. But the government of Spain was steadfast in its refusal to negotiate with ETA. It was always the policy of any Spanish government that ETA had to surrender its weapons, renounce violence and simply dissolve. This was not Northern Ireland nor Colombia. Spanish governments -- especially those of the center-right PP party -- were firm in not rewarding ETA for simply declaring a ceasefire. The government even rejected that the 300 members of ETA in Spanish jails be moved to prisons close to or in the Basque Country. The Spanish government's position was that there would be no negotiation. The most the terrorists could expect was shorter jail terms if they returned their weapons and dissolved ETA. And that is what eventually happened. In November of 2012, the group reported that it was ready to negotiate a "definitive end" to its operations and disband completely, and in April 2017 claimed that it had given up all its weapons and explosives.

Before ETA was defeated, there were many in Spain – especially among the left – who wanted the government to make concessions to the terrorists to facilitate an end to their campaign of violence. There were many who pointed to Northern Ireland as a model of how to resolve a decades-old insurgency by a terrorist group seeking independence from a strong Western European state. The Colombian government's agreement with the FARC guerrillas is deeply unpopular among many Colombians. It remains to be seen whether the Good Friday agreement will hold as Brexit proceeds and might put up a border between Northern Ireland and Ireland. In hindsight, the Spanish government was right in not making any concessions and we were all rewarded with ETA's unconditional defeat.

MF: I am glad to hear that ETA was defeated, and I offer my condolences to the families of the sixteen persons that were killed in the attack in Barcelona, as well as to the wounded. What else is going on?

AM: I made it to Bentonville, Virginia. I checked into a Motel 8 in Front Royal and drafted the op-ed on the terrorist attack in Barcelona for Cinco Días while listening to the latest political developments. The day's big story was that Steve Bannon had resigned as senior adviser to president Trump and was returning to Breitbart. The networks speculated how much damage his departure would cause Trump among his base. Fox News of course spun this development as a victory of the moderates and globalization hawks against the nativists. Chief of Staff John Kelly was really cleaning house. After firing Anthony Scaramucci as Communications Director, it was Bannon's turn to go.

It seemed that the generals, businessmen and senior economic adviser Gary Cohn were sidelining the radicals. I did not think that Trump would have the guts to dismiss Bannon. Officially, it was a resignation. But it was obvious that Bannon had become increasingly isolated after Chief of Staff John Kelly imposed a bit of message discipline and in terms of who was given access to the president.

MF: This is very good news.

AM: Sebastian Gorka, another nationalist and nativist, is likely to be the next to be fired. In fact, Trump has no issues with the globalists on some matters. He likes the fact that interest rates under Yellen have remained very low. Trump likes low interest rates. Yellen has not raised rates more often since unemployment dipped below 5% because she may feel that the labor participation rate is still very low. There is still a lot of slack in the labor market. As the economy has expanded and more jobs have been created, those who had left the labor market in despair are again actively looking for work.

In any event, Trump's pursuit of financial deregulation does require the dismissal of Janet Yellen. The current chairwoman of the Federal Reserve was critical of Donald Trump in public. This is something the president will not forget as he has a great memory. But in the last decades presidents have always re-nominated for a second term the chairmen of the Federal Reserve who had been appointed by their predecessors, even if the previous president was from the other party. Bill Clinton confirmed Alan Greenspan for another term and Obama did the same with Ben Bernanke. It might therefore rattle markets -- at least temporarily -- if Trump chooses a candidate to replace Yellen who must be confirmed by the Senate. The president and the business community are very keen on financial deregulation. But the Federal Reserve can undertake such a policy with Yellen at the helm because Trump has nominated Randall Quarles as Vice chairman of the Fed. He will oversee financial supervision and therefore can push for financial deregulation. Quarles' position had remained unfilled in recent years but was effectively carried out by Daniel Tarullo, who left the Fed earlier this year.

The other candidates who are being discussed as potential successors to Yellen as chairman of the Federal Reserve are John Taylor and Kevin Walsh. Taylor is a renowned academic from Stanford who came up with a mathematical rule that describes central banks' actions. Like other Republicans, Taylor wants the Federal Reserve to follow this algorithm when it sets monetary policy. I do not think such an approach would be compatible with Trump's eagerness to be flexible. Kevin Walsh served as a senior policymaker at the Federal Reserve from 2006 to 2011. Taylor is perceived as having fewer political skills, although he served at the Treasury during the George W. Bush administration. Both Taylor and Walsh opposed quantitative easing.

President Trump announced his new strategy on Afghanistan and South Asia in a speech on August 21st at Fort Meyer, Virginia. His entire cabinet and the Chairman of the Joint Chiefs of Staff, General Joseph Dunford, were in attendance. The media had portrayed Trump's announcement of the deployment of 4,000 additional US troops to Afghanistan as a U-turn imposed by the generals (Mattis, Kelly, Dunford) and which would be heavily criticized by the departed Bannon, conservatives and liberals.

Trump's speech was brilliant, with a lot of specifics. If only the president could always stick to the script and read the speeches drafted for him. Trump's speech did contain several newsworthy items. He admitted that he had changed his mind with regards to Afghanistan since becoming president, going against his instinct. The president also acknowledged that the war in Afghanistan had lasted far too long (seventeen years). He promised to pressure the government of Pakistan to crack down on the terrorist groups which operate in Afghanistan that still have havens in some of its provinces, especially in the northwest of Pakistan. He admonished the Afghan government and its people that the US commitment would someday end. Trump urged India, a strategic ally, to do more to invest in the economic development of Afghanistan. Trump made it abundantly clear that he would not telegraph to the terrorists in Afghanistan when and how they would be attacked or when the US would pull out. In one of several indirect swipes at president Obama, he insisted that his Afghanistan policy would not be based on a timetable. America's enemies would not be able to wait us out. The president repeatedly stressed that the US would not engage in nation-building.

The continued presence in Afghanistan is meant to crack down on Al-Qaeda and ISIS terrorists and the extremist Taliban that harbor and abet them. Trump referenced the egregious attack in Barcelona a few days earlier, in which a jihadist cell had killed sixteen innocent people. It is up to the people and government of Afghanistan to build up their institutions. Trump hinted at the possibility that the moderate elements of the Taliban could be included in political negotiations, but that such a move would only be considered from a position of strength. The president also called on the US's allies in NATO to help shoulder the military burden, while accepting that the US would continue to play the leading role.

Trump smartly used the devotion and sacrifice of those who bravely serve in the US armed forces and those who have given their lives or been wounded to deflect the criticism he received over his remarks on the violence in Charlottesville. He basically asked Americans to overcome their divisions to honor the service and sacrifice of the members of the military.

MF: As you know, during my career I always advocated a volunteer armed forces and firmly rejected conscription.

AM: Indeed. Unfortunately, president Trump's good speech on Afghanistan was just a fleeting moment. This is now a recurring pattern. On August 22nd, 2017, he flew to Phoenix, Arizona, to address a crowd of supporters. His 40-minute rant was filled with vitriol against the media and Republican senators. He did not back down on his statements about the violence in Charlottesville. Unfortunately, more than ten members of the Navy have been killed in two separate accidents in the past month. Unlike any other president, Trump did not mention them, let alone give his condolences to their families.

But Trump did berate Arizona's two Republican senators during his rally in Phoenix. Senator John McCain, a war hero respected by Republicans and Democrats alike, is fighting for his life after being diagnosed with brain cancer. But that did not stop Trump from chastising him for not voting to repeal and replace Obamacare. Arizona's other Republican senator, Jeff Flake, has written a book lambasting Trumpism. He has also become a target for the president. More surprisingly, the media has reported that Trump has often called some leading Republican senators and yelled at them for not stopping the bill that imposed sanctions on Russia or halting the special counsel's investigation into Trump's alleged ties to Russia and his campaign's possible collusion with its government.

Senator Bob Corker from Tennessee is the chairman of the Senate Foreign Relations Committee. He was on Trump's short list to be appointed Secretary of State. He is a man of great integrity and experience. Corker gave Trump the benefit of the doubt in the first few months of the presidency. But his latest remarks pointedly criticized Trump for not having the competence and character needed to be president.

Trump is also alienating Senate Majority Leader Mitch McConnell, whom he refers to as "Mitch" in his public remarks. McConnell has lately not minced his words. He expressed his belief in private that Trump might not be able to save his presidency. And McConnell has a vested personal interest in Trump being successful. His wife, Elaine Chao, serves as Trump's Transportation Secretary. McConnell is very upset that Trump proudly announced that he is endorsing primary challenges of extremely radical individuals against Republican incumbents such as Senator Jeff Flake of Arizona, Senator Dean Heller of Nevada and Senator Luther Strange of Alabama. McConnell has gone out of his way to praise Flake and Heller. Trump has endorsed a woman (Kelli Ward) who believes that 9/11 did not take place and blames Senator McCain for the rise of ISIS to take on Flake. Trump and McConnell have not talked to one another in weeks. The president also rebuked Republican Senator Thom Tillis from North Carolina, who is co-sponsoring a bill that would make it hard for Special Counsel Mueller to be dismissed and would enable any such dismissal to be challenged in court.

MF: It appears that not sufficiently denouncing the white supremacists after Charlottesville may mark a turning point. In 1940, I was appointed assistant professor in Economics at the University of Wisconsin-Madison. I was shocked to discover that anti-Semitism was alive and well at the Economics Department at Wisconsin-Madison. I therefore decided to return to government service. But I am shocked that a president in 2017 is at least indirectly condoning white supremacists.

AM: Yes, and after Congress returns from its recess, they will have a lot on their plate. The statutory limit on government borrowing -- popularly known as the debt ceiling -- has to be raised to avoid a default. Trump is already hinting that he will not prevent a government shutdown if funding for his wall on the border with Mexico is not appropriated.

The newly-elected president of France, Emmanuel Macron, is also facing a tough return from the summer break. Although he was elected in June, his approval rating at the one-hundred-day mark has already plummeted to 36% according to the polling firm IFOP. This is a man who could do no wrong a few months ago and came out of relative obscurity to be elected president at age 39 with 66% of the votes in the second round of the presidential election.

Many of those who voted for Macron in the second round were voting against the far-right Marine Le Pen, his opponent in the run-off. Macron has not helped himself with some self-inflicted errors since being sworn in. He tried to codify an official role for the French First Lady, in this case his wife, who is much older than him and has been one of his mentors since they fell in love while he was her pupil. Macron also had a run-in with a top general over cuts to the defense budget. And he has approved some tough but necessary reforms: cutting payroll taxes but offsetting it by increasing a charge that affects retired people.

MF: A French president who cuts taxes on business and finances them by hiking rates on retirees. That takes some guts! His tax cuts obviously need to be revenue neutral so that France will stick to its commitment to cut its budget deficit to 3.1% of GDP by the end of 2017.

AM: Yes but try convincing those impacted by the higher taxes about its virtues! Moreover, Macron has also frozen public-sector pay, which obviously has not endeared him with public servants in France. But the biggest test will come in September, when Macron will unveil his reforms to the labor market. He campaigned on a pledge to lower severance pay and to enable employers and employees to negotiate working conditions at the company level. In other words, agreements at the national level in a specific sector between employers and unions and which are the product of collective bargaining could be overridden at the company level. Needless to say, unions and left-wing parties have announced their opposition to both measures. Unions have already planned strikes for September 12th.

MF: Macron needs to keep his poise. He cannot cave in to labor unions as every French president or prime minister has done in the past two decades. It would send a signal to leftists everywhere that they can scuttle reforms by getting enough people to march on the streets. And proponents of populism would be given a shot in the arm. Macron was supposed to be the establishment's last best hope to reform the stagnant French economy! If he fails, populists everywhere will be emboldened.

AM: Yes, you are absolutely right. And Macron's surprising plunge in popularity in three months proves, in my view, that voters are increasingly whimsical and mercurial. They expect immediate results and do not have patience. The old rules about a newly-elected president or prime minister enjoying a "honeymoon" period seem to have gone out of the window. We are in an era of populism, social media and voter impatience. Macron needs to deliver reforms not just to shake up the French economy, but also to send a broader message to populists everywhere. He cannot afford to fail. It appeared that populism had been dealt a death blow after the presidential elections in Austria and the general elections in the Netherlands and France in 2017. But a failure of Macron's reforms would give populism a second wind.

MF: What about the general elections in September in Germany?

AM: The early polls are showing that the anti-immigrant populist *Alternative für Deutschland* will garner around 9% of the vote. That would give it about 60 MPs in the German Bundestag. It already has parliamentary presence in thirteen of the sixteen German regional (*Länder*) parliaments. The conventional wisdom is that the AfD is a nuisance which has peaked. Ninety-three percent of Germans surveyed asserted that the AfD presence in regional parliaments has gone unnoticed. Because of its history, mainstream German public opinion is particularly hostile to xenophobic right-wing parties. The AfD at first sought to capitalize on the eurozone debt crisis by advocating Germany's withdrawal from the eurozone. But Merkel's decision to allow about 800,000 (mostly Asian) immigrants into Germany in 2015 was seized by the AfD as an opportunity to become an anti-immigration party.

There is full employment in Germany. The AfD should not do better than the 9% predicted by current polls. But people who vote for extremist parties often do not tell pollsters the truth. Life in some parts of East Germany is still tough. The AfD could benefit from an ethereal protest vote. It is even conceivable that some of the discontented voters who usually support the post-Communist Left Party (especially in the former East Germany) could cast their votes for AfD. After all, political extremes attract.

At least, I can give you some good news. As I had predicted, another right-wing nationalist in president Trump's White House has been dismissed. It was Sebastian Gorka's turn to be fired.

MF: What is the latest regarding the Russia investigation?

AM: On August 31st, new information emerged about president Trump's mounting legal problems. Several newspapers, including the Wall Street Journal, disclosed interesting developments. President Trump's personal attorneys revealed that they had presented documents to Special Counsel Robert Mueller's investigators to prove that Trump had not committed obstruction of justice by firing former FBI Director James Comey because it is within his constitutional authority to do so. But the president could not fire Comey to prevent an investigation, which would be illegal. Although Trump has the power to fire the FBI Director, he cannot do it for an illegal reason. This obviously means that Trump and his personal attorneys feel that the Special Counsel is investigating a potential obstruction of justice. In fact, the Washington Post reported that shortly after Trump dismissed Comey, Special Counsel Mueller began to investigate the president for potential obstruction of justice.

According to another newspaper, Trump requested or even pressured both Director of National Intelligence Dan Coats and Admiral Mike Rogers, the Director of the National Security Agency, to drop any investigation into Russia's interference in the US elections in 2016 and the role the Trump campaign might have played. Moreover, the Internal Revenue Service (IRS) has begun its investigation about the possible evasion of taxes by some of the president's surrogates, including

Paul Manafort. There is speculation that Manafort's notes might prove that foreign contributions were illegally accepted by the Trump campaign. The IRS investigators belong to its criminal investigation unit and specialize in money laundering and tax evasion. They are held in high regard by Mueller because of their experience in preparing air-tight tax charges for prosecutors. These IRS specialists are accountants, have long track records and are experts in investigating money laundering.

President Trump never disclosed any of his tax returns. He routinely lied that, because he was the subject of an audit, he could not make his tax returns public. This is a lie. First of all, there is no evidence that Trump is being submitted to an audit. The president has never produced a document to prove his audit claim. But even if it were true, being subjected to an audit does not prevent a person from disclosing their tax returns.

Unfortunately, one of the worst hurricanes in American history pounded Texas and Louisiana for almost a week. It dumped record amounts of rain on several cities in Texas, especially Port Arthur and Beaumont. But Houston itself, the fourth most populated city in the US, was also extensively flooded. Images of people on boats on what used to be streets were tragic. Millions of people had to be evacuated and hosted in shelters because their homes were literally under water. Hurricane Harvey caused the most destruction in Texas since 1978 and has been described as a once in a thousand-year hurricane. The estimated property damage is at a staggering $75 billion. In comparison, the Federal Emergency Management Agency has a budget of $3.2 billion. A territory equivalent to the state of New Jersey has been completely flooded. There were not many fatalities, with the notable exclusion of a police officer. The winds did not cause damage, but Harvey lingered over Texas for almost a week, producing record amounts of rain. The flooding was very extensive, and many people's homes will not be insured. Pipelines and pumping stations had to be closed. Emergency services are distributing bottled water as tap water cannot be drunk. The outpouring of support and fundraising for the victims showcases Americans' generosity. Walmart and other big companies have donated millions and promised to match individual's contributions.

A chemical plant in a Texas city has suffered an explosion because its cooling systems broke down due to the flooding. An Arkema executive admitted that the smoke is noxious but -- despite journalists' insistence -- did not accept that the smoke caused by the fire could be toxic. Texas law does not require the company running the chemical plant to hand over to the public the chemicals stored at the plant. There was an accident fifteen years ago at a chemical plant in Texas that killed innocent people. The chemicals at the Arkema plant are stored in eight different containers, and the company admitted that there would be more explosions. The Environmental Protection Agency conducted tests of the smoke and air around the Arkema plant. In 2013, then attorney-general Greg Abbott (now the governor of Texas) changed a Texas law so that neither the state nor the companies that run chemical plants have to reveal to the public which chemicals are stored and used in their plants. Despite other deadly accidents, it seems unlikely that Texas will pass a right-to-know law regarding this matter.

MF: Enough about natural disasters! Tell me something new about finances.

AM: The Obama administration proposed putting Harriet Tubman on the $20 bill. She was a tough and brave black woman who worked as a spy for the Union and valiantly fought to abolish slavery. But president Andrew Jackson, who is on the $20 bill, is one of president Trump's favorite presidents. He has repeatedly extolled Jackson -- who was president from 1829 until 1837 -- as a maverick who took on the establishment and whose military prowess in Tennessee should be admired. Trump has even claimed that if Jackson had been president a little later in the

XIXth century, the Civil War would have been avoided. When asked about the potential replacement of Andrew Jackson by Harriet Tubman, Treasury Secretary Steve Mnuchin brushed off the question and made it clear that the Trump administration has bigger priorities. I agree with this decision. Harriet Tubman will not replace Andrew Jackson on $20 bills under a Trump administration. States can name boulevards, airports, train stations or ports after her.

On September 3rd, Kim Jong Un set off an advanced thermonuclear bomb. This was the sixth nuclear test undertaken by North Korea in its history. Kim Jong Un has carried out 84 missile tests since coming to power, and 18 since Trump was sworn into office. This pace far exceeds that of his father, Kim Kong II. Russia and China are helping North Korea despite UN sanctions which curb trade with North Korea. US sanctions are for Chinese companies that do business with North Korea. These are the so-called secondary sanctions. The sanctions are a good idea. But they must be followed up by negotiations because Kim Jong Un is determined to test President Trump. The sanctions approved by the UN would ban exports of North Korean coal and agricultural products. But this is insignificant. It is $3 billion in trade between North Korea and mainly China that keeps the North Korean regime in power. The Kim Jong Un regime conducts 90% of its legal trade with China. This is a drop in the Pacific Ocean as China's GDP is 11 trillion dollars.

The US and South Korea have conducted military maneuvers. According to a Gallup poll, 58% of Americans now support military action against North Korea if sanctions and diplomacy do not work. Among Republicans, the figure is 82%.

Russian president Vladimir Putin has as usual stepped up the pressure by sending military aircraft to fly over Korea while lecturing the US that it needs to negotiate with North Korea because the US is the bigger and richer country (he might have said the more intelligent one too). While this statement is true in isolation, Putin continues his determined strategy to expand Russia's influence beyond its post-Soviet near abroad and at least step up its intimidation of NATO allies such as the Baltic Republics and Poland. On September 24th, Russia and Belarus will conduct *Zapad* (West) military exercises. They will involve the armed forces of Russia and Belarus, which is a stooge regime ruled by Alexander Lukashenko since 2004. He is grooming his son to succeed him and remains the last dictator to Russia's immediate west. Ukraine is still making halting progress against corruption. But it is a democracy and its president, Petro Poroshenko, was elected fairly. He was a magnate in the chocolate industry, which is benign by east European or post-Soviet standards. He is like a post-Soviet Willie Wonka. The US and the West are not arming the Ukrainians but are advising them on the ground. Russian-financed paramilitaries still occupy parts of the eastern Ukrainian provinces of Donetsk and Luhansk. These Russian-financed islands of instability now join Transdniester in Moldova and the Kaliningrad exclave in eastern Europe.

Hurricane Harvey left 48 dead and affected 100,000 homes. I have thought about James Baker, the elder statesman of the Republican Party, whom I interviewed in Houston in 2003, greeted again at the Baker Center in 2010 and whose secretary also interacted with me when I tried to have a member of Baker Botts invited to the US-EU Energy and Technology Conference I organized while serving with passion as Director of Studies at the American Chamber of Commerce in Spain. My native country is the ninth on the ranking in terms of stock of foreign direct investment in the US. And it is second to the US in terms of investment in Latin America, particularly South America.

MF: Given my imprisonment in Venezuela, I do keep up with developments in the Bolivarian dictatorship. Maduro is still in power in Venezuela. Inflation has reached 1000% and the poverty rate 73%. Maduro's electoral commission rigged the elections to the constituent assembly by inflating the turnout. The opposition-controlled Parliament no longer exists. The opposition is split on how to confront Maduro. Some want to take part in the elections for governors that will take place in October, while others want to boycott them. The US imposed some limited sanctions after the Parliament was dissolved. Twenty-one high-ranking Venezuelan officials will be denied visas to come to the US, and US businesses will be forbidden from doing business with them. Moreover, the Venezuelan government and the state-controlled oil company, PDVSA, will not be able to raise money in bond markets in the US. Venezuela needs fresh funding to avoid defaulting on its $100 billion in foreign debt, which could prompt creditors to seize its oil shipments and other assets. As in other parts of the world, China and Russia are rushing to rescue Maduro.

AM: Well, sanctions will not work. The Venezuelan people must be braver and mount people power-like revolutions, as occurred in 1989 in eastern Europe. I called Professor Horst Teltschik in 2016 and convinced him to urge former Secretary of State James Baker to voice his misgivings or concerns about Trump. Baker has been on NBC's Meet the Press more than anybody in the seventy-year history of the program. He is 88 years old but regarded as the elder statesman of the GOP. And he is very close to president George H.W. Bush, whose entire family intensely dislikes Trump. Chancellor Helmut Kohl passed away on June 15, 2017, the day before I flew back to Washington, DC.

Texas is in a state of shock after hurricane Harvey. Trump's visits to the state have been pathetic. Governor Gregg Abbott is nowhere to be seen. Houston's mayor acted like a small-town mayor when responding to Chuck Todd. Houston is the US's fourth biggest city in terms of population, trailing New York, Los Angeles and your beloved Chicago.

And to add insult to injury, my former favorite preacher, Joel Osteen, whom I gave thousands of dollars to in 2009-10 and in exchange received nice handwritten notes (and more requests for money) and thereby sponsored a child in the Third World, refused to open his gigantic megachurch in Lakewood, Texas, to help those who needed shelter. It is a monumental mistake for a man whose ratings on FOX on Sunday morning are supposedly sky-high. Well, I will not be watching any more of his sermons.

MF: Well, what is president Obama saying?

AM: He is making sure that his eldest daughter settles in well for her first year in college in Illinois. The younger one, Malia, will be doing an internship for one year in Spain under the mentoring influence of the US Ambassador to Spain. Obama is being very wise in not speaking out now. He did break his bow of silence after President Trump threatened to rescind DACA and therefore make it possible to deport the Dreamers. Trump backtracked on this matter after his agreement with the Democrats in September of 2017 to raise the debt ceiling and pass a spending bill, and now wants a solution to keep the 800,000 Dreamers in the US.

The debt ceiling must be raised before the end of September. There are many holidays in September. The devastation caused by tropical storm Harvey adds to the urgency of the Trump administration and the president in particular not dialing up the rhetoric against North Korea, China or adopting mean measures like trying to overturn DACA. Trump holds the Dreamers hostage as a negotiating tool to pressure Democrats and Congress to fund his wall with Mexico in a surrealist repeat of the 2013 shutdown. The 2013 government shutdown did damage to the US's reputation. The greatest country in the history of the world cannot have its credit rating downgraded by one notch as occurred five years ago. Republicans were obsessed at the time with repealing Obamacare, officially called the Affordable Care Act (ACA). They had never accepted president Obama's 2008 historic victory and reelection in 2012. Moreover, the Supreme Court, despite a conservative majority, did not overturn the ACA. Chief Justice John

Roberts earned his place in history alongside other great chief justices by not bowing to Republican pressure.

This of course infuriated the Republican base and now president Donald Trump, who had embarked on his ridiculous and bitter failed attempt to prove that president Obama was not born in America. The birtherism movement was eventually defeated. Trump used the same tactic against Senator Ted Cruz in the 2016 Republican primary, claiming the sitting junior senator from Texas could not be president because he was a naturalized citizen of the US. This was also false. Ironically, it was Cruz's obsession with overturning the ACA which prompted him to speak for a very long number of hours on the Senate floor during the 2013 government debt shutdown. Cruz is a fanatic who is only somewhat moderated by the fact that his wife is an intelligent businesswoman and he has adorable daughters. Surprisingly, Cruz has not been one of the Republican senators who has consistently criticized Trump. In order of frequency and intensity of criticism and even a rejection to do Trump's bidding, the list starts with my hero, Senator John McCain, who is bravely fighting brain cancer and at the same time reminding Americans that they are not the subordinates of the President. It continues with Senators Lindsey Graham and Tim Scott from South Carolina, Senator Bob Corker from Tennessee, Senate Majority Leader Mitch McConnell, Senator Jeff Flake from Arizona, Senator Susan Collins of Maine (who voted against the repeal of the ACA in the Senate), Senator Lisa Murkowski of Alaska (who did the same) and Senator Dean Heller of Nevada, who is vulnerable to a right-wing challenge in 2018.

MF: Stop criticizing Republicans!

AM: I just named ten Republican senators who have the audacity of defying the president! I am proud of all of them, to varying degrees. Some are motivated by political ambition (Flake), sense of duty to the country (Rubio, Corker), lack of fear (Scott), and the instinct to protect women's health care and ensure they keep their seats in the Senate (Murkowski and Collins). The GOP is the party of Lincoln, Eisenhower, Reagan, Bush 41, James Baker, Brent Scowcroft and many distinguished senators and members of the military. I am not just referring to Country Club Republicans, the almost defunct Northeast moderate wing of the GOP. The Southwest, with is demographic boom, has become a bastion of Republican moderation with the likes of Dean Heller, Flake, and Colorado Senator Cory Gardner. Republican Governors Susana Martinez of New Mexico and Brian Sandoval of Nevada are not challenging Trump publicly but at least do not embarrass their states like former Arizona governor Jan Brewer did. Sandoval and Martinez surely have political ambition but do a reasonable job.

MF: What about the Midwest and my beloved Chicago?

AM: The Midwest is Trump country. Roy Blunt from Missouri was on Meet the Press on August 3rd and was full of praise for Trump, even hinting at his distaste for raising the debt ceiling. It is much the same across the rest of the Midwest. Republican Governor Bruce Rauner of Illinois has not criticized Trump once.

MF: Your memory cannot possibly be that good.

AM: I spend almost all my waking hours with the news on and watch CNN and MSNBC. Trump has a loyal base. His approval ratings are still in the upper-30s or low 40s, very low by historical standards but resilient.

Trump has never criticized Russia. Not once! He has criticized, offended, mocked or threatened many of America's allies and enemies but refused to do so even once in eight months in the case of Russia. Russia remains the second military superpower in the world with a Stalinist president bent of destabilizing Western Europe.

MF: Do not exaggerate!

AM: Milton, you have been away for twelve years. Putin has funded extremist right- and left-wing parties in all of Europe, except maybe in meaningless examples like Ireland and Portugal.

MF: Now you insult two EU members!

AM: No, Ireland and Portugal are wonderful countries. Their people are great. The Irish are very hard-working. But they are irrelevant in military and geostrategic terms. Ireland is not even in NATO.

And now Brexit threatens a border between Northern Ireland and Ireland, endangering the Good Friday Agreement that brought an end to the violence in Northern Ireland and a power-sharing democratic government made up of the Republican Catholic and Unionist Parties. And the UK will wind up paying a 100-billion-euro divorce fee to leave the EU.

Chapter 10: Hurricanes Harvey, Irma and María

After his conferences and meetings in Jackson Hole and on the West Coast, Milton Friedman returned to Washington, D.C. in late August. Hurricane Harvey, one of the most powerful in history, had just pummeled Texas. Friedman invited me to dinner at the Raku restaurant in downtown Bethesda, on Woodmont Avenue. He was eager to know more.

MF: How bad is the situation in Texas?

AM: Well, there have been some casualties, and the flooding has been extensive in Beaumont and some parts of Houston. There is a lot of fundraising going on by celebrities and corporations to finance reconstruction of affected areas and provide relief to those impacted by Harvey.

Milton, I think we should now focus on the horrific destructive power of Hurricane Irma. It is a category 5 hurricane with winds of 160 miles per hour and gusts of up to 195 miles per hour. It is the size of Texas. Experts are describing it as the most devastating and powerful hurricane in the history of the Caribbean and the southern part of the US.

We should pray for the twenty people who have passed away due to Hurricane Irma, and the thousands in Barbuda and the US Virgin Islands whose homes have been completely destroyed. Ninety-five percent of buildings in Barbuda have been totally flattened. The island is simply uninhabitable. Early estimates of the cost of reconstruction exceed $100 million. The airport and hospitals have been destroyed. Barbuda was cut off from the outside world for twelve hours. The prime minister of Antigua and Barbuda is working feverishly to gather support for the Caribbean country, whose main source of income is tourism. The situation in two of the three US Virgin Islands is the same. Aerial footage from helicopters show rubble where there used to be buildings in Saint Croix and Saint Thomas, the more inhabited of the three US Virgin Islands. Communications with the outside world have been cut. There are no ferries, no access to the Internet, electricity, and communications of any kind (telephone, mobile telephony) on the US Virgin Islands. The US National Guard and other units of the US armed forces will be deployed to assist the US Virgin Islands and its inhabitants.

The island of Saint Martin -- which is shared by France and the Netherlands -- also suffered a direct hit. The Dutch government has deployed troops to prevent looting on its side of the island.

Puerto Rico initially appeared to be relatively lucky as Irma tracked east of the island. But there was destruction caused by the outer bands of this massive hurricane. Puerto Rico will have trouble securing financing to get things back to normal because it has had to declare bankruptcy. One million people in Puerto Rico are without power, and it could take up to four or five months to restore it to everyone because FEMA's budget has been significantly cut.

Let us pray that Irma will not claim lives and devastate the Florida Keys, Marco Island, Naples and Fort Myers. Key West and Key Largo will suffer tremendously. Tampa and the western coast of Florida north of these cities could also be affected, albeit more modestly. Miami will be spared a direct hit, but Florida is only 45 miles wide. Irma's eye is 35 miles wide! Irma's width now doubles that of the entire state of Florida. There is complacency in Miami as it now lies outside of the hurricane's cone. Florida's building codes became much stricter after hurricane Andrew delivered a terrible blow and caused a lot of damage in 1992. Even if meteorologists' forecast for Irma to move up Florida's western coast does come to pass, Irma's outer bands will generate very powerful winds of 100 miles per hour or more in central and eastern Florida, affecting Fort Lauderdale, Miami and the Florida Keys. Meteorologists, state officials, the mayors of Florida's cities, top-ranking officials at the National Hurricane Center and FEMA are asking everyone to move to areas not in the hurricane's path. The brave military and civilian pilots who are flying through the eye of the storm to supply data on its size, intensity and path are all pleading with everyone to move to higher ground because the storm surge could reach 16 feet.

Florida governor Rick Scott has declared a state of emergency and described Irma as a life-threatening event. One fourth of Florida's population (6.5 million) has been ordered to evacuate their homes and move north or to shelters, which are filled to capacity. This is probably the biggest mass evacuation in United States history. People who believed that Irma would track over eastern Florida had to scramble to get in their cars, find a gas station with fuel and drive north. Interstate 95 obviously has bumper-to-bumper traffic. Although the science of predicting the path of a hurricane has progressed tremendously, there is no guarantee that Irma may not shift back to the east.

Irma of course comes on the heels of hurricane Harvey, which destroyed and flooded thousands of homes in the suburbs of Houston and other cities in Texas such as Beaumont and Port Arthur. And Irma will be followed by hurricanes José and Katia, which are already moving towards the Caribbean from the central Atlantic. At one point, there were two category 4 hurricanes in the Atlantic for the first time in history.

Everybody should pitch in to raise money to help the victims of hurricane Irma, which comes on the heels of Harvey and the damage it inflicted in Texas. These horrific category 5 hurricanes should remind us that we should stick together, that politics or ideology should not divide the people of the United States, a beacon of hope and opportunity for the world.

Irma is especially powerful because it moves at only 13 miles per hour. It feeds on the warm waters of the Caribbean and off the coast of Florida, which are as high as 86 degrees. Hurricanes pick up even more force when they move over warm waters. Hurricanes are weakened by mountains and cooler ocean temperatures, which obviously do not exist in Florida. Irma will make landfall in Cuba with winds of 160 miles per hour and storm surges up to 10 feet. Cuba does have mountain ranges, so it may slightly weaken Irma.

The early estimates of the devastation unleashed by Irma are $135 billion. CNN and MSNBC sent anchors (Anderson Cooper and Chris Hayes) to southern Florida. Their brave correspondents and reporters have also done an outstanding, selfless and noble job of describing the situation and emphasizing that people should evacuate their homes. The authorities and mayors of Florida have been on the air for hours warning people that they must evacuate coastal areas. In fact, the evacuation is mandatory for southern Florida, especially low-lying areas. Some people think they can ride out the hurricane by hunkering down in their basements. But that is a foolhardy proposition. Irma is one of the most powerful hurricanes in history. It has flattened Barbuda, the US Virgin Islands and Saint Martin, reducing most of their buildings to rubble. Some people in Florida are scrambling to buy power generators, food and gas. But they must evacuate to higher ground. In fact, after 3pm on Sunday, September 10th, 2017, there will be a curfew in many cities in southwest Florida. Those people found outdoors will be forcibly taken to shelters.

MF: Is there any hope that this cataclysmic hurricane will track further to the west, thus not making landfall in southwestern Florida but rather in the Florida panhandle?

AM: That is theoretically possible. But experts have consistently and accurately predicted that Irma would not make an east turn after pummeling the Caribbean but rather move over Florida.

The last category 5 hurricane that struck the US was Andrew in 1992. And even if Irma did move somewhat to the west, it might then bear down on southern Alabama, whose coast has often borne the brunt of hurricanes and tropical storms. One out of every twenty people in the US live in Florida. I hope you will now not continue to espouse the view that the government should not step in to help people.

MF: Of course, my comments on the inefficiency of governments do not apply to natural catastrophes. But the reconstruction should be funded primarily by donations from private individuals (millionaires and billionaires) and big corporations, whose financing can be leveraged to raise money from individuals.

AM: Well, I agree that the private sector can play an important role. But you criticize these big corporations and label them as big business, big multinationals that abuse their oligopolistic or even monopolistic situation to squeeze and even bankrupt smaller rivals. You rightly have pointed out that they stifle competition you deem essential for free markets to work. Walmart, to its credit, is mounting a big campaign to raise funding for the victims of hurricanes Harvey and probably will do the same for Irma.

Irma finally weakened as it made it to Florida. Fortunately, its eye and most of its inner bands turned eastwards and wound up moving over central Florida. It became a category two hurricane and caused much less damage than had been anticipated and predicted. There were five casualties in Florida linked to Irma.

MF: Well, let us turn to other topics. I do feel very sorry for the loss of life and the thousands who have lost homes. I will make a sizeable contribution to an entity financing reconstruction, a donation with a five-figure tag.

AM: Well, that is very generous of you! Although you are probably giving what you make by delivering just a couple of conferences. I thought you would be upset because your conference tour around the US will be disrupted! To make matters worse, some of the islands devastated by Irma will now be battered by José, a category 4 hurricane. In the country of Antigua and Barbuda, the latter island has a population of 1800. Its government is working feverishly to move the inhabitants of Barbuda to Antigua, which is in good shape.

So, Milton, do not even think of flying to Florida! It will not be safe anywhere in the sunshine state in the next few days. Miami International Airport cancelled thousands of flights and will remain closed at least until Monday morning. Senator Marco Rubio also went on national television to appeal to everyone to heed the authorities' instructions and orders. But some people want to prove they are tough or seek their five minutes of fame on TV or simply risk their lives to protect their homes. A house can be replaced, but a dead person obviously cannot.

Well, I feel that I should do something more than make a $50 donation. The Red Cross is accepting volunteers to fly out to the worst-hit locations. I am signing up. At first, I thought that only doctors and nurses were in demand. I inquired at a Red Cross office in Alexandria, Virginia, and an employee told me that they can use my languages. The estimated cost of reconstruction in the Caribbean countries and US territories of Puerto Rico and the US Virgin Islands ravaged by Irma is $13 billion.

MF: What is the latest regarding the Russia investigation?

AM: Don McGhan, who is Counsel to the President, has been asked to turn over documents to Special Counsel Robert Mueller's team. McGhan cannot claim executive privilege in terms of his conversations with the president if there is evidence that a crime might have been committed.

McGhan is not Trump's attorney. He serves as Counsel to the Office of the Presidency of the US. Taxpayers and not Trump pay his salary.

Michael Flynn's son, Michael Flynn Jr., is now also a subject of Mueller's investigation. He served as his father's right-hand man in their lobbying firm. Flynn Sr. retired from the US Army in 2014 after thirty-three years of service. He swiftly became a lobbyist and a key member of the Trump campaign as a foreign-policy surrogate. It is now obvious and well-proven that Michael Flynn Sr. pursued deals with Russia, Saudi Arabia and Turkey, and delivered well-paid speeches abroad. He concealed his speeches, his contacts with foreign officials and the deals he lobbied for (and benefited from) when he applied to get a top-level security clearance. He had been appointed National Security Adviser in Trump's administration. He lobbied on behalf of the authoritarian president of Turkey, Recep Tayyip Erdogan, after being paid almost $500,000 to deliver a speech in Turkey. Flynn also traveled to the Middle East in order to promote a deal whereby Russia would have sold civilian nuclear technology to Saudi Arabia. He was paid for this lobbying work. His failure to disclose these payments from foreign countries, foreign contacts and paid speeches abroad is enough to land him in jail. Mueller is undoubtedly putting as much pressure as possible on Flynn, so he will flip and provide incriminating information on Jared Kushner, Donald Trump Jr. and maybe the president himself. After Michael Flynn Sr. and Paul Manafort, Flynn Jr. is the third person to officially become a target of the Special Counsel's investigation.

Another outrageous disclosure on September 13th tarnished Facebook's reputation. It has been proven that Facebook accepted 3000 advertisements paid for by the Russian government during the 2016 presidential campaign. In addition, Russia's government used Facebook to drum up support in the US for anti-immigrant rallies, which were attended by Trump supporters. Facebook has not deployed the necessary human and financial resources to get to the bottom of the Russian interference. It is illegal for a foreign entity or government to purchase an advertisement on a TV channel. This should apply to social media as well, especially considering that up to one half of Americans get their news from Facebook. After months of denial, the social-media multinational admitted it had closed 50,000 accounts linked to Russia in the run-up to the French presidential campaign of 2017. But it only closed 4700 accounts in the US.

Senator Mark Warner, the ranking Democrat on the Senate Intelligence committee, tweeted that Facebook was paid for the advertisements in rubles. Special Counsel Robert Mueller has demanded that Facebook furnish more information. Mueller forced Facebook to turn over more information on the hundreds of accounts that Russia purchased from the social-media giant and used to target advertisements during the 2016 presidential campaign. The Special Counsel now has more information about the Russia-Facebook relationship than Congress. Mueller and his team can request search warrants, and the grand jury he impaneled can also issue subpoenas. But Mueller runs a tight ship and there are very few leaks about his investigation. Everyone in Washington, D.C. is trying to guess what Mueller's next big move will be.

The Kremlin onslaught against independent media of course does not spare Russian journalists. The latest victim is Yulia Latynina, an acclaimed Russian journalist. She has fled Russia. Her parents had already left the country. Latynina had bravely endured months of attacks and intimidation. Her car was set on fire and she was doused with a bucket of feces. Latynina hosted a weekly political-commentary show on the opposition-minded *Ekho Moskvy* radio station. She also writes sci-fi novels and was a regular contributor to the independent newspaper *Novaya Gazeta*. She has long been vilified by hardline Kremlin loyalists as an enemy of Russia.

September 14th was full of important headlines. North Korea again launched an intermediate range ballistic missile, the Hwasong-12, also known as KN-17. It flew over Japan's northernmost island of Hokkaido at an altitude of 700 km and landed 2,000 km east of Japan in the Pacific. South Korea believes the missile has a range of 3,700 km, which would allow it to reach the US territory of Guam, which lies 3,400 km from North Korea. With this launch, Pyongyang has now carried out a nuclear test and test-fired two intermediate range missiles within the space of seventeen days. This test had been expected on the anniversary of the foundation of North Korea. But there was a lot of fog that day over Korea. Kim Jong Un loves to show his people and the world footage of the missiles. He therefore delayed firing the missile until hurricanes Harvey and Irma had faded somewhat from the headlines and his launch would get maximum exposure in the media.

Japan's government and authorities ordered people through text messages, TV and blaring speakers to shelter in place. Both Japan and South Korea are beginning to ponder whether they should develop a stronger military deterrent. There is discussion in South Korea about deploying US tactical nuclear weapons, but president Moon Jae-in has rejected the move, which he feels would spark a nuclear arms race on the Korean peninsula.

Japan and South Korea do have anti-ballistic missile defenses: the THAAD system in South Korea, Aegis anti-missile defense batteries on destroyers and on land and Patriot anti-missile batteries. These anti-missile defenses proved to be somewhat effective, especially in the first Gulf War, when Israel shot down many Iraki Scuds. But some analysts now estimate that North Korea may have produced at least a dozen nuclear warheads. In the event of a North Korean attack, Seoul would have just 25 seconds to prepare. US territory in Guam and Hawaii is now well within the range of the Hwasong-12 and North Korea's ICBMs. The US requested a meeting of the UN Security Council on Friday, August 16th. But it is obvious that Russia and China are not just protecting Kim Jong Un. They are furnishing the rogue regime with oil, employing North Koreans and possibly providing technological assistance for Pyongyang's nuclear weapons program. The nuclear bomb that North Korea set off on September 3rd had a destructive capacity of 150 kilotons, far superior than the nukes exploded in its five earlier tests.

The US and South Korea cannot sit down to negotiate with Pyongyang under these circumstances. It would smack of appeasement. All of the president's options are bad. But maybe it is worth considering declaring a blockade (or quarantine) against North Korea, and deploying a naval flotilla of US, South Korean and Japanese vessels to enforce it, as John F. Kennedy did against Cuba in 1962. An embargo is meaningless as the US does not conduct any trade with North Korea. Ninety percent of the Hermit Kingdom's trade is with China. North Korea is a very poor country. In the late 1990s, hundreds of thousands and possibly more than a million of North Korea's 23 million inhabitants starved to death, despite Western humanitarian and food assistance. Income per capita is four dollars. North Korea's GDP is 4 billion dollars, a tiny fraction of the Pentagon's annual budget of $600 billion. It is sad that such a poor totalitarian state could soon threaten the United States and is already a risk to some of its allies, namely South Korea and Japan.

The Trump administration could warn Russia, China and North Korea that another launch of an intermediate range ballistic missile or ICBM over Japan will lead to a blockade or quarantine. The US would therefore maybe win over a few or most, (except Russia and China) members of the UN Security Council if it warned about the quarantine in the case of the launch of another missile. Russia and China would obviously veto a US resolution to approve the quarantine, but other countries in the Council might take the US's side. After all, North Korea is a proven proliferator of its nuclear and chemical weapons technology. It has been selling it to countries such as Iran. It also sells counterfeit currencies. The US hence has a case for clamping an embargo or even a quarantine on North Korea. The problem with a quarantine is that Kim Jong Un might react with an escalation, targeting Guam or sending a missile without a warhead to Japanese territory. The US administration would then have to stand down or take additional measures, possibly leading to a nuclear war on the Korean peninsula.

MF: And what is happening in Washington, D.C. with regards to the debt ceiling?

The media continues to have a field day reporting about president Trump's agreement with Senate Minority leader Chuck Schumer and House Minority leader Nancy Pelosi to raise the debt ceiling, extend funding for the federal government by three months, postponing the fate of Dreamers and earmarking $15 billion for the victims of hurricanes Harvey and Irma. The agreement also includes funding for securing the border, but not for the infamous wall on the border with Mexico.

MF: That seems like a betrayal to Republicans!

AM: Well, that is how some Republicans characterize it. Steve Bannon, who of course is back at Breitbart, denounced the president. Speaker Paul Ryan and other members of the GOP leadership in Congress did express support for the extension of the debt ceiling. But they were visibly upset over the fact that Trump is now negotiating with Democrats. They found out about the deal from the media. Senior Republican Senators accepted that Trump was negotiating with Democrats but emphasized that they would be the ones to work on the legislation with Democratic lawmakers. The backlash among conservatives was viral. Prominent conservative author and journalist Anne Coulter remarked that now everybody wants the president to be impeached.

Laura Ingraham has a nationally syndicated radio show. I had the chance to speak to her for a few hours when I was a guest at David Frum's house in the summer of 2009 and she came over for dinner with her son, who was just a toddler. After learning of Trump's deal with Schumer and Pelosi, Ingraham ironically pointed out that Trump was now advocating for the wall to be built a few pieces at a time, and that it would be funded by US taxpayers (and not Mexico). Ingraham railed against Trump and warned that Republicans would suffer in the 2018 mid-terms. "Let me just get this straight -- at these rallies during 2015, 2016, I don't remember hearing, 'Repair the fence! Repair the fence! Repair the fence and make Mexico pay for the fence.' Who said repair the fence?' He's going to get creamed on this and if this goes down the way I fear it goes, mark my words — this will be an electoral nightmare for Republicans." Ingraham was livid at Trump for cutting a deal late at night with Nancy Pelosi and Chuck Schumer. Steve Bannon also lambasted the president as "Amnesty Don" from the pages of Breitbart.

There was some disagreement over the details of the deal clinched between Trump and the Democratic congressional leadership over a dinner of Chinese food at the White House. Trump's spokeswoman claimed that the agreement did not rule out funding for the wall on the border with Mexico. Pelosi and Schumer ruled out any funding for the wall. This is a red line for Democrats. But Trump cannot further infuriate his base by openly giving up on the wall. He was at pains to explain to conservatives that the wall would be fully built later. He justified his U-turn on the Dreamers by pointing to the fact that the 800,000 covered under the program were children who were brought into the country illegally but through no fault of their own.

The president undertook another trip to Florida to personally interact with the victims of hurricane Irma and hand out sandwiches in Naples. He was ebullient on his flight back to Washington, D.C., welcoming questions from reporters on Air Force One. He asserted that his relationship with Republicans is still great. He reassured Americans that he is studying his options with regards to North Korea and that the US is safe. He highlighted the second-quarter GDP growth rate (3% over the first quarter at an annual rate), the record-low unemployment rate and the stock market records.

The media also underlined the fact that Treasury Secretary Steven Mnuchin requested a private plane for his honeymoon in Europe in the summer of 2017. Mnuchin claimed that it was all about having a portable office with secure communications, but he was forced to withdraw his request. This episode comes on the heels of his use of a government plane to fly to Kentucky. The official reason for his and his young wife's flight to Kentucky was to visit Fort Knox, where the US keeps much of its supply of gold. But the trip coincided with the solar eclipse. Mnuchin's wife insulted a woman who chastised her for flaunting her wealth during the supposed government trip. The Treasury Secretary has a net worth of hundreds of millions.

MF: Why would Trump risk alienating his base?

AM: Trump's relations with GOP leaders are very frayed. After the failure to repeal Obamacare, he felt personally let down by the GOP leadership in the Senate. He had heated telephone conversations with Senate Majority Leader Mitch McConnell. They are barely on speaking terms. Trump's relationship with House Speaker Paul Ryan is described as "frosty". Trump is also upset -- to put it mildly -- at Republican senators John McCain, Jeff Flake, Dean Heller, Bob Corker, Lisa Murkowski, Susan Collins and Ben Sasse for a variety of reasons, foremost among them that McCain, Collins and Murkowski scuttled his efforts to replace Obamacare in the Senate with the White House's plan. The president thus decided to cut a deal with Schumer and Pelosi. Trump takes pride on his ability to make deals. His aides describe him as being in an excellent mood. Chuck Schumer was caught in an open microphone boasting that Trump really likes him. They are both from New York, and in stylistic terms speak the same language.

Rachel Maddow today treated us to one of her best performances. Her glee at the Trump administration's challenges is contagious, especially for some of the staffers who work in the studio and cannot contain their laughter. She reminded viewers that seventeen persons working at high-level positions at the White House have been dismissed or resigned since January of 2017. Among them are Michael Flynn (National Security Adviser), top staffers at the National Security Council, Reince Priebus (Chief of Staff), Sean Spicer (White House press secretary), Anthony Scaramucci (Communications Director), Steve Bannon (senior adviser to the president) and Sebastian Gorka. Maddow also underscored that Vice President Pence has lost some key advisors, including a press secretary and his chief of staff.

But one senior cabinet official who has not lost his job is Attorney General Jeff Sessions. The New York Times revealed that the President yelled at him repeatedly and on one occasion called him an idiot. He was particularly incensed that Sessions had recused himself regarding the investigation over Russia's meddling in the US elections. The former senator from Alabama has admitted that Trump's humiliation was unlike anything he had endured in his life. At one point, he submitted his resignation. But Trump was persuaded to reject it. Sessions had been in the Senate for many years. He is accepting the abuse because, as Attorney General, he can implement policies which Trump supports and have always been very close to Sessions' heart. For example, increasing minimum sentences, cracking down on illegal immigration, overturning the legalization of marijuana in some states, and enacting measures to suppress voter turnout among minorities. Under Sessions' stewardship, the Department of Justice has also discontinued a program launched during president Obama's presidency that aimed at building trust between police departments and the communities they serve. In the past years there have been a lot of killings by police officers of men (especially blacks) whose behavior might have been illegal or suspicious according to the law but who posed no risk to the policemen's lives. In an NBC-Wall

Street Journal poll published in September of 2017, seventy-one percent of Americans asserted that race relations in the US are 'poor'. This percentage is close to a historical high.

There have been several high-profile shootings of black men by police officers. In many cases, the victims clearly did not threaten the officers' lives. It is understandable that policemen are sometimes nervous when confronting people with menacing intensions, especially given the easy availability of guns. But studies show that the number of policemen dying in the line of duty is near an all-time low. In addition to scrapping the Obama-era program that sought to improve relations between police departments and communities, the Department of Justice will appropriate funds so that policemen can better fight organized crime groups.

<u>**Chapter 11: Uncertainty at the Fed and the spirit of Gettysburg**</u>

In September of 2017 Milton Friedman was back in Washington, D.C. for meetings at the Treasury Department and conferences at Georgetown University, the Woodrow Wilson Center for International Scholars and the Carnegie Endowment for International Peace. We met in downtown Washington for lunch in a restaurant on 14th Street near Pennsylvania Avenue.

MF: I will be meeting with Treasury Secretary Steven Mnuchin and other Treasury officials in one hour. What do I need to know?

AM: There are new developments regarding the Federal Reserve. I think that you, Milton, should be nominated by president Trump to be the next chairman of the Federal Reserve. You should ask Mnuchin to recommend to the president that he appoint you. I believe that you would make an ideal chairman of the Federal Reserve. Stanley Fischer has retired for personal reasons as Deputy Chairman of the Fed. He was a very experienced central banker who served as the governor of the Central Bank of Israel and had been at the Fed for several years.

Fischer's departure means that there are now four vacancies on the Federal Reserve's Board, which among other tasks is responsible for setting interest rates. Janet Yellen's first term as chairwoman of the Federal Reserve will end in February of 2018. The past three chairmen of the Fed have all served two terms. But it is unclear whether president Trump will want to nominate Yellen to a second term. At times, he has been critical of her, and at others he has praised the fact that interest rates are relatively low. Yellen's critics have both accused her of hiking interest rates too soon and of raising them too slowly. The fact is that the Fed under Yellen started to increase interest rates in December of 2015. They are now at 2%. Inflation remains below the Fed's 2% target. It is a puzzle why inflation remains subdued despite unemployment having dropped to 4.3%. In fact, the current expansion of the US economy, which began in June of 2009, is now the third longest in its history. This is no small achievement. GDP grew at an annual rate of 3% in the second quarter of 2017. Since the Fed began to raise rates in December of 2015, the average monthly job creation number is 185,000.

In some regards, Yellen is not in sync with Trump's worldview. Trump and his Treasury Secretary, Mnuchin, want to roll back the financial regulation enacted during the Obama administration as a response to the financial crisis. Yellen is of course a proponent of such financial regulation and was nominated by Obama.

Moreover, Trump has to fill five vacancies at the Fed by February of 2018, if we include the decision about Yellen. His aides might convince him that it is best to nominate Yellen to a second term as opposed to choosing a divisive figure who would have trouble getting Senate confirmation. There are three persons who clearly want to replace Yellen. One is President Trump's current Director of the National Economic Council, Gary Cohn. But Cohn has no experience in central banking. It is also better for him to remain in his current position at the White House, where he can play a major role in steering the infrastructure package and maybe tax reform through Congress. John Taylor of Stanford University and Kevin Walsh also want to be the next chairmen of the Fed but have significant shortcomings.

Therefore, I believe the best solution would be for president Trump to nominate you, Milton, to be the next chairman of the Federal Reserve. Janet Yellen would not lose face as she would be serving as deputy chairwoman to the most influential economist of the second half of the 20th century. This would be a dream job for you. During your illustrious and extensive career, you did not have the opportunity to serve at an institution like the Fed that you studied, wrote about and did extensive research on. You clearly have unique insights as to how the Federal Reserve should operate. You are a monetarist. You believe that an economy's health is determined by the money supply. As chairman of the Fed, you would be able to prove that your theories are correct. You would also have ample human and financial resources to research and explain the enigma about subdued inflation despite more than eight years of economic growth and full employment in the past two years.

MF: That is a very interesting idea. I would like to be Chairman of the Federal Reserve. What about the debate about who should be on US dollar banknotes? Have there been any new developments since Secretary of the Treasury Steve Mnuchin rejected replacing Andrew Jackson with Harriet Tubman on the $20 bill?

AM: The whole debate about who should be on US banknotes has become very politicized. Let us first examine who is currently on the bank notes. George Washington is on the $1 bill, Abraham Lincoln on the $5 bill, Alexander Hamilton on the $10 bill, Andrew Jackson on the $20 bill, Ulysses Grant on the $50 bill and Benjamin Franklin on the $100 bill. The $2 bill featuring Thomas Jefferson still exists but it is rarely seen in circulation. Congress decided after much debate that only deceased persons would be featured on banknotes. There is also a $100,000 bank note but it is only used by the US government. Many regard the $2 banknote as unlucky.

The fact that the US does not need a bank note with a higher face value than $100 is a sign of monetary stability and that inflation has been contained since the seventies at low levels. Also bear in mind that there used to be higher-denomination bank notes of $200, $500 and $1000 dollars which were phased out in the late sixties. Some of the persons featured on these banknotes were presidents William McKinley, Grover Cleveland and James Madison.

It is very reasonable to make a case for more diversity in terms of gender and race on bank notes. But all of the personalities mentioned were either distinguished presidents or Founding Fathers. An exception would be William McKinley. His major accomplishment as president was leading the US to victory in the war against Spain in 1898. But he was assassinated by an anarchist very early in his second term. No serious historian would regard McKinley as a great president. But James Madison was one of the Founding Fathers and the drafter of the Bill of Rights. Many would argue that James Madison is more deserving of being on a banknote than Harriet Tubman.

The terms Founding Fathers can be somewhat hard to pin down. Some great Americans are considered to be founding fathers because they fought for independence from the United Kingdom on the battlefield (George Washington, etc.) or through political actions such as the drafting and signing of the Declaration of Independence on July 4th, 1776. Others are regarded as founding fathers because they took part in the Constitutional Convention that drew up the Constitution of 1787 and in creating some of the key institutions of the US federal government (Treasury Department, Coast Guard, etc.)

Historian Richard B. Morris in 1973 concluded that the Founding Fathers are John Adams, Benjamin Franklin, Alexander Hamilton, John Jay, Thomas Jefferson, James Madison and of course George Washington. Adams, Jefferson, and Franklin were members of the Committee of Five that drafted the Declaration of Independence. Hamilton, Madison and Jay were authors of The Federalist Papers, which argued in favor of ratifying the Constitution.

The Obama administration understandably tried to encourage diversity on banknotes by replacing Alexander Hamilton with Harriet Tubman on the $10 bank note. This idea may have been well-intentioned but was clearly ill-conceived. Alexander Hamilton may be one of the most underappreciated Founding Fathers. The fact that he was never elected president is one of the main factors. He was born in present-day St. Nevis in the Caribbean and could therefore not be elected president. He fought in the War of Independence, was a member of the Constitutional Convention, and an author of the Federalist Papers. He was the first Secretary of the Treasury of the United States under George Washington. Hamilton was a strong proponent of the Constitution and responsible for the creation of the US Coast Guard, the New York Post and the Federalist Party. Hamilton forcefully argued in the Federalist Papers and successfully accomplished while in office the establishment of a national bank and a strong central government with a robust executive. He fostered manufacturing, trade with other countries (and charging tariffs) and a normalization of relations with the United Kingdom.

Hamilton therefore clashed with the Founding Fathers who regarded these measures and institutions as an unacceptable intrusion into states' rights. These Founding Fathers arrayed against Hamilton were mostly from Virginia. They firmly believed that America had not fought to become independent from the UK in order to create a strong central government that would trample on states' rights. They were big landowners with slaves who did not have a stake in promoting manufacturing and industry. They opposed tariffs on imports, the rapprochement with the UK and were instead more inclined to align the US with France.

It was Hamilton who initially carried the day, but his opponents Jefferson and Madison created the Democratic-Republican party, on whose ticket Thomas Jefferson, James Madison and James Monroe were elected president. The Federalist Party withered away. But the Democratic-Republican party split into several camps after Monroe's presidency. Those still advocating hostility towards the federal government after 1830 eventually fueled secession and the Civil War. Therefore, replacing a statesman, Founding Father and the first Treasury Secretary of the United States (Alexander Hamilton) on the $10 banknote generated backlash.

Harriet Tubman was a slave who fought her way to freedom and was a hero in the Civil War. But there are other ways to honor women such as Harriet Tubman than removing the architect of the United States' original banking system on the $10 banknote. Airports, ports, train stations, boulevards, squares, streets and even stamps can be named after Harriet Tubman. The Obama administration realized that removing Alexander Hamilton was not realistic. They therefore attempted to have Tubman replace Andrew Jackson on the $20 bill. Andrew Jackson was the seventh president, a successful general and ironically detested the idea of a central or national bank. He told future president Martin Van Buren that he would destroy the national bank of the US before the bank undermined him. Despite strong opposition from Congress and his own Treasury Secretaries, Andrew Jackson did manage to dismantle the national bank. Until it was reestablished under president Lincoln to finance the Union in its struggle against the Confederacy, a private bank issued the US's currency.

Andrew Jackson was a maverick and an anti-establishment figure who correctly felt that he had been robbed of the presidency in the 1824 election. In that year Jackson ran against John Quincy Adams. Jackson defeated Adams in the popular vote (40% to 31%) and the Electoral College. But he was unable to secure a majority (131) in the Electoral College. The House of Representatives thus chose John Quincy Adams as the sixth president. This is the only presidential election in US history which was decided by the House of Representatives.

President Donald Trump has great admiration for Andrew Jackson. The current president identifies with Jackson's maverick spirit. He often describes his awe for Andrew Jackson and had a painting of Jackson hung in the Oval Office. Trump also paid a visit to Jackson's statue on

Lafayette Park. Therefore, the attempt to replace Andrew Jackson with Harriet Tubman on the $20 note will go nowhere under his administration, regardless of the liberal media's correct but one-sided portrayals of Andrew Jackson as a president who displaced Native Americans.

It may be controversial but worthy to point out that America's culture wars advise caution. One of the reasons that Trump won in 2016 is that a considerable percentage of America's white population felt and still feel that that the establishment was and is changing the United States too quickly. The establishment has advocated LGBT rights, trying to enact gun control legislation or symbolically changing the names or persons on dollar banknotes. At a time of bitter division in America, it is best to leave Alexander Hamilton and Andrew Jackson on the bank notes and find another way to honor the brave Harriet Tubman.

MF: I want to be able to focus on monetary policy as Chairman of the Federal Reserve and not have to worry about who should be on our banknotes. Andrew Jackson in fact prevailed and eliminated the national bank. It was Abraham Lincoln who established the predecessor to the current Federal Reserve in the context of having to finance the Civil War. I do think the Trump administration and Secretary of the Treasury Mnuchin are correct in asserting that they have bigger priorities than changing who is on the $20 banknote. Moreover, at a time of data breaches of big corporations like Target, Yahoo and now Equifax, the last thing we need is America's enemies tampering with our banknotes.

AM: Indeed, the Equifax data breach is scandalous as 143 million Americans have had their confidential information compromised. Top executives at Equifax sold their stock in the company before disclosing that its IT systems had been breached. They should be charged with insider trading and Equifax should really compensate its clients. This is one of the big three companies that furnish information on Americans' credit ratings to a wide range of companies. Equifax had the nerve to at first try to charge clients to ensure the protection of their confidential information. Only media scrutiny and outrage have forced Equifax to backtrack and try to really do right by their clients.

MF: What is the latest regarding Muelller's probe into Russia's behavior?

AM: The week of September 17th had some notable developments regarding the Special Counsel's investigation into Russia's alleged meddling into the US elections. Sources revealed that the Special Counsel's team has requested up to thirteen items of information from the White House. Former Press Secretary Sean Spicer kept copious notes during the time of Trump's campaign and his time at the White House until he was dismissed. The fact that Spicer keeps very extensive notes is well-known. Some of his colleagues joked that he was preparing to write a tell-all book. Spicer's notebooks will probably become a source for information for the Special Counsel's investigation. They can subpoena the notebooks. A young chief of staff at the Treasury Department had to testify before Congress in 1994 with regards to the Whitewater investigation because he maintained a diary.

Tom Price, who is the Secretary of Health and Human Services (HHS), has used private jets 24 times since May of 2017. This adds up to $300,000 in taxpayer-funded flights for Price. As a Congressman from Georgia, Price blasted (as is on the record on TV) congressmen who used private flights that were paid by taxpayers. Price was the subject of a criminal investigation into trading of stocks when he was confirmed by the Senate as president Trump's Secretary of Health and Human Services. At least HUD Secretary Ben Carson, Agriculture Secretary Sonny Perdue, Commerce Secretary Wilbur Ross (pays for private travel out of pocket), and Education Secretary Betsy DeVos (already has a private plane) are not engaging in this practice. The Inspector General at HHS is looking into Price's numerous flights on private planes to determine if they flout the rules. Cabinet secretaries are authorized to take private planes funded by taxpayer money, but only after an effort has been undertaken to rule out other possibilities.

Rachel Maddow was ebullient as she described one embarrassing item after another. The Trump Inaugural Committee has failed to account for the money it raised which was not spent during the inaugural and which the committee promised to hand over to charity. Maddow put it brilliantly when she referred to the administration's sense of entitlement to public finances. Maddow's team at MSNBC asked the Trump Inaugural Committee whether the money left over after the event was or might be used to pay for attorneys that are representing Trump officials with exposure to the Russia probe. The Committee replied: "No comment". If that were not the case, they would have flatly denied it.

Trump campaign funding and Republican National Committee (RNC) money may be helping pay Donald Trump Jr.'s attorneys. Donald Trump Jr. was not involved in the campaign and has no position in the government. He therefore, under the law, cannot use Trump campaign funds or RNC financing to pay for his attorneys. The Federal Election Commission grants approval on a case-by-case basis, and Donald Trump Jr. apparently has not submitted an application to the FEC. There are no rules or regulations, however, governing the money raised by the Trump Inaugural Committee. It can be employed to pay for attorneys or even be pocketed by Donald Trump himself. Rachel Maddow was flabbergasted when she was informed about this latter aspect by an expert on September 21st, 2017, on her show. Traditional campaign funds, however, are regulated, and cannot be earmarked for uses not related to a campaign.

New polling showed that 71% of Americans supported president Trump's agreement with Democrats to raise the debt ceiling, provide funding for the victims of hurricanes Harvey and Irma, some funding for border enforcement and a promise to work to resolve the situation of the 800,000 Dreamers.

MF: Well, thank you for all of the information about the Fed, the banknotes and the Russia investigation. How has the weather been? We must from time to time discuss more light-hearted matters. What do you think about the battle of Gettysburg?

AM: In July of 2018, the US will celebrate the 155th anniversary of the battle of Gettysburg. The battle lasted three days and took place from the 1st to the 3rd of July of 1863. It turned the tide of the war against the Confederacy. It was the deadliest battle in the Civil War, claiming more than 7000 lives. In fact, it is the biggest and bloodiest battle ever waged on US soil. The combined casualties of killed, wounded and missing of the Union and Confederate armies exceeded 53,000.

Robert E. Lee had been inflicting defeats on the Union Army in Virginia at the battles of Fredericksburg and Chancellorsville and in late June of 1863 marched north into Maryland and Pennsylvania. He wanted to deliver a fatal blow to the Union by seizing parts of Pennsylvania, which amounted to invading the north. Lee also hoped that a decisive victory over the Federal Army on its territory would spur sentiment against the war among public opinion and those who were financing it. In anticipation of crushing the Union's Army of the Potomac, the Confederate leadership had sent President Lincoln a letter which offered peace, and which amounted to an invitation to negotiate an end to the war on the South's terms.

Lee commanded his Army of northern Virginia made up of several corps and 70,000 soldiers as he pushed north behind the Blue Ridge Mountains and into Maryland and Pennsylvania. He wanted to draw the Union's Army of the Potomac into open ground and crush it. The death of General Stonewall Jackson a few months earlier forced Lee to rearrange his forces. Lieutenant General James Longstreet was Lee's most reliable, trustworthy and effective corps commander. According to biographer and historian Jeffrey Wert, Longstreet "was the finest corps commander in the Army of Northern Virginia; in fact, he was arguably the best corps commander in the conflict on either side." Longstreet remained in command of one corps, and Lieutenant Generals A.P. Hill and Richard Ewell each commanded another. Hill and Ewell, however, had reported to Stonewall Jackson as division commanders, and therefore lacked the experience of leading a corps before the battle of Gettysburg.

General J.E.B. Stuart was in command of the Cavalry Division, but disobeyed Lee's orders and did not report on the Union's movements. Stewart took his men too far to the north in an attempt to outflank Union forces from the east. He and his three divisions were absent for two decisive days at Gettysburg. Lee was forced to make decisions without intelligence on the strength and location of Union forces that Stewart should have furnished.

Longstreet desperately tried to talk Lee out of attacking the Army of the Potomac, which was made up of seven infantry corps, a cavalry corps, and an Artillery Reserve, for a combined strength of more than 100,000 men. George Meade had replaced Joseph Booker as supreme commander of the Union forces. The rebels' partial success on the first day of the battle convinced Lee that he had no choice than to attack Meade, regardless of troop strength and location of each side. Union forces were favorably ensconced on high ground on several hills. Longstreet beseeched Lee to redeploy to the south and east and let the Union forces pursue them, and thus fight on territory the Confederates could choose.

But Lee committed the biggest mistake of his career and the Civil War. He was outnumbered, the Federal Army held the high ground and possessed more artillery. Despite these odds, Lee was determined to launch a second major attack on the second day of the battle of Gettysburg. After the rebels were repulsed at the Little Round Top and elsewhere on the second day of the battle, Longstreet implored Lee not to go on the offensive again. Lee nonetheless ordered a charge of 15,000 men across a field one mile wide under heavy enemy bombardment. This charge is known as Pickett's charge because one of Longstreet's divisions was led by General George Pickett. Lee was convinced his forces could seize the low ground between the two hills. The charge was a bloody failure. Lee admitted that he had blundered and had to lead his depleted forces south. He and his forces would never again be in Union territory.

Longstreet survived the war despite being seriously wounded. He joined the Republican Party and worked for president Ulysses Grant as a diplomat and administrator. His criticism of Lee's tactics and post-war activities leading an African-American militia at the battle of Liberty Place in 1874 alienated him to southerners. That is probably the reason why the states in the south did not build statues of him in the 1950s, as they did of Lee, Stonewall Jackson and Jefferson Davis. Lieutenant General Ewell and others unsuccessfully tried to persuade Jefferson Davis to free the slaves and allow them to fight with the Confederate troops.

I am fascinated by the character of Joshua Lawrence Chamberlain, a coronel who commanded the 20th Maine regiment at the beginning of the battle of Gettysburg. He was a professor at Bowdoin College in Maine before the war. He signed up as a volunteer and was commissioned as a lieutenant colonel. By July 1863, he had lost almost two-thirds of the 1000-man regiment he commanded. Chamberlain was as idealistic and brave as they come. His defense of the Union west flank on the second day of the battle of Gettysburg at the Little Round Top was extremely heroic. Ordered by his superiors not to cede the high ground on Little Round Top, Chamberlain and his courageous men fought off several charges by swarming Confederate units from Alabama during an entire day. Outnumbered and out of ammunition after fending off several attacks, Chamberlain rallied his troops and ordered a famous bayonet charge down the hill, which managed to outflank and defeat the rebels. He was wounded during the charge, which obviously involved man-to-man combat. Chamberlain was awarded the Congressional Medal of Honor for his conspicuous gallantry and heroism at Little Round Top.

Chamberlain went on to bravely command Union forces at several more battles in the Civil War and was severely wounded several more times. At the second battle of Petersburg, Chamberlain was shot through the hip. He took out his sword, stuck it to the ground and held himself upright to inspire his men. After he finally fainted, doctors did not expect him to live. He was promoted to brigadier general by general Ulysses Grant as a deathbed recognition. But Chamberlain was soon back in command, and he was again seriously wounded when a bullet struck his chest and arm during the Battle of Five Forks in March of 1865. Confederate General Gordon approached Chamberlain with the Confederacy's surrender terms after a truce had been called. Chamberlain had been promoted to the rank of Brigadier General and was granted the honor of presiding over the Confederacy's surrender parade at the Appomattox Courthouse.

Chamberlain's fame helped him to win four consecutive terms as the Republican governor of Maine after the Civil War. After leaving politics, he returned to his alma mater, Bowdoin College, where he had been a professor before the war. He served as president of Bowdoin College. He was sorely disappointed when his wish to volunteer and fight in the Spanish-American War in 1898 was turned down. He was 70 years old at the time. He died in 1914 at the age of eighty-five. Chamberlain is considered the last casualty of the Civil War, because the cause of his death was complications from the wounds he sustained at the second battle of Petersburg in 1864.

Next July will mark the 155th anniversary of the battle of Gettysburg. At a time when many politicians seek to deepen divisions in democratic countries, it is worth listening to the inspirational and unifying speech by Civil War hero Joshua Chamberlain: "We are waging a war unlike any other, meant to set other people (slaves) free, and to uphold the idea that we all have value, regardless of origin or family lineage, and that in the end we must fight for each other."

Chapter 12: Private flights, Bannon versus the GOP establishment

In late September, Milton Friedman was fortunately back in Washington, D.C., in time for the IMF-World Bank Annual Meetings. We met in downtown Washington, D.C. so I could update him on the latest developments.

AM: The week that ended on September 30th featured more bad news for the Trump administration. Secretary of Health and Human Services Tom Price came under intense political fire for his use of private planes. In less than three months, the former congressman from Georgia flew on private planes with his staff on numerous occasions. This cost taxpayers half a million dollars. Several private flights involved a combination of personal and professional matters. Many of Price's routes were covered by commercial flights or even trains. Cabinet Secretaries can use private flights if there is no viable alternative. Price made a fool of himself, especially since he had heavily criticized the use of private planes by fellow congressmen when he was serving in the House. But Price is not the only case. Treasury Secretary Steve Mnuchin chartered a private plane to take his newly-wed wife to see the solar eclipse in Kentucky and tried to do the same for a trip to Europe. The private flight to Kentucky cost thousands of dollars. Another independent watchdog has revealed that Secretary of the Treasury Steve Mnuchin took flights on military jets to the tune of $80,000. In one case, an employee pointed out to him that a round-trip flight to Florida would cost less than nine-hundred dollars. Interior Secretary Ryan Zinke also flew on a privately-chartered plane to the US Virgin Islands for a fund-raiser that included snorkeling. Other cabinet secretaries actually own private planes, such as Education Secretary Betsy DeVos. At any rate, Price has also lost favor with Trump due to the failure to repeal and replace Obamacare with a Republican plan.

While almost three million Americans suffered in Puerto Rico with no electricity and shortages of basic goods more than a week after hurricane Maria pummeled the island, the optics of an HHS Secretary spending half a million dollars on private flights were awful. Trump dismissed Price on September 29th, 2017. He became the first cabinet-level casualty in the Trump administration, although several senior officials have been fired or resigned since January of 2017.

The Trump administration continues to have enormous difficulties filling the upper echelons of the federal departments. The president has the right to appoint around 500 persons to serve in the federal departments. These include the secretaries themselves, the deputy secretaries, the undersecretaries, the assistant secretaries and the deputy assistant secretaries. There are several reasons why the federal departments are so thinly staffed in these positions filled by political appointees. For starters, Trump and his core advisors do not believe in the mission of some of these departments. Secretary of Energy Rick Perry advocated doing away with the Department he now heads (in addition to the Education Department) when he campaigned for president in 2012. Similarly, Republicans intensely dislike the Environmental Protection Agency, whose head, Scott Pruitt, has cabinet-level rank. Trump's budget calls for a gutting of the State Department, with a proposed cut of 45% in its funding. Trump and his inner circle probably do not believe there is much value in the Department of Education, either. In other cases, the Russia probe and the many controversies the administration is embroiled in have dissuaded potential qualified professionals from wanting to serve in the federal government. After Price was fired by Trump, he was replaced as Acting Health and Human Services Secretary by a Deputy Assistant Secretary. That is four rungs below a secretary.

The administration has also failed to nominate a successor to General John Kelly as Secretary of the Department of Homeland Security. The acting Secretary, Elaine Duke, stoked the flames of discontent among the inhabitants of Puerto Rico by claiming that the administration's response was a "good news story". After being blasted by everyone, she took back her remarks.

Our thoughts and prayers should also be with the victims and the families of Mexico's second deadly earthquake this month. After more than 90 were killed in the quake in Chiapas and Oaxaca, more than 230 lost their lives after the tremor that shook Mexico City, Puebla and Morelos. It is encouraging to see Mexican civilians working alongside police, firefighters and other officials. They have rescued many from the rubble. And Mexico City's buildings have held up much better than in the 1985 earthquake thanks to stricter building codes.

MF: What is the alternative right in the US up to?

AM: There is ample evidence that Steve Bannon is waging an all-out war on the establishment since going back to his position at Breitbart. He has told *The Economist* that when he was a chief strategist to president Trump, he had influence.[8] Now that he is back at Breitbart, he claims that he has power. Bannon is publicly endorsing and backing Roy Moore, the Republican candidate for the Alabama Senate seat left vacant by Jeff Sessions. Moore has extremely radical views and was dismissed as Chief Justice of the Alabama Supreme Court twice for not following the law. On one occasion, Moore refused to remove a monument to the Ten Commandments from his courtroom despite a federal court order to do so. On another, he ordered judges in Alabama to enforce a ban on same-sex marriages even though it had been deemed unconstitutional. Moore has expressed support for criminalizing homosexual activity. He twice failed to win the Republican primary for governor of Alabama. But in the Trump era, he might defeat any Democrat and represent Alabama in the Senate.

Bannon, Breitbart and the Alt-Right are also supporting Kelli Ward, who is a proponent of not enforcing federal gun laws in Arizona and has called Senator John McCain "old" and "weak" in a futile attempt to get him to step down after his unfortunate diagnosis of brain cancer. Ward will take on the other sitting Republican senator, Jeff Flake, who has been publicly critical of Trump, and other candidates in the GOP primary to determine the Republican candidate for one of Arizona's two Senate seats. Arizona has not had a Democratic senator in quite some time. The victor in the Republican primary should beat the Democratic candidate, unless he or she is extremely controversial.

Trump has also weighed in on the Virginia gubernatorial race, that pits Republican Ed Gillespie against Ralph Northam, the Democratic sitting lieutenant governor. Gillespie served as Chair of the Republican National Committee, counselor to President George W. Bush and founded a lobbying firm. In 2004, he narrowly lost (by 0.8%) the race for a Senate seat to Mark Warner, one of the two current incumbent Democratic senators from Virginia. Gillespie is depicted by his opponents and in Northam's advertisements as the consummate Washington insider, which is not a positive attribute for voters. Gillespie is trailing in the polls. He is having trouble securing the support of Trump voters and the more moderate mainstream Republicans and independents who live in northern Virginia.

It appears that Gillespie is getting desperate as polls show he is not making progress in closing the gap with Northam. Gillespie's TV ads against Northam were harsh, but not anything beyond what is unfortunately customary in today's politics. In his latest TV attacks ads, Gillespie raised the vitriol and blames Northam for the murders committed by MS-13, a violent criminal group made up of people from El Salvador. It is true that MS-13 members have committed heinous and

---

[8] Reported on "All in With Chris Hayes", MSNBC (American news cable and satellite television network). October 6th, 2017.

barbaric murders in Central America and in the US, including some in Virginia. But blaming Northam is unfair and inaccurate. The commercial claims that Northam cast the deciding vote on protecting sanctuary cities, which are cities that protect illegal aliens from deportation. I do not know if that is accurate. The supposed connection is that protecting illegal aliens from deportation in general terms is beneficial for MS-13, whose members are mostly illegal aliens from El Salvador.

It is true that there are MS-13 members in the Washington, D.C area, which includes the northern Virginia suburbs. But the president's tweet that Northam "fights" for MS-13 members is beyond the pale. Gillespie had criticized Northam for being weak in dealing with MS-13. But Trump actually accused the current lieutenant governor of Virginia of doing MS-13's bidding. Gillespie clearly felt uncomfortable when reporters asked him about Trump's tweet about Northam "fighting" for MS-13. Gillespie is savvy, so he evaded the questions by asserting that it is customary for a Republican president to endorse and support the Republican candidate for the governorship of Virginia, which is true.

According to reporting by MSNBC, a right-wing supremacist aligned with Steve Bannon who sang to a group of white supremacists extending a Nazi salute has asserted that mosques are only a place of hate and that the main influence of Islam on the US was the September 11, 2001 attacks. Hayes also interviewed a very balanced and brilliant writer, Ta-Nehisi Coates, the author of "We were eight years in Power: An American Tragedy".[9]

MSNBC highlighted on the 6th of October that for the first time in seven years (since 2011), the US economy shed jobs in the month of September. The reporting did underline in fairness to MSNBC that the reason for the drop (33,000 jobs) is the extensive havoc and destruction wrought by hurricanes Harvey, Irma and Maria in Texas, Florida, Puerto Rico and the US Virgin Islands beginning in late August and throughout September. The unemployment rate, however, dipped from 4.3% to 4.2%. Economists had forecast an increase of 100,000 jobs for September. The case can be made that a loss of 33,000 jobs is reassuringly low given the massive destruction in parts of Texas, southern Florida, all of Puerto Rico and two of the US Virgin Islands. Business leaders are pointing to a quick recovery and reconstruction in Florida.

According to a poll by the Associated Press and the NORC Center for Public Affairs Research, president Trump's approval rating decreased to a new low of 32%. The poll was conducted in late September and early October of 2017. Trump's approval rating was approximately 46% when he was inaugurated and 42% in March. It has languished below 40% in the past few months, but the 32% must worry the Trump administration. It obviously means that 67% of Americans disapprove of the way Trump is handling his job. The same poll also showed that Trump's support is slipping among Republicans. Only twenty-seven percent of women approve of the president's performance. And a whopping 74% of Americans polled expressed their view that the US is on the wrong track.[10] In a Quinnipiac poll, 58% of Americans disapprove of his comments about the National Football League (NFL). Some pundits are half-joking that Trump is angling for the job of NFL Commissioner as he faces the prospect of not being reelected or even being impeached.[11]

According to an Associated Press poll, 65% of Americans feel that president Trump's comments about North Korea have worsened relations between the US and North Korea. Forty-five percent of those surveyed felt that Trump's bellicose language has made relations much worse. Only 8%

[9] Reported in "In All in with Chris Hayes", MSNBC, 6th of October 2017
[10] Reported in "The Last Word". MSNBC, 6th of October 2017
[11] Reported in "The Last Word". MSNBC, 11th of October 2017

of Americans think that Trump's remarks regarding the Democratic People's Republic of Korea (North Korea) are improving the situation.

Another survey conducted by Quinnipiac, a very respected institution, reveals that 55% of Americans believe Trump is not fit to be president, while 43% do think he is. Trump did get relatively good marks for his handling of the economy, with a narrow plurality (48%) approving of his handling of the economy, and 46% disapproving. According to the Quinnipiac poll, 70% want Trump to cut down on his tweeting, while 27% percent say he should continue[12].

Steve Bannon, the former chief adviser to president Trump, has declared war on Republican sitting senators whom he feels are not extreme enough or have not done enough to advance his nativist and extreme right-wing agenda. He and other radical groups will fund the primary campaigns of Republicans who challenge several sitting Republican senators. Bannon announced on Fox who will be "primaried" by his movement. More broadly, Bannon has declared war on the Republican Party establishment. Among those Republican senators targeted in the 2018 mid-terms are Arizona Senator Jeff Flake, Orrin Hatch from Utah and Dean Heller from Nevada[13]. But Bannon has actually upped the ante by stating that his mission is to replace all current Republican senators, except Ted Cruz from Texas. Bannon literally said on Sean Hannity's show on Fox that nobody in the Republican establishment would be safe from his crusade. He is an embittered fanatic.

This strategy has its risks. The GOP will win Senate seats in deep-red states like those in the South regardless of the candidate they field. But in purple (swing) states like Arizona, Nevada or Virginia picking a radical can result in a loss to the Democratic candidate. This happened in 2010, when the radicalism of the Tea Party prevented the GOP from taking control of the Senate, although they did regain control of the House. Sarah Palin and other GOP radicals raised millions for extreme right-wing candidates who won the GOP primary but were defeated in the general election. And Republicans only have a majority of two in the Senate.

The reason Ted Cruz is spared from Bannon's crusade is that they share a powerful and very wealthy friend and benefactor. His name is Robert Mercer. He has very deep pockets and his company funds the campaigns of Republican candidates. Like Bannon, Mercer does not believe the US needs a federal government and has other radical views. Mercer's company is a source of funding for Breitbart, which would otherwise not be as influential. But Mercer keeps a relatively low profile[14].

Senator Bob Corker from Tennessee, who is the Chairman of the Foreign Relations Committee, has announced that he will not seek reelection and will retire. He can now speak his mind. Corker was on the short list to be Trump's Secretary of State. He has been increasingly critical of Trump, questioning his temperament and ability to hold the office of the presidency. In the past few days, Corker admonished that Chief of Staff John Kelly, Secretary of State Rex Tillerson and Defense Secretary James Mattis are all that stand between chaos and possibly war, and specifically World War III. For good measure, Corker added that the White House has become an adult day care center – the president needing the "care". Corker is particularly upset because he and his staff have spent many hours and deployed great efforts working with Rex Tillerson and

---

[12] Reported in "All in with Chris Hayes", MSNBC, 12th of October of 2017

[13] Flake and Hatch announced they would not be running for reelection. Flake probably knows he would lose, having defied both Trump and the Alternative Right. Hatch has been in the Senate for decades and Trump unsuccessfully tried to persuade him to run again. Mitt Romney, a fierce critic of Trump who was governor of Massachusetts and is a Mormon, will run for the seat in Senate left vacant by Hatch's retirement.

[14] Reported in "All in with Chris Hayes". MSNBC, 10th October of 2017

the State Department on issues like North Korea and the nuclear deal with Iran. The president undercut Tillerson's work, tweeting that he was wasting his time in trying to negotiate with North Korea. This was more than Corker could stomach.

Trump obviously gave Corker a piece of his mind in response. He ridiculed Corker's height, calling him "liddle", and asserted he is not tall enough to be America's top diplomat. Trump also claimed Corker was set up by the New York Times in an interview (which is false) and that Corker had "begged" him to support his reelection.

President Trump has repeated in the past weeks that negotiating with North Korea is pointless and that we are experiencing the calm before the storm. Tillerson earned a rebuke from the president because the Secretary of State is keeping some communication channels open with North Korea. The "calm before the storm" reference by Trump might hint at possible military action against North Korea. Reporters repeatedly needle the president about what he has in store for North Korea. The president very correctly does not want to show his hand to Kim Jong Un. But his winks at reporters and casual answers (usually involving the sentence "you will see") in the context of a very serious and dangerous stand-off with North Korea make a lot of people nervous. MSNBC's anchors suggest that many high-ranking White House officials are worried sick about Trump having access to the nuclear code and arsenal. Trump of course threatened "fire and fury like the world has never seen" a few months ago after Kim Jong Un's missile launches and in his speech to the UN General Assembly threatened to totally destroy North Korea, arguably the first time in modern US history a president has done so in peacetime. The problem is that North Korea already has twenty nuclear warheads, multiple intermediate and long-range missiles and the capability to miniaturize warheads and install them on a missile.

According to military experts, a US pre-emptive attack against North Korea to destroy its nuclear program could result in one million victims -- North Koreans, South Koreans and expats from other countries -- and destruction of one trillion dollars. Kim Jong Un would unleash his conventional and nuclear arsenal on South Korea, whose capital Seoul is located only 35 miles from the border with the DPRK. Kim Jong Un's armed forces have thousands of artillery pieces on the border, which would immediately be fired against Seoul in the event of a US attack.

MF: Oh, do not exaggerate! Trump will not act militarily against North Korea unless Kim Jong Un attacks the US island of Guam, Japan or South Korea. The Trump administration is trying to move forward with tax reform, infrastructure and repealing Obamacare. These are just soundbites from the left. US taxes are simply too high, and this is undermining the country's competitiveness. We have the highest statutory corporate tax rate (35%) among developed countries. It is an imperative that it be cut.

AM: That is correct. But Trump often repeats that the US is the most "taxed country in the world", which is categorically false. The facts show that Denmark is the most heavily-taxed country in the developed world, and many other developed countries also surpass the US. But the real corporate rate that businesses wind up paying is much lower because there are many deductions they can resort to. Removing the deductions so the statutory corporate tax rate (35%) can be reduced is the crux of the matter. Therein lies the challenge, because there are legions of lobbyists who will defend each and every one of these tax breaks before Congress. But I wholeheartedly support diminishing the corporate tax rate and generally cutting taxes as long as the reform is revenue neutral and does not add to the US national debt.

I understand you do not have the time to watch the news as I do. But just consider the following. In today's White House news briefing by Press Secretary Sarah Huckabee Sanders, she had to answer, to, among other questions: why the vice president spent $200,000 in taxpayer money to make a brief appearance at an Indianapolis Colts football game; why Trump boasted that he is much more intelligent than his Secretary of State Rex Tillerson; why the president continues to repeat the falsehood that the US is the most heavily taxed country in the world; and why the president continues to attack and alienate Republicans in Congress whom he needs to enact legislation.

Huckabee Sanders has one of the toughest jobs in Washington, D.C. She has to downplay Trump's tirades against his own cabinet secretaries, Republican senators or anybody who is the target of the president's wrath. She also has to defend statements made by Trump which are utterly false. She does a reasonable job given the amount of controversial actions and statements spawned by the president and the White House. In many cases, she has to deflect or simply avoid answering a question. She has a southern accent and charm. But I wonder to what extent she is the president's Press Secretary because her father, Mike Huckabee, is a well-known conservative firebrand and former governor of Arkansas who jumped on the Trump bandwagon after he dropped out of the Republican presidential primary in 2016. I have certainly watched much better White House press secretaries over the years.

According to a Vanity Fair article, several anonymous sources within the White House have stated that president Trump is seething with anger, angrily repeats things, obsessively calls people and was quoted as saying that "he hates almost everyone in the White House". According to these sources, Trump is becoming "increasingly unfocused", "consumed by dark moods" and "unraveling". He is supposedly calling friends late at night from his cell phone.

Steve Bannon, his former chief strategist, was quoted in the Vanity Fair article as rating the chances of president Trump finishing his first term at 30%. Bannon of course is contributing to such an outcome by promising to wage a war against the Republican political establishment in the 2018 mid-terms by funding right-wing nationalists to challenge sitting Republican senators and members of the House of Representatives.

The Vanity Fair article claims that the chief of staff, General Kelly, has had several shouting matches with Trump. Kelly is particularly worried that the president is getting advice from people who are exacerbating his warmongering thoughts. At his property in Mar-a-Lago it is much more difficult for John Kelly to prevent radicals from fanning Trump's flames of anger at the networks, the NFL, the response to the Puerto Rico rescue and relief operations, or Senator John McCain, just to name a few people or situations that have incurred the president's wrath.

In the Vanity Fair article, Bannon warned Trump before leaving his position in July of 2017 that he could be subject to the 25th amendment. The president did not know about the 25th amendment to the Constitution. It allows the president's cabinet to vote by a simple majority to remove him from office because he is not mentally fit to be the commander-in-chief. The 25th amendment does not require the president to be incompetent or display a lack of knowledge. It just stipulates that the president is mentally not well. Senator Bob Corker's very measured statement that only General John Kelly (Trump's chief of staff), General James Mattis (Secretary of Defense) and Secretary of State Rex Tillerson are all that stand between chaos and a possible war emboldened some White House staffers to leak their descriptions of Trump's dark mood and rage to Vanity Fair and several newspapers.

General Mattis is not at the White House all day, and neither is Rex Tillerson. Mattis obviously works at the Pentagon and Tillerson at Foggy Bottom. John Kelly, who does work at the White House, is possibly the only person who is standing between Trump and chaos. There have purportedly been discussions about how to physically prevent Trump from accessing the "nuclear football" with the codes that allow a president to use the US's nuclear weapons. If a president decides to use the US's nuclear weapons, nobody in the chain of command can stop the order from being carried out. There are some experts who claim that members of the military can refuse to execute an order they deem unlawful.

It is obvious that John Kelly feels it is his duty to restrain Trump, and that is the only reason he has not resigned. National Security Adviser H.R. McMaster, a general, is often left out of the trio of responsible cabinet officials who are worried that the president may wake up in a foul mood and decide to launch a pre-emptive strike against North Korea. The president is particularly incensed that NBC reported that Trump supposedly requested a ten-fold increase in the US nuclear arsenal in a meeting with military officers at the Pentagon on July 20th of 2017. Trump was shown a chart detailing the evolution of the US's and the Soviet Union's/Russia's respective nuclear arsenals in the past decades. The president inquired as to why the US no longer has 32,000 nuclear warheads as it did in the late 1960s, as opposed to 4,000 today. His advisers were stunned but thought that Trump might not be serious. Military advisers explained to him that it was not practical nor necessary for the US to increase its nuclear arsenal. Moreover, a ten-fold hike in the number of US nuclear warheads would violate several treaties they US has signed (START, MNF). A nuclear build-up by the US would also prompt other countries (Pakistan, Iran, possibly Japan) to pursue the development of nuclear weapons. And it would be very expensive.

The president was walked through America's military assets, as well as soft power, with graphs and charts. The famous "tank" meeting at the Pentagon windowless office on July 20th did have the positive effect of convincing Trump to authorize the deployment of more US troops to Afghanistan, which Mattis, McMaster and presumably Tillerson were advocating. After or during that tense meeting, Tillerson allegedly made the comment about the president being a "moron".

Donald Trump's favorite person is now Sean Hannity, a right-wing zealot on Fox. He always fawns over Conservatives. He hosted an event with Trump supporters in Pennsylvania. He has apparently convinced Trump to go back on his promise not to deport Dreamers without securing financing for his wall with Mexico. The president had struck an agreement with the Democratic leadership to raise the debt ceiling and include funding in the budget for the victims of hurricanes Harvey, Irma and Maria without any money for his wall. Trump may have wanted to avoid his crowd of supporters from expressing dismay at his deal with the Democrats. Hannity also hinted that Julian Assange should be invited to come to the US to prove that it was an inside job within the Democratic Party and not the Russians who leaked the DNC's and John Podesta's emails. Assange is still holed up at the Embassy of Ecuador in London because he faces sexual harassment charges in Sweden from a former Wikileaks employee. Ecuador's current (Lenín Moreno) and previous president (Rafael Correa) are providing him safe haven from the United Kingdom, which would extradite him to Sweden.

The Trump administration continued to be distracted by relatively irrelevant issues. For example, the president did not let up in his criticism of NFL players who took a knee or raised their fists during the playing of the national anthem. He could have referred to the issue in a non-provocative way (I agree with Trump's position) and then allowed it to fade. But he added fuel to the fire by tweeting that the NFL's ratings had plummeted. On another front, the media revealed that Secretary of State Rex Tillerson had described the president as a "moron". Tillerson held a press conference and pledged his full support for the president, while praising his love of America. But he did not deny the claim that he had called Trump a "moron". The president had publicly remarked that his Secretary of State should not waste his time trying to negotiate with the North Korean regime. That probably did not go down very well with the former CEO of ExxonMobil. There had been other media accounts to the effect that America's chief diplomat was unhappy and considering resigning. The chief of staff, John Kelly, probably had a lot to do with dissuading him.

On October 11th, the media was indulging in a frenzy after a New York Times investigate reporter revealed that famous Hollywood producer Harvey Weinstein has a history of sexual harassment and abuse. He and Miramax have paid off several women, mostly actresses, that were harassed by Weinstein. Famous stars like Gwyneth Paltrow and others confirmed that Weinstein has a troubled history.

MF: What will happen with the nuclear deal with Iran?

AM: President Trump launched an attack on the media which he claims is unfavorably covering him. He mentioned NBC in particular. It is true that MSNBC has an agenda and is biased against Trump and his administration. But Trump threatened to revoke the licenses of TV stations, and he singled out cable news channels and NBC. This is something that the president does not have the authority to do. The first amendment to the US Constitution of course protects freedom of speech and the freedom of the press. CNN and MSNBC were very quick to denounce Trump's threats. They also pointed out that the president does not have the authority to revoke the licenses of local or national TV stations. The Federal Communications Commission is the US government agency that regulates the airwaves and would have to have due cause to shut down a TV station. President Richard Nixon apparently also tried to intimidate some TV channels. The Washington Post was of course on a quest to get to the bottom of the Pentagon Papers and later the Watergate scandal, and Nixon banned all Washington Post reporters and photographers from the White House.

Trump is moving to decertify Iran with regards to its compliance with the nuclear agreement signed with the US, Russia, China, Germany, France and the UK in 2015 under the Obama administration. The international inspectors who are monitoring Iran's compliance on the ground have repeatedly concluded that Iran is not engaging in any illegal activities, such as enriching uranium or building more centrifuges. Defense Secretary James Mattis and the Chairman of the Joint Chiefs of Staff, Joseph Dunford, have also confirmed this conclusion and recommended to the president that he certify that Teheran is complying. Trump has twice certified that Iran is fulfilling the agreement. But in October of 2017 it appeared that Trump had made up his mind to decertify Iran in the future, whilst not imposing sanctions. In pursuing this course, he is basically passing the hot potato to Congress. He is also sending a signal to our allies and rivals that they cannot trust Trump. The president emphasized on October 11th that he is not seeking an increase in the US nuclear arsenal but that he wants it to be "in tip-top shape", meaning modernized and ready for use.

MF: I have to be a speaker at several IMF and World Bank (WB) events on the occasion of their Annual Meetings, which are coming up in the next few days. You were the speechwriter and assistant to the president of the World Bank. You therefore know how busy the Annual Meetings are, with the attendance of the Ministers of Finance or chairmen of the central bank of each of the IMF's and the World Bank's 189 member countries. And, of course, thousands of journalists from around the world, members of NGOs and many others descend on Washington, D.C. for the Annual Meetings. I therefore please need you to keep me updated in the coming days on international and national political, economic, business, financial and social issues. I will not have time to even read the newspaper. At most I may glance at the headlines.

AM: I understand. I will be more than happy to give you a summary of key breaking news and developments. I have done the same for many of my bosses. It is a pleasure to do it for you.

Some Republican senators did criticize president Trump's threats to revoke the licenses of local TV channels or cable news networks and rambling on how there is so much fake news. Specifically, Republican Senator Ben Sasse from Nebraska (who is not retiring) alerted the president to the implications of his threats for the First Amendment of the US Constitution, which of course protects the freedom of the press (and of speech, assembly and religion).

Republican Senator John McCain and many Democrats are publicly asking why president Trump has not yet implemented the sanctions on Russia which Congress overwhelmingly approved and which were supposed to go into effect on October 1st, 2017. The sanctions were passed by the Senate 98 to 2 and in the House by 415 to 3. That is almost unanimity. The president signed the legislation on August 1st, as he obviously did not have the votes to override a veto. Trump privately signed the sanctions bill and left it to Rex Tillerson to publicly declare on August 1st that the president and himself disapproved of the measure adopted by Congress. The deadline for implementing the sanctions was October 1st. By the 12th of October, nothing had happened, and two of its co-sponsors in the Senate (Republican John McCain and Democrat Ben Cardin) wrote a letter to the president seeking an explanation as to the reason for the delay. The Trump administration is stalling on applying the Russian sanctions overwhelmingly passed in the summer.

By all accounts, president Trump is spending a lot of time calling Sean Hannity, one of his best friends, after his daily show on Fox in the evening. Trump also watches Fox and Friends in the morning. A contributor to MSNBC pointed out that this is actually therapeutic for him, as he is surrounded by his followers and supporters at many of Hannity's outdoor shows.

The talk about the 25th amendment to the Constitution is very premature and inaccurate. In order for a president to be considered mentally unfit to serve, a majority of his cabinet and the vice president have to reach that conclusion and actually vote. Mike Pence is not going to vote or seek to persuade a majority of cabinet secretaries that president Trump is mentally unfit. He would look like a traitor. Mike Pence may be very conservative but does not fit the profile of a scheming opportunist. And even if he did try to persuade a majority of secretaries in the federal government that Trump is unfit, he would probably not get secretaries like Steve Mnuchin (Treasury), Rick Perry (Energy), Ryan Zinke (Interior), Sonny Perdue (Agriculture) to agree. If his rage and legal troubles mount in several months and his behavior gets worse, it is conceivable that James Mattis (Defense), Rex Tillerson (State), Jeff Sessions (Attorney General, whom the president ridiculed and insulted), Elaine Chao (Transportation, whose husband is Mitch McConnell) and conceivably Sonny Perdue (who already has a good legacy), Perry, Labor Secretary Alex Acosta and maybe Zinke might go along with a determination that the president is unfit. But the president, under the 25th amendment, would have the right to challenge his supposed inability to serve before the Congress, and two-thirds of the members of the House of Representatives would need to ratify the determination made by the vice president and a majority of his cabinet. With a big Republican majority in the House, that will simply not happen. Even if the Democrats were to seize control of the House in 2018, the Republicans will always have more than one-third of the members of the House. The 25th amendment is also meant to deal with presidents who have to undergo surgery or may be unconscious for a few hours due to a medical operation.

It was passed in 1967 to clarify presidential and vice-presidential succession in the wake of John F. Kennedy's 1963 assassination. We have all seen pictures of vice president Lyndon Johnson's stressful taking of the oath of office as president aboard Air Force One on the afternoon of November 22nd, 1963. Federal District judge Sarah Hughes administered the oath to Johnson as Air Force One was still on the tarmac at Love Field, Dallas' airport. Johnson and Hughes were friends and the vice president had sought her promotion to a federal judgeship a few months earlier. Attorney General Robert Kennedy ruled against the promotion because the Department of Justice underlined that she was 65. The Department of Justice later reversed its decision and Hughes was made a federal judge without consulting vice president Johnson, who felt disrespected. In the hours that followed JFK's assassination, there was reasonable concern that there might be a foreign conspiracy and that Johnson and others might also be at risk. Johnson did insist on waiting for Jacqueline Kennedy to be on Air Force One before taking the oath. Jacquie, for her part, was not going to leave Dallas without JFK's casket. Johnson called Bobby Kennedy to offer his condolences and also tell him that he would be taking the oath as president before taking off. Bobby Kennedy was the Attorney General, and he was in Washington, D.C. on that tragic day, November 22nd, 1963. Bobby felt that Johnson was in too much of a rush to become president. He was obviously stricken with great grief, but this somewhat clouded his judgement. JFK was unfortunately dead, and Johnson had to become president. This is an example of historical trivia that explains why people design conspiracy theories.

Lyndon Johnson in fact was very courteous in understanding Jacqueline Kennedy's desire to not depart before the casket was brought on board. Johnson, his wife, their children, Judge Hughes, Jacqueline Kennedy, JFK's personal secretary, several police officials and the Secret Service waited on Air Force One until JFK's body was brought on board. The oath was administered before taking off.

The 25th amendment has been invoked three times. On one occasion it involved President Gerald Ford bringing in Nelson Rockefeller as his vice president. When Ronald Reagan was shot by John Hinckley on March 20th of 1981 outside of the Hilton Hotel in Washington, D.C., he was rushed to George Washington University Medical Center. Vice president George H.W. Bush was traveling in the US. Former Secretary of State Alexander Haig infamously stated to reporters: "As of now, I am in control here, in the White House, pending the return of the vice president." Reagan underwent very serious surgery to remove a bullet from his lung. Despite the president's life-threatening wounds, operation at George Washington University's Medical Center, and several days of recovery at the hospital, Article III of the 25th amendment was not invoked in order to make Bush president until Reagan recovered. The 25th amendment was invoked in 1985 when Reagan underwent surgery for colon cancer and power was provisionally transferred to George Bush.

Chris Matthews, who is very intelligent and fair, has pointed out that it is not wise at this point to seek impeachment or try to prove that president Trump is mentally unfit to serve. He referenced the medical dimension of the 25th amendment and urged president Trump to sit down with the Republican (Speaker Paul Ryan and Senator Mitch McConnell) and Democratic leadership of Congress (Nancy Pelosi and Senator Chuck Schumer) and see how something tangible such as an infrastructure package or a repatriation with some amnesty for the $2 trillion that US companies have stashed away overseas can be approved by both chambers of Congress with some bipartisan support.

Chapter 13: Tax Reform and Mueller's first indictments

Green Bay Packers' star quarterback Aaron Rodgers was the victim of a vicious hit by a Ravens linebacker who threw him to the ground after he had already thrown a pass. The Ravens linebacker was out to injure him. He just walked away as Aaron was lying on the ground. Rodgers was not able to cushion the fall. The Ravens linebacker pinned him to the ground on his right shoulder and arm, which is his throwing arm. Rodgers broke his left collarbone a few seasons ago. But this is much worse. His right collarbone was broken, and he is right-handed. But he is a real man. He actually got up and walked off the field with a broken collarbone. He was of course upset at the unnecessary viciousness of the sack. The back-up quarterback, Brett Hundley, took over but the Vikings prevailed, 23 to 10. The Packers fell to 4-2. Rodgers is probably out for the season. He got very little sympathy across the NFL. As Rodgers has inspired me, I decided to drive to Green Bay. I have been to Wisconsin before, to the capital Madison and Kenosha in southern Wisconsin. But I had never spent a night in Wisconsin nor visited Green Bay, a city of 104,000 near Lake Michigan.

Wisconsin obviously reminds one of Northern Europe. There are of course many names of German, Dutch or French origin. There are towns named Belgium, Denmark or Font du Lac. It feels like being in Germany or the Netherlands. It is a mixture of America, northern Europe and Indian-American heritage, all close to Canada. I liken Wisconsin specifically to Denmark. They have exactly the same population (5.7 million), both produce a lot of dairy products and beer, both have lakes and are flat, and are not densely populated.

Milton Friedman was on a swing of the Midwest delivering conferences and joined me in Green Bay. He inquired about the NAFTA negotiations.

MF: As you know, I taught at the university of Wisconsin-Madison for one year. It is interesting to hear about this great state. But what is the state of the NAFTA negotiations?

AM: Hundreds of government civil servants and lobbyists will huddle in meetings in Arlington, Virginia, until the 17th of October of 2017 for the fourth round of negotiations on the future of NAFTA. President Trump's setbacks in other policy fronts have hardened his position with regards to the revision of NAFTA. The Trump administration demands, among other measures, a five-year "sunset clause" which would automatically end the agreement unless all parties decide to renew it after five years, the disappearance or weakening of NAFTA's dispute-resolution system, revisions to the intellectual property provisions, barriers for Canadian and Mexican companies in bidding for public-sector projects and more protection for US agricultural products. The first two demands are red lines for Mexico and Canada. Moreover, the Trump administration wants the percentage of parts from the NAFTA members for the manufacture of vehicles to rise from 62% to 85%, and that at least 50% of the components be from US companies.

During his trip to Washington, D.C., Canadian Prime Minister Justin Trudeau will again highlight that Canada is the US's top export market. Mexico's Foreign Minister warned that bilateral cooperation with the US (in combatting drug trafficking, for example) would be downgraded if NAFTA is unilaterally scrapped by the Trump administration.

Tom Donohue is the president and CEO of the US Chamber of Commerce, the world's biggest business association. He warned that the $1 trillion in yearly trade flows between the US, Canada and Mexico are seriously threatened by the White House's demands. Donohue this week sent a letter to president Trump advocating the maintenance of NAFTA, which was co-signed by 300 US regional business associations. The US's agricultural and parts of its manufacturing sector also support NAFTA. It is ironic that US business associations are teaming up with Mexico and Canada against a Republican administration. Tom Donohue predicted that a clause requiring more US- or NAFTA-made vehicle parts would lead to North American car manufacturers importing more parts from Asia. Mexico is more vulnerable because its trade surplus with the US is $64 billion, whereas Canada's trade account with the US is balanced. The Trump administration also seeks to restrict Canadian exports to the US of some types of lumber and dairy products. The WTO did rule against Canadian subsidies of dairy products, but prior US administrations had not allowed the dispute to undermine NAFTA. Trudeau has been a moderating influence on Trump. But the recent Trump administration announcement that the US is applying preliminary anti-dumping duties against the Canadian manufacturer of airplanes Bombardier foreshadows a tense summit.

President George W. Bush indirectly criticized Trump in public remarks by condemning how nationalism has evolved into nativism, how "discourse has degraded into casual cruelty, how argument turns too easily into animosity." Kudos to the former president. George W. Bush also added that "discontent has deepened partisan conflict." Bush, like other former presidents, usually avoids criticizing the sitting president.

On the same day, president Obama eloquently addressed a crowd at an event in Richmond for Lieutenant Governor Ralph Northam, who is facing Republican Ed Gillespie for the office of governor of Virginia. Obama stated that "politics is infecting our communities." "Instead of looking for ways to work together, there are some who demonize people who have different opinions." This is being done to "fire up the base in order to achieve a short-term advantage."

Although the two speeches were not coordinated, it is clear that both George W. Bush and Barack Obama are worried about the divisiveness stoked by Trump. George W. Bush did not even vote for Trump and remarked that he might be the last Republican president, hinting that Trump could tear the GOP apart, taking his base with him. The two former presidents' speeches and John McCain's denunciation of Trump's handling of the Niger raid added momentum to the campaign to discredit Trump. Hopefully, support for the president among his base will diminish after his mean-spirited call to the widow of a fallen Sergeant, giving himself a "10" on his response to the hurricane in Puerto Rico and other gaffes and embarrassing comments.

Milton Friedman traveled to China as an observer of the Communist Party's five-year Congress. It was a calculated invitation to burnish Beijing's pro-business image. Why would they otherwise invite the champion of free markets, tax cuts, deregulation and privatizations? The Economist featured Xi Jinping on its cover, with the caption: "The world's most powerful man". The Congress has enshrined Jinping's thoughts and beliefs into the Chinese Constitution, something unprecedented by a Chinese leader since Deng Xiaoping in the early 1980s. I understand that Milton could not resist the temptation to be in Beijing and talk to Chinese leaders. After his return to the US, he needed a briefing on the latest political, economic, business and financial developments.

MF: What is happening in the US with tax reform?

AM: Paul Ryan, speaker of the House, is making an all-out push to get tax reform through the House before the end of the year. Republicans in general are aware of the fact that they have not enacted any major piece of legislation. Repealing and replacing Obamacare is no longer their priority, as they do not have the votes. But the Trump administration is doing its best to undermine the Affordable Care Act (ACA) by stopping payments to states and health-insurance companies, thus weakening the exchanges and prompting many insurers to pull out of many counties in many states. There is a bipartisan bill in the Senate which would precisely shore up the exchanges. It is co-sponsored by Republican Senator Lamar Alexander (Tennessee) and Democratic Senator Patti Murray (Washington) and the non-partisan Congressional Budget Office has scored the draft bill as cutting the budget deficit by $3.8 billion in the next ten years. But a judge has ruled that the Trump administration's decision to stop payments to health-insurers under the ACA is legal. This is major blow to Obamacare and the Alexander-Murray effort in the Senate. The administration is also not enforcing the individual mandate, which fines individuals who do sign up to have health insurance.

The big infrastructure package does not appear to have traction. Tax reform is therefore what Congress will be wrestling with in the next months. There are some details regarding the administration's plan for tax reform. It would cut the corporate tax rate from 35% to 20%. It would allow small businesses to pay an even lower tax rate. Moreover, the threshold for paying the estate tax would be increased to over $11 million. With regards to income tax, there would be three rates. The lowest one, which is now 8%, would be raised to 10%. This would obviously hurt the middle class. The administration claims that its tax plan will cut taxes by $6 trillion over ten years.

MF: Alex, you should be thrilled. Tax cuts for corporations, small businesses, etc.

AM: I agree that the corporate tax rate should be cut. But without an elimination of deductions, this plan will blow a hole in the deficit and the national debt will soar. It is beyond the pale that the richest will benefit through the higher threshold of the estate tax and tax cuts for the richest, while some in the middle class will pay more.

Republican Senator Jeff Flake from Arizona has announced he will not run for reelection in 2018. He was behind by thirty points to Kelli Ward, a firebrand conservative backed by Steve Bannon and Breitbart who unsuccessfully tried to unseat John McCain when the senior senator from Arizona ran for reelection. Flake has written a book which is very critical of Trump. Flake could see the writing on the wall. His approval ratings are very low and he knew the hard right would lavish a lot of money to fund Ward's campaign. McCain, Corker and Flake can thus be counted upon to heavily criticize the president until November of 2018.

It has also emerged that the billionaire Mercer family is bankrolling Breitbart, the Alternative Right and the election campaigns for nationalist Republican candidates. News also broke that Trump's campaign had sought information from Cambridge Analytica about what dirt Russia had on Hillary Clinton. The Mercer family also funds Cambridge Analytica. The Trump administration is counter-attacking by claiming that Hillary Clinton was instrumental in getting the Obama administration to approve a deal between the Canadian company Uranium One and the Russian company Rosatom. This happened in 2013. Rosatom is the Russian government-owned uranium monopoly which purchased Uranium One for $1.3 billion. The terms of the agreement stipulate that the uranium can never be shipped to Russia. The Committee on Foreign Investment in the US (CFIUS) did approve the deal. CIFIUS is an inter-departmental committee that is in charge of examining and recommending to the president which deals which involve US companies or others operating in the US with those from hostile countries can threaten US national security. Although Uranium One is Canadian, it does operate in the US and owns 20% of the US's uranium. But the State Department is only one of the players that has to sign off when the CFIUS process is activated. The Treasury, Pentagon, Commerce and Justice Departments also have a say. Hillary Clinton, for her part, asserts that she delegated the decision to an expert on nuclear issues when she was Secretary of State.

According to the latest Fox News poll, support for Trump has dropped from 42% to 38%. Other polls have Trump's approval rating at 32%.

Milton Friedman stayed in Washington, D.C. after the IMF/World Bank Annual Meetings. He needed some rest after all of the speeches he gave and the events he attended during the Annual Meetings. The Annual Meetings can be stressful, given the thousands of journalists, members of NGOs, government officials from the IMF and the World Bank's 189 member countries. Milton hence needed to de-compress and to find out what had happened while he was busy attending the Annual Meetings. Milton was even eager to leave downtown and come to my neighborhood, so we met at the McDonald's in Fort Washington.

AM: Milton, I want to tell you something that will cheer you up. The Economist, the newsmagazine, ranked you as the most influential economist of the second half of the XXth century, and "probably" of the entire XXth century. As opposed to the BBC and a survey of your peers, The Economist is placing you at the same level as Keynes.

MF: Well, that is thrilling to know. But the IMF and World Bank are riddled with Keynesian economists.

AM: What did you expect. After the onset of the financial crisis in 2007 and the Great Recession, governments, central banks and international institutions had to resort to policies that spurred demand in order to avert a deeper crisis. As you know, they cut interest rates to almost 0, implemented stimulus programs, increased deficits and debt to foster demand and put in place public-work programs.

MF: Yes, Keynesianism.

AM: Well, call it whatever you want. But it is what the international economy needed.

MF: And look at the huge debt levels. At any rate, what has been going on?

AM: On October 29th, Special Counsel Robert Mueller publicly announced his first indictments in the Russia investigation. Paul Manafort was indicted on twelve counts, including conspiracy against the United States, failure to register as a foreign agent that represented foreign governments, money laundering and tax fraud. Manafort has not been charged with tax evasion yet because this requires documents from the Internal Revenue Service, and such a procedure would take months. Mueller was under pressure to produce indictments and might put off the tax evasion charges until later. If Manafort were convicted on all or most of these counts, he could spend the rest of his life in jail. Manafort was ordered to surrender his passports and is being allowed to live in his home. But he has to check in with the court every day and can only leave his residence for medical reasons or to attend religious services. In a long career over several decades of lobbying for foreign companies and governments, Manafort had amassed over $20 million dollars, which he illegally held in foreign bank accounts. He paid for his expensive collection of suits, ties and purchased real-estate with the millions stashed in accounts in foreign banks. Manafort was an adviser for the Ukrainian Party of Regions, the pro-Russian party headed by former Ukrainian authoritarian president Viktor Yanukovich. Manafort advised Yanukovich and other politicians in his party on domestic politics as well as how to present themselves as democrats in Western capitals, make their case and even how to appropriately dress.

Manafort was first hired by Ukrainian steel magnate Rinat Akhmetov in 2015. He later teamed up with energy oligarch Oleg Deripaska, who has very strong ties to the Kremlin. Yanukovich was overthrown by a popular revolution in 2014 and is living in exile in Russia to evade the charges against him in Ukraine. According to Ukraine's investigators, between 2007 and 2012

Yanukovich's Party of Regions paid Manafort $12.7 million for his consultancy services. Manafort had offices in Ukraine, which he only closed after he joined Trump's campaign team in 2016.

The court ordered Manafort to wear an ankle bracelet and argued that he is a flight risk because of his financial resources and overseas connections. The indictments which Mueller's team sought from and obtained from a grand jury against Manafort were expected. His home in Virginia had been raided by the FBI after obtaining a warrant from a judge in search of documents. For the record, Manafort's attorney protested that his client is innocent and added that there was no case against the Trump administration in terms of working with Russia. Manafort of course served as Trump's Campaign Chairman. Manafort's business partner, Rick Gates, was also indicted on similar charges. Both Manafort and Gates pleaded not guilty to the charges.

A hitherto unknown Trump campaign staffer named George Papadopoulos has pled guilty to lying to the FBI about his contacts with Russian officials who offered him "dirt" on Hillary Clinton in the spring of 2016. Papadopoulos was approached by a supposed Russian professor with contacts to the Russian Foreign Ministry, who offered to furnish the dirt on Hillary Clinton in the form of thousands of emails and set up a meeting between President Vladimir Putin and the highest echelons of the Trump campaign. The White House dismissed Papadopoulos as a little-known young volunteer whom Trump and the principals in the campaign did not even know. A Trump ally referred to Papadopoulos as a "coffee boy". But Sarah Huckabee-Sanders and Trump surrogates cannot wish away a picture of then-candidate Trump chairing a meeting attended by Jeff Sessions and which included Papadopoulos – who was three seats away from Trump. In an interview during the campaign, Trump listed members of his foreign policy team. In addition to Michael Flynn and Carter Page, Trump singled out Papadopoulos as an "energy consultant" and referred to him as "a great guy". Papadopoulos started cooperating with the Special Counsel back in the spring of 2017, and therefore nobody outside of Mueller's team knows all the information that Papadopoulos might have provided as part of his plea agreement.

MF: Things are getting complicated.

AM: Yes, indeed. An article in Vanity Fair described an irate president Trump lashing out at Jared Kushner and getting phone calls from Steve Bannon, who is trying to persuade him to hire aggressive attorneys and appoint an independent counsel to investigate the sale of 20% of the US's uranium stockpile to a Russian company (Rosatom) by the Canadian one Uranium One. The Rosatom-Uranium One deal was approved during the Obama administration after being reviewed by sixteen government department and agencies, as the CFIUS process requires. Bannon hopes that Mueller himself could become the target of an investigation, which would undercut his power and credibility as Special Counsel tremendously. The United States House Permanent Select Committee on Intelligence is investigating the Uranium One deal.

In November of 2017, Milton Friedman accompanied president Donald Trump and his delegation during a whirlwind tour of Asia, which included visits to Japan, South Korea, China, Vietnam (for the APEC summit) and the Philippines. The trip was packed with high-level events. President Trump delivered an eloquent speech before South Korea's Parliament, honoring the sacrifice, hard work and entrepreneurship of South Koreans since 1950. The president also denounced and listed some of the unspeakable crimes committed by the Kim dynasty in the gulag that is North Korea. Moreover, Trump reassured the Republic of Korea about the US's commitment to its defense. The president's speech contained no bombast nor fiery rhetoric. I was disappointed that even CNN did not give him credit, as MSNBC managed to somehow downplay it or just outright ignore it. The harshest line that president Trump uttered in the thirty-minute speech before South Korea's national legislature was that the North Korean leadership should not "try us". It was very mild, even by the standards of other presidents. Trump was unable to make it to the demilitarized zone with South Korean president Moon Jae-in because Marine One helicopters could not fly in the very heavy fog.

After he returned to Washington, D.C. from the Asia tour, Milton was as usual eager to know what he had missed during his absence. As was sometimes my custom, I opened up with information he might not be initially interested in. This always piqued him and often sparked intellectual debates.

AM: Milton, they featured people on CNN who do ultramarathons in Alaska. They have to ski or run for 100 miles, which means non-stop for thirty-three hours for one guy who finished second. I do not think I could ever do that. Well, I would if I had people coming along. Thirteen out of thirty-four finished. They had apparently done it in the winter because it was dark for a long time. They have to take a backpack full of emergency supplies. One runner who was featured was terribly overweight (400 pounds) and began to jog because he did not want to be a father who was unable to keep up. He wanted to actively parent his little kids. So, who knows, maybe we could do it?

The Economist had a long article on Protestantism, with numbers and distribution by continent, and expanded on how a Catholic country like Guatemala after its 36-year-old brutal civil war and natural disasters (the 1976 earthquake) is now predominantly (60%) Protestant. I also found a prelude to the movie Gettysburg. It is called *Of Gods and Generals*, and features many of the same actors in the same roles as in the more acclaimed film *Gettysburg*. It is part of a trilogy written by novelist Jeff Shaara. This one got bad reviews partly because it glorified the "Lost Cause"[15] of the Confederacy and showed a very human side to general Stonewall Jackson, for example. It covers the action in the Civil War between the first Battle of Bull Run (Manassas) through the battle of Chancellorsville in the spring of 1863.

MF: That is all very interesting. But what is happening now in the US? What about the Virginia governor's race?

AM: Democrat Ralph Northam defeated Republican Ed Gillespie to succeed Terry McAuliffe as the next governor of the Commonwealth of Virginia. Northam is a medical doctor who had been serving as lieutenant governor. His triumph was expected, but not his eight-point margin of victory. Gillespie alienated voters in the moderate counties in northern and eastern Virginia (Fairfax, Loudon, etc.), where he lost by over 20 points. Gillespie was unable to run the table in the rural and conservative southern and southwestern counties in Virginia to make up for the shellacking in the north. In fact, Gillespie performed much worse in the northern Virginia counties (which account for a large percentage of Virginia's population) this time around than he did when he lost to current Democratic senator Mark Warner. I am pleased. I do not like Gillespie, but Democrats are overreacting. Virginia is a blue state now. There is a debate among pundits as to whether Gillespie's defeat was a rejection of a very flawed candidate. Gillespie is a former lobbyist who is part of the establishment and he resorted during his campaign to divisive identity and culture issues such as the NFL, gangs, and sanctuary cities. Other analysts, especially Democrats, see in Northam's victory a repudiation of president Trump. Both versions are compatible, in my view.

---

[15] A version of the Civil War according to which the Confederates gallantly fought for their way of life and traditions against a Union bankrolled by money-grubbing industrialists and bankers.

After Northam's victory, Trump promptly distanced himself from Gillespie, tweeting during his Asia trip that the former lobbyist Gillespie had not fully embraced him. It is true that Gillespie did not seek Trump's participation in his campaign. I find myself feeling guilty for thinking the left is on a mission to redefine America's history. Do you know they are putting up a bust or sculpture to honor Mayor Marion Barry?

MF: I beg your pardon? You must be joking. A statue or bust for former mayor Marion Barry! He was dreadful.

AM: Yes, you heard it right. That pot-smoking corrupt and inefficient joke of a mayor who spent time in jail for dealing in drugs will be getting a memorial too. And he certainly did not improve the plight of Washington, DC. He once remarked that the city should be cleansed of Asian shop-owners. And statues of even Thomas Jefferson are being taken down in Virginia as we speak. Of course, the South was on the wrong side of history. But not everyone in the south was an evil person. And America was hardly the only country that practiced slavery. I find the middle ground is being lost. Besides, taking down statues of Lee, Jefferson and even George Washington and Thomas Jefferson will just beget a reaction. And millions of dollars would have to be spent to revise maps and GPS systems with the new names of streets, boulevards, parkways and streets should a massive elimination of places named after Lee be undertaken. We have Jefferson Davis highway (Route 1) right here in the Washington, D.C. area, in addition to Robert E Lee's house at the top of Arlington.

As you know, my Civil War hero remains Colonel Joshua Lawrence Chamberlain, who rose to the rank of major general. Wounded six times in the Civil War, he left his cushy tenure as professor of oratory, rhetoric and religion at Bowdoin College in Maine to volunteer to command the 20th Maine regiment. He played a very key and brave role at Gettysburg and received the Congressional Medal of Honor. Chamberlain was seriously injured five more times and was a successful four-time governor of Maine after the war. He was given the honor of presiding over the surrender ceremony of Robert E. Lee's army at Appomattox Courthouse. Chamberlain, who was a very idealistic and honorable person, made it a point to not humiliate the defeated Confederate soldiers during the ceremony. Chamberlain risked his life and was wounded six times during the Civil War. He almost died after being shot at the Second Battle of Petersburg and at Quaker Road. Chamberlain died in 1914 at age eighty-five of complications from the gunshot in Petersburg. And he was a fierce advocate of abolishing slavery from the beginning.

Chamberlain came as close to death as possible after being shot in the hip and groin at the Second Battle of Petersburg in 1864. After being struck by the bullet, he withdrew his sword and stuck it into the ground to stay upright and rally his retreating soldiers. The "Lion of the Round Top" stood for several minutes until he fainted due to the loss of blood. The division's surgeon predicted Chamberlain would not survive. Chamberlain's incorrectly recorded death was even reported in Maine newspapers, prompting Ulysses Grant to award Chamberlain a battlefield promotion to the rank of brigadier general. With his usual tenacity and willpower and support from his brother Thomas, Joshua was back in command of his brigade in November of 1864. His wife Fanny begged him to resign. He had nothing to prove. But the father of three surviving children continued to lead and inspire both his men and even Confederates. During Grant's final push against Lee at Quaker Road, Chamberlain was again shot, this time in the chest. His own men and even the Confederates were awestruck. Even the enemy cheered his determination to continue to lead his men. His incredible valor helped his men rally to victory. On this occasion, it appeared he would lose an arm to amputation, but again the Bowdoin professor defied the odds and recovered.

Chamberlain served in a total of twenty battles during the Civil War. He was cited for bravery four times, was awarded the Congressional Medal of Honor, had six horses shot from under him, and was wounded six times. He underwent surgery six times after the war to heal the wound from Petersburg, which inserted a primitive form of catheter that Chamberlain would have to wear the rest of his life. He also suffered other complications from the unhealed wound such as fevers and inflammations. Chamberlain endured pain for the rest of his life. He defeated his Democratic rivals by wide margins (double digits and even more than twenty points) in four successive elections to serve as Maine's governor (1866-69). The term for governor of Maine was only one year at the time. He served his alma mater, Bowdoin College, as its president after retiring from politics. He successfully resolved a violent 12-day dispute in 1880 as to the victor of an election to be Maine's governor that included threats to kill him and armed men taking over the State House in Augusta.

Joshua Lawrence Chamberlain declined an offer to run for the US Senate because both sides were trying to bribe him. He worked as an attorney in New York City and traveled in the West to work on railroad work and public improvements. With the outbreak of the Spanish-American War, he volunteered as an officer, but was turned down because he was seventy years old. He called this rejection the most disappointing of his life. Despite his ongoing pain, he continued to visit Gettysburg until shortly before his death in 1914 to deliver speeches. He is considered the last Civil War veteran to have died from an injury sustained during the conflict. He did not receive the Congressional Medal of Honor until 1893. The citation partly reads: "Daring heroism and great tenacity in holding his position on the Little Round Top against repeated assaults and carrying the advance position on the Great Round Top". A town in Bristol, Maine, bears his name, as well as a bridge in his home state.

MF: Enough about Chamberlain. What about Special Counsel Robert Mueller's investigation into Russia?

AM: As usual, Robert Mueller is running a tight ship. But the media have reported that his team has been interviewing former National Security Adviser Michael Flynn and will continue to do so through the end of the week of November 13th. The former lieutenant general can already be accused (there is plenty of evidence) of failing to register as an agent of a foreign government, which is a felony. He did extensive consulting work for both Russia and Turkey and failed to disclose this fact as well as the amounts he was paid. There are now allegations that Flynn planned to have Fetullah Gulen extradited to Turkey as a *quid pro quo* or as part of his work for the Turkish government. This would be a more serious act if proven guilty. And Flynn's son also has legal exposure.

Those cheering for Trump's downfall are speculating that Flynn has not been indicted by the Special Counsel yet (as Manafort and Rick Gates have) because he might be cooperating with Mueller's team. A former Mueller colleague was quoted in the media as describing how Mueller is an ace at flipping persons who already have legal liability and potentially face charges to obtain even more damaging accusations about others in the Trump administration. This former Mueller colleague predicted that before the investigation is wrapped up, people will be running to the Special Counsel's office to seek deals.

MF: Well, I need to know more about what is going on in the US and the world.

AM: Settle down, Milton. You are beginning to sound as demanding as many of my bosses or my late father, for that matter. What about what is happening to me?

MF: Any progress on the infrastructure package that will improve this situation in America?

AM: Not in the rest of 2017 and I doubt it will happen before the mid-terms. The Republicans' focus right now is on tax reform. And approving any major legislation has been elusive since Donald Trump came to office a year ago.

MF: Do not be unfair. The Dow Jones is up 28% since Trump defeated Hillary in November of 2016. The NASDAQ has climbed from 5300 to over 6700. The Russell 2000, which encompasses companies with a smaller capitalization, has risen 9% in the year to date.

AM: Yes, but there is exuberance in these financial markets.

MF: It is not irrational. GDP grew at more than a 3% rate in the second and third quarters of 2017. Unemployment stands at a 17-year low of 4.1%. In the month of October of 2017, 266,000 jobs were created.

Another of my heroes from the Civil War is General Winfield Scott Hancock. After an illustrious military career, he was the Democratic presidential candidate in 1880. The Republicans nominated James A. Garfield, a congressman from Ohio and a skillful politician. Hancock and the Democrats expected to carry the South but needed to add a few of the northern states to their total to win the election. The practical differences between the parties were few, and the Republicans were reluctant to personally attack Hancock because of his heroism during the Civil War.

The one policy difference the Republicans were able to exploit was a statement in the Democratic platform endorsing "a tariff for revenue only." Garfield's campaigners used this statement to paint the Democrats as unsympathetic to the plight of industrial laborers, a group that would benefit by a high protective tariff. The tariff issue diminished Democratic support in industrialized Northern states, which were essential in establishing a Democratic majority. In the end, the Democrats and Hancock failed to carry any of the Northern states they had targeted, with the exception of New Jersey. Hancock lost the election to Garfield. James Garfield polled only 39,213 more votes than Hancock. The final popular vote was 4,453,295 for Garfield and 4,414,082 for Hancock. The electoral count, however, had a much larger spread: Garfield obtained 214 electoral votes and Hancock 155. There are similarities between Winfield Scott Hancock and Hillary Clinton: both are/were Democrats who lost the industrial northern states to a Republican, Garfield in Hancock's case and Trump's in Hillary's case.

Next July will mark the 155th anniversary of the battle of Gettysburg. At a time when many politicians seek to deepen divisions in democratic countries, it is worth listening to the inspirational and unifying speech by Civil War hero Joshua Chamberlain: "they (Union soldiers) wage a war unlike any other, meant to set other people (slaves) free, and to uphold the idea that we all have value, regardless of origin or family lineage, and that in the end we must fight for each other".

After the trip to Ecuador during February of 2018, I had to brief Milton Friedman on the latest political, economic and business developments.

AM: Well, Milton. You were finally proven right. With many developed economies growing at healthy clips and with full employment, inflation has begun to creep up. That has prompted the Federal Reserve to announce that it will hike interest rates at least three times in 2018 and another three times in 2019. As markets realized that the era of ultra-low interest rates is coming to an end, the Dow Jones suffered one of its worst single-day losses on February 2nd, 2018. All of the stock markets' gains in 2018 were wiped out in one day. In the following days, volatility was extremely high.

You should also know that President Trump announced that he has accepted an invitation by North Korea's dictator, Kim Jon Un, to hold a summit meeting by the month of May. South Korean president Moon Jae-in had managed a rapprochement with North Korea during the Winter Olympics, which were held in South Korea. They produced high-level meetings between a North Korean delegation which included Kim's sister and the head of state, and the South Koreans. The two Koreas also marched together in the opening ceremony of the Olympic Games. Vice President Mike Pence and Ivanka Trump attended the Games, but they did not hold face-to-face meetings with the North Koreans.

After the Olympic Games were over on February 25th, 2018, Seoul announced that president Moon Jae-in would meet with Kim Jong Un. There have been summits between South Korean presidents and the North's dictator (Kim Jong Un or his late father, Kim Jong II) on three occasions in the past. But they are extraordinary, considering that the two countries are still technically at war and that the North has been firing missiles and conducting nuclear threats at an accelerated pace – among other hostile actions – in the past few months. The unanimous reaction to President Trump's acceptance of a meeting with Kim Jong Un has been that diplomacy and talking is better than trading insults and threatening war. But the president may not be in a position to negotiate anything of substance within two months. And accepting the first-ever summit between a sitting US president and a North Korean leader is a propaganda coup for Pyongyang, which has tried very hard for decades to achieve recognition from the US. The North Koreans have always wanted to negotiate directly (and only) with a US administration and drive a wedge between the US and its allies in the region – namely South Korea and Japan.

Chapter 14: The Kennedys and President Trump's first tariffs

I have read numerous books about the Kennedys, visited Arlington National Cemetery dozens of times, and done research about them for my own books, articles and other work. I therefore believed there was not much of great substance for me to find out about the main characters of the greatest American political dynasty -- Joseph Kennedy Sr., Rose Fitzgerald, Joseph Jr, John F. Kennedy, Bobby (RFK) and Ted.

CNN's documentary series *The Kennedys* proved me wrong. I learned a lot. The CNN documentary series pays particular attention to the relationships between the main male characters – and extends it to the eldest daughters, Kathleen and Rosemary, as well as to the spouses and children of John F. Kennedy, RFK and Ted.

Before *The Kennedys* aired in March and April of 2017, I was well aware of the fact that Joseph Kennedy was tremendously ambitious and, after making a fortune on Wall Street in the 1920s, was appointed as the US's Ambassador to the United Kingdom by president Franklin D. Roosevelt. At that point, Joseph Kennedy was among the twenty richest men in America. He had his sights set on the White House. But in failing to recognize the inherent evil in Adolf Hitler, he sowed the seeds of his downfall. Joseph Kennedy forcefully advocated for a negotiation with the Nazi leader. Hitler attacked Poland on September 1st, 1939, and the UK and France declared war against Germany. Yet Joseph Kennedy continued to publicly call for negotiations with Germany and asserted that the UK would not withstand an invasion by the Nazis. Joseph had already sent all of his family home. The same media that had welcomed him to London with much fanfare a few years earlier and fawned over his adorable family now blasted him as a defeatist. Roosevelt had not option other than to recall Kennedy and dismiss him.

With his personal presidential aspirations crushed, Joseph transferred them to his eldest son, Joseph Jr. Tragically, Joseph Jr. was killed when the aircraft he was piloting crashed in the British Channel during a test in 1944. John F. Kennedy was the next in line. But unlike his older brother, JFK was a scrawny young man with a deadly affliction: Addison's disease. This ailment cripples the immune system. JFK thus suffered from numerous health problems in his short life: malaria, chronic colds and terrible back pain.

I did not imagine to what extent Joseph Sr. went to make sure JFK would fulfil his own dream of becoming president of the US. John F. Kennedy (Jack) was a womanizer who felt his father's pressure very intensely after Joseph Jr. was killed in World War II. Joseph made sure that JFK would be elected to Congress by paying off an older congressman's debt so he would retire. His second son was thus able to win the 11th district of Massachusetts. Joseph also ensured that the PT Boat disaster in the Pacific would not result in a court martial. Technically, JFK was in command and during a moonless night he did not see the Japanese destroyer that split the PT Boat in half. JFK did of course rally his surviving men in the water and, surrounded by fire, urged them to swim to escape the Japanese. He dragged a wounded crew member who was much heavier than him by his teeth and swam for several hours until they reached an island that was controlled by the Japanese, in the Solomon Islands. With the aid of local inhabitants, JFK sent a message using a coconut and he and the surviving crew members were rescued. There was no court martial. In fact, Joseph Kennedy deployed his connections and money to make sure JFK was portrayed as a great hero. A movie about the episode was produced, as well as a magazine article. JFK did start to come into his own during the 1950s. His book *Profiles in Courage* describing the leadership of other Americans earned him the Pulitzer Prize in 1957. At that point he was the junior senator from Massachusetts.

MF: I have heard enough about the Kennedys, and your disillusionment due to the fact that they were such a close-knit family with ample financial resources. I was around during JFK's presidency. That is when I began to roll back Keynesian policies. In 1962, during JFK's presidency, my book *Capitalism and Freedom* was published. In the book, I advocated a volunteer military, freely floating exchange rates, abolition of medical licenses, a negative income tax, and school vouchers. How are the markets doing?

AM: Well, Milton, remember that JFK cut taxes, so you should like him somewhat, if only for that reason. I watch the Kennedy documentary series on CNN and another on the Papacy in order to not let the dreadful performance of the stock market get to me. All of the increase so far in 2018 in the stock market in the US and most countries has been wiped out completely because of a combination of Trump's tariff announcements and the expectation of several interest rate hikes in 2018, which the Federal Reserve has warned investors about.

Milton, you have a lot of prestige. You have to convince the president that he needs to scrap the $15 billion in tariffs that he has announced will be applied on Chinese robotics, biopharmacy and some machinery. The US has an annual trade deficit of $385 billion with China, which means that the tariffs only amount to 3.8% of the Chinese trade surplus. There is a two-month period to review the proposed tariffs until they go into effect. The Chinese have already announced that they will target $3 billion worth of US exports to China, mainly fruits, soya, wine, steel pipes and recycled aluminum by slapping a 25% tariff on these products, if the US tariffs do indeed go into effect.

MF: This is a horrible idea! Who came up with it?

AM: Well, the president campaigned on the pledge to reverse large trade deficits with several countries and get tough on China. His Secretary of Commerce, Wilbur Ross, and his Trade and Industry Advisor, Peter Navarro, were able to convince Trump to disregard the opposition to the tariffs expressed by the so-called globalists (advocates of free trade) in the White House and cabinet, namely the Director of the National Economic Council, Gary Cohn, and the Treasury Secretary, Steven Mnuchin. Cohn resigned the day that Trump announced the 25% tariff on imported steel and 10% on imported aluminium. Mnuchin is staying, but Ross and Navarro have been appearing on television to explain how this so-called modest tariff will hardly impact the prices that Americans pay for Chinese imports. Ross explained that most cars have a ton of steel -- $700 -- whose increase would add more than $150 to the price of a mid-range $35,000 car. I am not sure all Americans would consider this amount to be small, as Ross described it.

MF: How did the markets react?

AM: The tariffs on China were announced on March 22nd, a Thursday. The Dow Jones plunged more than 1000 points between Thursday and Friday and dropped 1400 points in that week.

MF: But the tariffs amount to only 3.8% of China's trade surplus with the US!

AM: Yes, and annual bilateral trade between the US and China is worth $648 billion. China is the US's third export market after Canada and Mexico. Almost one million jobs depend on US exports of goods and services to China, and the US has a small surplus in trade in services with China. But the markets had already been caught by surprise with the announcement on the steel and aluminum tariffs, which prompted another steep sell-off. Moreover, the excellent job reports have spooked investors, who know that the Federal Reserve will increase interest rates at least three times in 2018 and in 2019.

The Trump administration also lodged a formal complaint against China before the World Trade Organization (WTO) regarding the alleged theft of intellectual property. Some analysts speculate that Beijing may be willing to make some concessions to prevent a trade war. Some Chinese authorities have hinted at the possibility of diminishing tariffs on US vehicle imports and opening up the financial sector to US institutions. The Trump administration would have more credibility in pursuing its case against China at the WTO if it did not continue to hold up the naming of judges to the WTO's Appellate Body, which examines cases after an initial verdict has been rendered if any of the parties (countries) in the dispute decide to appeal.

I do agree with the Trump administration with regards to the unfairness of China's IP and technological transfer policies. Many Western companies that invest and operate in China are forced to transfer their technology to the Chinese company they partner with. In fact, it is a requirement if a foreign company pursues a joint partnership with a Chinese one. The Chinese companies then turn over the technology to the government. This is the reason that in the past years both presidents Barack Obama and Donald Trump have vetoed investments of Chinese tech giants in US companies. China unabashedly has declared that it seeks global dominance in strategic sectors. Given these practices, the US has to protect itself.

With regards to investments in the US and deals with US companies, the Committee on Foreign Investment in the United States (CFIUS) is an inter-agency process that makes recommendations to the president as to whether the acquisition of a US company or a foreign investment threatens US national security. Chaired by the Treasury Secretary, CFIUS involves input from sixteen US federal government departments and agencies, including the State Department, the Defense Department, the Commerce Department and the Department of Homeland Security. The president has the final word when it comes to approving a deal or investment.

Some deals in the technology sector which have been quashed on the basis of CFIUS recommendations in recent years are purchases by the Chinese telecommunications giants Huawei and ZTE, Broadcom's merger with Qualcomm, a Chinese consortium's (including the giant Tencent) bid for European mapping company NV Here, the acquisition of Lattice Semiconductor Inc. by the Chinese-backed private equity group Canyon Bridge and Barack Obama's veto of a Chinese company's purchase of the German semiconductor-equipment supplier Aixtron SE.[16]

The US government memo advocating a government-built 5G mobile wireless network explicitly labeled Huawei a strategic threat. All these vetoes have the common denominator of trying to prevent China from beating the US in the race to develop 5G and other technologies such as self-driving cars. NV Here is owned by BMW, Volkswagen's Audi unit, Daimler and Intel. NH Here is developing 3D maps for driverless cars and location-based services used by logistics and online companies.

On another note, the monthly job numbers in the US continue to be excellent. The Federal Reserve hiked interest rates as expected by 25 basis points. It also revised its forecast for US GDP growth in 2018 to 2.7%. The new benchmark funds rate is now at a target of 1.5 to 1.75%. This was the sixth rise since the policymaking Federal Open Market Committee began to increase rates in December 2015. The Federal Reserve's forecast remains just 1.9% for both core and headline inflation in 2018. For 2019, the Fed prediction for core personal consumption expenditures was raised slightly to 2.1% from 2%. The US's central bank also forecast that

---

¹⁶ "Red Hot", *The Economist*. March 31st, 2018, page 65.

unemployment would dip to 3.8% by the end of 2018. The Fed believes in the Phillips curve, which indicates that as unemployment diminishes inflation rises.

Although president Trump did not name you to head the Fed as I had hoped, new Fed chairman Jerome Powell and his colleagues will continue to try to raise rates without stifling growth, while also keeping inflation in check. The markets were alarmed when hourly earnings rose to a recovery-high 2.9% in January of 2018, partly sparking the massive sell-off on Wall Street on February 2nd. Hourly earnings climbed by 2.6% in February.

MF: Great. It is reassuring to hear Powell and the other governors are committed to containing inflation and believe in the Phillips curve and my theories. The Fed is raising rates and GDP growth is not slowing! But unemployment needs to rise. Otherwise inflation will soar. That is what my theories predicted. I described a "natural" rate of unemployment, below which inflation inevitably rises. As you should know, William Phillips was an economist from New Zealand who spent his academic career at the London School of Economics. His main contribution to macroeconomics was the Phillips curve, which stipulates that increased employment (or diminishing unemployment) inevitably result in a higher rate of wage hikes. Phillips came up with his curve in 1958. I was the one who in 1967 took the additional step of linking higher employment to rising inflation and therefore popularized the Phillips curve. In 1968, I stated that the Phillips curve was only valid in the short run, and that in the long run inflationary policies do not lead to lower unemployment. I then correctly predicted that in the 1973-75 recession both inflation and unemployment would climb, a phenomenon named stagflation, which I coined.

AM: Well, for some time the US and other developed economies with full employment or very low unemployment and strong growth were showing no signs of an uptick in inflation, despite rises in wages. Hence, some had begun to question the Phillips curve and your theories. Maybe the Phillips curve was wrong, some argued, mainly because automation and technology allow companies to replace workers with machines, and the labor participation rate is still below its historical average. But technology can only go so far. Workers have managed to elicit higher wages, and combined with strong monthly job reports, investors realized that the bull market is nearing its end, as higher interest rates are inevitable.

MF: Is there any evidence that Trump's negotiation tactics on trade are working?

AM: Yes, with South Korea. It is the first real and tangible success. The US and South Korea have agreed on a renegotiation of the US-South Korea Free Trade Agreement that Trump had heavily criticized. The agreement exempts South Korea from the tariff on steel and aluminium. But it sets a quota for exports of steel to the US at 70% of South Korea's average annual exports in 2015-2017, which translates into 2.68 million tons of steel that will be tariff-free. But South Korea will not be able to export steel to the US in excess of that amount. The US also obtains better access for its vehicles to the South Korean market. South Korea is the third-largest steel exporter to the United States and the world's top importer of Chinese steel, which prompted concerns it enabled China to export its excess capacity to the rest of the world, thereby depressing the international price for steel.

The renegotiated US-South Korea trade deal is a pretty reasonable agreement, as the quota is set at 70% of South Korea's recent level of exports. It does violate the spirit of WTO rules, which seeks to eliminate quotas, and to do so by replacing them with tariffs, which are a less harmful trade barrier. The new US-South Korea FTA does the opposite, namely convert tariffs into a quota.

On another front, the Trump administration in a coordinated action with many of our NATO and EU allies – as well as Australia and Ukraine – ordered the expulsion of more than one hundred Russian diplomats from US territory along with the closure of the Russian consulate in Seattle. There is now no chance of a US-Russia rapprochement. We need to push back against Russia on social media and the wealth of the Kremlin-backed oligarchs and businessmen who live in the US and the EU. In my view, Putin miscalculated. He thought he had figured out Trump and "owned" him because he could leak more embarrassing details about his past business deals in Russia or the 2016 campaign. But Trump allegedly told a source that he would look forward to impeachment. He would obviously only want it if he thought it would not succeed. President Trump has many flaws, but he is not a coward, in the back-handed way that Putin and others are. Putin may have been trying to drive a wedge between the UK and US at the time of the Brexit negotiations, or between the UK and the EU, but it backfired in either case.

The attempt to poison Sergei Skripal was a Kremlin-ordered assassination attempt against a British citizen and his daughter in a park in Salisbury, which also injured a policeman. The former Russian spy and his daughter are fighting for their lives in the hospital. The park had to be cordoned off because of the threat to the public from the nerve agent used by Russian spooks. Theresa May finally took charge of a bad situation. Corbyn, the neo-Marxist Labor leader, blundered badly. The nerve agent used to try to kill Skripal and his daughter is only manufactured in Russia.

Russia has responded to the expulsion of more than one hundred of its diplomats from more than two dozen countries by retaliating against the nations that kicked out their officials. Putin has also indirectly threatened the US by test-firing a new generation ICBM that can fly over the North or South Pole and strike the US even faster than the traditional ICBMs Russia still has in its arsenal. Putin underscored that the new missile -- nicknamed Satan 2 by the West -- can reach any part of the US. The Satan 2 has a range of 6800 miles and a supersonic speed of 16,000 miles per hour. In the wake of the biggest expulsion of Russian diplomats ever, Russia has carried out tit-for-tat expulsions and threatened to carry out more. Moreover, the Kremlin has announced it will sue the US because of the closure of its Consulate in Seattle and test-fired the Satan 2.

Donald Trump wanted to be Putin's friend and ally. The way things are unfolding, we are quickly headed in the opposite direction. Some analysts talk about a descent into a new Cold War. If Russia continues to expel more diplomats from so many countries, it will just make it harder to have the appropriate personnel and channels of communications to improve ties and foster cooperation between Russia and the West in the fight against terrorism and other global scourges.

Vladimir Putin might have miscalculated in trying to kill Skripal with a nerve agent in Salisbury. The response by more than two dozen countries which expelled Russian diplomats in solidarity with the United Kingdom is a hopeful sign that the Russian president will get the message that he can no longer divide and conquer, at least when dealing with Western countries. Putin needs to continue to saber-rattle and thump his chest to show Russians he is still the strong czar they need. But so much provocation by the former KGB lieutenant colonel (Putin) is somewhat puzzling. He has just won another term as president after silencing or jailing his critics and opposition politicians, allowing him to stay in power indefinitely. He is in good health and the Russian economy is growing at a slow rate after years of recession. He faces no internal opposition after his repeated crackdowns and jailing of opposition leaders, civil society activists and journalists. The key is whether Putin will calm down and not escalate the confrontation after Russia expels more diplomats.

On the trade front, China is floating possible compensation for the US for its technology-transfer practices and lack of enforcement of intellectual property rights but also underscoring it may retaliate. Some speculate that China will seek to placate Trump by lowering tariffs on car imports, liberalizing its financial sector and opening it up to US companies. But Trump's gambit could backfire if Beijing calls his bluff and decides to retaliate with more than the token measures it has announced so far.

The West faces China's attempt at economic domination and a Russian president bent on restoring his country to the status it had during the Cold War. Let us hope Western politicians, diplomats, business leaders, civil society and the media do not lose sight of this worrying menace for democracy and free markets.

On April 14th, Milton was on his way from Chicago to Florida. He had a layover in Washington, D.C. and managed to arrange his flights so we could briefly meet and I could update him on the latest news.

AM: Milton, you should know that yesterday, Friday the 13th of April, British, French and US warships and bombers carried out precision strikes against Syrian targets related to its R&D, stockpiling and production of chemical weapons. This measure was in response to Bashar al-Assad's decision to once again gas his own people, specifically in the rebel-controlled town of Douma east of Damascus. The heinous chemical attack involved the use of chlorine, and possibly sarin.

Let us pray for the brave British, French and US pilots and personnel who are involved in the punitive strikes against Bashar al-Assad's repeated use of chemical weapons against his own population. Since 2011, more than 400,000 people (possibly half a million) have been killed in the Syrian civil war, and about half (12 out of 23 million) of Syria's pre-2011 population is either living in exile in Turkey, Lebanon, Jordan or Europe, or internally displaced.

Most of the 400,000 dead and refugees are the result of the brutal repression unleashed by Assad and his Iranian and Hezbollah allies. Assad routinely orders his air force to drop barrel bombs on civilians who live in rebel-held parts of Syria. Assad has undoubtedly committed war crimes. Russia was a guarantor of the 2013 agreement whereby Assad committed to giving up all of his chemical weapons stockpile, and Putin has obviously condoned the Douma chemical attack, as well as the one last year.

The Organization for the Prohibition of Chemical Weapons has 192 signatories, which encompass 98% of the world's population. After World War I, chemical weapons were banned. One million people were killed or wounded in World War I due to chemical weapons. Let us also pray for the long-suffering Syrian people, who have endured arguably the worst humanitarian catastrophe since World War II. And let us also pray for the brave reporters who are covering the events on the ground.

While there can be cynicism about whether these strikes will change the military situation on the ground, the West and the United States could not have stood by and looked on after so many uses of nerve agents and use of chlorine and sarin by Bashar al-Assad. On April 4th, as the UN concluded in a report, at least 74 Syrians were killed and 557 were injured when Al-Assad employed sarin gas against his own people in Douma. And there are reports that Assad has gassed more people since April 2017.

The West can only do so much. Turkey, which has admittedly paid a high price in accepting more than 1 million refugees from Syria, Saudi Arabia, the United Arab Emirates and other Gulf countries need to ramp up their financial, logistical and military support for the moderate opposition to Assad. Saudi Arabia and the Gulf nations' interests are much more at stake in Syria than in Yemen. And Saudi Arabia and other Gulf countries should take in Syrian refugees, something they have not done. The slaughter in Syria since 2011 cannot go on. It will eventually destabilize the region to a greater extent. Diplomacy should be undertaken after the strikes.

MF: How is populism faring?

AM: Donald Trump's election and Brexit in 2016 created the narrative that the punished middle and lower classes would bring to power Marine Le Pen and the extremist Geert Wilders in the Netherlands. That prediction was proven wrong by the overwhelming victory of Emmanuel Macron and the Dutch moderate parties. The growth forecast for the international economy is 3.9% for 2018. For the first time since the international financial crisis of 2007-08, developed as well as emerging and developing countries achieved high rates of GDP growth in 2017. Below this apparent stability, dangerous trends point to an end of the cycle.

Key economies such as Brazil, Mexico and Colombia may be led by populists by the end of the year[17]. Andres Manuel López Obrador will not show Peña Nieto's containment in the face of the forced renegotiation of NAFTA when he will probably win Mexico's presidential election in July. Right-wing extremist Jair Bolsonaro -- dubbed the Trump of the Tropics -- may be the winner of the Brazilian presidential elections in October. A former leader of the Colombian M-19 leftist rebel group leads the polls of the presidential elections in the largest US ally in South America. And in June, Doug Ford, who boasts of being a populist, can become premier of Ontario.

It still seems unlikely that Trump's cabinet will allow him to open more trade confrontation fronts than those already unleashed against China, NAFTA and to a lesser extent the EU. Instead of working with Washington to make sure that through the World Trade Organization (WTO) and in a reasonable manner China is forced to end its practices of forced technology transfers and intellectual property theft, the EU Trade Commissioner has no choice but to prepare the list of American products (Levi's jeans, Harley-Davidson motorcycles, bourbon whiskey) that will pay higher tariffs if Trump does not maintain the EU exemption from tariff increases on steel and aluminum on June 1st.

President Obama was working with the EU and through the WTO to prevent Chinese technology companies from controlling Western manufacturers of semiconductors and other components of the digital revolution. The Trump administration has also imposed severe limitations on Chinese technology companies, for example by banning the sale of components to the Chinese smartphone manufacturer ZTE. To the dangerous cocktail of populism and protectionism we can add the end of the era of low interest rates, which will wreak havoc especially in countries with high levels of public and private debt.

Fortunately, the much-resented German austerity in the management of the eurozone crisis means that not only the eurozone hard core, but also Spain (1.25%) and Portugal (1.63%) pay

---

[17] In Colombia, the populist candidate did not win the presidential elections. In the second round, Iván Duque Márquez was elected president. He belongs to the political party founded by former president Alvaro Uribe, who successfully crushed the FARC guerrillas during his term in office. Uribe subsequently fell out with his successor, Juan Manuel Santos, who negotiated a treaty ending the decades-long war between the FARC and the Colombian government. The agreement was initially rejected in a referendum but later adopted after amendments were made. Nonetheless, Uribe, president-elect Duque and a considerable percentage of the Colombian population continue to oppose key provisions of the accord, especially the lack of punishment for FARC leaders and members who committed crimes and their participation in the political process. Duque is unlikely to tinker with the free-market policies pursued under Uribe and Santos but will probably modify parts of the agreement with the FARC.

significantly less than the US (3%) to sell their 10-year bonds. Stock market declines were inevitable because central banks were able to keep interest rates at very low levels to promote growth and inflation remained subdued. If Trump suspends the agreement with Iran, it will exacerbate the rise in oil prices that Saudi Arabia is achieving with production cuts. The European Union has to import 54% of its energy. Thanks to the shale oil and gas revolution, the US has become the world's leading combined producer of shale oil and gas, exported natural gas in 2017 for the first time in 60 years, and reduced the share of energy in its trade deficit to 10%.

MF: Tell me how big tech companies are doing? Will they be regulated?

AM: The valuation of US technology giants (Facebook, Amazon, Netflix, Google, the so-called FANGs) is vulnerable to regulation. Since 2016, the FANGs have contributed 20% of the increase of the S&P 500. It is impossible to rigorously predict the evolution of so many political, economic and trade variables. The philosopher Popper warned that "tribal spirits" foster a desire for a world without personal responsibility and is the source of nationalism and religious fanaticism. The EU must continue to protect the only rule book of the international community that has delivered so much prosperity and peace over the past 60 years: economic integration, multilateral institutions and reasonable trade agreements. The EU ranks first in the world as the leading trading partner of 59 countries. Assured by this fact, the Commission and the European Court of Justice must apply the rulebook both internally with governments such as that of Poland and Hungary against the threats posed by a multipolar world.

MF: Update me on the Mueller probe.

AM: Mueller has announced that he will issue a subpoena if Trump does not voluntarily sit down to answer some of his 49 questions. Trump's attorneys will never accede to a voluntary interview. Trump has a penchant for lying or exaggerating and would incriminate himself. Taking the Vth amendment is an option. CNN's senior legal analyst and former federal prosecutor Jeffrey Toobin insists that Trump will opt for taking the Vth amendment. Others stress that taking the Vth would be politically very harmful. Taking the Vth legally is not a recognition of guilt. But for ordinary people it smacks of fear of being prosecuted for a crime.

The consensus is that Trump's new legal team -- the Raskins, Giuliani and one of Bill Clinton's impeachment attorneys -- will appeal a subpoena to testify from Mueller all the way to the Supreme Court, a process which could take up to a year and take us beyond the November 2018 mid-terms.

Over 100 million Uber drivers have assaulted, harassed and even kidnapped passengers in the past years. Uber settled all of these cases by paying the victims in exchange for non-disclosure agreements. This is a disgrace. CNN's excellent investigative reporting team uncovered the case and first reported it on May 1st. I cannot imagine how anybody can still defend this lousy idea of putting cab drivers out of work by indulging in people's desire to be gratified instantaneously with a non-professional driver. Uber has had many scandals and resignations. But there was no reporting about the scandal today. I do not know if some people in high places are pressuring the media to stop the reporting. This would also be revolting as CNN pursues cases that deliver high ratings.

In 2015, I decided to rank the world's top twenty economies by volume of GDP according to four metrics. I labeled them the TIDE challenges: "T" stands for technological competitiveness, "I" for inequality, "D" for demographics/ageing population and "E" for energy security. There are obviously many macroeconomic and microeconomic parameters that researchers, international institutions and governments employ to determine how an economy is doing and might perform in the future. Any choice of parameters, therefore, is bound to be somewhat arbitrary and incomplete. But I nonetheless chose four metrics that I believe -- and many analysts might concur – certainly shape a country's economy and determine its ability to succeed in the medium to long term. The first one is competitiveness, the second inequality, the third ageing of its population and the fourth energy security.

Some analysts might object that other metrics are just as important, for example productivity, the quality of infrastructure or the population's education level. But nobody can argue that the four I chose *do* matter. Moreover, a country's competitiveness as measured by the very prestigious World Economic Forum's (WEF) Global Competitiveness Index (GCI) is itself determined by many categories, from education or infrastructure to the strength of institutions. In terms of measuring a country's competitiveness, the WEF's GCI is the current gold standard.

Given the rise of populism and nationalist economic policies, the increase in inequality is at the top of policymakers' concerns. Inequality has risen both between and within countries. The global financial crisis and the slow recovery have contributed to the jump in inequality. The universal metric for measuring a country's inequality is the Gini coefficient. The third variable I have measured is the ageing of a country's population. As many countries' populations have aged, their ability to continue to finance generous welfare states is being jeopardized. Many advanced and some emerging countries have fertility rates below 2.1, the level needed to replace the population if there is no net immigration.

Inward migration flows have slowed down this ageing problem, but engendered problems when natives feel overwhelmed by the arrival of people from different cultures and who practice different religions. Countries like Germany, Italy and Spain in Europe and Japan and South Korea in Asia all have fertility rates well below 2. How will future Japanese or Italians receive universal and free health care, reasonable pensions and free education if fewer people are working, life expectancy has climbed significantly and large segments of the population want to drastically restrict the arrival of more immigrants? In terms of energy security, I have resorted to the World Energy Council's Energy Security Index.

For each of these four metrics, I ranked the top twenty economies in the world by volume of nominal GDP. For example, the country with the highest Global Competitiveness Index from the World Economic Forum in 2017-2018 among the top twenty economies is the United States, with a GCI of 5.9[18]. It is thus given 25 points. The country with the second highest GCI (within the top twenty economies) is the Netherlands (5.7), which is therefore awarded 24 points, and so on. For inequality, the country with the least inequality (Gini coefficient closest to 0) receives 25 points. In this case, Germany is the top performer with a coefficient of .289, and hence receives 25

---

[18] The World Economic Forum's Global Competitiveness Index ranks almost 140 countries. The US's 1st place is in terms of its placement among the top twenty economies in the world by volume of nominal GDP.

points, the country with the second-best performance in terms of inequality obtains 24 points, and so on.

With regards to ageing and the fertility rate, the country that comes closest to having a fertility rate of 2.1 receives the 25 points, and so on. The same applies to energy security. The points from each category are tallied and therefore result in a final number of points for each country which reflects all four categories – competitiveness, inequality, ageing of its population and energy security (see tables below).

In 2015, in the research for my prior book, the United States ranked first in the composite index with 85 points. This makes sense. The US's fertility rate (1.8 in 2015) is higher than that of most developed countries. The world's only superpower boasts a highly competitive economy, has a reasonable degree of inequality and has dramatically reduced its energy dependence as it has become the world's top combined producer of oil and natural gas. The Netherlands, another competitive economy with even lower inequality and its own energy supplies (natural gas) finished second in 2015 with 80 points. Canada and the United Kingdom tied for third place with 79 points.

In the 2018 ranking, the Netherlands has overtaken the United States and finished first with 88 points, Germany second with 87, Canada third with 84 and the US and France tied for fourth with 81 points.

Below a pie chart with the top twenty economies' nominal GDP. The US still is far ahead of China, regardless of the methodology employed – GDP at Purchasing Power Parity or nominal GDP[19].

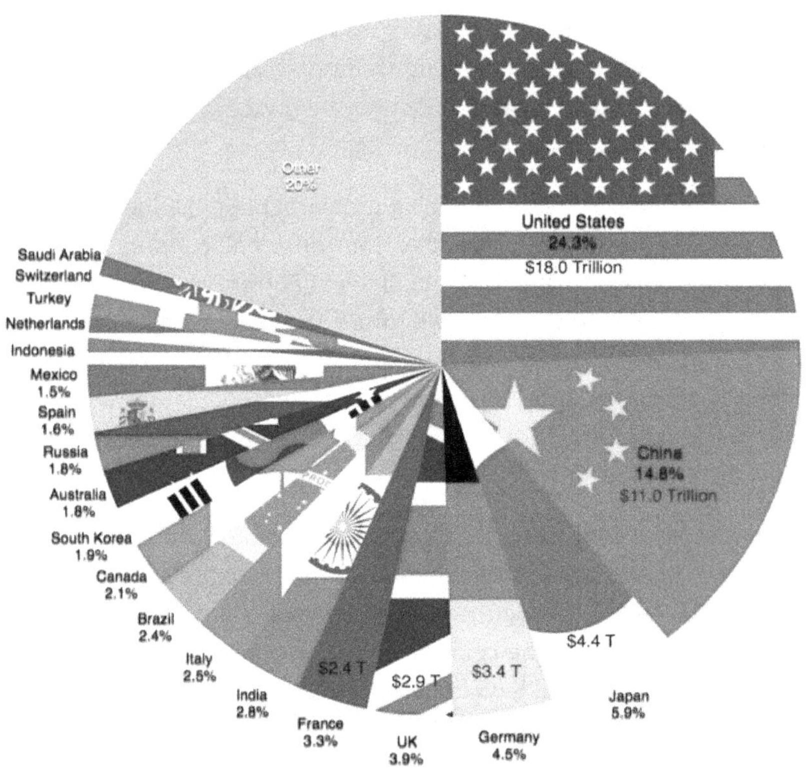

Rank 2015	T Points 2015	Rank 2018	T points 2018	GDP (nominal) IMF, 2017	COMPETITIVENESS WEF Global Competitiveness Index, 2017-2018 2017 GCI rank and score (maximum 7)	Ranking in top 19	best 25 Points[a]	INEQUALITY OECD, World Bank Gini coefficient	Ranking	Points
1	85	4	81	United States	2 (5.9)	1	25	0.39	14	12
10	58	10	58	China	27 (5.0)	10	16	0.421	16	10
9	60	6	67	Japan	9 (5.5)	5	21	0.33	7	19
5	74	2	87	Germany	5 (5.7)	3	23	0.289	1	25
6	72	4	81	France	22 (5.2)	8	18	0.297	2	24
3	79	6	74	United Kingdom	8 (5.5)	4	22	0.36	11	15
13	52	14	49	Brazil	80 (4.1)	19	7	0.547	18	8
9	60	6	67	Russia	38 (4.6)	14	12	0.376	12	14
14	48	7	66	Italy	43 (4.5)	16	10	0.326	6	20
15	45	12	53	India	40 (4.6)	15	11	0.339	9	17
3	79	3	84	Canada	14 (5.3)	6	20	0.313	5	21
4	78	5	80	Australia	21 (5.2)	7	19	0.337	8	18
8	63	8	64	Spain	34 (4.7)	12	14	0.347	10	16
9	60	15	47	Mexico	51 (4.4)	17	9	0.459	17	9
12	53	7	66	South Korea	26 (5.1)	9	17	0.295	3	23
7	71	9	63	Indonesia	36 (4.7)	13	13	0.381	13	13
11	54	13	50	Turkey	53 (4.4)	18	8	0.398	15	11
2	80	1	88	Netherlands	4 (5.7)	2	24	0.303	4	22
6	72	11	55	Saudi Arabia	30 (4.8)	11	15	0.459	17	9

Demographics and Energy Security

	Demographics/Ageing Population			Energy Security	World Energy Council's 2017 Ranking on Energy Security	
	Fertility rate (World Bank, 2015)	Points	Rank top 19	Energy security rank	Energy security among top 19	Points
United States	1.8	20	6	8	2	24
China	1.6	18	8	18	12	14
Japan	1.5	17	9	77	16	10
Germany	1.5	17	9	12	4	22
France	2	21	5	44	8	18
United Kingdom	1.8	20	6	26	9	17
Brazil	1.7	19	7	46	11	15
Russian Federation	1.8	20	6	2	5	21
Italy	1.4	16	10	17	6	20
India	2.4	24	2	76	15	11
Canada	1.6	18	8	4	1	25
Australia	1.8	20	6	37	3	23
Spain	1.3	15	11	20	7	19
Mexico	2.2	23	3	57	10	16
South Korea	1.2	14	12	64	14	12
Indonesia	2.4	24	2	59	13	13
Turkey	2.1	22	4	82	17	9
Netherlands	1.7	19	7	10	3	23
Saudi Arabia	2.6	25	1	31	10	16

China passed a law in 2016 to promote renewable energies. It will soon be able to produce enough electric batteries per year to power 1.5 million Tesla cars. In contrast, president Trump basically disavows climate change and wants to bring back ageing and polluting coal plants

Trump has approval ratings of over 60% in West Virginia, and over 50% in Wyoming and Kentucky. All three states have a long tradition of producing coal. Trump carried West Virginia by 40 points. He visited the states often and drew large crowds. The president is very proud of the fact that since he took office eight-hundred jobs have been created in coal mines that have reopened.

Donald Trump may be trying to resurrect or maintain certain sectors or companies on life support. These sectors will indeed become obsolete in the medium to long-term, and they are sometimes inefficient, uncompetitive and polluting. Their only advantage is that they preserve jobs in depressed economic areas and do not force workers into abandoning the labor force or attempting a professional reinvention at a relatively old age. But in the next few pages we will examine several cutting-edge technologies. They all hold out great potential and promise investors and consumers an almost fantastic world where people will be driven in self-driving cars, live in intelligent homes and be assisted in their daily lives, travel and work by dozens of devices seamlessly connected to the internet. The Internet of Things makes for some visionary stuff. We will also examine drones, on-demand wireless insurance and the prospects for the 5G mobile wireless internet network.

As we shall see, these technologies will certainly at some point deliver fat profits for companies and investors. But they also need to be regulated. There are national-security, equality, economic and other considerations that need to be factored in. China openly admits it seeks global dominance in strategic sectors. Many people cannot afford current technologies, let alone future ones. A lack of competition and regulation can turn certain technology sectors – in developed as well as developing countries -- into price-gouging and consumer-unfriendly environments where a few inefficient companies carve up the market. Telecommunications and the provision of Internet are among some of them. Technology is a great tool. But it should be deployed in a way that makes common and economic sense. Surveys show that more than 20% of people will not want to be in self-driving car, and a similar percentage will get dizzy when it tries to read or work while being chauffeured by a self-driving car. Does it not make more sense to use technology to improve traffic and relieve chronic congestion – which causes great inefficiencies and pollution – before moving on to self-driving cars?

Bill Peduto, the current mayor of Pittsburgh, rejects the appeal to coal and steel as nostalgic and not realistic. He ought to know. His father lived and worked in Pittsburgh all of his life. Coal was discovered in Pittsburgh before the US gained its independence from the UK. At one point during World War II, the city of Pittsburgh was manufacturing more steel than Nazi Germany, fascist Italy and Imperial Japan combined. It was the arsenal of democracy. But as coal mines aged and they lost competitiveness, the domestic demand for coal plummeted and Pittsburgh's unemployment rate reached 19%. In the 1970s, skeptics were writing the city off.

Even in the city's heyday, the city was described as "hell with a lid on" because coal and steel production generated a terrible cloud of smog. The lights had to be kept on during the day so residents could see through the pollution. Pittsburgh abandoned coal and steel production and consumers switched from coal to natural gas to power their heat furnaces. And Pittsburgh staged a renaissance on the back of high-tech companies, biomedicine, education and tourism. Its mayor and locals would want the US to return to the Paris climate change agreement.

<u>Drones</u>

The exceptional power of Artificial Intelligence, the cloud, big tech companies, robots and big data has to help drive down prices for products and services and increase competition for those in the lower classes. Let us take an example. Most lower-class people are not going to own a sophisticated drone. At most, they might purchase a small one as a toy. They probably do not see a great benefit in the exponential growth of drones. In fact, the skyrocketing number of drones presents dangers. They have and can affect airplanes taking off or landing, as well as other kinds of traditional air travel -- small planes or helicopters -- that first responders rely on. They also pose a national security threat. If foreign enemies can use Facebook and bots to influence our elections, they can surely deploy drones. According to the consultancy Gartner, 174,000 drones were sold worldwide in 2017 for commercial use, and 2.8 million to individual consumers. Richer people want them to take cool pictures, pull of stunts at outdoor events and other kinds of recreation. How can this benefit poorer people?

<u>On-demand insurance for cars and other vehicles and instruments</u>

Drones have to be insured if they fly at a certain altitude and exceed a certain size. There are already regulations in place to ensure that drones do not hurt people. I strongly believe that these regulations need to be tightened. Technology is always several steps ahead of regulators. There have already been accidents and many incidents involving drones. I am surprised to read that a British insurance company (Insure4drones) charges only $1000 per year to insure the DJI Phantom, a best-selling drone[20]. Progressive charges me more than that to insure my 2013 Honda Civic Si, and I am 49 and have never had an accident since I started driving at age eighteen. Progressive does allow me to install a Snapshot device which has lowered my monthly premiums to $114 because I have performed at an A+ level when monitored by the plug-in.

A start-up company named Flock will offer insurance to British commercial operators of drones on a flight-by-flight basis. According to the German insurance giant Allianz, costs will be only 5 British pounds per hour. Flock will be able to offer such low rates to insure commercial drones because it benefits from data generated by other tech companies. IBM's investment in The Weather Channel enables it to furnish very accurate weather forecasts[21]. A software company called Snowflake furnishes data about planes that are close to the drone. Flock's software also captures data about the drone, where it is flying, over which kind of terrain, etc. so it can build a risk profile. Flock's software then adds up all of the numbers and offers the drone operator a quote and tips on how to steer the drone more safely. Based on this data, Allianz generates a final insurance price.

This is apparently a win-win situation, right? Small companies like Flock and Snowflake expand, add more employees, and bigger ones like Allianz and IBM acquire more clients. But there is a catch. Humans are no longer needed to come up with a business plan that results in an insurance quote. That is the reason that most mainstream car-insurance companies in the US do not offer rates that vary too much given a certain car model and make, miles driven, driver and zip code. The existence of Geico, Progressive, Liberty, Allstate, Amica and other car-insurance companies in the US would seem to guarantee competition and lower rates. That is not the case. After you call them yet again after getting a letter in the mail, their employee on the phone will just insert

---

[20] "Real-time Insurance: Pay-per-risk", *The Economist*, September 23rd, 2017, p. 68.
[21] *Ibidem.*

the aforementioned data (plus driving record, average miles driven per year) into a computer that will produce an algorithm. That is why I do not waste my time any longer calling car insurers when they target me.

Therefore, when it comes to insuring commercial drones, Allianz will no longer need humans to write up the price. With all of the data gathered by the other tech companies, an algorithm completely replaces humans. We thus face a destruction of some jobs.

With the plethora of sensors available to companies, they can offer real-time insurance based on real-time risk. Verifly is competing with Flock to lure commercial drone operators in the United States[22] with the same kind of technology and data. But all of these fancy new products and services basically benefit the rich and upper middle-class. There is a company called Root, however, which purportedly offers car drivers insurance based on their behavior while driving. I want to check it out. Such tech companies can and should deliver benefits to those who simply drive a car. Tech types want to push things too far. Flock's chief executive asserts that in the future he wants to insure taxi rides and rolling delivery pods. I beg to differ. Let Flock prove that it can safely insure drone operators first. Cabs can already choose from a wide array of insurers, and they have correctly pushed back against Uber, given its lack of security and sexual harassment culture. Rolling delivery pods are taking jobs away from persons who deliver products to homes and offices. In sum, on-demand insurance is a great idea and can benefit the rich and upper middle-class with their Ubers, drones and automated delivery pods. But how about benefits for poorer people or the middle class?

<u>5G mobile wireless internet. Faster speeds but more need for antennae and fiber-optic cable</u>

Several countries and companies are competing to build the next generation of wireless mobile internet, 5G. To those who may not be tech enthusiasts, creating a new network when the existing one (4G) only reaches a limited percentage of the territory and the population might not seem fair or logical. But the fact that 4G does not work better cannot be attributed entirely to technology issues. In many countries, there is simply not enough competition among the providers of mobile technology, so the established companies can charge higher prices without improving their product. Regulators are also at fault, as they do not remove barriers to entry nor hold the established companies accountable for abusive practices and successful attempts to stifle competition and innovation.

A case in point is Comcast, an American giant which includes the large movie studio Universal, one of the big four US networks (NBC, and its sister channels MSNBC and CNBC), and the delivery of cable television, Internet and fixed telephony. No other company in America can compete with such an array of the physical infrastructure (towers, Comcast's outdated copper cables) necessary to transmit data, voice and cable and the content itself. Universal is one of the biggest movie studios in the world, so Comcast has a menu of thousands of on-demand for-pay movies. Comcast clearly abuses its dominant position, which its attorneys make sure to defend before the Federal Communications Commission.

Some of Comcast's unethical -- and possibly illegal -- practices include charging for the service ahead of time. Customers like myself pay for Comcast's service before it is actually delivered. I have complained about this practice for years. There are few companies that can get away with this, even in the services sector. Car-insurance companies do not bill for insurance to be provided the next month, for example. It is true that Comcast does not force its customers to be bound by yearly or time-related contracts. A customer can dump Comcast and switch to a competitor at

---

[22] *Ibidem.*

any time after returning the equipment (cable boxes, modem) which it rents from the communications giant. But Comcast has many ways to ensure that its clients do not get away with not paying their bills. For example, it charges late payment fees, and eventually disconnects the service if the client does not pay. The requirement to pay for the next month's or billing period's services is therefore unnecessary, unethical and should be illegal. In my case, as I have no family, whom would Comcast return the credit of an unused service if a car runs me over and kills me?

Moreover, when Comcast equipment or content malfunctions, it credits the customer in the future billing period. It therefore has the best – and for the consumer worst – of all worlds. Charging ahead of time for a service not rendered and crediting a customer in the future for a breach of its terms, failure to deliver the service or mishaps such as slow or no Internet, the loss of signal or the deletion of all of my recordings (this happened to me). I currently have two cable boxes and am paying $190 per month. But most months I wind up paying $230-260. I recently dropped the sports channels in my package, which supposedly should diminish my monthly payments. Calling Comcast is one of the most unpleasant features of my life. On October 30th, I had to put everything aside and engage in a tough conversation with a Comcast supervisor to seek to bring down my monthly payment – to no avail. No, eliminating the On-demand movie function for the second box (the one in my bedroom) is not possible. I do not need thousands of channels. Just the main cable news ones and the networks. Yet the supervisor claimed that their lowest package (with Internet) is $150 with taxes. I have not ditched Comcast because it does not bind me into a contract. As my long-term future in the US is not guaranteed (if I do not get citizenship), switching to Verizon, Direct TV or another competitor (which do require contracts) is unwise. Nonetheless, Comcast's abuses are real. Many people I interact with get their Internet and cable from other companies (sometimes two) and pay less, although it is true that they do not have access to the thousands of movies that Universal can offer nor the DVR recording function.

The movies are not free, however, and can even cost more than watching a film at a movie theater. I do not watch many movies and use a small fraction of Comcast's channels. Yet I am stuck with these outrageous bills. I told the supervisor on March 30th that another bill over $200 would prompt me to ditch Comcast.

Beyond my personal struggle with Comcast, there is no question that they highlight what happens when regulators do not force monopolies or very powerful companies to divest some of their assets and allow them to engage in abusive and uncompetitive practices towards consumers and competitors. The Department of Justice is investigating AT&T and Verizon over alleged collusion. Together they account for 70% of the US's cell phone subscriptions. President Donald Trump is extremely upset at the very negative news coverage he receives from the mainstream media.

MSNBC in particular does not even try to tell both sides of a story. Although they may be reporting true stories, some of their anchors (whom I personally like) do not disguise their total contempt for the president and his administration and steer their panels of analysts in a direction which is critical of Trump. I am not claiming that they behave like a state-run television news channel in a dictatorship or banana republic. Yet they are undoubtedly biased and have an agenda. NBC is somewhat less biased, but nonetheless also has trouble covering both sides of a story all of the time. In this regard, CNN is much more balanced. Donald Trump is an avid consumer of cable news. It mystifies me that he has not sought to weaken NBC and MSNBC by having the FCC weaken Comcast's stranglehold on consumers.

The aforementioned situation underlines the importance of getting 5G done right. Proponents of 5G mobile wireless internet promise that it will be faster, reach a higher proportion of the territory, have a more powerful signal capable of going thorough physical hurdles and be more flexible, meaning that it will multiply the number of devices that can be online and thus make the Internet of Things (IoT) possible. The IoT is the not-too-futuristic proposition that people will live in homes where not just TVs, laptops, computers, tablets and alarm systems are online, but also smart refrigerators that order food, smart AC systems that self-regulate the temperature, self-driving cars that will take people from point A to B, etc.

The debate surrounding the development of the 5G network has national-security implications. The Chinese government outlined in its "Made in China 2025" a plan for global dominance in strategic sectors. China forces foreign companies to share and turn over technology when they form partnerships with Chinese ones. This is often a pre-condition in order to be able to operate in the country. This abuse also facilitates its intellectual-theft practices. The Trump administration in March of 2018 threatened tariffs of 25% on up to $60 billion dollars of Chinese exports to the US in aerospace, ICT and machinery if it does not stop these practices, and also lodged a formal complaint with the World Trade Organization regarding the forced technology transfer and intellectual property abuses and violations.

Given China's ambitions and abuse, the Trump administration in 2018 floated the idea that the US government should build and operate its own 5G network. The proposal was withdrawn after heavy criticism. But the US has been vetoing certain Chinese investments in advanced sectors on national-security grounds. This is not a Trump invention. Since its creation by executive order by president Gerald Ford in 1975, the Committee on Foreign Investment in the US (CFIUS) is an inter-agency process that makes recommendations to the president as to whether the acquisition of a US company or operation or a foreign investment threatens national security. Chaired by the Treasury Secretary, CFIUS involves input from 16 US government departments and agencies, including the State Department, the Defense Department, the Commerce Department and the Department of Homeland Security. The president has the final word.

Some deals in the technology sector which have been quashed on the basis of CFIUS recommendations in recent years are purchases by the Chinese telecommunications giants Huawei and ZTE, Broadcom's merger with Qualcomm, a Chinese consortium's (including the giant Tencent) bid for European mapping company NV Here, the acquisition of Lattice Semiconductor Inc. by the Chinese-backed private equity group Canyon Bridge and Barack Obama's veto of a Chinese company from purchasing German semiconductor-equipment supplier Aixtron SE.[23]

The memo advocating a government-built 5G mobile wireless network explicitly labeled Huawei a strategic threat. All of these vetoes have the common denominator of trying to prevent China from beating the US in the race to develop 5G and other technologies such as self-driving cars. NV Here is owned by BMW, Volkswagen's Audi unit, Daimler and Intel. NV Here is developing 3D maps for driverless cars and location-based services used by logistics and online companies.

<u>Mexico's public-private partnership to build 5G: Red Compartida</u>

Mexico is not the world's leading military and economic power. It therefore has approved a more inclusive project to develop a 5G network. Under outgoing Mexican president Enrique Peña Nieto, the telecommunications sector has been liberalized, although Carlos Slim's company, América Móvil, still controls 70% of the market for mobile and broadband and runs its own network. Movistar (a subsidiary of Spain's Telefónica) and AT&T are the only other competitors,

---

[23] "Red Hot", *The Economist*. March 31st, 2018, page 65.

and they own and operate their own networks. The Red Compartida (shared network) is described as one of the most ambitious telecommunications projects in the world[24]. It is part of the liberalization of telecommunications undertaken by the Peña Nieto administration in 2014. It aims to cut mobile and Internet prices, expand access and create a viable business environment for 5G.

Red Compartida is a $7.2 billion public-private partnership (PPP) that will create a new 5G network. The government will furnish 18,000 km of fiber-optic cables and spectrum in the 700 MHZ band. Altán Redes is a private consortium that won the right to build the network and will pay for most of its construction, which is slated for completion by 2019. It will not be able to directly sell mobile and broadband to customers but rather to providers. The government will approve each deal between Altán Redes and a mobile and broadband provider. The aim is to create a fair and efficient 5G public network that expands access, increases speeds and enables new companies to enter the market and challenge the established giants -- América Móvil, Movistar/Telefónica and AT&T.

Mexico has one of the lowest mobile penetration rates in the OECD. In 2016 there were only 60 mobile-broadband subscriptions per 100 mobile customers because many Mexicans are still poor and because existing providers do not offer service to many parts of the country. Red Compartida covers 30% of the population now and is projected to cover 50% by 2020[25]. It is certainly a worthy endeavor when it comes to expanding access, lowering prices and creating a sustainable PPP in a key sector. The Peña telecommunications reforms have already delivered results. Broadband rates in 2013 in Mexico were 30% above the OECD average in 2013 and have dropped to 30% below the OECD average in 2016.

In order for Red Compartida to be successful, it will have to spur the entrance of new providers into the market. In many developed countries companies rent access to networks owned by other providers. These companies are known as Mobile Virtual Network Operators (MVNO's). In Mexico, MVNOs have a market share of only 1%, whereas in most European countries, the US and Canada the equivalent figure is 10 to 15%. Red Compartida's success depends on its ability to entice companies to become MVNOs. Otherwise, Altán Redes will not have any customers, as it will not be allowed to deliver mobile and broadband directly to consumers. It will therefore be a publicly-regulated but privately-run operator and provider of access to telecommunications services, namely 5G.

But some argue that 5G will be expensive to build. It will deliver faster speeds, lower response times and more flexibility, a requirement for the Internet of Things to work. But 5G employs higher-frequency radio waves that have more difficulty going through physical obstacles. This means that 5G operators will have to build more antennae and connect them to more fiber-optic cable in order for 5G to be both better and cheaper than 4G.

<u>Tesla's struggle to mass produce the Model 3</u>

Tesla has been a trailblazer and is America's biggest producer of electric vehicles. The models it has manufactured so far are expensive (starting at $74,000) and have been produced in limited numbers. Unfortunately, Tesla is greatly struggling to mass produce its Model 3 (retail price $35,000) at its car plant in Fremont, California. According to analysts, Tesla's CEO Elon Musk has excessively complicated the task of assembling a mass-market car.[26] Tesla discarded the

<hr>

[24] Ibidem
[25] Ibidem
[26] "Driving to the next circle of hell". *The Economist*. April 7th, 2018. Page 52

traditional manufacturing methods employed by most carmakers, which still rely on humans to play a significant role in the assembly of vehicles. Musk, in contrast, wanted the Fremont factory to be hyperautomated, a "machine that makes machines", with robots doing most of the work and humans reduced to a minimum. Robots are not able to efficiently use a fork-lift or insert plastic parts into the interior of cars, for example[27]. Most global carmakers have understood that a combination of robots and humans delivers the most efficient assembly of cars[28]. Elon Musk, Tesla's CEO, is now promising that his company's factories will roll out 6000 Model 3s every week by the end of June of 2018. Tesla posted a loss of $2 billion in 2017, and Moody's downgraded the company's debt in March of 2018. Analysts project that Tesla will have to invest billions more to successfully mass produce the Model 3, and its traditional rivals like Volkswagen and others are also investing in the production of electric vehicles.

Moreover, in March of 2018 a Tesla car using its autopilot software crashed into a barrier in California, killing the driver. Tech enthusiasts shrug off such mishaps as growing pains for self-driving cars. But regulators will surely pay more attention. Tesla's travails highlight the limits of automating the assembly of products.

---

[27] Ibidem

Carlos Baradello

Lecturer, Hult International Business School, University of San Francisco. Adviser to Fortune 500 companies.

Dr. Carlos Baradello is a university professor, investor, advisor and public speaker. A leading innovation and entrepreneurship practitioner, Carlos draws his understanding from his broad global business and academic experience, deep technical knowledge and understanding of the realities innovators face. Carlos' interests include new global business creation, venture funding, business acceleration for "born global" startups and global scaling for "foreign born" startups in emerging economies. In addition, Carlos has teaching responsibilities as a member of the faculty at Hult International Business School and the University of San Francisco in the United States, the Danish Technical University (Denmark), CENTRUM Católica (Perú) and the University of International Business and Economics (Beijing).

He founded the groundbreaking Silicon Valley Immersion program while serving as Associate Dean for Global and Executive Programs at the University of San Francisco. He is public speaker and corporate adviser to Fortune 500 companies, Economic Development Agencies and NGOs across the world. Carlos is also a Founder and General Partner of ALAYA-CP, Córdoba, Argentina's first venture capital firm, and Founder and Managing Partner of Sausalito Ventures, a firm that enables Latin American ventures to scale globally.

Carlos earned an Engineering Degree from Argentina's Catholic University of Córdoba, his MSc from the Eindhoven University of Technology (The Netherlands) and his PhD in Electrical Engineering from Carnegie-Mellon University. For over 30 years, Carlos held progressively senior positions in telecommunications and computer companies such as ITT, NYNEX, Digital Equipment Corporation, Advanced Fiber Communication and Motorola, where he served as the company's Corporate Vice President for Latin America and the Caribbean. He has authored over fifty technical and management papers and has been awarded six USA/EU patents for his inventions.

<u>On Technological change</u>

Technological change has been part of human history for thousands of years. What is different now is the speed of change, and that is what is unsettling. Nonetheless, we have been dealing with technological change for a very long time. There is no other way or alternative to this change than personal reinvention. And we are all having to reinvent ourselves. The problem arises when society or the labor market expects of some people that they reinvent themselves, namely acquire new skills, while others can continue to do what they have been doing. And now almost everyone is being affected -- although to varying degrees -- by technological change. Everyone at some point in their lives will have to reinvent themselves, and probably more than once. This situation spawns fear and uncertainty, which are very fertile ground for demagogues, who are able to attract people who feel vulnerable.

I can convey some ideas through my family history. My father had a third-grade elementary education. He worked in a leather factory, but he took risks and improved his situation. The factory produced many kinds of leather. He had no choice but to reinvent himself. My father had the foresight to seek and succeed in attaining a generational improvement. It was his life's crusade to ensure that his children would receive a better education. My brother and I both have advanced degrees. Hence, in my family's case, in one generation we went from a third-grade education (that of my father) to both my brother and I having a PhD. My argument is that this kind of generational improvement needs to be repeated again and again, generation after generation. There is no other way out, if one wants to remain competitive in today's challenging labor market in the context of a globalized economy.

The second point I want to make is the following. We have been undergoing a process of change for hundreds of years. But in the past fifty years this process has taken on great speed. We are more interconnected and interdependent than ever. This has raised the expectation of a global professional meritocracy. In a sense, the world and the labor market is becoming a global Olympics. Continuing with this metaphor, you can get a medal (a good job) regardless of where you come from. But there is only a limited supply of medals to be awarded in this global Olympics. We have to train for the global Olympics. There is no other way out. Building walls and isolating ourselves is unthinkable, because the bridges are already established. The Internet connects everybody and levels the playing field. The genie is out of the bottle, the toothpaste is out of the tube. We cannot put it back in the tube. Hence, it is foolish to try to build walls and borders, because ideas flow regardless of the establishment of these obstacles. In order to carry out work and projects, our physical presence is not required. There is no need for a passport or visa. Therefore, the idea that we can build walls flies against common sense and the laws of gravity.

I grew up in Argentina, which is an emerging country. My parents lived in northern Italy and had been rendered economic refugees because of the Great Depression of the 1930s. I was born in very humble economic means. I do not consider myself or my life as special in any sense, except that I have and continue to work very hard. I put in 50, 80 or 100-hour weeks, as I saw my parents do, and I continue to do.

The market economy has an infinite appetite for people who flip hamburgers for a living or have similar jobs. This a completely viable and highly-respectable option. The problem is the consumption aspirations that exist today. The consumption of the rich and famous is very visible. But many people want to enjoy those levels of consumption but their income comes from low-paying jobs like flipping hamburgers. And this mismatch generates a lot of frustration among people.

Question: As companies continue to automate more and eliminate jobs, some argue that corporations will assign their remaining employees more innovative tasks. But others fear that if replacing workers with machines is very effective, the number of jobs for people will diminish very substantially. And some economists point out that, despite automation, productivity is not increasing. Moreover, cyberattacks, hacking, maintenance of machines and other factors mean that humans have to stay in the loop. In early 2018 there were two malware attacks and the big Internet companies had to scramble to provide companies and individuals with patches. And even if there were no cyberattacks or hacking, machines also break down.

All of the technological and scientific advancements have to benefit society. We are not developing technology for the sake of it. Society should benefit from technological progress. But we are losing sight of the human factor. There should be humanity behind everything we do. And there is no doubt that we risk losing that humanity. People can now get divorced by clicking a few boxes on an electronic document. Technological progress can sweep aside long-established human traditions. Life, to a certain extent, has become disposable. Three mouse clicks can order euthanasia. These kinds of developments raise the question as to whether we have lost sight of the equation *between having more and being more.*

You and I probably agree regarding the fact that in the past forty years society in general and individuals have been able to attain very high levels of consumption. The access to better goods and services, as well as the ability to pay for them, has spread at great speed. That is true today.

But we must ask ourselves whether these developments are helping us to become more humane, more altruistic, to show more solidarity, generosity, integrity, and ethics.

I would argue that we have lost the right balance, that we have broken the equilibrium between *having* and *being* to the detriment of the latter. Someone can have as many things as he or she wishes as long as that also results in that person being a better human being. But if the equilibrium is broken, it leads to excesses and some individuals' quest to have more becomes harmful. The quest to have more becomes harmful to the existence of some individuals.

<u>On the dysfunctionality of our political system</u>

We are already eight months into the 2018 fiscal year and we still do not have a budget. Congress keeps passing two- or three-month budget extensions. Most politicians do not have any courage. In the United States, they are just worried about the November (2018) mid-term elections. That is the time horizon for most politicians.

<u>On how to approach the increasing use of robots, and even a tax on robots</u>

This question cannot be answered with a simple "Yes" or "No" in isolation, without first looking at the broad picture. The reality is that the economy and technology have always created more new jobs than those they have destroyed. This has been the case throughout the history of mankind. The current situation, however, is problematic because we have certainty about who is going to lose their job but uncertainty with regards to which new ones will be created. A mailman, for example, knows that email will make his job disappear. I am leaving aside parcel delivery and strictly describing delivery of regular mail. A photographer working in a dark room making prints also faces a 100% certainty that such a job will be eliminated. But we cannot predict how many new jobs will be created by manipulating photography with the advent of photoshop and other technology, for example. Hence, a person in the photography sector needs to acquire new skills. Her or she can excel in terms of making beautiful prints with light and chemicals in a dark room. But those skills are not easily transferrable to operating in the photoshop environment.

Hence, at the core of the issue you are raising are factors such a fear and uncertainty. And such fears and uncertainty about the future of jobs obviously have economic consequences for individuals. This challenge is compounded by many individuals who have an infinite appetite for consumption. This is fertile ground for demagogues like Donald Trump, who repeats one lie after another. Unfortunately, some people like to listen to lies because it provides them a false sense of comfort.

There are studies showing that more young people have attention-deficit disorders because of their excessive use of certain technologies, especially cell phones. As the pace of technological change accelerates, even white-collar jobs such as that of a university professor could soon be eliminated and replaced by a robot.

But instead of referring to a person replaced by a machine or robot, we should view this development differently. We sometimes use the wrong vocabulary. A white-collar professional will not be *replaced* by a robot. The professional will be *liberated* from having to perform tedious and repetitive tasks and given a unique opportunity to apply his or her imagination and creativity to performing much higher value-added tasks.

I do accept that it is difficult to demand life-long professional reinvention because people want to at the same time maintain high levels of consumption. As parents, we have to do a better job of teaching the right skills to our kids. We have raised children who spend too many hours playing video games or on Facebook publicizing the globalization of superficiality. A lot of parents have failed in this regard. Family as an institution has been under considerable strain for decades. The number of marriages that end in divorce is growing. Many children are born into broken families where the right values are not instilled in them.

It all starts at the top. We need to look no farther than to the president of the United States. The current president has been married three times and has a collection of different kids with different wives. He is unable to distinguish between the truth and lies, between good and bad. It is all a reality show for him.

Question: Germany's apprenticeship system guarantees everyone who studies a profession a top-rate internship at a company in a system that brings together the federal and regional governments and the private sector. Not everybody needs to graduate from the university. This is a stigma that society needs to part with. In fact, many people with a non-university technical degree earn more than university graduates.

I have written extensively about the virtues of the German apprenticeship system. I can again reference my family history. How did my father become the supervisor of a leather shop, where they processed products? He only had a third-grade education at age eleven or twelve. But he worked hard and learned the necessary skills that enabled him to climb the professional ladder and make more money in the leather company. By his early twenties he had become a supervisor of the company that manufactured leather products. His success can be attributed to an "informal" kind of apprenticeship that he undertook since he joined the leather company. The German model, of course, involves formal internships at companies that must be successfully completed as part of the graduation requirements. We should aggressively promote an apprenticeship system like that of Germany.

<u>On the application of technology to the health-care sector</u>

The disruption of health care in the coming years is going to be amazing. Some of its parts will be automated, but the whole system as such will undergo what Joseph Schumpeter (the Austrian-born US political economist from the XXth century) called a shower of icy water that will jolt it into greater efficiency.

There will be great transformations in both the management and delivery of health care in the coming years. Do we need pathologists and radiologists? If we examine the time period between 1900 and 1950, we retired 90% of the horses used for transportation because we evolved from road traction into motor traction. I believe that in the next ten years pathologists and radiologists will be made redundant by technology. They will be liberated from the boring job of looking at an image of a body in order to come up with a diagnosis. This task will be performed in a much better, cheaper and faster way by small equipment that does not require coffee breaks or vacations. Such a development will drive down the cost of health care in general and of diagnostics in particular, which are currently extremely high. Those who manage to introduce such technologies into health care will be regarded as heroes, as driving down the cost of health care has eluded policymakers for decades.

Question: Some of these developments have already taken place in the health sector and they have led to the outsourcing of the less-skilled health-care jobs to countries like India. The current global economy allows freedom of movement of goods, services and capital, but it does not permit it for workers. How do we get around this obstacle?

With technological progress in the health-care sector, there will be no need for mobility of labor because these tasks will be carried out by small robots ("bobs") that will examine images and speed up the diagnostic process. And diagnostics performed by small robots will be better than those carried out by humans in 90% of the cases. This will of course dramatically cut the costs of health care.

I will furnish you with another example from the health-care sector. Every drugstore or pharmacy currently needs an employee with an advanced degree in pharmacy. This position originated 150 years ago when a chemist mixed different ingredients and came up with medical solutions. When was the last time you saw a pharmacy that worked with chemicals and formulas and developed treatments? We do not really need pharmacies. They have been reduced to the role of counting pills. They buy wholesale medical products and then disburse a certain number of pills to each patient according to what the doctor prescribes. It does not make sense to pay a pharmacist a salary over $100,000 and for that person to spend seven years in college so that he or she is reduced to the role of counting and disbursing pills.

There are certain sectors and people who may prefer a human to deliver a service even if a machine or robot can perform the task. This is especially true in the case of care for the elderly. Yet this care for the elderly does not have to be provided by a doctor, someone who spent up to ten years in medical school. This can be left up to a social worker -- or a companion – in order to substitute for something that society is increasingly neglecting, which is respect for our elders.

<u>Adam Bartha</u>

Director, European Policy Information Center (EPICENTER). London

Adam Bartha is the Director of the European Policy Information Center (EPICENTER), with the responsibility to enable the cooperation of the network and organize the private and public events program in Brussels. He was previously European Outreach Manager at EPICENTER and a Koch Summer Fellow in the Publications Department of the Independent Institute in California. He also has experience in domestic party politics in Germany and Hungary. Adam has a Bachelor in Arts (Hons) in Politics and International Relations from the University of Sheffield and a Masters in Science in Political Theory from the London School of Economics. Adam is fluent in English, German and Hungarian.

Question: Some of the causes of populism are that middle- and lower classes have struggled to recover from the financial crisis and the Great Recession despite the current growth. They are also witnessing the destruction of millions of jobs as robots, Artificial Intelligence and machines displace humans. Those without the right degrees or skills fear for their jobs and how their children will be able to make a living. Do you share this assessment?

The "Economic Divide" and the fast pace of technological progress are only part of the explanation for the surge in populism. The power of politicians, their actions and their words should not be underestimated in any analysis of the rise in populism. Depending on the interests of the political elites, a lot of things can change in society. For a long time the political elites were interested in maintaining the status quo, as well as managing the pace of economic development and social change. But in many countries new actors emerged onto the political scene and became involved in politics. Their interests clashed with those of the traditional political elites. These newcomers to politics were very skillful in using feelings that already existed in society and channeling them into simple messages and policy proposals. Poland, Hungary and the new governing parties in Italy are good examples of this development. Populists have been able to tailor their messages very effectively, as opposed to the existing elites, whose ideas have not evolved. A shift has thus taken place whereby citizens realize that it is now possible to change the course of politics in a fairly short period of time.

Examples of such shifts are the election of Donald Trump as president in 2016, which analysts thought was impossible, as well as the British people's decision to vote to leave the European Union and the election of populist governments in Poland, Hungary and Italy. These developments highlight the divergence from what had been mainstream politics.

Question: In the case of Hungary, would you agree that the success of Prime Minister Viktor Orbán's[29] populist Fidesz party has many causes. Hungary does not have an Indo-European language and lost two-thirds of its territory at the end of World War I in the Treaty of Trianon (1920). Orbán and his people flirt with irredentist claims and have successfully exploited the false idea that the rights of Hungarian minorities in Romania, Slovakia and Serbia are being trampled on. Moreover, as is the case in Poland with the right-wing populist ruling Law and Order (PiS) party, Fidesz justifies its interference in many domains (the judiciary, media, activities of NGOs) by

---

[29] Viktor Orbán served as Prime Minister from 1998 to 2002. After eight years in opposition, his Fidesz party returned to power after the 2010 elections, and subsequently also won in landslides in 2014 and 2018. Orbán is now the third-longest serving prime minister in Hungarian history.

The factors you mentioned were always there. The question is how ruling elites were able to cope with them. The circumstances in these countries changed at a slow but constant pace. How politicians utilize these changing circumstances is a different matter. Populists learned how to exploit the existing frustrations in their societies.

Question: The breakneck advance of technology will destroy millions of jobs, not just among blue-collar workers but also white-collar ones. One obvious policy response is lifelong training. The German apprenticeship system is always praised. Will people accept that jobs for life are a thing of the past?

Flexibility is a key on the part of individuals. The more diverse skill-set you have, the easier it will be to adapt to new circumstances. For our generation (people in their 20s, 30s and 40s), it is fairly obvious that in twenty years we will not be performing the job we are in today. In twenty years we will not employ the same tools and we will be surrounded by different technological equipment. People in these age groups have already come to terms with this reality. It is not a shock to them that in twenty years we will be using very different tools and technologies. The real problem is for the people in my parents' generation -- individuals in their fifties and early sixties. They were told that if they studied they would have a job for life and would be able to climb the corporate ladder and become managers or hold high-level positions in the companies where they started out. Those times have long gone.

It is true that the German education system is more flexible than the ones in the United States and the United Kingdom. In Germany, pupils are able to choose at an early age several paths that are skills-based as opposed to paper-based. A lot of individuals in the UK who do not know what to do with their lives attend university with the hope that while they do so they will figure out what they want to do professionally.

In Germany, the apprenticeship system allows young people to work at a company for half a year and to study during the other half. If the person later decides to pursue a different career, it is easier to do so as the student will not have wasted four or five years of paper-based study. He or she will have learned practical on-the-job skills which will always be valuable.

One disadvantage of the German apprenticeship system is that kids are sorted out according to their skills at a very early age. Hence, if a youngster does not perform well at age twelve or thirteen, he or she is not recommended for entrance into a college-oriented high school. They are instead advised to attend a technical high school. Pupils from underprivileged socioeconomic backgrounds often feel that the college-oriented high schools are not for them because they are not confident in their ability to perform well. We therefore need to ensure that students have enough freedom to switch career paths and are not trapped in an apprenticeship system. Otherwise moving up the social ladder between generations becomes more difficult.

There is not much evidence that the apprenticeship system constrains social upward mobility in Germany except for certain groups with an immigration background. Second and third-generation Turkish individuals perform worse than first-generation ones. This is an aspect of German education that merits more research.

Question: The left or center-left favors a minimum universal income, for example for people who are very old and cannot be retrained. As life expectancy rises, some cannot survive on the low pensions they are entitled to. How do you feel about such schemes?

A lot depends on how well they are implemented. The trial conducted in Finland was not successful. I would be in favor if a universal minimum income could replace a lot of the other welfare benefits[30], which are very difficult to test. All of the welfare benefits cost taxpayers a lot of money, in part because testing to determine eligibility is expensive. If a universal income payment could replace the bureaucratic welfare state, I would not be opposed to it. On the other hand, one very big disadvantage is that it could become a bargaining chip between political parties seeking to form coalitions after elections. We constantly hear politicians running for office who vow to raise the minimum wage they deem to be too low. They commit to increasing the minimum wage by 10% because they feel it is outrageously low. This would also probably happen with the minimum income.

Success for a minimum income would hinge on the level of political discussion and how the policy would be crafted in a specific country. I would trust certain Nordic countries with a minimum income trial much more than countries in southeastern Europe, where welfare becomes part of the daily bargaining by populist parties and could actually widen the divide between populist and non-populist parties. In sum, I do not think a minimum income would be a solution for the economic divide.

Question: In 2015-16 Europe experienced a massive influx of non-European refugees and asylum-seekers, particularly from the Middle East and Africa. All attempts at forging a common European migration policy have failed, and eastern European countries are adamant in rejecting a quota of refugees. Nevertheless, was the influx of such an extraordinary magnitude in 2015-2016 that we can hope that immigration as a topic that spurs support for populist parties could revert to a lower level?

I think immigration and its consequences are here to stay. I do not foresee changes in US or European foreign policy, which I believe are the drivers of this current migration crisis. In the medium and long-term migration will remain as relevant as it is now. The magnitude of immigration is an interesting aspect to discuss. If you consider the total population of the European Union and the number of migrants who have arrived in the past two to three years, the latter amount to less than 1% of the total population[31]. A one-percentage increase in a country's immigrant population should under normal circumstances not be a major issue. The main cause of people's fear is how this migration happened. We had not witnessed mass migration in Europe for a long time[32]. When immigrants crossed from Serbia into Hungary, and from there they traveled north to Austria and Germany, they did so in trains or on foot. This migration was covered on television and was very visible to the general public, which had never encountered this kind of mass migration before.

I was disappointed at the time of the 2015-16 immigration influx and remain so today with our inability to integrate these individuals. Syria was among the best-educated societies in the

---

[30] Welfare benefits can include work-based pensions, payments for disability, payments to widows and housing allowances for the poorest.

[31] In 2017, there were 728,470 applications for international protection in the EU. This represents a reduction of 44% compared to 2016, when there were almost 1.3 million applications.
European Parliament http://www.europarl.europa.eu/news/en/headlines/society/20170629STO78630/eu-migrant-crisis-facts-and-figures

[32] With the partial exception of the migration flows spawned by the wars unleashed by the break-up of Yugoslavia in the 1990s. But the refugees from these conflicts were European.

Middle East. Studies show that most refugees and asylum-seekers from Syria are highly-trained, and a significant share of the immigrants were fleeing the civil war in Syria.

If we are unable to integrate highly-qualified people, there are serious issues with our social culture and our employment regulations. In Germany it is a major problem that the newly-arrived migrants are obliged to live off of state benefits and cannot work until they acquire certain qualifications and language training[33]. This system has proven too rigid. The employment system in Europe is too rigid and makes it very difficult for newly-arrived migrants to become productive members of the labor force. We should therefore address issues that prevent integration from taking place. Once we have removed these obstacles, we will find that integrating a group of people that amount to 1% of our population is not a major challenge.

Question: As the Brexit negotiations proceed, is there any chance that the British population will determine that the result of Brexit will not be beneficial for the UK? The result of the Brexit referendum, after all, was very close. The British population might conclude that cutting immigration sharply starves the labor force of qualified workers. The UK's financial sector will suffer if its financial institutions cannot retain passporting rights, and in any event outsourcing of staff from London to other European capitals is already happening.

I really struggle to witness a scenario where the result is a complete reversal of Brexit. I can imagine a scenario where it remains a matter of debate for the next ten years and politicians on the right and left debate how close the UK should remain to the EU. But I rule out a majority of the British population concluding that the country should revert to its previous situation of full membership in the European Union.

I think the EU and the UK could agree on a system of economic migration that is similar to that implemented in Switzerland. Only if an individual has an offer of employment, is he or she free to move to Switzerland. There are no quotas as such in Switzerland. But a foreigner cannot just move to Switzerland, decide to live there, not work and claim state benefits. One of the three items that British Prime Minister David Cameron negotiated with the EU in advance of the Brexit referendum in 2016 is that it would *not* be possible for EU migrants to claim benefits for a certain number of years[34]. Hence, EU migrants already cannot claim social benefits in their first years residing in the UK. If there are additional negotiations between the British government and the EU on this matter, I do not foresee strong opposition among the British population.

On the subject of immigration, even the populists in the UK admit that we need migrants. But it has to be quality migration. The state is not in a position to ensure this quality migration because a bureaucrat is not in a position to knowj whether a specific migrant is qualified to work in a particular company. The free market provides much better solutions. If the political elites

---

[33] In 2017, EU countries granted protection to more than 538,000 people, a 25% drop from 2016. Almost one in three of these were from Syria while Afghanistan and Irak rounded up the top three. Of the 175,800 Syrian citizens granted international protection in the EU, more than 70% obtained it in Germany.
European Parliament http://www.europarl.europa.eu/news/en/headlines/society/20170629STO78630/eu-migrant-crisis-facts-and-figures
[34] "EU reform deal: What Cameron wanted and what he got". BBC News. 20 February 2016.
The Council would authorise that Member State to limit the access of newly arriving EU workers to non-contributory in-work benefits for a total period of up to four years from the commencement of employment. The limitation should be graduated, from an initial complete exclusion but gradually increasing access to such benefits to take account of the growing connection of the worker with the labour market of the host Member State. The authorization would have a limited duration and apply to EU workers newly arriving during a period of 7 years.

manage to convince their voters that a deal that is struck makes sure that people moving to the UK have qualifications and skills, I think this matter will be solved.

__Veronica Bertozzi__

United Nations Fellow, Italian Agency of Development and Cooperation.

Bertozzi holds a Bachelor's degree in Political Science and International Relations from a joint program between the Universitat Autónoma de Barcelona, Marmara University and the University of California at Los Angeles (UCLA). She was a researcher at the Yala Institute in Israel. Her academic publication most relevant to the title of the book is titled "The Power of Institutions: A Comparative Analysis of the US and the Eurozone in dealing with the crisis." Bertozzi worked at YALA, a Middle Eastern organization, and as a volunteer for the African Refugee Development Center in Tel Aviv, where she dealt with legal topics and asylum seekers' applications.

Populism in Italy is not a recent phenomenon. We must remember that Silvio Berlusconi served three terms as Prime Minister of Italy. The media tycoon was prime minister from 1994 to 1994, from 2001 to 2006, and from 2008 to 2011. The nine years Berlusconi served make him the longest-serving post-World War II Italian prime minister. The majority shareholder of the Mediaset media empire is not a populist in the current incarnation of this phenomenon. Berlusconi had a long political background and track record before becoming prime minister. He was a deputy in Italy's Chamber of Deputies for nineteen years (1994-2013) and a senator for one year before being appointed prime minister in 2013. Most current populists enjoy public support precisely because they have not been involved in politics. In fact, being an outsider of the political system is one of the defining features of current populists.

Berlusconi did benefit from the longing for a strong and new leader after decades of mostly weak, unstable or short-lived coalition governments made up of Italy's traditional post-World War II parties – the Christian Democrats, Socialist Party, Liberal Party, etc. In taking on the discredited political establishment, Berlusconi can be considered a populist to a certain extent. But the policies he espoused and adopted in his three terms as prime minister were not radical. Berlusconi pursued a center-right agenda with very limited success in terms of liberalizing and modernizing Italy's economy. His public behavior, comments and numerous charges, indictments and convictions on corruption practices did lend him the aura of a populist in the eyes of his diehard supporters, who remained loyal despite Berlusconi being charged and, in some cases, convicted of tax fraud, paying bribes, defamation and abuse of office, among other charges. Berlusconi was able to avoid conviction and jail time because of legislation his governments enacted, statutes of limitation and his age. Nonetheless, Berlusconi was and remains a figure of the establishment. In 2017, Forbes ranked him as the 199th richest person in the world, with a net worth of $7 billion.

The new development is the rise in the number of Italian populist parties and their impressive performance at the polls, especially in the general elections held in March of 2018. The anti-establishment left-wing Five Star Movement (M5S) placed second in the elections in number of votes (32.6%) and garnered 133 members in the Chamber of Deputies. The center-right coalition obtained 37% of the vote and 157 deputies. Unlike the M5S, the center-right coalition is made up of several parties: The League (formerly the Northern League), Forza Italia (led by Berlusconi) and Brothers of Italy. The center-right coalition obtained the most deputies in the Chamber of Deputies, edging out the M5S. But no party nor coalition captured an absolute majority, thus creating a hung parliament. Under the leadership of Matteo Salvini, the League has rebranded itself as a national populist party that is skeptical about European integration -- especially membership in the eurozone -- and very hostile to immigrants, particularly to those who arrived in the wave of 2015 and ensuing years. At the time of writing, it appears that Salvini will be able to cobble together a coalition and will become Prime Minister[35].

Ironically, Berlusconi is now one of the politicians in Italy trying to check the power of the new populists. He remains an influential figure (though not dominant as he was before) in the center-right coalition as he leads its second-biggest party, Forza Italia.

From the left to the right of the political spectrum, in Italy's politican landscape we can find demagogues who simplify reality and pretend to find solutions to virtually each problem merely by pointing their finger against something or someone. Among the favorite scapegoats of Italian populists are the adoption of the euro (in their view the cause of Italy's economic stagnation), immigrants who "steal" Italians' jobs, German chancellor Angela Merkel, banks and the traditional Italian establishment. This Manichaean description of reality is something that is common to all populists. Populists offer catchy slogans to a hungry crowd. The modus operandi of populists is to be simple and fast. The solutions that populists propose must be linear and follow the basic cause-effect rule. The measures populists promise to enact should require just a few and easy quick steps. For example, populists argue that the solution to Italy's secular economic stagnation and lack of competitiveness is to leave the eurozone. Populists repeat that creating jobs simply requires expelling immigrants. Populists do not accept complexities and have no long-term strategies.

<u>How did we get here?</u>

The classical democratic political divide between effectiveness and representativeness seems to be tipping in favor of the former, while populists loudly advocate for the latter. The Internet and social media reward speed. To be the first to report about an issue or to be among the first ones who live stream about an incident is what catches the public's interest. #breaking became one of the most used hashtags on social media outlets such as Twitter. The quantity of information that the public is exposed to has soared, while deep investigative and quality reporting has diminished. The possibility to view news in real time and have unlimited access to news sources and social media though our smartphones made most users of these products want to be able to actively share news, opinions and comments. This technology, which could empower people, also has the risk of creating cacophonic rooms where users are echoing their prejudices and personal views. An example of this is the Facebook news-feed bias, according to which the social media's logarithms will tend to show us opinions of people like us. This circle of assent prevents discussion, reinforces existing opinions and offers a simplified vision of the world. The lack of knowledge of others' opinions could also be one of the downsides of what the social media project to us. Thus, this superficial and biased knowledge became a very fertile ground for populism to breed in.

Democracy is the best political system. But it is undergoing a deep crisis. The acceleration that is taking place in the field of science, technology, mobility and transformational cultural changes is generating a new and challenging context for democratic political systems based on elections, negotiations and agreements. Changes require time and in order to adopt long procedures in a democratic system the majority must agree. The time that governmental bodies require to debate and enact new procedures and laws is frustratingly long for part of the population, especially the young. Younger people are coming of age politically in an era when technology and

---

[35] Matteo Salvini did not become Prime Minister. But Italy's prime minister, Giuseppe Conte, is arguably less powerful than Salvini, who is Deputy Prime Minister. Salvini has a tight grip on the League, the party which has allied itself with the left-wing Five Star Movement to form western Europe's first openly populist government.

social media spawn impatience. Democracy requires that society listen to the concerns, fears and arguments from all sides on a given issue. Drafting a proposal which considers different points of views, backgrounds and opinions and debates them obviously requires time. Such proposals need to be thoroughly analyzed and debated and should incorporate the biggest number of views. The aforementioned long process of debate, deliberation, and inclusion of all points of view and eventual adoption is anathema to how modern populist politicians operate. Populists present very firm views, and do not tolerate that they be subject to discussion. Instead of fostering a constructive debate, populists present us with repeated slogans. Populists thrive in social media echo chambers, where they channel and amplify opinions that coincide with theirs.

Nowadays geographical distances have been reduced thanks to modern transportation and technology, and borders are more open than ever, especially in the West. All social indicators -- if we exclude the Middle East -- show an improvement in the quality of life of citizens and a clear reduction of poverty and violent conflicts. Although the world is getting better, the public perception, which is influenced by populists and social media, paints a darker picture of the present. Most Western countries are currently registering strong growth. But the relatively slow recovery after the global financial crisis and the Great Recession has taken a toll on the endurance and confidence of middle and lower classes. The mass media tend to report mostly about the conflicts around the world, crimes committed in our communities, and often emphasize bad news which reflect an excessively pessimistic picture of reality. Moreover, globalization has fostered several reactions, which culminated with the revival of local cultures. Communities, regions and religious groups want to be autonomous. They want to clearly draw a line of separation between their local culture and that of the rest of the world. We see these phenomena happening all around the world. Voices that advocate independence for regions from the existing states have increased in Europe: from Belgium to Spain minorities are trying to attain international recognition and support, as is also the case of the Kurds in Turkey and Irak.

Populism draws its strength from this return and enhancement of local cultures, religious affiliations and love for the homeland. Populism tends to resist globalization, and its international cooperation, agencies and laws. Multilateral international institutions such as the United Nations are more often considered as a complex and slow burden, unsuited to deal with the current situation and, as populist leaders like to describe it, the current catastrophe.

<u>How can we move forward?</u>

A main premise of the answer is the enduring validity of the democratic system, which citizens need to cherish despite its imperfections, delays and bureaucratic institutions. Another basic premise of the answer is that reality is far more complex than what populist leaders want us to believe. There are no simple straightforward formulas to tackle complex problems, as different sides and views must be taken into consideration. Finally, another premise is the positive role that globalization can play in our lives by allowing international laws and regulations (labor, environmental, anti-corruption) to be applied for the benefit of all human beings. When these assumptions are threatened, populist forces benefit. We need remedies to stop the erosion of confidence in democratic institutions. Education must play a key role by instilling values and a sense of the duties of citizenship in the young. We need to deploy tools that identify fake sources of information and the accuracy of news. We also require the capability to differentiate between slogans and valid arguments and data that the educational system must convey to the new generations.

Unfortunately, many teenagers are growing up having more friends on social media than in the real world. Leaders such as Vladimir Putin and Donald Trump are role models for some young people. We are witnessing a deep radicalization of society. On the other hand, youth have great potential as most countries -- and all of the developed ones -- in the world have never achieved such high standards of living. For this reason, the biggest step we can take to fight populism is to invest in education, which is an investment in the future of the younger generation. It provides them with tools to accept differences and understand nuances. We should all be held accountable for the kind of education that we give to our children. We should try, since they are little, to treat them as adults, to talk to them, and to describe to them realities from different perspectives. In sum, we need to teach and encourage them to imagine different scenarios, and to think out of the box. Populism appeals to people's instincts and emotions, so solutions that defeat it have to include rationality that can negate its empty claims and slogans.

Pierre Bessard

President and Member of the Board of Trustees, Liberal Institute. Geneva.

Pierre Bessard is Executive Trustee and President of the Liberal Institute, Switzerland's independent research and educational think tank. Founded in 1979, Bessard joined the Liberal Institute in late 2007 and has helped expand it with a new team. He also serves on the scientific committee of the Cercle de Philosophie Politique Benjamin Constant and the Center for Tax Competition. He was an editor at Agefi, the Lake Geneva region's financial newspaper, where he wrote on political economy from 2002 onwards. After schooling in Lausanne, London, and Berlin, Bessard studied economics and finance in New York and Shanghai. He is the editor and author of 16 books in French and German on Swiss liberalism and current affairs, and a member of the Mont Pèlerin Society and the Hayek-Gesellschaft.

Question on the causes of populism

Some of the causes of populism are that middle- and lower classes have struggled to recover from the financial crisis and the Great Recession despite the current growth. They are also witnessing the destruction of millions of jobs as robots, Artificial Intelligence and machines displace humans. Those without the right degrees or skills fear for their jobs and how their children will be able to make a living. Do you share this assessment?

Answer

All political parties are to some degree populist, and this is especially the case of social democrats, with their promise of unlimited consumption and living off other people's or future generations' money. The truth is that living standards in relatively free economies have never been so high, considering not just disposable incomes, but the goods and services that these incomes can buy. Even households viewed statistically as "poor" today own automobiles, giant flat-screen televisions and smartphones. It is more likely that the rejection of traditional parties, which are often populists or opportunists of a different kind, takes place because of the disillusions arising from the costs of bloated welfare states, not because of productivity-enhancing new technologies.

On the one hand, the welfare state implies an increasing tax burden that has long passed its tolerable weight. Ever larger shares of tax revenues are used to pay people to do nothing, which is doubly destructive: The tax burden takes away productive resources from investors, consumers, and savers, depressing economic activtoity and growth. Moreover, disincentives to work apply both where the taxes are levied and where they are redistributed. The ridiculously low legal retirement age between 60 and 65 in many countries despite higher life expectancy and advances in medication cause an enormous waste of human and financial resources. In addition, for many years ultraloose monetary policy has favored the financial over the manufacturing sector and debtors over savers. These are systemic imbalances that lead voters to seek alternatives to "more of the same", even if these alternatives are objectively suboptimal or really bad.

In parallel, the loss of orientation arising from the bloated welfare state has been identified as an opportunity by political "entrepreneurs" seeking power above anything else. Anti-immigration sentiment and group collectivisms have been a universal strategy for cheap vote grabbing, as it flatters patriotic sentiments and give weaker-minded individuals the feeling of being more than themselves, namely a part of a great "people" or "nation". In addition, foreigners typically do not vote, so the political risks of this strategy are limited. It is much easier to build a power base on that basis than by promoting sensible policies strengthening individual freedom and upholding the ethics of personal responsibility, without which a free and prosperous society cannot be sustained. The welfare state thereby becomes acceptable if it is reserved for the "nationals", and immigrants are given a hard time. Empirical studies show that xenophobia is especially prevalent in countries with large welfare states. This welfare chauvinism arises from income redistribution. Even people of good faith and intellect find superficial appeal in such policies because they give the impression of standing in for the "national" interest, although interests and preferences necessarily vary within a nation. The collectivist narrative is powerful, as the tragic 20th century in Europe and its different brands of socialism exemplifies. I would therefore call today's type of populism "national social-democratic".

Question on how individuals will adapt to destruction of jobs by technology

The breakneck advance of technology will destroy millions of jobs, not just among blue-collar workers but also white-collar ones. One obvious policy response is lifelong training. The Swiss apprenticeship system is always praised. Will people accept that jobs for life are a thing of the past?

Answer

I do not think this analysis is correct at all. Technological advances not only create new jobs, but higher-paying jobs. Goods and services that were unaffordable in the past offer many new employment opportunities and lower costs of living for lower-skilled individuals. This is the story of the last 250 years, where yesterday's luxuries are today's ordinary conveniences. For example, there has never been so much food and so few farmers. The number of farming jobs has dramatically dropped over the past decades. Moreover, the food budget for a typical household has dropped from about 40% of disposable income one hundred years ago to less than 10% today. There have never been so many and so many well-paying jobs, and this is largely driven by markets and technological progress.

The American Marxist ideologue Jeremy Rifkin predicted in his 1995 book "The End of Work" with the subtitle "The Decline of the Global Work Force and the Dawn of the Post-Market Era" that jobs were being destroyed and not replaced. This was of course mere socialist wishful thinking. What has really happened between 1995 and today? Not only did the global workforce grow from 2.3 to 3.4 billion people, but world gross domestic product per capita rose 150% from $6,400 to $16,000. Over the same period of time, extreme poverty decreased from 28% to 10% of the world population, and these trends continue to improve. The factor of success or failure of any country is precisely the opposite of Mr. Rifkin's prediction, namely the degree of economic freedom. The freer the economy, the more prosperous people are. And this is remarkably not just about more money. Economic freedom and higher incomes go hand in hand with greater life satisfaction, environmental quality, better health outcomes, longer life expectancy, higher educational levels, and other positive indicators.

Skepticism toward innovation is as old as the first invention, but the fact is that innovation leads to more jobs, not less. Innovation increases the productivity of work and reduces its cost: As a result, demand for labor rises, and more employment opportunities are created. This is also why robots, or automation, benefit work, and do not harm or replace it. As the productivity of labor increases through automation, more value is created and wages rise. In turn, rising labor productivity makes more people employable, creating new jobs. In addition, wage earners benefit as consumers from better and cheaper goods thanks to the increase in productivity and output. In other words, markets work in the exact opposite way of the gloom-and-doom authors' predictions. Unfortunately, sound economics is not as sexy as catastrophism for those who seek to write bestselling books for the unthinking masses.

To destroy jobs and instill chaos and shortages in an entire economy, there is a way, which is commonly called socialism. Venezuela today is a case in point about how policy can instill mayhem and a humanitarian catastrophe. Under milder regimes, unemployment is typically a policy phenomenon as well. Inadequate monetary and credit conditions (such as the euro in southern Europe), taxes (government spending), labor regulations, industrial policies depressing the productivity of capital and labor, welfare benefits (as disincentives to work), minimum wages artificially raising the costs of labor, and labor unions as drivers of bad policy are all causes of higher unemployment. Markets and technology are just the opposite. They raise employment and incomes.

The Swiss apprenticeship system, which allows further academic and technical specialization later on, is a success story that is rightly praised and should be carefully examined elsewhere, in particular in countries that produce far too many unemployable university graduates. The apprenticeship is a powerful social integration tool where 16-years-olds have the responsibility of a job and earn a salary for their work. It is based on the ethics of reciprocity of the market. That is why Switzerland has a very low youth unemployment rate and no problem with youth from immigration backgrounds, although 25% of the resident population in Switzerland is non-Swiss. Young people learn a profession and become full and useful members of society, rather than feeling frustrated for a lack of academic skills. One of the country's strengths is precisely its relatively low percentage of university graduates. It is not very useful to have a plumber with a degree in art history who doesn't know his craft. Many highly skilled individuals start their career with a technical apprenticeship before earning higher degrees in engineering later on in life if they have the inclination to do so.

Question on a universal minimum income

The left or center-left favors a minimum universal income, for example for people who are very old and cannot be retrained. As life expectancy rises, some cannot survive on the low pensions they are entitled to. How do you feel about such schemes?

Answer

This is just socialism in disguise. A minimum universal income amounts to a childish revolt against reality in that it promises that money can fall from the sky and can be paid out without providing any reciprocal value. This unrealism is a typical feature of socialism. More than that, I believe the proposal to be deeply immoral for two reasons. First of all, it denies people the dignity of self-responsibility and autonomy for their own lives and makes every citizen a dependent of the state. Second, it denies that to finance a minimum universal income, someone has to be taxed, that is, that money must be taken somewhere to be redistributed elsewhere. In a wild dream we might indeed wish that we could deplete a little bit of Bill Gates's or Jeff Bezos's wealth to live comfortably without having to work. Yet in plain language, this is theft. Proponents of a minimum universal income are in effect suggesting employing the legislative process to loot the rich and allow others to live off their back. I can understand the superficial appeal of such a proposal with those who do not think far, but if we look at it honestly, the minimum universal income is a very disturbing proposal. It reflects the decadence of a post-modern society brought up by the welfare state "from the cradle to the grave". I personally think that the minimum universal income is a terrible idea. It is a relief that in Switzerland, 77% of voters rejected such a plan in 2016.

Regarding older workers, this very much depends on incentives. In Switzerland, the occupation rate of over 55-years-olds has risen from 66% to 76% over the last 15 years. The idea that older workers are at a disadvantage in the job market is a myth. Their unemployment rate is lower than the average or than that of young people. Also, companies are very much willing to invest in the continuing education of older workers if they can expect that they will keep on working for a number of years. The problem, again, is not the market, but policy, where pension systems place disincentives to work and incentives to retire much too early in light of life expectancy and health conditions.

<u>Question of the influx of migrants, refugees and asylum-seekers</u>

In 2015-16 Europe experienced a massive influx of non-European refugees and asylum-seekers, particularly from the Middle East and Africa. All attempts at forging a common European migration policy have failed, and eastern European countries are adamant in rejecting a quota of refugees. Nevertheless, was the influx of such an extraordinary magnitude in 2015 that we can hope that immigration as a topic that spurs support for populist parties could revert to a lower level?

<u>Answer</u>

We should distinguish between two types of immigration: contractual and state-sponsored. Most people would agree that contractual immigration does not cause any problem. This is typically an extended freedom to contract work, as happens in Europe with the free movement of people. This kind of immigration is typically well-integrated into the fabrics of society and adds value to an economy in a free exchange relationship, contracting work, housing, and living a "normal" life like any other residents. Contractual immigration is basically beneficial, otherwise it would just not occur, as contracts are not signed unilaterally. The free movement of people in Europe is a wonderful achievement, which was self-evident before World War I. It necessarily operates at the margin because of the language differences and the many other distinctive features of European countries, but it is nevertheless an important freedom, along with the freedom of movement of goods, services, and capital.

The story is very different as regards state-sponsored immigration, managed by the bureaucratic automatisms of asylum systems and supported by the welfare state, i.e., taxpayers. This is generally bad policy. From a humanitarian point of view, it is a catastrophe. It has given rise to a large and growing human trafficking and people smuggling segment in organized crime that has become more profitable than drug trafficking. The United Nations Office on Drugs and Crime estimates its turnover at $6.75 billion a year. And when these migrants arrive in Europe, they are unable or not allowed to work, which has some rationale since they were not "invited" by an employer as in the case of contractual immigration. This creates frustrations and very high social and financial costs for the populations involved. Since migrants often come from regressive cultural realms and repressed economies very distant from the free and industrialized West, their assimilation is difficult.

Basically, there are far more humane and intelligent ways to help people fleeing war and repression. One such way is the establishment of charter cities near their current location. The Marron Institute of Urban Management at New York University, for example, researches the conditions for the successful implementation of this concept. In any case, "welcoming" migrants who are uninvited by market agents is generally a bad idea, for the migrants themselves and for the societies disrupted by a sudden influx of people with completely different perceptions, ethics, and values about essential features of social life. From a humanitarian point of view, this is bad policy, regardless of the problematic socioeconomics of it.

<u>Question about the EU</u>

Switzerland has remained outside the European Union and concluded many bilateral agreements with the EU. However, the relationship might prove more difficult in the future, as the EU demands further concessions to integrate new EU law into the agreements without having to renegotiate them. Is the current Swiss position sustainable, also in light of the difficulties experienced by Brexit?

<u>Answer</u>

The European Union has always been attractive for less competitive European states, and it is unquestionable that countries with traditionally deficient national governance or a preference for protectionism and interventionism have benefited greatly from the EU single market economically, despite all the remaining national shortcomings. For Switzerland, not out of arrogance but simply out of reality, the EU proposition was never attractive, since the country (with the notable exception of agriculture) is economically more open, freer, and more competitive than the EU as a whole. In terms of economic freedom, Switzerland ranks fourth in the world and number one in Europe, so EU membership would mean regressing on many accounts: monetary policy, labor, product, and financial regulation, global trade, size and decentralization of government, or legal system. Currently, 92% of the Swiss population opposes EU membership, and it is unlikely that this will change in the future.

It is unquestionable that the four freedoms of the EU's Single Market have been a great achievement of post-war Europe. At the same time, the pretense of a European superstate, as evidenced by the unsound euro or the ineffective and costly European Parliament, is understandably deeply alienating for many voters in Europe who cherish local democracy. Generally, I believe that EU institutions are largely overvalued in the debate. They are far less important than it is generally perceived. What is important are the freedoms implemented in Europe, for which it is sufficient to get rid of (legal) barriers. It is not necessary to create an all-encompassing bureaucracy to sustain them.

The Swiss economy is more integrated into the EU economy than most EU countries, yet the relations do not happen between "Switzerland" and "the EU", but between individual agents: workers, consumers, entrepreneurs, suppliers, investors, buyers, sellers, or even lovers. I am a firm believer in good diplomatic relations between neighbors, and sincerely hope that Switzerland and the UK can shape their future relationship with the EU in a mutually profitable way. Unfortunately, the EU Commission and some EU leaders have often expressed an imperialist ambition to expand their jurisdiction. They should demonstrate more humility, especially considering their dismal rate of approval and general lack of credibility in light of their actual performance.

Howard Bloom

Best-selling writer and scientist. Member of the American Association for the Advancement of Science

Bloom's area of expertise is mass behavior, from the mass behavior of quarks to the mass behavior of human beings. He has lectured at Yale, Stanford and Columbia University. He has published on theoretical physics, cosmology, neurobiology and evolutionary biology. Bloom is the author of six books, including "The Lucifer Principle: A Scientific Expedition into the Forces of History", "Global Brain: The Evolution of Mass Mind from the Big Bang to the 21st Century", "The Genius of the Beast: A Radical Re-Vision of Capitalism", and "The God Problem: How A Godless Cosmos Creates". Bloom is the founder and head of the Space Development Steering Committee, a group that has included astronauts Buzz Aldrin, Edgar Mitchell (the sixth man on the moon) and members of NASA, the National Science Foundation, and the National Space Society. Bloom is also the founder or founding board member of the International Paleopsychology Project, The Darwin Project, and the Epic of Evolution Society. He is a member of the Board of Governors of the National Space Society and a member of The New York Academy of Sciences, the American Association for the Advancement of Science, and the American Psychological Society.

On How to Bridge the Digital Divide

First it is important to recognize the following fact: there is a division between cosmopolites and small-town folks. This division can be found within big cities. There are people that live in New York City, for example, who have been part of cosmopolitan culture all of their lives. They have lived in other cities, gone to college in other cities, and are as comfortable adjusting their schedules in order to talk to professional acquaintances in Paris or Tokyo as they are talking to their friends in the city where they live. They are cosmopolites: the people who live as part of global culture. And these cosmopolites have existed, at least, since the days of Erasmus of Rotterdam, in the second half of the XVth century, who maintained a big international network of friends. And then there are the small-town folk. They do not build bridges, they build walls. They are part of an enclave, and they are against cosmopolitan culture. These are people who grew up in a certain environment and never left it.

We had an incident in Howard Beach Queens in 1986 in which a black man accidentally walked through a white neighborhood. Queens is, after all, one of the boroughs of New York City, one of the most diverse cities in the world. But because some of the people in that neighborhood were white supremacists, they beat the black man up. This became a big international story. It was a result of a small-town mentality alive and kicking in a big city.

When I first came to New York City in 1964 and was registering as a student at New York University, I met a woman who had grown up in Brooklyn. She told me that she had not left Brooklyn until she was eighteen years old. Think about that. She had not seen Manhattan until she was eighteen years old. The neighborhood where I live – Park Slope, Brooklyn – was ranked recently by Money magazine as the most upscale and advanced neighborhood in North America. But even in this neighborhood -- in Park Slope -- there are people who were born on 9th street, who grew up on 9th street, who married somebody else who was also from 9th street and who are still living on 9th street. These are the small-town folk. And now we have a small-town person in a position of great power -- the presidency of the United States. Donald Trump comes from Queens. He comes from neighborhoods where people would rather build walls than bridges. How do we bridge this gap?

There are certain dichotomies that seem to be a necessary part of society and it has always been that way. For example, if we go back and examine the Carthaginians in the first millennium BC, they had a War Party and a Peace Party. In Carthage, sometimes the Peace Party managed to become the eyes and ears of society, and sometimes it was the War Party that took on that role. Sometimes the Peace Party was right -- commerce was the best way to grow Carthage. And sometimes the War Party was right -- Rome was conspiring to dismantle Carthage by military means. A military emphasis was hence crucial for survival. Dichotomies allow a society to see both sides of a question. Therefore, I do not think that we are going to be able to do much to break down our dichotomies. Including the dichotomy between the small towners in big cities and the cosmopolites. But what we are really talking about is who owns the eyes and ears of the culture, who owns its means of expression.

The conservatives, parochial and small-town folk complain that the left is prejudiced against them because of what they label the mainstream media. The mainstream media is basically a mouthpiece for the left, and that media had been dominant until about fifteen years ago. The right at that point began to create its own version of the mainstream media, which now features the Washington Times, The New York Post, Fox News, Breitbart, the Daily Caller, and a host of right-wing personalities on talk radio. Nobody on the right complains that its mainstream media is biased and that its statements are highly prejudiced. It is always the other side's mouthpieces that we complain about.

Recent studies on the effects of training have revealed that job training has not been effective at finding people jobs. Instead, I support trying to establish an apprenticeship system like the one in Germany. The Germans have one of the world's most competitive economies and have been one of the world's top three exporters for decades. Germany's system does not operate on the premise that everybody should get a university degree. They foster apprenticeships. And in the context of an apprenticeship, a company can train you to be the worker they want. We now hear a lot of repetition of the phrase that the economy has plenty of jobs but not the workers with the skills to fill them.

Tim O'Reilly of O'Reilly Media is one of the most prominent insiders in the computer community. He has just published a book titled WTF. In WTF, he puts forth the notion that we should not complain that we cannot find the right workers but instead that we should make the workers we need. We should train them. Apprenticeships work. I myself used apprenticeships in my career in the music industry. My background is science. But in 1976, I founded the biggest PR firm in the music industry, the Howard Bloom Organization, Ltd. The Howard Bloom Organization had a problem. We had a unique approach to public relations. I called it perceptual engineering. No potential employees were going to be trained in this approach if they had worked at other companies. In fact, for Howard Bloom Organization purposes, those who were trained in competing firms were educated all wrong. We therefore trained people internally with a two- to three-year training process based on apprenticeship. We did not assume that people would come to us as ideal employees, especially as we were inventing new public relations methods and new ways of thinking about public relations. We therefore had to start with good material, with people who were intelligent and articulate, and trained them methodically in the new public relations philosophy and techniques we were developing.

This should be happening all over the country. The problem becomes acute in a small town like Janesville, Wisconsin (population 63,500). The local General Motors plant shut down in 2008 and put roughly 9,000 people out of work. The workers who were laid off could not move to another town because they had very strong ties to their community. By the way, the Speaker of the House, Paul Ryan, was born in Janesville, and he and his family still live there. Something that would help in cases like the lost jobs in Janesville is that workers recognize that they need entrepreneurs and businesspeople, creative thinkers who will find a useful way to employ their skills. A useful and cost-efficient way to employ their skills. A profitable way. And the mayors of these towns that have lost vast amounts of jobs in the manufacturing sector are trying to find these entrepreneurs. But this is easier said than done.

Before we discuss taxes on robots to pay for training, examples of the kind of entrepreneurship that can help displaced workers are Uber and Lyft. They have apps that enable a free driver to find a passenger who needs a ride in real time. If the negotiation between a person who badly needs a ride and a person who has a ride to offer can be handled with such swiftness and efficiency, then surely, we can come up with apps that can do the same for jobs. In other words, we need apps that can let a person who wants a job to know where there is a job that can fit his or her abilities swiftly. Task Rabbit already does this. If you have a small job you need done -- let's say rewiring your sound system or installing Internet of Things remote control devices on your lighting system -- Task Rabbit finds someone capable of doing the job, makes an appointment, and handles the billing. All with a laptop or cellphone app.

There are also people who are unfortunately too old and whose health does not enable them to be retrained. These are low-income individuals without savings and without a right to a pension on which they can survive. The idea of a guaranteed minimum income is becoming increasingly popular. Secondly, for those people who are too old to be retrained, if they are (physically) capable they can play a role in providing care. There is a far greater need for providers of care than is recognized. This is something which the economy, society, and individuals need. People need human contact. Little kids do better in school if they have older people who can sit with them and help them do their homework. Older people can do that. Older people need somebody who wants them and cares about them, and such people can be put in touch especially if you have an app that can bring people with common interests together. People need to have their hands held and they need to be in face-to-face conversations with their fellow human beings. Older people have the time to be interested in what other people are doing. We can turn for an example to the relationship between grandparents and their grandkids: the grandparents just adore having little kids that need them and love them, and the little kids just adore having grandparents who need them, love them, and have the time to pay attention to them. We need more of these social hook-ups taking place in society to take advantage of the fact that people need to be needed. That provides an opportunity both for those who need and those who can fill those needs, those who can provide care.

Society is not going to run out of needs, wants, and wishes anytime soon. It is not going to run out of demand. Now the trick is to hook that demand and supply up in new ways. Even if it is a supply of emotions like caring.

Alexander Burns

Research services administrator, Australian National University

Alexander Burns is a research services administrator at The Australian National University's College of Asia and the Pacific, and a PhD candidate at Australia's Monash University. He has published on Australian and United States counterterrorism and national security policy, internet sociology, journalism, and strategic foresight. He is past editor of the popular counterculture news site Disinformation. He is a member of the Australasian Research Management Society.

Bridging Australia's Digital and Skills Divide

Australia faces what economist Ross Garnaut once called the *Dog Days* macroeconomic scenario (2013): a current sociopolitical environment of income inequality, political gridlock from minor parties, and growing anxieties about the post-2008 decline in Australians' living standards. Housing markets in Melbourne and Sydney look like overheated, speculative bubbles. Australia has had five Prime Ministers in ten years. Its mining and commodities boom has ended the economic growth enjoyed by the Hawke, Keating, and Howard-led governments. Major infrastructure projects such as the National Broadband Network (NBN) have significant delays, are over budget, and are cautionary case studies in policy implementation. At the time of writing, the Australian Labor Party (ALP) and the ruling Liberal National Party (LNP) coalition are locked in bitter disagreements about company and personal tax reforms, and how to deal with sovereign risks.

This pessimism suggests that a post-2008 phase shift has occurred in Australian sociopolitical identity. It eclipses a prior period of optimism which had suggested a different, more preferable future would occur. In 2004-05, I worked on a Smart Internet Technology Cooperative Research Centre project called *Smart Internet 2010*. The research team developed four conceptual 'schools of thought' to consider the internet's future: its major growth drivers included social media, mobile use, e-health, and digital games. The research team also considered potential dangers as well, including hacking and security risks.

Smart Internet 2010's lead industry sponsor Telstra took these research findings on board in its planning of internet and telecommunications consumer services. An important aspect of this was to bridge Australia's urban and rural divide for the delivery of internet-enabled services, particularly for e-health, and for disaster and emergency response. However, the NBN's troubled rollout has meant that *Smart Internet 2010*'s optimistic vision is still to be fully realized.

In 2015 the Turnbull federal government launched the AUD $1.1 billion National Innovation and Science Agenda (NISA) to address microeconomic reforms. NISA's four pillars addressed fiscal policy tax levers; university-industry sectoral collaboration; focusing on STEM (science, technology, engineering, and mathematics) disciplines and a visa program to attract young entrepreneurial talent; and streamlining government and public services via the Department of Finance and a new Digital Transformation Agency. One important aspect of NISA was to provide support for small and medium enterprise (SME) entrepreneurs, and to overcome the 'valley of death' problems faced by a risk-averse venture capital sector in Australia.

The Turnbull government has also committed to continued funding of the Medical Research Future Fund established by the previous conservative Abbott government. Mirroring this decisive funding shift, Australian state governments also support recent initiatives such as the Brisbane-based Translational Research Institute (TRI) facility. Here, industry partners and universities collaborate together on pioneering, intensive medical and biopharmaceutical research.

In 2017-18, I worked with The University of Queensland's Professor Ranjeny Thomas at TRI. Her spinout company Dendright Pty Ltd is conducting a Phase 1 clinical trial to test new immunotherapies that may successfully treat rheumatoid arthritis, and other autoimmune diseases. Professor Thomas' immunology laboratory attracts an international cohort of young, talented research scientists who are also creating methodological advances in related areas such as computational biology. A viable research program, a close relationship with potential funders and knowing the funding landscape, and commercialization skills such as knowledge of patents will underpin their continued success.

The Turnbull government has also recently emphasized tax enforcement, in several initiatives announced in the 2018 Federal Budget that responded to the Australian Treasury's Black Economy Taskforce. Part of this targets the Black Economy's use of internet payment systems for tax avoidance. This dichotomy illustrates that in Australia there is both funding pressure to innovate in medicine and science, and simultaneously there are also domestic concerns over fiscal and monetary policies.

The latter influence the policy platforms of Australian micro parties such as Pauline Hanson's One Nation and Cory Bernardi's Australian Conservatives: Hanson rails against growing government debt, whilst Bernardi critiques the political elite he calls the 'Canberra Bubble'. Debt-aware counter-elite sentiment now affects the Australian Senate's oversight and review function -- which makes it more difficult for the major political parties to pass new legislation that will continue to address needed microeconomic and productivity reforms. The micro parties are able to attack incumbents but they also largely lack the policy expertise to propose new and viable policy solutions.

A lack of bipartisan consensus also affects the institutional reforms in Australia's higher education sector for new skills training. Australia's federalist structure has led its States and Territories to implement different skills training guarantees for apprenticeships. Successive ALP and LNP governments have de-funded and then re-funded the network of Tertiary And Further Education (TAFE) colleges that oversee a significant number of Australia's apprenticeships and work-based training.

This uncertainty has led to adverse selection and moral hazards for Australian and overseas students. For example, the Victorian state Education Department in 2015-16 conducted a sector-wide crackdown on registered training organizations (RTOs) that used incentives to enroll students (such as offering free laptops), used subcontractors, and delivered ineffective training. The RTOs had sought to gain market share from the TAFE colleges -- and to use high pressure sales tactics reminiscent of Trump University -- on a more widespread scale.

A deeper challenge is the neoliberal assumption of economist Gary Becker's human capital framework which underpins the sector's current emphasis on lifelong learning. Successive LNP governments have used efficiency dividends to focus universities on employment and vocational outcomes. In turn, university administrators have emphasized funding for STEM disciplines, and applications in areas like machine learning and robotics. Malcolm Harris (*Kids These Days: Human Capital and the Making of Millennials*) contends that Becker's human capital framework has had negative impacts on Millennials; George Mason University professor Bryan Caplan (*The Case Against Education*) argues that between 30% to 80% of higher education involves signaling to potential employers rather than mastery of course content.

Australia's Treasury considered some of these long-term and structural issues in its 2015 intergenerational Report. The conservative Abbott and Turnbull governments' emphasis on budget repair, tax reforms, government service delivery reform, and the Digital Transformation Agency's establishment were part of the Intergenerational Report's agenda. Now, the Turnbull government's focus is on enhancing Australia's competitiveness and productivity.

<u>Australia's long-term challenges</u>

First, the commodities and mining boom's end now means that Australia needs to develop new industries in order to replace falling revenues. The fate of the domestic coal industry – and rising electricity and gas costs – is a political flashpoint for micro parties and voters. Recent investment in STEM and medical research under NISA signals the Turnbull government's preferences for innovation and investment in new skills. One commercialization model for this is The University of Queensland's Professor Ian Frazer's discovery of the Gardasil vaccine for human papillomavirus -- and his successful defense of the scientific patents involved. Intangible assets like an intellectual property portfolio and holding companies thus become more important.

Second, Australia needs to address growing income inequality and to ensure that the economic benefits of globalization and negotiated free trade agreements flow through to all Australians. The ALP and LNP debate over company and personal tax reform is in part about who benefits from fiscal policy. Sally McManus, the current Secretary of the Australian Council of Trade Unions (ACTU), has run a high-profile campaign of union membership renewal and targeted perceived 'wages theft' by employers. McManus and the ACTU have also criticized ride-share companies like Uber whose disruptive innovation of the taxicab industry relies on independent contractor agreements, regulatory arbitrage and tax minimization strategies. Whilst the Australian Greens advocate for a Universal Basic Income (UBI), the ALP and LNP's reticence to increase unemployment benefits to meet the poverty line means that a UBI is not likely to be adopted in Australia in the near-term future.

Third, Australia needs to address skills shortages and provide more effective pathways to full-time employment. In March 2018, the Turnbull government replaced the 457 visa for skilled migration with a new Temporary Skill Shortage visa overseen by the new Department of Homeland Affairs. Eligibility requirements for employers and visa applicants were tightened under the new scheme. However, Australia's skilled immigration levels and the flow-on effects for primarily urban infrastructure and population growth remains a political flashpoint for several micro parties including Pauline Hanson's One Nation Party.

Further microeconomic reform is also needed to address skills gaps. A National Skills Needs List defines the Australian Government's priorities to provide financial support under the Australian Apprenticeships Incentives Program to interested employers. The National Skills Needs List needs to be revised and updated to reflect emerging skills and new industries such as those emerging from STEM disciplines. As noted above Australia's RTO sector has faced adverse selection and moral hazard for Australian and overseas students: the Australian Skills Quality Authority needs to strengthen its regulatory oversight in order to combat the perverse incentives that are involved.

Fifth, Australia needs to resolve the troubled NBN rollout and to consider emerging technology infrastructure for internet services delivery. Its oligopolistic telecommunications industry structure has created perceptions of regulatory arbitrage over the past decade. Australia now lags regional leaders like Japan, Singapore, and South Korea in average internet speeds. New services have been envisioned since *Smart Internet 2010* in 2005 but are yet to be fully implemented due to technology rollout bottlenecks. Different ALP and LNP solutions have made the NBN a case study in troubled policy implementation. There is a significant risk that the NBN will be already outdated prior to its full rollout. This needs to be addressed but an oligopolistic industry and government policy brinkmanship means Australia's average internet speeds are likely to continue to fall, comparative to regional leaders.

Economist Ross Garnaut's forecasted *Dog Days* macroeconomic scenario has now arrived: with the end of the commodities and mining boom, most Australians face declining living standards, polarized political decision-making, slower average internet speeds, and political flashpoints over fiscal policy and skilled immigration. To-date the Turnbull government has relied strongly on medical and STEM innovation. The five major challenges outlined in this chapter need bipartisan support in order to be urgently addressed so that Australia's economic growth can be secured and shared more widely.

Naomi Campbell

Renown Interdisciplinary Artist

Born in Montreal, Canada, she comes from a background in both art and science. With an interdisciplinary practice with multiple media for over 30 years, Campbell's work has won many accolades, including several gold medals of honor. Featured in 21 book publications, she has exhibited in almost 200 exhibitions. She has been an instructor of the dynamic contemporary figure in watercolor at The Art Students League of New York for over ten years. Her work is in national and international public, corporate and private collections. Her permanent public commissions include the MTA Art & Design Bronx Zoo subway station, the City of Geochang (S. Korea), the City of Irving (Texas) and SWIFT Pan-Americas (New York). She has also designed the LIA London International Awards, New York, London, and the ASPCA Humane Award both used in perpetuity.

Ms. Campbell has been distinguished as an interdisciplinary artist pioneering new directions in three-dimensional stained glass and watercolor. Her recent work with Columbia University's neuroscience lab and its studies with genetic engineering has helped her expand her ongoing investigation into the role of perception in our lives. Campbell's resulting installations explore the fear, loss, power and fragility associated with the ecological environment in the natural world. Her work explores sense and perception in art and science, and her recent sculptures and installations look at the biodiversity of food.

Naomi Campbell lives and works in Brooklyn.

<u>On the causes of populism</u>

The idea of divide and conquer still seems to be popular. It is sad to to see such drastic changes occurring in our society and the divisions between social rankings. The role of labor is changing. How it will be replaced by the idea of pleasure as a new way of living is still evolving and will apply unequally to different groups in society. We do not have an idea of what to expect. The idea of having a strongman to look up to also explains the rise of populism, although it is more of an image than a realitistic proposition.

There are a lot of developments going on, and they are related and interwoven. Technology is a doubled-edged sword. It is pulling us away from the way of life we have led for decades or centuries. We are looking at a very different kind of Life on this planet. We have already catapulted ourselves into an unstable environment. This creates a high level of uncertainty for individuals, which in turn has political and economic consequences.

There are no simple answers or solutions to the causes that have spawned populism. We live in a rapidly changing world. We have launched ourselves into Internet lives. But how many images are we bombarded with daily? The human mind has to adapt to this new situation. And it is doing so. Scientists can make a lot of predictions as to how the human brain copes and adapts. Yet there is still a large degree of uncertainty and lack of knowledge.

I hesitate to make predictions. I come from a scientific background but am also active in the artistic world. We have seen a huge shift globally in agriculture. The idea of how to feed the world in the future is something I am concerned about in general terms, and the role that genetic engineering plays in particular. Family farming is being phased out. Big corporations in many countries are taking over the harvesting, packaging and delivery of food products. Farmers may be pushing back against this trend towards agribusiness, but many family farms are disappearing at an alarming rate.

Economic insecurity is therefore very real, in the manufacturing sector as well as in agriculture and even in white-collar professions. This economic insecurity compounds the insecurity from the threat of terrorism, global warming and other negative developments. People are reacting by innovating. The role of startups is essential and interesting. It emphasizes individual thinking at many levels. We need to encourage young people and professionals to obtain a degree or skills in one of the STEM fields (Science, Technology, Engineering, Mathematics). How the rest of the population that does not have such degrees or skills will fit into the labor market remains to be seen. The role of education has always been important in any technological revolution. Now, in the fifth industrial revolution we are undergoing, it is more important than ever.

The availability of the Internet to billions around the world has engendered a new way of learning, especially by universities that now offer online courses. How does this new method of learning affect group behavior or individual thinking,

Is it better to have people working on an individual working and researching on their own? This is open to debate

We live in an era that is amazing and horrifying at the same time. Those who can move around and relocate and have the right degrees are in an advantageous positions. Otherwise it is much more difficult to adapt to the digital revolution. Innovation

How do we finance lifelong learning and training? If factories and even farms are going to be staffed primarily by robots and machines, shoudn't these corporations that employ them pay some kind of tax or contribution so that the benefits of the welfare state – or at least a part – can be funded? Bill Gates is on the record as favoring contributions by companies.

I do agree with the general proposition. I am not sure if the wording – in terms of a tax or contribution by corporations -- is the appropriate one. But the basic idea would revolve around the fact that at the same time that technology is replacing persons, there is also a desire by many – especially in developed countries – to lead a more organic form of living and thinking

We have to move forward. There is no other way. Big corporations and the individual have to come to an agreement that allows for a collaboration. That would of course be ideal. But if it is not possible to reach an agreement, establishing a baseline now is more important than ever. Once everything is set in place, it will be harder to make profound changes. But it is hard to set down or establish any ideas and parameters when there are so many elements that are evolving. These transformations are not just affecting individuals, but also companies and countries. Corporations and nations have to cope with technological transformations as well as phenomena such as global warming and climate change, whose evolution even scientists cannot unanimously predict. The timeline on changing weather patterns has accelerated. It makes sense to have coportation make some kind of contribution. Companies will also have to as flexible as individuals and nations. Climate change is creating serious problems which we may not yet realize but will have to mitigate and cope with in the near future.

Startups are essential. Many people have started on a very small scale with modest means and have scaled up and been very successful. Corporations will experience a lot of problems themselves. It will be a very plastic and evolving world.

Should there be a universal income for older people who are too old to be retrained? Life expectancy has increased dramatically and will continue to rise, especially in developed countries, but also in emerging ones. In the Netherlands, there is a universal income for people who turn 65 regardless of whether they have worked or not. Individuals receive a 900 euro payment from the time they turn 65 until they die. Such policies are espoused or not opposed by

Coming from Canada, we have had a very stable system that took care of the elderly. People are ageing in a different manner, so some older people can be retrained. But we do have to help older people. They have put in a whole life of work. Limiting population growth would also be desirable, although it has not been successful everywhere. Certain countries have decreased their birth rates, which has been helpful and is desirable.

Everybody wants to have a university degree, especially in developed countries. But technicians make more money than university graduates, especially those in the humanities. Germany has an excellent apprenticeship system. Not everybody needs to attend university.

I absolutely agree on the need to foster apprenticeships. The idea of degrees has worled for a long time. But we now have to shift to a system of more individualized learning. People have to learn on their own, according to their own trajectory. Individuals therefore are required to take their education and acquisition of knowledge into their own hands and cannot expect to benefit from a passive learning system. They need to take the initiative. If they do so successfully, they can develop their own individual strengths. Individual skills can then be adapted and scaled up to benefit a group, which adds to collective knowledge.

University systems are wonderful, but it depends on the field you are in. For many years, graduates in the humanities have encountered difficulties in obtaining well-paying jobs, as opposed to those in scientific and technological ones. Training and self-training is the key. It requires a degree of self-motivation. Universities are diversifying. Everybody is looking at the structure of education. Universities are rethinking their role, and this puts educators in a new situation. Depending on which field you are in, whether you study invidually or in a college system, taking your acquired knowledge and skills in a direction which enhances your natural abilities is a very positive development.

The International Labor Organization has published studies on the millions of jobs that will be destroyed, including in a vast array of white-collar professions, as machine- and AI-activated services in every field from law to medicine will further advance. Pro-tech enthusiasts assert that companies will assign more value-added tasks and jobs to their remaining employees. Do you think this will happen? Do you see evidence to prove such predictions?

The idea of Artificial Intelligence and its role in our future concerns me and is a topic which I have worked on. The idea of replacing the organic body with the non-organic (machines) or merging the two is fascinating, for example in the medical field. There are going to be negative consequences for which there are no easy answers now.

Going back to the subject of production of food, it will be redefined. Looking far down the road, expanding into space is one of our trajectories. Unfortunately, it will involve a lot of mechanization and many jobs will be destroyed. There will be an imbalance between individuals with the right knowledge and skills and those who do not have them.

Miguel Cervantes

Lecturer, Burgundy Business School and EM Lyon Business School

Mr. Cervantes, who is originally from Mexico, holds a Bachelor's and Master's degree in Economics from the University of Texas at El Paso. He has been a lecturer at HEC Business School and Vanier College, both in Montreal. Cervantes carries out international research for the Fraser Institute. He is the co-author of several issues of the annual Survey of Mining Companies, Global Petroleum Survey, and currently works on the Economic Freedom of the Arab World report. He currently lectures at several business schools in France: Burgundy Business School, EM Lyon Business School, EM Normandy Business School and South Champagne Business School.

Exploring the causes of Populism

The past years have seen the rise of economic populism, demagoguery and nativism. Populism represents a threat to freedom and poses a threat to economic liberalism.

But the question is what is the source of populism? Is it the result of technology that has displaced jobs to less developed countries? Is globalization the culprit? Is it free trade? Others blame the spread of populism on political correctness.

Let us consider whether technology is the cause of unemployment. The charge that machines have replaced people is a fallacy on many levels. It is a philosophical mistake called scientism. It is also an economic mistake that does not take into account that, without human capital, the marginal product of capital is zero. Very advanced software has zero productivity if there is no human capital to work with it. For instance, there have been programs in Mexico that have brought electronic blackboards to poor schools. But these programs have been a failure because there was no human capital to make them work. Physical capital enhances human capital and frees people from tedious tasks. Let us think of cashiers in supermarkets. Today many supermarkets operate with machines that enable self-check-out. These advances in technology help the former cashiers, who have become supervisors who ensure the self-check-out system and machines work smoothly. Moreover, cashiers no longer have to worry about making a mistake and getting a complaint from a customer.

One job that cannot be done completely by machines is translation. Software can be useful in terms of making translations more accurate. But they will never completely replace humans when it comes to translating because of the many nuances that languages have. Teaching is also another task that can be performed partly by machines. Even though some classes can be delivered by videos, they are the most basic ones. Watching these tutorial videos actually help students to be ready for the real and more complex lectures. Each professor has a unique method of teaching. It is therefore impossible to completely replace teachers with online platforms.

The engineering impossibility of perfect adaptability of machines and labor had already been proven. That is the idea that you can perfectly substitute labor for capital. In this theory, there is an assumption regarding the existence of a production function $Q= f(x1, x2)$. Q is the output per unit of time, X1 is a service flow called man hours and X2 is a service flow called machine hours. The equation allows for the variation of the rates of use of man hours and machine hours with perfect adaptability. This equation is supposed to be the only efficient maximizing technical alternative. But there is a challenge. When changing the rates of use of machine hours, the capital stock which generates the service flow must be instantaneously and costlessly adapted to the changing rates of the variable service flow that is men/person hours. The perfect adaptability is false *a priori*, and a logical impossibility, because perfect adaptability implies a costless metamorphosis of the capital input (Roth 17-18). I invoke the theory of Timothy Roth who criticized the neo-classical social welfare theory to illustrate the impossibility that all the activities of life are completely interchangeable between man hours and machine hours.

Furthermore human capital exists in many differentiated forms. The service flow of a cardiologist, for example, is not the same as that of a heart surgeon.

We have heard from many quarters that globalization has caused the uniformization of cultures, created inequalities, and the concentration of capital. Such assertions have been made by not too serious economists. But prestigious ones such as Joseph Stiglitz, and more recently Thomas Piketty, have also staunchly advocated these claims. Let us take a closer look at their arguments.

Mass production done by big multinationals cannot replace everything. Big companies produce for the average tastes and preferences. However, there are always special tastes and preferences that cannot be satisfied by mass production. All production done in an artisan way is based on monopolistic competition, not perfect competition. In a monopolistic competition producers will make a similar good but will differentiate from others. A good example is artisanal beer. There are small artisanal producers in most countries. For instance in France there are producers in the regions of Britany and Alsace.

<u>The complexity of today's trade flows</u>

Furthermore, today's trade is not based on a simple equation like in the past. In the past a country -- for example -- exported wine and imported wool. Trade flows have become more complicated. This is what is called intra-industry trade. These are international exchanges within the same industry. For instance, France exports Bayonne cured ham, but imports from Spain *pata negra* cured ham.

Trade enriches a culture, provides it with new ideas and makes it more competitive. When a country faces competition, producers will listen to consumers around the world, and will imitate the best practices. Countries more open to trade will learn the best practices from the rest of the world much faster. There are dynamic effects of learning by doing, but the learning by doing can only happen in a competitive environment.

The debate about globalization has led to an abuse of language. A lot has been said about globalization, but the key question is whether we are more globalized than at other times in history. The traditional international economics textbook by James Gerber reveals that in 1913 six economies (France, Germany, Japan, Netherlands, the United Kingdom and the United States) were already globalized, as measured by trade over GDP. They then suffered a decline and bounced back in the seventies to the same levels they had attained in 1913. So globalization has slowly increased since the 1970s but has not been grown radically. The Netherlands in 1913 were more globalized than many countries are today.

In 1913 immigration was more mobile than today. In Canada, the US and France, immigrants accounted for about 10% of the population. There was labor mobility even within the British Commonwealth. Indian people, for example, were allowed to work in South Africa. The city of Winnipeg in the 1910s had a large share of inhabitants of Ukrainian origin. In the case of labor, the world is less mobile than before.

It is therefore inaccurate to state that we are witnessing a radical wave of unprecedented globalization. In the 1800s, globalization was enhanced with the invention of the steam train, the telephone and the telegraph, as well as by improvements in shipping. This wave of globalization was abruptly cut short by the Great Depression of the 1930s and the enactment of the Smoot-Hawley Tariff Act in 1930. This protectionist law compounded the 1929 stock market crash, unleashed trade wars and competitive devaluations and lengthened, deepened and spread the Great Depression. In 1944, before the conclusion of World War II, more than forty countries gathered at the Bretton Woods conference in New Hampshire. They were determined to craft an international economic order and create international institutions that would prevent a repeat of the breakdown of international cooperation that took place in the 1930s. In addition to the creation of the International Monetary Fund to oversee the monetary system and the International Bank for Reconstruction and Development to assist in rebuilding Europe, the countries gathered also agreed in principle that an institution to regulate and liberalize trade should also come into being. The United States administration of president Harry Truman led such efforts. The Havana Charter in 1948 called for the creation of the International Trade Organization. After the US Senate failed to ratify the creation of the ITO, the countries that had signed the Havana Charter successfully pushed ahead with reductions in tariffs on the exchange of industrial products within the framework provided by the General Agreement on Tariffs and Trade (GATT).

The efforts of the successive GATT rounds from 1947 until 1986 helped to decrease tariffs on industrial products across the board. However, the GATT was not as successful in decreasing non-tariff barriers for industrial products, and in liberalizing and regulating trade in agricultural products, services and intellectual property. But the Uruguay Round of the GATT, held between 1986 and 1994, was the most successful exercise in regulating and liberalizing international trade in history. The GATT's member countries managed to agree on additional cuts to tariffs on trade in industrial products (the GATT 1994 agreement), adopted a first-ever agreement on trade in agricultural prouducts, the first agreement on trade in services (the GATS), another for textiles and one to protect intellectual property (TRIPS). The Uruguay Round also produced a robust mechanism to resolve trade disputes among the signatories and the World Trade Organization (WTO).

Unfortunately, since 2001 the WTO's Doha Round has been a dismal failure. The membership of the WTO is much bigger (164 countries) than during the GATT's early years or even during the Uruguay Round. Moreover, the vast array of matters that must be agreed upon -- industrial products, agriculture, textiles, services, intellectual property, investment disputes, anti-dumping -- is daunting. The so-called Single Undertaking requires that all countries reach an agreement on all of the aforementioned topics for the round to be concluded. This approach has scuttled the Doha Round.

The Doha Round's failure has fostered the multiplication of regional and bilateral trade agreements, described by Bhagwati as a spaghetti bowl. In addition, we must bear in mind that there are several countries that are not members of the WTO, such as Algeria, Irak, Somalia or Timor Leste. While 189 countries are members of the IMF and the World Bank Group, the WTO's membership stands at 164. The GATT and WTO have achieved a lot, but much work remains to be done.

But coming back to the idea of globalization, it is important to have specific benchmarks that measure globalization in order to ascertain reality and examine how it can be improved. There are many nations that are not integrated into world markets as the KOF Globalization Index indicates. Many countries rank very poorly in the globalization index. The DHL index measures the hotspots for international trade, such as the cities which are trade hubs. It shows that there are several in Asia and Europe but few in Africa.

Even closer to Europe, in northern Africa, there are practically no infrastructure or trade links between Algeria and Morocco. The fact that Algeria supports the independence of the Western Sahara has created tensions between Morocco and Algeria for decades, therefore hampering economic integration in northern Africa.

But to really understand why some countries are more open to trade and are more prosperous, we need to define the concept of economic freedom. Economic freedom is a way to measure how free people can engage in voluntary transactions without interference from others and government. The traditional ranking is the Fraser Institute's Economic Freedom of the world. Using the Economic Freedom ranking is a good tool to measure free markets. The Economic Freedom ranking includes several components, such as the size of government, the adequacy of the legal system, sound monetary policy and trade and regulation. Economic freedom is related positively to different variables such as GPD per capita, GDP growth, the income of the poorest, and political and civil liberties. In the places where economic freedom has taken hold, there is more prosperity and social cohesion.

Around the world there are success stories and stories of countries where economic freedom has diminished. In Europe, the Baltic republics (Estonia, Latvia and Lithuania) that became independent when the Soviet Union collapsed have made great progress in increasing economic freedom and liberalizing their markets. Georgia is another outstanding example of a country that has cut import tariffs unilaterally, liberalized its labor market, has low barriers to foreign investment and low taxation. Ireland is another country that has improved drastically in terms of economic freedom and is posting very high rates after undergoing a painful but necessary internal devaluation and bail-out supervised by the IMF, the European Central Bank and the European Commission.

In Western Europe the excessive size of the welfare state, high levels of taxation and rigid labor markets are holding it back from experiencing an economic miracle like the one that took place in the 1950s and 1960s. The rigidness of the labor market is one of the reasons for the rise of right-wing parties in Europe. Labor markets in many countries in Europe include two very different kind of employees. These two-tiered labor market pits well-paid workers on indefinite contracts who are expensive to fire and have accrued many benefits against temporary workers with no job security and minimal benefits. The latter group of employees is obviously prone to be attracted by and vote for left or right-wing populists. We have seen this happen recently in Italy, a country suffering from a decades-long economic underperformance, corruption and extremely low growth in GDP and income. In the past general elections in Italy, the left-wing populists of Five Star Movement and the right-wing populists of the League placed first and second. They have formed Western Europe's first populist government. It not only wants to increase spending in breach of the EU's budget deficit targets and raise spending for many constituencies. The new government will never adopt the structural reforms – such as liberalizing the labor market – that would unleash job creation and growth. We are thus caught in a catch-22. Economic underperformance in several countries produce populist governments, which upon taking office only make matters worse by adopting irresponsible policies.

In the region of the Middle East and northern Africa, there are countries that are open to free markets and trade such as Bahrain, Jordan, the United Arab Emirates, Qatar and Oman. These countries have very low taxation, low barriers to trade, and sound legal and monetary systems. They are integrated into world markets and are not too dependent on oil revenues. On the other hand, there are countries that have not integrated into world markets, such as Algeria, Egypt, Libya, Somalia and Sudan. Even in Northern Africa, there is a wall between Morocco and Algeria as the latter supports the Polisario Front in its quest for independence for the Western Sahara. This conflict has thus poisoned the economic and trade relations in Northern Africa in general and between Morocco and Algeria in particular. The Middle East and northern Africa region needs urgent integration in world markets.

The Asia region has had some positive examples of increasing economic freedom, such as the Asian tigers and jaguars. India and China started dismantling their centrally-run economies decades ago. China started in the late 1970s, and India started in the 1990s. However, further liberalization has stagnated. The world needs further economic liberalization in China and India, that would produce a domino effect in the rest of the world. In southeast Asia, Burma has undergone a profound political transition but not the economic transformation it requires.

In the former republics of the Soviet Union there was great hope when communism was dismantled in 1991. Some countries, like Estonia, Latvia and Lithuania, quickly embraced free markets, opened up their economies to trade and investment, cut taxes, privatized state-owned companies and developed sound institutions. They were rewarded by very high GDP and income growth rates and membership in the eurozone. More recently Georgia and Armenia have made much progress. On the other hand other countries such as Belarus, Kyrgyzstan, Moldova, Uzbekistan, Tajikistan, Ukraine have not adopted market reforms and are still lagging well behind the best performing former Soviet republics. Russia after the fall of Communism experienced the chaotic 1990s and a sovereign debt crisis in 1998. Afterwards it enjoyed a period of healthy growth delivered by high prices for its oil, natural gas and metals. Growth in Russia stagnated in 2014 when commodity prices tumbled. The Russian economy is still heavily dependent on exports of fossil fuels, minerals and metals and has not fostered the creation of enough modern or high-tech industrial and service companies which produce goods with more value added.

The aforementioned failures we described around the world in the underperformance of any economies are not a crisis of globalization, but rather a lack of globalization. The regions that are not linked to world trade flows are the ones that have stagnated. These countries simply are not implementing free market reforms, whether because they are ruled by crony dictators or by populist parties. What is happening today is the failure to further integrate trade and further unleash the power of free markets. Populism thrives in places with a lack of free markets.

<u>Reviewing Mexico's post World War II economic development</u>

Let us take this approach and analyze the troubling rise of populism in Mexico. During the period between 1940 until 1980, Mexico adopted the protectionist and interventionist model involving import substitution and industrialization. This model was based in the idea of producing goods nationally and putting up stiff barriers to trade. Its purpose was to build up an industrial sector that would be a source of national pride. The import substitution did not live up to its promise of glory for Mexico. The import substitution policy did not create new competitive industries. It simply forced multinationals to produce locally, often churning out goods of lower quality than those manufactured abroad. Due to the overvalued currency, the policy harmed exports. In order to maintain the peso's fixed exchange rate, public debt began to soar as the country's treasury was forced to buy dollars.

Import substitution was accompanied by economic nationalism, thereby creating state-owned enterprises in electricity, oil, fertilizers, buses and other sectors. The import substitution and economic nationalization drive created huge social, economic and legal inequalities. Every city in Mexico has huge poverty belts. These policies protected the elites and did not unleash economic competitiveness and innovation. By the 1970s, the import substitution model was falling apart. The 1968 students protests were a testament that the import substitution was not creating prosperity at all. The governments of Luis Echeverria and Jose López Portillo in the 1970's did not respond to the crisis by opening the economy. Instead, they borrowed and spent without any accountability in order to redistribute wealth and prevent unrest. Furthermore, the discovery of oil off of Mexico's Pacific Coast compounded the government's sense of security and its profligate borrowing and spending. The result was increasing corruption at all levels. In 1982 Mexico was one of several Latin American countries that suffered a severe debt crisis. It experienced massive capital flight and double-digit inflation. Mexico was forced to resort to the IMF to prevent a complete default. The new administration of president Miguel de la Madrid (1982-1988) undertook some liberalizing reforms, which were nonetheless foisted on Mexico by the IMF and its foreign creditors, which did restructure and even write off some of Mexico's public debt.

One significant reform was for Mexico to join the GATT. Under the next president, Carlos Salinas de Gortari (1988-1994), Mexico negotiated and became a member of the North American Free Trade Agreement, which profoundly fostered Mexico's economic integration into North American supply chains. Moreover, under the Salinas administration privatization of state-owned enterprises was carried out in the telephone, bus and fertilizer sectors. However, big companies such as the oil and electricity monopolies remained in state hands. Under the ensuing governments of president Ernesto Zedillo (1994-2000) there was further privatization of marginal corporations such as the railroads and macroeconomic stability was maintained.

<u>The post PRI era in Mexican presidential politics</u>

In 2000, after many decades in power, the Institutional Revolutionary Party (PRI) lost the presidency for the first time in seventy years. The governments of center-right president Vicente Fox (2000-2006) of the National Action Party (PAN) ushered in much-needed democratic reforms. During the Fox administration, macroeconomic stability was also maintained. But the first president from the business-friendly PAN was unable to enact the structural economic reforms that Mexico needed in order to become more competitive. Some of these necessary reforms were of the labor market and the education and energy sectors. The next right-wing government under president Felipe Calderón (2006-2012) ensured macroeconomic stability and was successful in attracting foreign companies to participate in the exploration and drilling for oil in Mexico through service contracts. It was a step in the right direction but was not sufficient in luring massive foreign investments into the energy sector. Calderon's other modernizing reforms were scuttled by the opposition in Parliament. Despite enjoying a period of macroeconomic stability and solid growth, prosperity did not reach enough Mexicans, especially in the rural southern states. In the 2012 elections, voters opted to choose a PRI president, Enrique Peña Nieto.

During Peña Nieto's term, the president successfully negotiated with the PAN-controlled Parliament the adoption of substantive and wide-ranging economic reforms. The power of labor unions in the education sector was significantly curtailed. The implementation of additional reforms in the energy sector attracted foreign direct investment through profit-sharing contracts. These arrangements will open up the possibility of shale gas exploration and production, which have unleashed an energy revolution in the United States in the past years and put in on a path to energy independence.

The Mexican electricity sector was also opened up to foreign direct investment under Peña Nieto's tenure. These reforms will deliver investment and prosperity to Mexico in the future. They are key for improving Mexico's competitiveness. The benefits will take time to be felt. The period of exploration and production of oil and natural gas can take several years. Even though the Peña Nieto government accomplished important reforms that will engender benefits in the future, his administration was riddled by corrupt practices in several contracts for infrastructure projects. The corruption undermined the success of implementing far-reaching reforms.

The long-time left-wing populist firebrand Andrés Manuel López Obrador (popularly known as AMLO) finally managed to win the presidential elections held in July of 2018 after several unsuccessful tries in the past. AMLO's mantra is that during the past thirty years Mexico has been subjected to neoliberalist policies and globalization that have not worked, and which have generated more inequality, poverty and externalities. Where AMLO misses the point is that Mexico has never experienced extreme globalization nor truly implemented liberalizing reforms in a sustained manner. Mexico has never placed among the top 10 countries in the Freedom Report.

But there has been poor communication by the other mainstream parties and academics. Even though Mexico opened up to foreign trade when it joined GATT, NAFTA and some bilateral trade agreements, it still has variable tariff rates with other countries. Some special interests like car distributors have created barriers to the import of cheap used cars from the US. So people are bombarded with the message that Mexico has joined the globalized economy but they often fail to see the tangible benefits in the form of cheap foreign goods. Despite the energy reforms, people cannot pump cheap gas or natural gas into their vehicles because it takes time for the investments to materialize.

The president-elect, López Obrador, has been telling people that the increase in the gas prices are the result of the energy reform. Unfortunately, people in Mexico think that Mexico underwent a period of sustained liberalization in many sectors which has not worked. People think that capitalism has created poverty and exclusion. People believe that the energy reform was a disaster which will take at least a decade to yield benefits. Most of the reforms in Mexico have been of the crony-capitalism variety but dressed up in the language of free markets. In Mexico, the elites took control of assets through crony capitalism from the public sector, privatizing state-owned enterprises to friends. Mexico has experienced free trade for the elite but protectionism for the poor, as the privileged engage in rent-seeking behavior. Instead of unleashing an entrepreneurial drive, privatizations have often protected privilege. As long as people are not informed and truly understand that Mexico never wholeheartedly and efficiently experienced free markets but rather crony capitalism, López Obrador's popularity will remain high. He won the presidency in the first round with over 50% of the vote.

Another factor that has contributed to López Obrador's increased popularity is the anti-immigration sentiment and measures taken by the US administration under President Donald Trump. Mexico had pushed through economic reforms that finally opened up the oil, gas and electricity sectors to foreign direct investment. It was a time to celebrate and support Mexico. It was very irresponsible to attack Mexico and Mexicans with inflammatory speeches, precisely at a time when the country had taken very bold steps in strategic sectors to attract FDI and relegating decades of anti-imperialist rhetoric to the dustbin of Mexican history.

<u>Alan K. Chan</u>

Independent business consultant to North American companies in China.

Alan K. Chan was born and raised in Hong Kong and educated in the United Kingdom. He started working and living in China after graduating with a Bachelor's in Science from the University of London in 1989, a time when multinational firms began to enter the Chinese market. Over the following years, he witnessed the transition of China from a "state-owned enterprise" economy to a market economy, and how this evolution changed people's mentality. Through his work as Regional General Manager of a Fortune 500 company, Alan became acquainted with many government officials, managers of state-owned companies and university academics. Alan hired hundreds of local graduates as part of the first wave of foreign company employees, many of whom have become lifelong friends. As economic reforms continued, many of them have experienced changes in their lives which were unthinkable just 20 years ago. Alan was later seconded to Canada where he also completed his MBA and has since settled down with his family in Toronto. Among other things, he helps North American companies develop their business in China as an independent business consultant. In his private time, he focuses on his studies and research on comparative sociology between China and the Western countries, often tapping into the insights of his friends whom he met back when China was still the "sleeping dragon".

China: The unexpected guardian of Globalization and Universal Digital Access

I was born in Hong Kong in 1966, the year when Mao Zedong started the "Cultural Revolution" in China. Obviously, as an infant, I had no idea that it was happening, not to mention that it would become such a tragedy for at least two generations of Chinese people. The only recollection I have is watching the trial of the "Gang of Four" on TV at the end of that horrible era in 1976. Other than that, life was uneventful for this schoolkid in the then British Colony of Hong Kong.

Fast forward to the spring of 1989. I was about to graduate from university and was preparing for my final exams in my dormitory in Chelsea, London. However, it was a challenge to stay focused on my studies, as there was non-stop news coverage of the student-led protests in Beijing on TV. I had never been to Beijing at that time, or anywhere north of the Hong Kong border for that matter. Nonetheless, I had always felt a tie to the Chinese people. My grandfather worked for the Chinese government and owned many businesses in China after graduating from the University of California in the early 1900's. Eventually I passed my exams and graduated, but the ending of the mass demonstration in Tiananmen Square became another tragedy in Chinese history.

I bring up the Cultural Revolution of 1966-76 and the Tiananmen protests of 1989 not only because they mark two important milestones in my life. I believe they are two important benchmarks in recent Chinese history, against which we should measure the progress China has made and to analyze developments in the right context. According to World Bank data, in 1976, after ten years of brutal mismanagement during the Cultural Revolution, there were over 800 million people living in extreme poverty. Since then, over 700 million Chinese have been lifted out of it. Per capita GDP has increased from a mere $168 in 1976 to over $8,000 today. Sixty eight percent of the Chinese urban population is considered to be in the middle class today, with more than $9,000 in disposable household income. More importantly, people are generally happier. There is no denying that China has made some incredible progress in a relatively short time to improve the quality of life of its people. And let us not forget that China accounts for almost 20% of the world's population.

That being said, there are growing pains. Inequality was rising. Property rights were often overlooked in the name of development, especially at local levels of government. Corruption by government officials was rampant until the crackdown in recent years. More importantly, in the pursuit of social stability which the government values above all as a precursor to economic growth, civil rights are often violated. We will revisit this matter at the end of my contribution.

<u>Deng's decisive reforms and WTO accession</u>

So how did the Chinese government achieve such an incredible turnaround, after the decade-long Cultural Revolution had destroyed much of the economy? It all started with Deng Xiaoping's economic reforms in 1978. At the core of the reform was the "Open Door Policy" which opened China up to foreign businesses and investments. Reform in the agricultural sector led to the accumulation of wealth among the rural population, which in turn drove demand for modern goods and services. Foreign businesses saw the opportunity and began to trade with and invest in China. Small, private enterprises in the rural areas (the so-called Township and Village Enterprises, TVE) emerged to replace state-owned enterprises as the engine of economic growth. As a result, total trade volume increased steadily from $20 billion in 1978 to over $470 billion in 2000.

The pivotal moment came in 2001, when China officially joined the World Trade Organization (WTO) after a long and controversial negotiation. Even within the Chinese government, many had viewed the WTO as a "club of the rich", in which wealthy countries imposed rules on poor and developing nations. China's commitment to privatize and open up major industrial sectors as a result of its accession to the WTO would mean massive layoffs from state-owned enterprises, which had been the main provider of not only jobs but also everything from housing and healthcare to retirement welfare. Foreign investment would have more control of the local economy. There were worries of compromised national security if foreign firms entered key strategic industrial sectors.

These are the same challenges that many developed countries face today in the globalized economy and the digital era. However, instead of turning inward and maintaining its protectionist policies, China decided that the benefits of being a player in the global economy outweighed the risks and costs. Massive layoffs did turn out to be a major headache in the years that followed China's accession to the WTO in 2001. But the inflow of foreign direct investment and foreign goods and services also benefited the economy and consumers and allayed the impact of unemployment. Many of those who were laid off went on to become entrepreneurs in foreign trade or the emerging services sector or were retrained and rehired for new manufacturing jobs. With foreign investment and an ample supply of labor, China became "the world's factory". New technologies and management expertise also contributed to the development of local capabilities. A case in point is the many local university and medical school graduates that my company hired at the time, when it was making a major investment in China for manufacturing, research and commercial operations. I was utterly impressed by those young talents, and how hungry they were when given the opportunity to learn and grow.

It was such open-mindedness, rather than xenophobia, that drove the exponential growth since China became an active player in the global economy. Today, China is not only the world's biggest exporter, but also the second largest importer. It has signed 14 regional and bilateral free-trade agreements with international trading partners from all over the world. It has also become a major player in outward foreign investment, with more than $120 billion invested in various projects in over 170 countries. The current leadership under President Xi Jinping has signaled repeatedly in many international forums that global economic integration will remain a key commitment and strategy for growth for the next decade and beyond. It is safe to say that

China is not turning its back on globalization, despite the increasing nativism and protectionism displayed elsewhere in the world.

<u>Record investments in infrastructure and technology</u>

Domestically, the government invested heavily in infrastructure, with a clear objective of improving connectivity and productivity. Since the first highway was built in 1988, there is ongoing construction of an expressway network to connect all provincial capitals and cities with a population of over 200,000. At the end of 2017, the total length of China's expressway network reached 136,000 kilometers, the world's largest expressway system by length. High speed rail (HSR) passenger trains travelling at 250 - 350 km/h have been another major investment by the government. They are also a case study of successful implementation of international technology transfer agreements. Leading manufacturers from around the world participated in the initial HSR construction. Today, the total HSR network in China exceeds 25,000 kilometers, and accounts for over two thirds of all commercial HSR networks in the world. New airports are also being built every year and are expected to reach 260, covering most medium-sized cities by 2020.

But perhaps the most important infrastructure that the Chinese government has built is the mobile telecommunications network. China had a unique opportunity to leapfrog to mobile communications, as landlines were largely damaged during World War II and the civil war that followed and were never fully restored. When mobile telecommunications technologies became available in the late 1980's, the government seized the opportunity and went directly with mobile to develop a national network. Telecommunications is one of the key strategic industries that the government maintains a tight control of. The industry is dominated by three state-owned companies (these are the mobile network carriers, namely China Mobile, China Unicom and China Telecom), which were spun off from the Ministry of Telecommunications. Following the government's mandate, these companies had to provide access to remote rural areas when they developed their mobile networks across the country. The result is almost universal access to mobile signal, and more importantly, to the Internet. According to the China Internet Network Information Center, there are 772 million people in China who have access to the Internet, 98% of whom access it through their mobile phones. Based on this prevalent access to the Internet, new technologies thrive. In 2017, $120 billion of private equity and venture capital were invested in Chinese technology startups, most of which provide Internet-based services ranging from mobile healthcare to microfinancing to bicycle sharing.

The more established technology giants such as Alibaba and Tencent provide online platforms for e-commerce and mobile payments, significantly reducing the cost and barriers for entrepreneurs across the country to sell their products to the world. Now a farmer in a remote rural village can sell his produce online to customers in North America and collect payment easily. Similarly, the owner of a small pop-up store no longer requires expensive point-of-sale systems. Instead, all he needs is a QR code on a cardboard for customers to scan with their phones for payment and transaction records. The exponential growth in e-commerce also drives demand for many supporting services, and the logistics industry in particular. More than 30 billion packages are delivered every year in China. This requires sophisticated logistics and distribution companies, which in turn employ a massive labor force that covers every corner of the country. The latter plays a key role in providing employment for rural migrant workers who move to the cities (the "courier brothers") and afford them an opportunity for upward mobility in the big urban centers. Going forward, the government has committed to its "Internet Plus" strategy as a key driver for further economic growth, especially with the development of Artificial Intelligence based on data collected from the vast 1.4 billion registered mobile users across the country. The 1.4 billion registered users include people who have more than one phone, which is common in the big cities.

<u>Development of the National Social Credit System</u>

Mobile technology and widespread Internet access has therefore been a key driver of China's economic growth. But the government also depends on them for another project. In 2014, the State Council announced the development of a "National Social Credit System" by 2020. Just like the credit score system in many western countries, which collects user-specific data on financial transactions to establish financial creditworthiness, the Social Credit System would look at individual data but with a much wider scope. Instead of just getting the data from financial institutions, the Chinese Social Credit System collects data from various online platforms, based on activities related to individual mobile phone accounts. It is important to note that all mobile phone accounts in China are registered to verified individuals based on government issued IDs. Mobile phone numbers are *de facto* proof of people's online identity. As more and more of people's daily lives migrate online, the resulting "big data" has become a rich source for evaluation of one's "social credit worthiness". Today, verified individual mobile phone numbers are required for opening bank accounts, social media accounts, and most online transactions from buying airplane tickets to concert tickets.

In the State Council document that outlines the plan for the Social Credit System, the government stated the objective of building a trustworthy and harmonious society. That seems to be a thoughtful goal, as the lack of trust among individuals and corporations has been a problem in China. Ideally, it can be an effective way to address real life problems such as financial scams or counterfeits including harmful food products, which are common in China. Ironically, by creating the Social Credit System and using it to encourage trustworthy behavior, the government would need people to trust that the system will not be abused and used as a surveillance or controlling tool. Skeptics point to the possibility of the system being used to punish political dissidents. Or that the government can easily use the system to turn China into a police state where everyone's every move is under constant monitoring. While the latter is probably the case in China even today, it would be naïve for anyone to think that our privacy is in much better shape elsewhere in the world. The hard, cold fact is that our behavior on social media, online shopping and Internet searches are already tracked and analyzed on a daily basis for commercial purposes. Occasionally we hear about the data being misused for malicious manipulation, such as the recent Facebook/Cambridge Analytica scandal. It is not even unfathomable that ongoing government surveillance is already happening in a lot of countries.

As for the concern about punishment, early experience from pilot programs of the Social Credit System being implemented in selected cities suggests that the Chinese government is using the system more for positive reinforcement. People get points for their "social credit scores" by performing good deeds such as donating to charities or volunteering. A high social credit score would get the individual perks like a rebate on the utilities bill or being able to use a bike-sharing service without paying a deposit. Points are deducted when law-breaking acts are committed, such as getting a fine for traffic offenses or other reasons. Someone with a poor social credit score can be put on a blacklist and be banned from buying plane tickets or applying for certain types of jobs. There are some grey areas that will test people's trust in the government. For example, points will be deducted when an individual is deemed to have spread rumors on social media. Again, this is not a unique problem to China. However, it remains to be seen if people will trust the government as the judicator of "fake news" as opposed to legitimate reporting.

<u>Confucianism and attainment of a harmonious society</u>

From the conversations that I have with my friends, I have the feeling that people in China do trust their government much more than their fellow citizens and corporations. This intuition is supported by data from the World Value Survey, which is led by an international team of social scientists based in Vienna. Most people in China I talk to agree with the government's goal that it is important to have a stable social environment, where people can work out their differences harmoniously for the common good. This is attributed to learning from the often-turbulent Chinese history over thousands of years, and to Confucian teachings which are at the core of Chinese culture. Confucius, a social and political philosopher who lived circa 500 B.C., taught that the key to good governance lay in each citizen carrying out his duties as prescribed by his position within the hierarchy. He stated that good government consists in "the ruler being a ruler, the minister being a minister, the father being a father, and the son being a son" (*Analects 12.11*). He also taught that "the head of state worries not about insufficiency, but about uneven distribution. Not about poverty, but about instability. If there is equity in distribution there will be no poverty; if there is harmony in society there will be no uprising" (*Analects 16.1*). Following these deeply ingrained principles, it is not hard to understand why many people in China are oblivious to government surveillance, as long as the government is doing a good job in a fair and equitable way. And indeed, according to a recent study by economists from Cornell University and Peking University, income inequality in China has been falling since it peaked in 2010. Most attribute this to the improved social policies implemented by the current government, including minimum wage legislation and better social security. This is happening at a time when inequality has become a major issue in other leading economies, contributing to rising protectionism and angry populism around the world.

Conclusion

From being an autarchic state just 40 years ago, China has become an unexpected guardian of globalization in a world that is increasingly turning inward towards protectionism and nativism. History, opportunities and government leadership all play a key role in it. Coming from one of its lowest points in Chinese history after the Cultural Revolution, consecutive governments have taken the right path to embrace global economic integration and foreign technologies. The result is a quantum leap from mostly primitive systems (e.g. a limited fixed-line telecommunication network, no financial credit system) to cutting edge infrastructure and one of the best eras in Chinese history, which has changed the lives of generations to come. Whether the current political system can support continuous economic growth is the subject of much debate. However, if we consider China's aforementioned cultural idiosyncrasy and what the current system has accomplished in the last 40 years, perhaps it deserves the benefit of the doubt. Looking from outside, perhaps we should help create the stable and harmonious society that the Chinese people are looking for, while keeping a close eye on any signs of abuse of the trust that the people have given their government. That would be an honorable goal for all global citizens.

<u>**Alexander Chirkov**</u>

Director General, EuroAsia (Russian import company)

Chirkov was born in Rostov (Ukraine) in 1965. After his secondary education, he served in the Soviet armed forces in Afghanistan for two years. He earned a Law degree from the Russian University Patrice Lumumba in 1990 in Moscow. He also obtained a degree in foreign languages from the Russian University Patrice Lumumba, which is now named The Peoples' Friendship University of Russia. From 1991 to 1993, he served as Councilor at the Russian embassy in Nicaragua. He moved to Spain in 1993 and took up a position at a private company. Since 1999 he is the Director General of the company EuroAsia in Russia.

After the fall of Communism in Russia, along with snickers, jeans and microwaves, a wave of foreign industrial equipment and computers swept into the country. Before the country opened up to imports, I still remember labels on electrical equipment that read: "Sovnarhoz of the USSR. Plant named after Comrade Stalin." Twenty-six years later I see modern Russia with all its advantages and disadvantages.

It is worth remembering that it is ordinary people that carry out any revolution. In the case of industrial revolutions[36], those at the forefront are scientists and academics. Chinese, Japanese or American scientists do not have to worry. They are carefully trained, financed and promoted in every possible way because the world's leading countries understand that "prodigious minds" will bring good results.

By 1939, when industrialization was not yet complete in the USSR, over 50% of the working-age population in the country was still employed in agriculture. In 1959, only 38.8% of the working-age population was employed in agriculture, and now it is only 7%. At the same time, the production of agricultural products grew continuously.

The scientific and technological revolution in the USSR began in the 1950s. In a short time, several scientific institutions were founded and started operating, such as the Institute of High Pressures Physics. The Institute of High Pressure Physics, founded in 1958, received international recognition because it successfully synthesized a diamond and cubic boron nitride. The original equipment and subsequent technology developed at the institute were adopted by more than 45 organizations and established the basis of the diamond industry in the USSR. The first Central Institute for Nuclear Research located in Dubná, Moscow oblast was founded in 1956.

Most of the research was conducted in secret at several locations. Well-equipped scientific and technical organizations, such as Arzamas-16 and Chelyabinsk-70, were established. For the development of the first Soviet computer, Professor Segey Lebedev and his team took over an entire wing of the two floors of a secret laboratory, which was hidden in the oak forests near the village of Feofania, on the outskirts of Kiev. In the autumn of 1948, Lebedev decided to focus the work of his laboratory on computer design. Lebedev's first computer, BESM-1, was completed by the end of 1951.

Lebedev later began working on a more powerful computer, the M-20. In 1958 the machine was accepted as operational and its mass production was started. At the same time, the BESM-2, a

---

[36] Analysts now refer to four industrial revolutions. The current digital age is the fourth industrial revolution

development of the BESM-1, also went into series production. The BESM-2 was employed to calculate satellite orbits and the path of the first rocket to reach the surface of the moon.

During the 1950s, spending on science increased more than tenfold, and the number of scientists increased six-fold. New machines and technologies were urgently mastered. Rail transport adopted electric traction, and the first nuclear power plants were built. The nuclear icebreaker "Lenin" was launched on its first voyage and the world's first artificial earth satellite was sent into space. An especially important victory for the Soviet Union was to beat the United States in putting the first man in space, namely Yuri Gagarin, who became the first person to journey into space in 1961. However, due to several factors, scientific and technological progress in the USSR soon -- certainly by the seventies -- began to lag behind the pace of the West. Many workers continued to toil by hand, in agriculture as well as in factories. This allowed the Soviet Union to proudly declare the absence of unemployment. But productivity and competitiveness declined sharply, and the Soviet Union fell behind western industrial powers in developing and using new technologies.

Until the early 1990s, the USSR was making slow but steady progress in technology, even if it lagged behind the West. The Soviet Union's space program continued to reach milestones, such as the creation and launching of the Soyuz rockets and spacecraft beginning in the 1960s. The Soyuz rocket is regarded as the most reliable launch vehicle in the world to date and was originally designed by Sergey Korolev in 1962. The Soyuz spacecraft started to operate in 1966 and were originally designed for the USSR's moon program. But since then they have been used primarily to carry cosmonauts into orbit and back. It continues to transport astronauts and devices into space more than fifty years after its first launch. The USSR was also the first country to successfully operate a manned space station, the Salyut, which existed and conducted research between 1977 and 1986. Moreover, advanced ships, submarines and aircraft were designed and built, although funding prioritized their development for the military. Despite the disaster at Chernobyl in 1986, the USSR mastered the capability of building civilian nuclear reactors. The country's education produced the scientists, engineers and mathematicians who made these developments possible.

But as the USSR opened up under Mikhail Gorbachev and his *perestroika*, the subsequent economic and social upheaval prompted many of the best scientists, engineers and doctors to leave the country. They were welcomed with open arms in the West, especially in the United States. The USSR suffered a terrible brain drain before it was dissolved and fell apart in 1991.

Unfortunately, Russia has hardly taken part in the Fourth Industrial Revolution, the digital revolution. It does not have anything remarkable to showcase over the last twenty years in terms of developing new technologies. Yotaphone ("Yotafon") is an exception. It is a smartphone developed in Russia which is compatible with Long Term Evolution (LTE), a standard for high-speed wireless data communications for mobile phones and data terminals. The Russian company Yota Devices launched it in 2013. The device is equipped with two independently operating screens. It has been successfully mass produced and sold, although it is assembled in China.

Attempts are being undertaken so that Russia can keep up or not fall further behind the more advanced technological powers. Although research and investment are being pursued, there are many gaps. It is not clear, for example, how research centers such as Rosnano and Skolkovo should operate. They were built so that Russia could compete in the Fourth Industrial Revolution. Since the Skolkovo project was launched, it has come up against skeptical opponents. The very concept of a scientific center designed from scratch, and not building on the knowledge and technology of existing scientific centers in Novosibirsk or Obninsk, raised objections. But at the time many wanted to believe in technological miracles, and it seemed that with the proper funding and investment in science Skolkovo would soon deliver results in the form of cutting-edge industrial applications and technologies. Above all, the new Russian research center in Skolkovo summoned up images of a magical place where intelligent scientists were creating all kinds of advanced projects.

The Skolkovo Innovation Centre is a state-of-the-art center being built in Skolkovo, in the Moscow region of Russia. It is also known by the name of Russia's Silicon Valley. It should be a modern complex of scientific and technological innovation for the development and commercialization of new technologies, the first in the post-Soviet period in Russia. The complex will provide special economic conditions for companies operating in the priority sectors of the modernization of the Russian economy: telecommunications and space, biomedical technology, energy efficiency, information technology and nuclear technology. It was founded by the then President of the Russian Federation, Dmitry Medvedev, on 28 September 2010.

The 400-hectare area will be home to some 21,000 people, while another 21,000 will arrive at the innovation center every day to work. The first "Hypercube" building is now ready. The objects of the first stage of Innograd have been put into operation in 2014, and the construction of the facilities will be completed in 2020.

However, to the best of our knowledge, the advances and progress that the aforementioned research centers were supposed to achieve have not come to our attention. Despite the unique designs for the research centers -- who took everyone's breath away -- and the big amount of money that authorities proclaim they have invested in them, it is hard to know what they have specifically attained.

These research centers are now under pressure. They received a lot of funding, but their efficiency is low; they consume a large amount of resources but yield weak returns. Many ambitious projects will be closed, and the lack of results is a sufficient reason to stop additional funding. In other words, it is necessary to reform rather than abolish funding for fundamental science in Russia. The issue is how to improve efficiency. Funding will be appropriated and disbursed, but for specific tasks, rather than for "abstract science" for which there is no money, at least now.

<u>Technology at an international level</u>

People are gradually moving into virtual space. The World Wide Web is dragging us deeper: today it is impossible to imagine life without a mobile phone, a tablet or a computer. Scientific and technical progress is racing ahead. But it should also be noted that younger generations have a completely different mental and spiritual attitude. If people used to read books, they now read electronic publications in digital format. Many young people have knowledge not of specific content, but of how and where to find it if they need it.

It seems that humanity is striving to create a society where people will not have to think or do anything. Soon, factories will manufacture robots for our use. At the same time, advanced technologies are constantly evolving, machines are acquiring new capabilities and artificial intelligence is processing more and more information and proposing solutions on a variety of issues. Current achievements in the field of robotics now allow us to predict in which areas robots will replace people completely or at least to a large extent in the future.

<u>Could technology lead to mass unemployment?</u>

In recent years, more and more media outlets are publishing articles about the introduction of a variety of intelligent and high-tech devices, the threat of destruction of jobs, how robots will replace people in the near future in large amounts of professions. Of course, there is some truth to what these articles describe. But it is wrong to talk about when robots will completely or almost completely replace a worker. It is unlikely that machines with artificial intelligence can take over all our tasks because they lack many human qualities. These are, among others, imagination, the ability to find non-standard solutions, the ability to create in the broadest sense of the word, and to invent something new.

One of the professional sectors where jobs are at risk is the financial system. In three or five years, the traditional banking system will have disappeared. This will happen due to the automation and implementation of technologies. Banks working under old procedures will be forced to withdraw from the market. Not only is there talk of automation in the financial sector. It is actively being implemented. In January of this year, it was announced that Russia's largest bank, Sberbank, will cut about 3,000 employees and replace them with computer systems. In total, Sberbank intends to reduce its workforce by 8 percent as a result of the transition to online banking. Instead, they plan to hire 200 analysts who will be involved in a new activity for financial institutions: customer data analysis.

Optimism about technology is felt in the reports of the most important Russian financial regulator, the Central Bank of Russia. The Central Bank believes that half of the world's bank branches will close in the next ten years, and its employees will lose their jobs due to the introduction of new technologies.

Automation cannot be stopped. "This is part of capitalism, a constant desire to increase productivity." Robotization of production is beneficial to almost everyone, except for workers without academic qualifications, and it is they who are most affected by mass robotics.

<u>Other sectors of human activity vulnerable to substitution by robots</u>

The scientific and technological revolution and medicine are also in contradictory interaction. On the one hand, there are new opportunities to apply medical knowledge in areas of human health that had not been previously explored. New techniques are employed, which positively impact the achievements and capabilities of doctors. On the other hand, as technological progress has enabled medicine and doctors to become more specialized, unforeseen problems have arisen. In the past, a single doctor examined, diagnosed and cured you. As medicine has become more specialized, a patient has to visit several doctors, which increases the bureaucratic cost of delivering quality health care. The tight relationship that existed between a patient and his or her (family) doctor is disappearing. Therefore, we see that technological progress, like any other phenomenon, has its advantages and its negative aspects. Nonetheless, we consider it progress.

Technological development will inevitably affect taxi drivers, and drivers in general. Transportation will be automated. Self-propelled and self-driving vehicles will replace taxi drivers and public transport operators, excavator operators and truck drivers. Factory transporters are going to control robots.

Guards - this is the sphere of security services that will also be computerized. Janitors, security guards and security guards will be replaced by identification systems. The machines will screen a person's face and immediately determine if he or she has a criminal record, is potentially dangerous or not, and was seen in contact with the offenders.

Many and soon most vendors and cashiers will scan devices automatically to determine the product and its price and withdraw money from the account. This is a real revolution in shopping.

Automation will also affect interpreters, postmen, doctors, pharmacists, builders and teachers. On the other hand, by 2030-2035 there will be many new professions of which we are not yet aware. Many of them will be associated with advanced technologies, including robotics and specialists in related areas.

At the International Economic Forum in Saint Petersburg in 2017, Russia's minister of Labor and Social Affairs, Maxim Topilin, pointed out that in the 21st century the working day is likely to be 4 hours instead of 8 hours. This may sound like science fiction to us now, but it could happen.

I take comfort in the fact that there are jobs that are not going to be replaced by robots, jobs that are important and require purely human empathy. Human resources will continue to be in demand - those areas where the machine simply cannot replace the component of both physical and emotional human warmth. The work of volunteers cannot be replaced by robots. Robots also cannot care for the elderly, an important sector that requires special attention based on respect, and especially for the generation of our parents, supporting victims and helping people with disabilities.

For the same reason, psychologists will continue to be in demand, as a profession that requires emotions and direct contact with a person. None of the robots with highly developed artificial intelligence is fully capable of replacing human beings. We have advantages over machines currently in existence, as robots have no creative thinking, no consciousness and no intuition. Therefore, to be successful, it is necessary to develop skills that robots do not possess: creativity, imagination, initiative, leadership qualities. But even if you are not a good painter, singer, music composer and you did not get a PhD from Harvard or a prestigious university, you should not panic. Technological progress kills certain professions and generates new ones.

Labor automation will reduce the number of jobs. But it will also allow companies to cut production costs and, at the same time, lower product prices, which in turn will increase people's ability to consume. Therefore, there will be an increase in citizens' purchasing power and the creation of new jobs in other sectors. In addition, robots will still need a person's supervision for a long time to come. There will be a need for a robotics profession: a professional who trains robots and makes sure they do not harm people.

<u>Winners and losers of globalization</u>

Clearly, there is a gap between the winners and losers of globalization. At the moment this gap is growing and nobody seems to know very well what to do. Optimists, on the one hand, believe that a window of opportunity is opening and that new jobs will be created that we are not able to imagine right now. But the lack of certainty about the nature of these jobs is not reassuring for the pessimists. In any case, we will have to interact with artificial intelligence. Modern children are adapting quickly: they learn to handle a tablet before they speak. Older people, of course, will have more difficulty adapting to new technologies. Human beings have no choice other than to adapt to the new technological paradigm. Progress cannot be stopped.

As for Russia, we can point to great scientific discoveries in areas as diverse as thermodynamic physics, archaeology, biomedicine and quantum technologies. We are also advanced in military technology. Moreover, Russia will probably once again be able to take advantage of a considerable gap with the most developed countries, for instance by learning from the mistakes of other researchers. There is no such thing a zero risk, especially in the transition phase.

Russia portrays itself to the rest of the world as an advanced country. In 2018, the FIFA World Cup will be held in Russia. It will feature technological advances such as the broadcasting of matches in 4K format, a ball with a built-in NFC chip, and repetition of VAR plays. In addition, the

Kremlin is considering creating a parallel Internet to prevent cyberattacks and offering an alternative wi-fi service to tourists.

In the labor market, the need for the humanities will grow. Some of the skills that will be in demand in the coming years are:

A robot does better than a person no matter how large databases are and easily manages to solve simple and clear tasks. But in some cases, the problem that needs to be solved cannot be recognized immediately. In these cases, artificial intelligence cannot do without the help of a person.

For example, if a patient gradually stops taking medication, the algorithm will sense the change but not understand what the problem is. Besides, artificial intelligence will not know what questions to ask the patient. A person has a better understanding of such a situation because he or she knows what life with a chronic illness is like, whereas a robot does not. The medical specialist will be able to ask the right questions and organize an appropriate course of treatment.

<u>Curiosity</u>

The ability to explore the world and draw conclusions from observations is an important property that distinguishes a person from a robot. For the time being, technologies do not allow machines to be programmed to develop living creative thinking and the ability to notice irregularities. Any attempt that artificial intelligence work in a creative environment is based on large data and randomization. Robots cannot yet construct concepts based on observations.

In the era of information bubbles, thousands of television channels and social networks, critical thinking is valued more than ever. It is important that companies have people who can value things from an ethical point of view. Specialists are already required to monitor robots. In an era when opinions often prevail over facts, people with the ability to critically evaluate reality will be especially valued. A company cannot rely completely on algorithms because of reputational risk. This trend will only grow over time, and each company will need its own ethical risk assessor. Nobody knows how the rapid acceleration of technology will shape our societies in the decades to come. In any case, I am a proponent of humanity, and not of replacing humans.

<u>**Aad Correljé**</u>

Professor, Economics of Infrastructure, Technical University of Delft

Dr. Aad Correljé is a professor of the Economics of Infrastructure Department of the Faculty of Technology, Policy and Management at the Technical University of Delft. He is also a research fellow for the renowned Clingendael International Energy Program of the Netherlands Institute for International Affairs Clingendael. In 1989, Correljé graduated in Political Sciences (International Relations and European Law) from the Social Sciences Department of the University of Amsterdam. He combined Political Sciences and Economics in his PhD thesis: "The Spanish Oil Industry: Structural Change and Modernization", which he wrote and defended in 1994 at the Centre for International Energy Studies (EURICES) of the Erasmus University in Rotterdam. He has been involved in academic research, teaching and consulting on many water, energy and transport related issues for several public and private organizations. From 1998 until 2001, he was scientific coordinator of the multi-disciplinary research program Tackling Environmental Resource Management (TERM) Phase II of the European Science Foundation. Correljé's current research involves an economic/institutional approach to public policy and private strategy development and analysis in infrastructure-bound sectors, particularly oil, gas and water. His focus is on the theoretical and empirical of public and private decision-making processes on these issues and in particular with the specific role of institutional analysis and economics therein. Correljé is a member of the Editorial Board of the academic journal Energy Policy and an instructor at the Florence School of Regulation.

<u>On raising revenue for more training</u>

I think that taxing robots as such may be difficult to start with. Normally, we tax things that have some degree of scarcity, and which are retrievable and measurable, such as energy. But I do believe that the fact that a lot of technology is replacing people is a very important issue. Technology is eliminating jobs which people could do, make a decent salary and lead a dignified life. A lot of these jobs are being taken over by some kind of technology -- computers, robots, Artificial Intelligence and other devices.

We should also highlight the fact that an increase in technology leads to people feeling like they are living and operating in a dehumanized system. These people feel ignored and not taken seriously. They feel that their lives and work are more linked to technology and machines than to the interactions of traditional society. This alienation must be addressed. Whether taxing companies that use robots is a good idea is questionable. But there is no question that people feel that they are being ignored and not taken seriously.

In the Netherlands, many people feel that they can no longer access services which they could in the past on a fairly equal basis. These services are increasingly distributed according to the capability and the ability to pay for them and the ability to use and access them. This applies to energy, but also health services and housing. The Netherlands has a serious difficulty regarding the availability of sufficient affordable housing. Home prices have risen substantially in the Netherlands in the past years. The combination of all of these factors makes people feel that their lives are currently quite uncomfortable.

First of all, there is a group of people which can be retrained and receive the skills necessary to perform new jobs. But of course there is a segment of the population -- elderly people -- for whom this is not feasible as it is too late to retrain them. For the latter group, retraining obviously cannot help. But for the former group, it may make sense to transform or adapt the taxing system and tax corporate activity -- whether robots or something else -- to generate the revenue to finance this training. Currently, most of training is concentrated on young people. These young people start working and make a living, but they do not obtain additional skills and must continue to work with the skills from their original training. Therefore, in the Netherlands we do refer to "eternal training or schooling", whereby people at older ages would have the time and opportunity to learn new skills and therefore change jobs if necessary. There are many ways to generate revenue for this additional training. Taxing robots is questionable. But raising taxes on capital may be a solution.

<u>The apprenticeship system in the Netherlands</u>

The German apprenticeship system is very efficient and praised around the world. It ensures that young people studying a trade can do an internship at a private-sector company. It is a partnership between Germany's public administrations and its private companies that delivers a high quantity of skilled young people. Not everyone has to attend and graduate from a university. In fact, many non-university-trained technicians earn more than university graduates with non-technical and non-scientific degrees (especially in the humanities). How does the apprenticeship system work in the Netherlands?

The apprenticeship system in the Netherlands does not work as well as in Germany. We do have vocational schools where young people can learn a trade as opposed to attending university. But the funding for these schools has diminished as a result of the financial and economic crisis of a decade ago. Since 2008 it has become increasingly difficult to provide apprenticeships and internships for young people pursuing a trade or craft. The owners and managers of private-sector companies argue that it takes a lot of time to train and supervise young people. Therefore, in the Netherlands in several sectors -- such as nursing, health care and certain technical fields -- there is a shortage of qualified workers at the same time that there are not sufficient internships available. Many young people who do study a trade have a lot of difficulty obtaining an internship. That is why they do not become available to the job market at the right level of their qualification.

My own son was trained at a high-level vocational school, at a level slightly below that of a university. It is in the field of water management. He had to wait for a year to access an internship with which he could finish his schooling. This is a pressing problem in the Netherlands. There is also a shortage of nurses for hospitals and for occupations where a large part of the skills has to be learned and trained for on the job and not from books.

<u>On a minimum universal income</u>

Several political parties -- especially on the far left and right -- advocate paying a universal income to everybody to help them cope with the wrenching transformations brought about by globalization and the acceleration of technology. Is a universal income desirable for elderly people who have not earned the right to a decent pension and are too old to be retrained?

The Netherlands does have a pension available to everybody which is sufficiently high to enable a decent life for older people. This income support begins when people reach the age of 65 and lasts until they pass away. This income support for older people is a complement and is added to the pension that is accumulated as a result of the number of years worked. Many people in the Netherlands who are older than 65 live on this basic non-work payment. Hence, the Netherlands does have a system that furnishes an income to older people regardless of whether or not they have worked.

In the Netherlands, any man or woman who is older than 65 receives a net minimum monthly income of about €900. This is supplemented by the traditional pension, whose level is determined by the number of years worked, the income or salary paid and the sector. Combining both payments, many people who are retired receive funding which is equivalent to 75% of the salary they made. If an elderly couple live together, they are paid €1200 as opposed to €1800 to reflect the fact that, proportionally, the cost of housing for two persons is lower than for one. This supplemental income for older people at the level I have described -- €900 per person -- requires that the person have spent his or her entire life in the Netherlands. If they have only spent a part of their lives in the Netherlands, the payment is lower.

<u>Technology and jobs in the energy sector</u>

Tech-friendly people argue that as more technology replaces people, companies will employ their remaining employees in more value-added jobs. Do you think this will happen?

No, I do not think this will happen. In the fields of energy and infrastructure employees are expensive. There is not much value-added job that employees can perform in the energy sector. As the energy sector becomes more automated, the number of employees will decrease. Over the next 25 to 30 years a lot of work in the energy sector will involve the transition that changes energy systems in houses and cities. And there will be a lack of qualified people to perform this work. Hence, in the near future the problem will be a scarcity of qualified employees in the energy sector.

Each round of lower prices for energy in general and oil and gas in particular leads to more automation and new technologies which carry out tasks that were previously done by people. But there will always be a need for employees who monitor, repair and keep track of machines and technology, as well as advanced analysts.

Energy production will move from large-scale centralized production systems -- like oil and gas -- towards more local and decentralized generation of energy. More complex and interconnected systems in which gas, electricity and storage are combined will also be developed. Such systems require more supervision than the large-scale centralized technical facilities. A drilling platform in the North Sea, for example, can operate without people. They just require a few employees that are flown to the platform every few days to ensure everything is operating well. But these kinds of platforms are designed to stand alone and not require humans as long as the technology works.

But other energy systems are not built for such long periods of time and need much more overall continuous control and repairs. For the latter energy systems, more employees will be required. Energy transformations in the past have destroyed jobs. It happened, for example, when labor-intensive energy sectors such as coal were partially replaced by oil and gas production, which employ fewer people.

The Netherlands used to extract a lot of natural gas. But production of gas in the Netherlands has been scaled down. There were earthquakes in the region of Groningen in the north of the country. According to the current governmental projections and policy, gas production in the Netherlands will be terminated in twelve years.

The shale gas revolution will definitely not occur in the Netherlands as things stand now. And the same goes for other European countries given the current state of technology. It is feasible in largely unpopulated areas of the United States. Shale gas production also requires a quick and flexible responsive transport system for gas, something which does not exist currently in Europe given our deregulated system. There is also a need to obtain the relevant slew of permits and to fulfil environmental standards. Population density in Europe is much higher than in the United States. Given all of these obstacles, it will be quite difficult to produce shale gas in Europe.

<u>On the EU's energy dependence and the potential for US exports of Liquefied Natural Gas (LNG)</u>

The European Union has to import more than 50% of its energy. On current trends, this percentage will rise substantially. Reserves of oil and natural gas in the North Sea are running out, are becoming more expensive to extract and even face opposition in the case of natural gas in the Netherlands. Many EU countries have never had nuclear power plants (Italy, Austria), others are phasing out nuclear power plants (Germany) and in many there is a de facto moratorium on building new ones due to political opposition. Extraction of shale gas is also very controversial because of the consequences of fracking and Europe's high population density, especially compared to the United States. In this context, exports of US Liquefied Natural Gas to Europe is an option worth pursuing. The US has become the world's top producer of natural gas due to the shale gas revolution. The Obama administration began to issue permits to allow exports of LNG. President Trump is a strong proponent of LNG exports. Can LNG from the US displace some Russian gas supplies to Europe?

Russia can still provide and sell large amounts of lower-priced gas to many parts of Europe than LNG from the United States can. The problem is that Russia's reserves of natural gas and production and transport capacity are such that it can underbid exports of LNG from the United States in terms of pricing. It can also do so by partially adjusting the long-term existing contracting structure. Russia will be able to continue to do this in the near future.

In some parts of Europe such as Spain, which is rather unconnected by pipelines from the European gas system, LNG can play an important role. This can also be the case for the United Kingdom, which is also only partly connected to Europe's gas network in terms of its needs. We also have to take into account the way that gas prices are set in Europe and the organization and regulation of the transport system. For all of these reasons, for Germany, France, Italy, the Netherlands and large parts of central and eastern Europe, Russian natural gas will remain dominant for quite a long time.

<u>On the US's and President Trump's desire to export more LNG</u>

It is true that Spain boasts seven out of the 23 existing regasification plants for Liquefied Natural Gas in the UE. But exports of Liquefied Natural Gas (LNG) from the United States to Europe are more expensive because of the distance involved in shipping the LNG from the US to Europe, and also because of the transport costs for such LNG *within* Europe. This is a very important factor. Moreover, there is quite a margin between the sales prices of Russian natural gas and its production cost. That means Russia can substantially lower its sales price of natural gas if it wants to maintain its market share in Europe in the face of, for example, exports of LNG from the United States. This means that US LNG prices would have to be much more competitive in order to capture a sizeable part of the gas market in Europe. Obviously, there are variations in gas prices depending on the time of the year. In addition, because of the reduction of the production of natural gas in the Netherlands, more LNG is reaching the Netherlands. But it is Russian and not US LNG which is being shipped to the Netherlands. It is a matter of how competitive US LNG can be in reaching the northwestern and Mediterranean shores of Europe. If it does become more competitive, it could raise its market share.

<u>Additional thoughts on how to tackle populism</u>

Education is of course important in order to change the mindset of people who vote for populists. But it is also about the need for traditional parties to come to grips with reality and see that things are going wrong. Non-populist parties need to adjust their policies and objectives to offer a more inclusive perspective on how society functions and should function. In education, health services, housing and other services, people feel they are being handed over to neoliberal private entities that charge them. These privately-run services also have a lot of variation in their quality, and access is limited or affected depending on people's income and what they can afford to pay. This dismay creates a society which is a breeding ground for populists. Many people have lost faith in what traditional and non-populist parties can do for them. As long as this feeling – which is quite strong -- persists, populism will thrive. In the Netherlands, even the Dutch Socialist Party retains a neoliberal approach in many of its policies, even if it publicly denies it. If the necessary changes are not made, populism will not go away.

Stephen Eule

Vice President for Climate and Technology, US Chamber of Commerce

Stephen D. Eule is vice president for climate and technology at the U.S. Chamber of Commerce's Global Energy Institute (GEI). With more than two decades of experience, Eule is a recognized expert on the nexus between energy and climate change. He engages with business groups across the world and is asked frequently to testify before Congress. He is also responsible for GEI's two authoritative energy security reports -- the Index of U.S. Energy Security Risk and the International Index of Energy Security Risk. They have been cited by the International Energy Agency and are used by universities and think tanks across the world. Previously, Eule was director of the Office of Climate Change Policy & Technology at the Department of Energy. There he oversaw the development of the U.S. Climate Change Technology Program Strategic Plan in 2006 and ran President Bush's Climate VISION program. Internationally, Eule represented the Department of Energy as part of the U.S. government delegations to the UNFCCC, Intergovernmental Panel on Climate Change, the G20, and other multilateral forums. Eule earned a Master of Arts degree in geography from The George Washington University and a Bachelor of Science degree in biology from Southern Connecticut State College. The views expressed in his contribution are his own and not necessarily those of the U.S. Chamber of Commerce.

The shale gas and shale oil revolution are putting the United States on a path to an energy surplus early in the next decade, something the country last saw during the Dwight D. Eisenhower administration in the early 1950s.

The US is already the world's top producer of natural gas and oil with an estimated 16% share of total global combined output for these fuels in 2016. Moreover, in 2011 it became a net exporter of refined petroleum and in 2017 a net exporter of natural gas for the first time in sixty years. Exports of US crude oil also are on the rise.

The United States is now producing more oil than it ever has in its history, and the U.S. Energy Information Administration's 2018 forecast suggests that domestic crude oil production, mostly tight oil, soon will breach 11 million barrels per day and fluctuate between 11 and 12 million barrels per day out to 2050 -- a sustained annual rate that is about 2 million barrels per day higher than the previous U.S. record of 9.6 million barrels per day set in 1970.[37] As a result, the amount of America's crude oil supply met by imports has over the past 10 years plunged from 66% to 42%,[38] and it could go lower still. Indeed, the International Energy Agency projects that on current trends in production and efficiency, the United States could find itself a net exporter of total crude oil and refined products, a notion that would have been deemed absurd a decade ago. These trends will bring -- indeed, already are bringing -- both enormous economic and geopolitical benefits. The Trump Administration has embraced these trends as the central feature of its "energy dominance" policy, which is aimed at ensuring that the US's combined production of oil, natural gas, coal, and renewables will both turn the country into an energy power as well as prevent its reliance on foreign sources of energy.

Technology is powering this revolution. For instance, it is now possible to remotely search for deep underground or underwater oil or gas deposits without having to involve persons in risky operations. And we have seen how the shrewd application of hydraulic fracturing, horizontal drilling, and advanced seismic imaging continues to unlock vast amounts of oil and natural gas

---

[37] Energy Information Administration. *Annual Energy Outlook 2018.*
[38] U.S. Energy Information Administration.

from shale formations across the country. It was not just technology that was responsible for this revolution, however. The U.S. also has other advantages that make it an ideal place for this type of energy revolution to occur. Much of this production from shale formation takes place on private land, and because US landowners also own the minerals to the land -- some almost unique to the United States -- property owners have a clear incentive to work with producers. The technology also was invented in the United States and the infrastructure and expertise needed was at close hand. America's entrepreneurial culture was another big factor. How these attributes are replicated or approximated in other countries will determine to a large extent whether other countries with large shale formations -- and there are a lot of them -- will successfully launch their own shale revolutions.

The extraction of shale gas and oil from shale deposits is generating wealth and creating jobs in parts of the United States that traditionally had no major role in the fossil fuel sector. Take Pennsylvania, for example. A decade ago it accounted for about barely 1% of total domestic natural gas production. State output from the Marcellus shale formation has pushed the state's share of the total to about 20%. North Dakota is another example. From less than 100,000 barrels of oil per day, its production of more than 1 million barrels per day would place it, if it were a country, in the top 20 oil producers, and it has for all practical purposes "0%" unemployment. But traditional oil-producing states like Texas and Oklahoma are also reaping the rewards of new exploration and extraction. Moreover, some states will also benefit from the expansion of the Keystone XL Pipeline network, which will probably add a new pipeline to transport Canadian oil from Alberta through Montana, South Dakota and Nebraska to link up with the existing pipeline network south through Kansas and Oklahoma to the refineries in the Gulf of Mexico.

President Trump reversed the previous administration's rejection of the new pipeline. On November 20th, Nebraska's Public Service Commission also approved the construction of the pipeline. The $8 billion project still has to overcome some regulatory hurdles and landowner issues, and also ensure its financial viability,[39] but it is likely to proceed if the business case remains strong. Transportation of oil through pipelines has a smaller environmental footprint than doing so by rail or trucks. And it will create direct and indirect jobs, in addition to those involved in the construction of the new pipeline.

The record production of oil and natural gas in the United States has wider implications for the country's foreign policy. In a book titled "Windfall", Meghan O'Sullivan argues that, among other benefits, the shale revolution has dissipated any concern about American decline, allowed the imposition of sanctions on energy-exporting countries, created a global gas market, and lessened the threat posed by China's aggressive expansion into the South China Sea[40].

It is difficult to understate the importance of the US achieving energy independence with regards to fossil fuels. The US's dependence on its traditional oil suppliers (Saudi Arabia, other Gulf countries, Venezuela) has already dramatically diminished. This is obviously of great geostrategic importance for the United States. In fact, Saudi Arabia and other OPEC members are losing their capacity to influence world oil prices through production or price hikes or cuts. OPEC recognizes the threat posed by the shale gas and oil revolution and has tried to drive U.S. frackers out of business. Saudi Arabia's excess production capacity traditionally enabled it to be the "price maker" in global markets, leaving the US in the disadvantageous position of being a "price taker." America's producers can now swiftly increase output in response to international oil price hikes

---

[39] "EX-XL". The Economist. November 25th, 2017
[40] O'Sullivan, Meghan: "Windfall: How the New Energy Abundance Upends Global Politics and Strengthens America's Power". Simon & Schuster, 2017.

thanks to large and growing inventories of untapped wells. The US is thus becoming the world's "price breaker" able to apply the brakes and keep prices from rising too high. The 2017 edition of the Global Energy Institute's Index of U.S. Energy Security Risk concludes that U.S. energy security is improving and achieving one of its highest levels in decades.[41] Back in 2007, gas prices were at record levels, America's dependence on foreign oil was rising and our energy security was dramatically deteriorating. In 2008, the US had to import oil and natural gas worth $500 billion. Our energy trade deficit soared to a record $416 billion in 2008, accounting for half of our trade deficit. By 2016, the import bill of oil and natural gas had plummeted to less than $100 billion, and in the first ten months of 2017 our energy deficit had plunged to only 53 billion, one-tenth of our total trade deficit.[42]

The Global Energy Institute's US Energy Risk Index uses 37 different energy security metrics in four major areas of risk: geopolitical, economic, reliability, and environmental. A lower Index score indicates a lower level of risk. The eighth annual edition of the Index covers 1970-2040. In 2016 -- the most recent year available -- the risk score for the US dropped another 1.3 points to 76.0, the lowest score since 1995. The biggest reason for the dramatic drop in US energy dependence is the shale gas revolution and the technological breakthroughs that made it possible and, as importantly, allowed it to continue under trying market circumstances.

The shale gas and oil revolution has dramatically cut the cost of energy prices in the United States. Between 2014 to 2016, U.S. energy expenditures decreased by over $400 billion, resulting in average cost savings of over $1,000 per person. And the shale revolution is still in its early stages. According to the International Energy Agency, by 2025 the shale revolution will have delivered for the US a higher amount of oil and natural gas in fewer years than any country has been able to tap in its history, including Saudi Arabia from 1966 to 1981[43].

The shale revolution also has created an energy price advantage for the United States. Data from the International Energy Agency show that U.S. industry pays anywhere from two to four times less for natural gas, coal, and electricity than many of its global competitors, especially in Europe. It is no wonder, then, that many foreign companies are making or expanding productive investments in the US precisely because they can harness these lower energy prices. This fossil fuel revolution is therefore enhancing the attractiveness of the United States as a place to invest. Given the emphasis President Trump has placed on revitalizing U.S. manufacturing, it is unlikely that his administration will do anything that could jeopardize the energy price edge the United States enjoys.

There is another long-term benefit from shale gas and oil which can be exploited: The US is beginning to ship liquified natural gas (LNG) to other countries. The world market for natural gas -- really a collection of regional markets -- is much different than the market for crude oil. The biggest difference is that it is relatively easy to ship oil via tankers. Not so with natural gas. Spot markets for oil also are more numerous. In most parts of the world, too, the price of natural gas is pegged to the price of crude oil (the shale revolution severed the link between crude oil and natural gas for good in the United States). There are signs, however, that an abundance of natural gas is changing the way the global gas market operates, and US exports of LNG may further this.

By law, the Department of Energy has to sign off on LNG exports, as they obviously cannot go against the country's national interest. The Obama administration already undertook actions to

---

⁴¹ Index of U.S. Energy Security Risk. US Chamber of Commerce's Global Energy Institute. June 2017
⁴² "Special Report: The Geopolitics of Energy". The Economist. March 17, 2017
⁴³ Ibidem

promote exports of LNG. The current administration is stepping up these efforts. President Donald Trump has personally often voiced his determination to increase US exports of LNG. Analysts have hinted at the possibility that China might import oil and natural gas from the US as a concession to defuse the current trade row between the two powers. Europe has many regasification plants and is building more. Importing LNG from the United States would enable Europe to cut its dependence on Russian natural gas. As opposed to the United States, Europe has a very high dependency on foreign sources of energy, and the percentage is expected to climb on current trends. More than half (54.0 %) of the EU-28's gross inland energy consumption in 2015 came from abroad[44].

Germany and many central and eastern European countries are particularly reliant on Russian natural gas, and its government exploits this fact. Former German Chancellor Gerhard Schröder (Social Democrat) struck a deal late in his second term to allow Russia to build an underwater pipeline in the Baltic Sea that supplies Germany with natural gas. Schröder was aware that his unpopular internal economic reforms doomed his chances for a third term. The Nord Stream pipeline completely bypasses Poland and the Baltic Republics of Estonia, Latvia, and Lithuania, thus seriously undercutting the European Commission's efforts to forge a common European energy policy. It is puzzling that current German Chancellor Angela Merkel (a Christian Democrat) has given her blessing to the construction of Nord Stream 2, which will again directly supply Germany with Russian natural gas and further weaken any chance of developing a common European energy policy. Many are voicing concern at the national security risk of building Nord Stream 2. The fear is that Russia, which has used energy as a geopolitical weapon in the past, would again be in an even better position to use shipments of gas via Nord Stream 2 as a wedge to divide European countries.

Germany's need to import Russian natural gas is in part a consequence of its extremely expensive determination to carry out its energy transformation policy -- the so-called *Energiewende*. Chancellor Merkel's decision to accelerate the decommissioning of Germany's nuclear power plants in the wake of the Fukushima disaster in Japan in March of 2011 reinforces Germany's need to subsidize renewable energy and import fossil fuels. Germany has developed its renewable energy sector at the price of very high energy costs. As electricity generated by wind and solar energy cannot be stored, the excess supply of electricity is wasted. Germany has not sufficiently integrated its energy grid with France, thus preventing the export of electricity spawned by renewables when it exceeds internal demand. The population in Germany is paying very high electricity bills, as the government is forced to pass on some of the cost of subsidies to consumers. But most Germans are proud of their contribution and sacrifice in attaining the transition to a very environmentally-sustainable energy model. This explains the lack of popular rejection to the high price of subsidizing renewable energy. The difficult and ongoing negotiations to form a coalition government in the wake of Germany's general elections in September of 2017 appear at the time of writing to point to a renewed CDU minority government headed by Chancellor Merkel with the support of the Social Democratic Party. As opposed to the Green Party and Liberal Party, which initially tried but failed to negotiate a three-way alliance with the CDU, the Social Democrats are staunch supporters of Nord Stream 2.

There are certainly many other European countries with the capability to further imports of LNG from the US. Spain does not import natural gas from Russia and has more regasification plants than any other country in Europe. A pipeline to supply more Algerian natural gas to Spain is under construction. It will run under the Mediterranean and from southeastern Spain north along the Mediterranean coast, potentially hooking up with networks in Europe. It is in the US and EU

---

[44] Eurostat, June 2017

interest to reduce imports of natural gas from Russia, which far outstrip the exports of natural gas to Europe from Norway and Qatar.

Japan also should benefit from US LNG and coal exports. Its decision after the Fukushima Daiichi accident to shut its fleet of nuclear reactors, which generated 25% to 30% of the country's electricity, has increased its need to import fuel for power generation, including from the United States. As the world's largest importer of LNG, Japan (like all countries) benefits substantially from US-driven decline in oil prices, and therefore natural gas prices.

The US government is laying the groundwork for increased exports of LNG. In addition to the aforementioned permits, storage capacity is being ramped up. Under Secretary of Energy Rick Perry, the Department of Energy is financing the construction of storage facilities for natural gas. With regards to coal, the current administration is keen to preserve national production. Coal miners in traditional coal-producing states like West Virginia are more sympathetic to efforts to save their jobs, as opposed to initiatives to retrain them and close down coal mines.

There have been negative headlines stemming from the US's decision to abandon the Paris Climate Change Agreement. Many foreign leaders, including US allies, have been critical of the move. But underneath the official pronouncements, technical cooperation between the US and its allies has not been affected. And the United States has continued to foster renewable energy. Wind generating capacity and generation have more than doubled since 2010 due to production subsidies, allowing wind to furnish nearly 6% of US power production in 2016. Solar energy is also the beneficiary of production subsidies, although its share of US power production is only 1% but growing rapidly.

Carbon dioxide emissions from the electric power sector have dropped significantly as a result of the rise in natural gas and renewable energy production. As of 2016, US power sector emissions had dropped 595 million metric tons from 2005 levels, a much bigger fall than in any other sector in the US and any other developed country.

The United States is therefore pursuing an energy agenda which features increased production of oil and natural gas, their export to friendly countries, continued production of coal and development of renewables. Although the US is not ready to lead the world in a German-style transition to a sustainable but still expensive energy model with a heavy emphasis on renewable energy, it is on a path to energy self-sufficiency and enhancing its competitiveness by achieving significant cuts in energy prices.

Francesc Granell

Professor, International Economic Organizations, University of Barcelona.

A Professor emeritus of Applied Economics (International Economic Organizations) from the University of Barcelona, he earned his Bachelor's degree in Political, Economic and Trade Policy from the University of Barcelona. His PhD versed on multinational corporations and development. He pursued post-doctoral studies at the Institut Universitaire d'Études Européennes in Geneva under the tutelage of the renown European federalist Denis de Rougement, at Harvard/Tufts's Fletcher School of Law and Diplomacy under Leo Gross and at the International Marketing Institue in Cambridge.

Between 1968 and 1980 Granell served at the Center for International Trade GATT/UNCTAD, as a consultant for the United National Industrial Development Organization (UNIDO) and as Director of the International Economics Research Center of Barcelona's Chamber of Commerce. After Spain's accession to the European Community in 1986, Granell became one of Spain's first civil servants in Brussels. During a long career at the EU, Granell oversaw food assistance to developing countries and relations with the World Food Program and International Fund for Agriculture Development. Granell was promoted to Director General within the European Commission and led development missions to almost one hundred countries. He played a key role in the EU accession negotiations of Austria, Sweden and Finland. Professor Granell authored or edited twenty books on European Integration and the EU's and Spain's trade and development assistance. He was awarded Europe's Star Award in 2012 and is the recipient of numerous European and Spanish awards. He is a member of the Spanish Institute's Royal Academy of Economic and Financial Sciences and a member of the founding board of the Jean Monnet Foundation for Europe.

<u>An increasingly expensive welfare state</u>

It is indisputable that in today's world there are great differences between the levels of resources that citizens receive from their respective welfare states. The data also proves that European countries are the ones at the forefront of protecting their citizens through their welfare states because they have heretofore had the resources to do so.

The membes states of the European Union account for approximately 7% of the world's population, 25% of the world's GDP and 50% of the social expenditure that we encompass under the label "welfare state", and which is made up of four pillars:

1) universal access to free education and public heath care;

2) payment of pensions for the handicapped, disability pensions, orphan's pensions, widow's pensions;

3) unemployment benefits;

4) public financing for assisted care.

Many Europeans are pondering whether this level of social protection is sustainable considering the current demographic trends and an analysis of the evolution of production processes brought about by the fourth industrial revolution. The sustainability is even harder to maintain if a part of the population continues to demand even more social spending which states cannot reasonably provide given their budget constraints and the high cost of such protection.

Most European countries have low and declining fertility rates and an ageing population due to the technological progress of health care and all types of medical advances which allow people to live much longer lives while still requiring health care. This care is increasingly costly due to the use of more sophisticated medical equipment, medication and health-care professionals. The challenge is that this increase in the costs of delivering high-level health care is not matched by a corresponding rise in the state's revenue to finance it.

Life expectancy has grown substantially in developed countries, and in Europe in particular. But the number of years that people are part of the labor force has diminished. People join the labor force at a later age because of the length of their education or training, which is the result of a labor market that demands a higher level of skills. On the other hand, people by and large do not want to accept a raise in the retirement age despite the fact that they are living much longer.

Therefore, there is an intense debate regarding the future of the pension system as one of the pillars of the welfare state. Some argue that individuals should save during their years of employment. Others advocate that the state should design such financing schemes, working alongside the companies where the individual has been employed.

<u>The future of work and its compensation</u>

Secondly, there are many uncertainties regarding the future of work and the salaries that those who are still working will earn, as well as the salary aspirations of those who will gradually join the labor force in the years to come.

The new technologies linked to the fourth industrial revolution demand a much higher skill level. But we are now confronted with a paradox. The individuals with the most knowledge or who possess the qualifications to fulfil a job do not earn more than those who are less knowledgeable and lack those skills. The latter group may earn more if they have been employed in a company for a long number of years, even if their professional profile is partly obsolete due to an unwillingness to expand their knowledge to technological progress which has taken place in their line of work.

This leads to an economic aberration according to which the median cost of employing a semi-obsolete worker is high while the median cost of employing one with a higher knowledge and skill level is lower than his or her performance. Similarly, we could compare the marginal employment cost and performance of the latest workers hired by companies to those who are comfortably protected by long-term contracts in their jobs and who have not been willing to upgrade their skills.

If we extrapolate this latest conclusion to society as a whole and take into account the fast technological progress, we find that the number of workers with a lower marginal performance than their salary is growing, as well as the number of workers with salaries inferior to their marginal performance or output. This in turn leads to the discontent of workers who feel they are underpaid relative to their productivity. These individuals are more likely to be captivated by populist political parties, which results in political instability that is not easily overcome in traditional democratic Western countries.

Politicians and others must have very high levels of leadership and the right convictions to address the social demands of those who feel left behind by the fourth industrial revolution we are experiencing, with its robots, three-dimensional printing, drones, and other cutting-edge technology.

<u>The transformation of work</u>

These problems are compounded by the transformation of employment that the fourth industrial revolution is bringing about. Decades ago, the worry in developed Western countries was of an insufficient workforce, which fostered immigration-friendly policies as well as emigration from the countryside to cities. The current challenge is how to tackle a substantially higher level of structural unemployment and the adaptation of employment to the demands of the aforementioned fourth industrial revolution.

Let us briefly describe the four industrial revolutions. The first industrial revolution employed water and steam power to mechanize production. The second used electric power to create mass production. The third utilized electronics and information technology in order to automate production. Now a fourth industrial revolution is building on the third, which is the digital revolution that has taken shape since the middle of the XXth century. The fourth industrial revolution involves the fusion of technologies that blur the lines between the physical, digital, and biological spheres.[45]

<u>Xenophobic attitudes, nationalist parties</u>

Xenophobic attitudes have emerged and led to the creation and success -- to varying degrees -- of far-right nationalist parties. Unfortunately, these xenophobic parties have achieved good results in elections in several European countries in the past years, thus leading to complex governance situations whereby traditional moderate parties cannot attain absolute majorities or form stable coalitions with one another.

It is also obvious that globalization does not distribute costs and benefits in a homogenous way. According to research carried out by the International Labor Organization (ILO), the expected transformations in production and distribution will destroy jobs in the following sectors:

a) Civil service: Due to an unwillingness to raise taxes, it will be necessary to rationalize and distribute employment functions without hiring additional civil servants or employees.

b) Manufacturing and industrial production because of the widespread use of robots, automation and artificial intelligence.

c) Low-skilled labor in the construction sector due to the creation of more advanced construction techniques.

d) In the field of law due to a greater willingness by indviduals to engage in arbitration and consensus-based dispute-settlement methods.

<u>On the other hand, the ILO expects</u> a growing demand in employment in sectors such as:

[45] Schwab, Klaus. *The Fourth Industrial Revolution: What it means, how to respond.* World Economic Forum, 14 January 2016. Accessed https://www.weforum.org/agenda/2016/01/the-fourth-industrial-revolution-what-it-means-and-how-to-respond/

a) Business and finance after the current restructuring period involving electronic banking and the closure of branches, and the appearance or development of new financial and banking business needs.

b) Highly-qualified business administration and management with executives capable of adapting companies to new paradigms and the features of the fourth industrial revolution.

c) IT and mathematics will require very highly-skilled professionals capable of designing new programs and systems capable of addressing new needs.

 d) The design of robots which can perform repetitive household tasks or fit into industrial production processes, retail, or health care for individuals that does not require direct human intervention.

e) Intelligent architecture, conservation, rehabilitation and different domains of engineering that adapt to new needs and paradigms.

f) Sale and marketing of goods and services.

g) Education and training geared towards providing the knowledge and skills required by the new employment paradigm, as well as the re-training of professionals to fulfil new tasks stemming from the fourth industrial revolution.

h) Leisure activities and their organization.

This enornous upheaval in employment and the excess supply of labor in traditional jobs that do not adapt to the new realities will have enormous consequences. Combined with the ageing of the population and the rise in the number of retired peopled, it will foster a great difficulty: how to rearrange the social surplus which heretofore was distributed according to the employment and capital that each individual contributed towards production.

As the number of low-skilled jobs diminishes, there will be a growing number of unemployed individuals who are unable to access and perform sophisticated jobs. This development will require much wider income redistribution mechanisms than the current ones, which regard unemployment as an anomaly.

The idea of redistributing work by shortening the number of working hours currently is not feasible -- as it might have been in the past -- since such a reduction would not benefit those displaced from the labor market.

<u>Leadership and the redistribution of costs and benefits</u>

The welfare state enabled low-income individuals to receive the benefits financed by the taxes paid by high-earning individuals. This arrangement will not work in the future. The difference between revenues and expenditures, namely the sustainability of the welfare state, will not be sufficient. It would also be unfair to burden future generations with servicing the debt left behind by our generation if we are not able to meet the financing demands of the welfare states with sufficient current revenues.

In this context, it is necessary to explore solutions and outcomes that deal with this redistribution of costs and benefits among the new employment structure's winners and losers. Such solutions must also allay the hostility spawned between winners and losers. This clash must be managed within the parameters of a democratic society which we must preserve in the present and future despite transformations that could spawn anti-establishment challenges.

These are not the only worries and challenges that need to be addressed. Those who feel left behind – the losers – feel entitled to receive benefits and/or pensions which are explicitly supported by certain political parties and NGOs which would rather bankrupt the welfare state with unsustainable additional expenditures and add to the public debt in order to try to close our societies' growing inequalities.

Another option is to try to persuade the losers of globalization that the welfare state can no longer provide all of the benefits which they have become accustomed to. But politicians competing for election or re-election rarely convey such messages to their current potential voters as well as to those who might or not vote for them in the near future.

Such persuasion can only be successful by authorities with true leadership capability. Such leaders must also underscore that in a globalized world an excessive welfare state can render our exports and economies uncompetitive vis-à-vis the emerging powers which do not have such a welfare state.

Daniel Griswold

Co-Director of the Program on the American Economy and Globalization at George Mason University

Daniel Griswold is Senior Research Fellow and Co-Director of the Program on the American Economy and Globalization at George Mason University's Mercatus Center. From 2012 until 2016, Griswold was President of the National Association of Foreign-Trade Zones (NAFTZ), representing its members in Washington before Congress and regulatory agencies. Prior to NAFTZ, Griswold was director of trade and immigration studies for the Cato Institute in Washington, D.C. Griswold is a nationally known expert on U.S. trade and immigration policy. The author of the 2009 book, "Mad about Trade: Why Main Street America Should Embrace Globalization", Griswold has testified before congressional committees, commented for TV and radio, authored numerous studies and articles, and addressed business and trade groups across the country and around the world. He holds a bachelor's degree in journalism from the University of Wisconsin at Madison, and a Masters in the Politics of the World Economy from the London School of Economics.

Question:

In his 1962 book Capitalism and Freedom, Milton Friedman advocated deregulation, lower taxes, privatization of enterprises and floating exchange rates. The Bretton Woods system of fixed exchange rates was designed at the end of World War II. The dollar acted as its anchor currency with a fixed exchange to gold ($35 per ounce of gold), and other currencies in turn had fixed exchange rates to the dollar (which were difficult to modify). Nations could only enforce gold convertibility on the anchor currency – the dollar. The causes and forces that unraveled the Bretton Woods system and prompted the US administration under president Nixon to abandon where an excessive printing of government debt to finance the Vietnam war, an insufficient expansion in the supply of gold to keep pace with the issuance of dollars and the higher growth rates and prosperity of other developed countries (Western Europe, Japan), the stagflation of the early seventies and the US's growing trade and current-account deficits with the rest of the world in comparison to the situation at the end of World War II.

In designing the current system of freely-floating exchange rates and abandoning pegs, was the International Monetary Fund merely accepting the reality of the causes that led to the downfall of the Bretton Woods system or also coming under the liberalizing influence of Friedman's theories – in this case for exchange rates?

The collapse of the Bretton Woods exchange-rate system in the early 1970s was probably inevitable, given the lack of fiscal and monetary discipline in the United States at that time. The system really only worked as envisioned for a relatively short period, from 1958 to 1973. Western governments turned to floating exchange rates out of necessity, not out of any ideological conversion to Milton Freidman's view. But Friedman's ideas were ready on the shelf when the system of fixed rates broke down. And with more than four decades of hindsight, Friedman has been proven right. It is a lot more efficient for exchange rates to adjust instantaneously to changing market conditions and perceptions than for governments to wrestle over painful decisions about whether, when and by how much to devalue or revalue their currencies. And it is much easier for real exchange rates to adjust through a change in nominal rates than through a change in the domestic price level, especially if an adjustment requires a domestic deflation.

Question: *Do you believe that a system of freely-floating exchange rates not only fosters trade but also is at fault in crises such as the one that Southeast Asia experienced in 1997, Russia in 1998, several countries in the European Exchange Rate Mechanism in 1992-93 (UK, Sweden, Ireland, Spain) and others caused by severe capital outflows brought about by a loss of market confidence arising from falling competitiveness and/or an excessive accumulation of public or private debt? One could argue that with fixed exchange rates these crises would not be as severe, and countries would have more time to address and correct the underlying problems that spawn a loss of confidence in their currency.*

A system of floating exchange rates is clearly compatible with an expansion of global trade flows. In fact, the era of floating rates has coincided with one of the great expansions of globalization and trade in human history. We have had successive rounds of the General Agreement on Tariffs and Trade (GATT) which started in 1947 that have lowered barriers globally, a proliferation of bilateral and regional agreements that have further liberalized trade, and also extensive unilateral liberalization, especially in emerging economies. Just as importantly, floating exchange rates have helped to liberate the international flow of capital. Under the "trilemma" of international economic policy, nations can choose two of three policies -- an independent monetary policy, a fixed exchange rate, and the free flow of capital across the border -- but cannot choose all three. With a floating rate, nations can now exercise independent monetary policy while also enjoying the benefits of more openness to foreign investment.

Floating rates and freer capital flows are not to blame for the various economic crises we have seen in recent years. The crises you mention -- Sweden and the UK in the early 1990s, East Asia and Russia later in the decade, or more recently Greece -- were primarily the fault of domestic government policies. The problem is not that foreign investors can withdraw their funds or sell the currency, but the underlying policies that cause a loss of confidence. In fact, fixed or managed rates can mask the underlying problem for a time, postponing needed reforms. Then the dam breaks and a true crisis ensues. With floating rates, there is still a reckoning for policy mistakes, but the exchange or capital markets can start sending signals sooner and the adjustments can be more incremental rather than everything falling apart on a Friday afternoon. I would argue the crisis in Greece was made more severe by its membership in the Eurozone because it was deprived of the valuable adjustment tool of a floating exchange rate.

Question: *Since 2001, the World Trade Organization (WTO) has been unable to conclude the Doha Round launched in that year partly because its single undertaking requires that member states reach agreements on all areas of trade, meaning agricultural products, manufacturing, services, intellectual property and others, before the round can be wrapped up. Since agriculture is basically the only stumbling block preventing a conclusion to the Doha Round, should the system be changed so that the requirement of the single undertaking is eliminated?*

If another WTO round is going to succeed, it may in fact need to be a more plurilateral, multi-track agreement. It may simply be too difficult for all of the WTO's 164 members to reach consensus on an ambitious agreement for a single undertaking. The current impasse is unfortunate because the elements are there for a win-win agreement for all members, with the rich western countries giving up their remaining barriers and subsidies for agriculture and tariffs on consumer goods such as clothing and footwear, in exchange for emerging economies liberalizing how they treat investment, technology goods, commercial services, and other issues important to the richer countries. Maybe the best we can hope for in the current environment are plurilateral agreements in the WTO on services and technology combined with regional and bilateral agreements, such as the new Trans-Pacific Partnership with 11 members (without the US), that are truly trade creating.

Question:The Trump administration seems to be focusing on a few countries (Mexico, Canada, China, South Korea) and on a few sectors (steel, aluminium, dairy products, vehicles, airplanes, some types of lumber) where the US has trade deficits. But in the current round of the NAFTA negotiations, the US is insisting on some conditions which are red lines for Mexico and Canada: sunset clauses which would force a renegotiation of the agreement after a few years and a dismantling of NAFTA's dispute-resolution system. The Trump administration's demands on the rise of NAFTA- or US-sourced components in cars built in one of the three NAFTA members has also sparked criticism from the US Chamber of Commerce, Mexico, Canada, and US agricultural and manufacturing associations. What do you foresee happening in the next few months on the trade front?

Where the Trump administration will go with the NAFTA renegotiation is more uncertain than ever. With the departure of the free-trader Gary Cohn as the Director of the National Economic Council (the president's Chief Economic Adviser) and the re-ascendance of the protectionists Wilbur Ross (Secretary of Commerce) and Peter Navarro (Director of Trade and Investment Policy), the Trump administration seems to be barreling toward a more confrontational approach on trade. The announcement of the imposition on March 8th of steel tariffs of 25% and 10% on aluminium have poisoned the atmosphere even further, making a constructive agreement even more difficult. NAFTA, for its part, is an important and successful commercial agreement for all three North American economies. It has delivered lower prices and more choice for consumers. It has created a more competitive North American platform for manufacturing, especially for the auto and energy industries. And it has institutionalized Mexico's turn away from a closed and centralized one-party system to an open and competitive economy and pluralistic democracy. U.S. belligerence on NAFTA will not only inflict economic damage, but it could also unravel decades of progress in U.S.-Mexican relations. U.S. business interests, Wall Street, the US Chamber of Commerce, farmers and ranchers, and most members of Congress -- Republican and Democrat -- are against withdrawing from NAFTA, but with this president and his core mercantilist beliefs, the demise of NAFTA must be considered a real possibility.

Question: Milton Friedman once famously remarked that if the government were put in charge of managing the Sahara desert, it would run out of sand in a few years. But do you believe that given the complexity of the global economy, the acceleration of technology, and other factors the public sector does have to play a role in mitigating phenomena such as income inequality, climate change, the growing digital divide, the impact of ageing of the population on the funding for entitlements, etc. Or can the private sector with some guidance by regulators and governments develop adequate tools to tackle these challenges?

Governments do play a key role in providing the institutional space for trade and globalization to continue to expand for the benefit of the large majority of mankind. Governments need to provide security for shipping lanes and certain key infrastructure such as ports. They also need to address the management of common resources such as environment quality and fishing stocks. But the main problem today is not a lack of government involvement, but too much intervention. Significant barriers remain to the free flow of goods, services, capital, and people in the global economy. In the past quarter of a century, according to the World Bank, the number of people living in absolute poverty has dropped by more than 1 billion. This historic achievement of mankind has not been attained because of any concerted government effort, but because of the spread of global capitalism -- because of the ideas of thinkers such as Milton Friedman and Peter Bauer, not Keynes and certainly not the school of "development" thinkers who called for massive foreign aid and import substitution policies for poor countries. The well-spring of human progress remains the expansion of human freedom.

<u>**Orhan Güvenen**</u>

Director of the Institute of World Systems, Economies and Strategic Research, Bilkent University (Turkey).

Professor Güvenen holds a Bachelor of Sciences degree in Econometrics from the University of Istanbul. He earned a Master's in Science in Econometrics from the University of Paris I, and a PhD in Econometrics and International Economy from the University of Paris (Sorbonne). Güvenen specializes in Strategic Decision Systems, Information Systems, Econometrics and the International Economy. Since 1988, Güvenen is professor of Strategic Decision Systems and Econometrics at Bilkent University. He is also the Founder and Director of the Institute of World Systems, Economies and Strategic Research (DSEE), and Chairman of the Accounting Information Systems Department at Bilkent University. Moreover, he serves as Chairman and member of the Executive Committee of the Advisory Board on Strategy, Economy and Industry of the National Nanotechnology Research Center (UNAM). Professor Güvenen is president of the Applied Econometrics Association. He is a visiting professor of the University of Paris Pantheon-Sorbonne and a Fellow of the World Academy of Arts and Sciences. Among other awards, Güvenen has received the "Award for Great Achievers of the World -- International Gusi Peace Prize" (2013); the "Turkish World Lifetime Achievement Award" (2012) and the Order of Merit of the Italian Republic (1994). In 2016, he was one of only two individuals in the world to receive the Transdisciplinary Distinguished Achievement Award by the Academy of Transdisciplinary Learning and Advanced Studies (ATLAS).

In 2016, the Academy of Transdisciplinary Learning and Advanced Studies (ATLAS) awarded me the *Transdisciplinary Distinguished Achievement Award* for my research[46]. I have been conducting research on the subject of transdisciplinary science and methodology for thirty-seven years and continue do so. The article related to the award contains some answers to the matter of globalization, nativism and the Digital Divide.

First of all, the social sciences for more than fifty years have been operating in an under-optimal way. Social sciences are difficult subjects to begin with. Their task is complex. Why? Because the object of their research -- human beings -- are complicated, irrational and, driven by their basic instincts, seek to accumulate power. Therefore, my research and academic articles employ transdisciplinary methods. The *Academy of Transdisciplinary Learning and Studies* published a book on the topic which contains my academic articles. They also have a journal with articles by engineers and mathematicians.

There are many problems in terms of research and decision-making systems. For decades we have been in a case of operating in an under-optimum situation. Why? Because in the past fifty years social sciences -- including statistical social sciences -- have become subjective in their research. When this happens, it is not possible to achieve an optimum solution. This is a big mistake. What I am describing can be proven mathematically. For more than fifty years, the social sciences have been operating in an under-optimal way. This leads to under-optimal information and under-optimal decision systems. The social sciences in general, and certainly economics, have been operating in such a way for more than fifty years. One of the results is that in the field of economics the ideas associated with liberalism (in its British meaning as pertains to

---

[46] Professor Güvenen was one of two individuals to receive the award in 2016, the other being Bosheng Zhou, founder and honorary dean of the Beijing University of Aeronautics and Astrophysics.

markets) have become the dominant force. I am not opposed to liberalism per se. But liberalism as the result of under-optimal economic research has led to a maximization of money and power, despite all of the theories linked to democracy. There is something wrong in academic terms. Therefore, in terms of the application of decision-making systems or political systems, I believe the analysis is not properly done.

In the current international order, individuals do not have much choice. They do not have much choice unless the world's 7.6 billion human beings through time dynamics can raise consciousness at a global level. Spanish universities, for example, can summon the will to take action not only in their country but globally. This means overcoming inaction both in the decision-making system as well as in the market system. One individual's actions can be amplified.

At the international and national level, the decision-making systems are not driven by politics. Politics act only as a kind "spokesmen" for greater powers. These greater powers are transnational corporations. They are extremely powerful. They can attain market capitalizations of more than 100 billion dollars. The knowledge concentrated and accumulated at the highest level of transnational corporations -- top management -- is also highly powerful. This knowledge is much better than that of the average politician's capacity. Secondly, transnational corporations have tremendous financial capacity, which translates into great freedom. They have networks spread around the entire world, in one hundred or more countries. Nation states cannot afford to create and sustain such networks. Transnational corporations can hire labor from wherever they want. They can, for example, decide to shut down a factory in Belgium in order not to have to pay employees $20 an hour, relocate to China or Indonesia and pay an hourly salary of $1, and still make their products. Transnational corporations can decide to transfer their operations from one continent to another without much efficient resistance by international institutions, governments or labor unions.

Globalization has been moving in the direction I have described for more than thirty years. Nobody is behind globalization. It is not fostered by academia and it does not have a strategy. Transnational corporations have done their homework. It is not their fault. Engineers developed laptops, which have facilitated the use of computer power exponentially. This means that instead of having to go to laboratories, entrepreneurs can go home and research on their laptops how markets are evolving. After the necessary market research, these entrepreneurs can create small corporations. And the probability is very high that if these small corporations (especially in the technological sector) are successful, a transnational corporation will want to acquire them and pay their creators and founders millions of dollars. Globalization began in the financial sector more than thirty years ago with the liberalization of financial systems and flows of capital and has gradually taken over the real economy as well.

I do not think the solution to globalization's problems will come from international organizations or nation states. Nation states try to achieve their optimal situation and pursue their own interests. Or even from NGOs. We have to analyze who is financing NGOs. Some are moderate but others are more unreliable because we do not really know who is financing them. In such a world, the individual does not have much of a choice. Unless over a period of time each of the world's 7.6 billion inhabitants brings a consciousness to bear. We have to create what I would call a global consciousness. If politicians' promises are not fulfilled, there is no need to take to the streets and throw stones and behave aggressively. For example, when a politician reneges on a campaign promise, in the next election each voter has to politely but firmly hold that politician to account and tell him or her that he will not be obtaining that person's vote. If millions and eventually billions of individuals behave this way, they will generate a global consciousness. In order to amplify their message, technology can have a very strong and positive impact. Politicians would therefore be obliged to change the current decision-making systems.

At a second level, we have to deal with the markets. We have to confront transnational corporations which have not behaved ethically. Let us say there is a transnational corporation or big firm which controls a market for a specific product or service in Latin America or Africa. But they may have paid a dictator to achieve this market dominance. There is nothing wrong with their production, but there is in the way they have financed their market domination. At an economic level, certain individuals without the proper ethical values who own a company may have a monopoly or a dominant market position in a particular sector. This big corporation may make financial contributions to a political party in power that sells weapons to other countries. This unfortunately happens, even in democracies. As a result of these sales of weapons employed in wars, thousands of innocent people die. Individuals can reject buying these companies' products. Individuals can calmly say they will not purchase products from such companies. These kinds of boycotts have been successful in the past. This is the best approach to correct markets and the market economy. It has to come from the grass roots. It is not a matter of a country ordering others to change their behavior. Only through multilateral cooperation between countries through international institutions can real transformations come to pass. But the basis for this cooperation must be laid first by a grass-roots campaign. For example, countries that used to finance dictators eventually stopped this practice and began to increase their funding for development, thereby providing finance for education and protection of the environment in developing and emerging nations.

At the time of the May 1968 democratic revolution in France, at least 60 or 70 percent of the members of the French cabinet (ministers, deputy ministers) were Marxists or Maoists. I was working in France at the time. There was nothing wrong with these people in terms of their humanity. But real revolutions take place in the mind. They have to take root in peoples' minds. There has to be a certain level of sensitivity in peoples' minds in order to be able to generate a global consciousness that brings about real transformations. These transformations mean real change in terms of accountability, the sciences, better education, etc.

Many analysts and academics use the term "multinational" corporations. But this is the wrong terminology. These companies are transnational corporations, they go beyond the nation-state. They transcend the nation-state, which cannot control them, and can operate in 120 o 130 countries and amass tremendous wealth. People in governments who have the responsibility to raise revenue know that transnational corporations are a very important source of funding. But that does not mean that governments can control these powerful transnational corporations.

Regarding the proposal to tax transnational corporations that employ a lot of robots and technology in order to finance more training, who would in practice be in charge of and be responsible for applying and collecting these taxes from transnational corporations? Transnational corporations are very powerful, and because of their size they can in many cases choose where they want to pay taxes. They therefore choose to register for tax purposes in countries with low levels of taxation. And if a country tries to apply a level of taxation that the transnational corporations deems to be too high, they can take their operations to another country. They can recruit workers from around the world and move their operations to optimize paying the fewest possible taxes. Transnational corporations that operate in more than one hundred countries, for example, have a great degree of freedom and power. Which government can force them to pay a tax rate of 20% -- the average of OECD member states -- instead of 5%?

It is therefore very difficult for developing countries, in particular, to raise taxes on transnational corporations. If they hike taxes for transnational corporations from 5% -- for example -- to 20%, which is closer to the OECD average -- these corporations may take their operations elsewhere.

I have held senior positions at the OECD for many years. And the Paris-based institution has achieved a lot in terms of holding transnational corporations accountable and making policy recommendations to governments. The OECD has also made a lot of progress in tackling money laundering. But the OECD and other international institutions need to make more progress. We do not know how much time they will need to address the challenges of globalization.

Tysun Ihm

Attorney. Advisor to technology companies.

Tysun Ihm is a Washington-based international lawyer with decades of experience in providing counseling to small technology startups, multinational corporations in joint ventures and strategic alliances in biotech, IT, and alternative energy, as well as large international trade organizations. With executive management and Board experiences at public international companies -- and an Executive at Stanford University's first-ever high-tech spinoff. He has also served as Counsel to South Korea's leading democratic dissident leader turned President in 1992. More recently, he manages investment projects in Silicon Valley while focusing on promoting cultural exchanges between China and the West through the Ren Foundation. He is engaged in original research relating to a book on Great Wars in East Asia: How China, Korea, and Japan Came to War and Peace in 1600 and 1953. Mr. Ihm is a Magna Cum Laude graduate from Yale University (B.A., 1980) and Harvard Law School (J.D., 1983).

"The World Is Too Much With Us", lamented Wordsworth in 1807, at the dawn of the First Industrial Revolution. What was once lamentable is now a passionate loathing, of all places, in advanced nations that prospered most from globalization in the past half-century.

British fishermen in Grimsby massively voted to leave the EU to regain control of British waters to avoid competing with foreign trawlers. [47]Coal miners of West Virginia fell prey to a guiling promise of resuscitating coal mining. Fears and frustrations resonate across rust-belt states to and beyond Pacific waters. Everywhere the saga is familiar -- the interest of those in the disrupted industry is pitted against those in the new and expanding businesses. Wisdom of clinging to the romance of the fading pastoral, or sustainable seafaring life aside, fears about immigration, jobs, sovereignty and the loss of a way of life are real and persistent.

Societies excessively bent on material greed, further distancing from sustainable, interconnected living, are tested now more than ever as artificial intelligence, automation and foreign lifestyles rapidly impinge on us all.

Like Japan and Germany, South Korea faces acute demographic issues with declining fertility rates and a rapidly ageing population. Like the rest of East Asia, South Korea has tried to increase birthrates, offering childcare bonuses, fertility treatments, and even gifts of beef for newborn babies without much improvement.[48] Such measures are shortsighted without assuaging job insecurity, costs of raising children, or redirecting hedonistic impulses embedded in our mass-consumer culture. Between 1975 and 2015, Korea's median age soared to 41.2 from just 19.6.

More so than Japan, South Korea has recruited about two million foreign workers today, from fewer than 50,000 in 1990. Guest worker programs allow about 275,000 foreign workers up to five years without offering a path to citizenship. Undocumented migrant workers exceed 200,000.[49] These foreign workers, mostly from China, Vietnam, and other parts of Southeast Asia, mainly fill shortages in agriculture, construction and manufacturing jobs that most locals eschew.[50]

While youth unemployment hovers at 10%, there is a mismatch of college graduates who gravitate toward lucrative jobs either at large, global companies or smaller, dynamic start-ups.

---

[47] David Segal, NY Times, April 23, 2018
[48] Brook Larmer, NY Times, February 20, 2018
[49] Ibidem
[50] Ibidem

For the highly skilled, well-educated entrepreneurial graduates, there are more incubators, more funds for startups and better networking between people and work in startups in many of these leading economies. Many universities hope to replicate the success of the Stanford-Silicon Valley nexus.

Japan, more resistant to immigration, opted for automation and limited immigration. To some experts, immigration is a solution to Japan's ageing, declining population, which caused labor shortages. Others assault Japan's less inclusive national policy. However, the immigration issue has to be examined in the context of a society's tradition and norms, not as a quick fix for labor shortages only.

Temporary guest workers programs are favored in Korea and Japan to maintain social stability and a consolidated identity. In their view, this would prevent or minimize the anti-immigrant problems and violence seen in Europe and other countries. In Hungary and Austria[51], among the more homogeneous countries in the EU, the defense of sovereignty of the nation and culture has fueled anti-immigration parties and even governments in the case of Hungary and Poland[52].

South Korea and Japan have long had cultural and ethnic homogeneity. More importantly, education, family bonds, mutual obligation (more than individual freedom) as core values of Confucian culture provided social cohesion. As these values have eroded in the past decades, high divorce rates, hyper-consumer oriented, hedonistic lifestyles set in. Korea's left leaning government came to power in 2017 with promises of social justice and income-led growth at a time of rising discontent over inequality, youth unemployment, stagnant incomes, and growing elderly poverty. It campaigned on promises such as:

> --A basic income (Finland model);
> --To create hundreds of thousands of public sector jobs for college graduates;

---

[51] This statement applies to certain provinces of Austria. Of a population of 8,773,686 residents (as of 1 January 2017), including 1,342,758 foreign citizens (15.3% of total population). In 2016, an average of1,898 million people with migration background lived in Austria, that is 21.6% of the entire population, one of the highest percentages of any EU member state.

[52] Austria was shunned by the EU and part of the international community when it elected Kurt Waldheim, who had a Nazi past, as its president in 1987. He served out his term until 1992. Waldheim has been Secretary General of the UN for 9 years (1972-81). The far-right anti-immigrant Austrian Freedom Party (FPO) led by the deceased Jörg Haider headed the government of the federal state of Carinthia, and Haider was premier of Carinthia for two terms. The FPO was also the junior coalition partner to the center-right Austrian People's Party (OVP) in a government that again drew widespread rejection from the EU and beyond (although Austria had become an EU member state in 1995). The Freedom Party split up before Haider's death in an automobile accident in 2008, and unfortunately the FPO is again the junior coalition partner to the Austrian People's Party since December of 2017. Moreover, the current president of Austria, Alexander Van der Bellen, narrowly defeated the far-right candidate in the 2016 presidential election in the second round.

Austria is fairly homogeneous in terms of its population, but the Vienna metropolitan area attracted hundreds of thousands of immigrants for decades, especially during the wars that broke up Yugoslavia in the 1990s. The far-right has not managed to turn the Austrian People's Party into an openly hostile and xenophobic party that actually expels immigrants and condones violence against foreigners. But the OVP clearly has moved to the right. Austria's troubled history at the gates of the Ottoman Empire and its Cold War neutrality and non-membership in NATO have to be also considered. The governments of Hungary, Serbia (not an EU member) and Poland have adopted more specific hostile policies, such as building fences in Serbia's case. Poland's government is undermining the rule of law by packing the judiciary and media with party loyalists. The EU is moving ahead with plans that could enable Brussels to reduce the financial transfers to Poland, as a suspension of its voting rights under article 7 of the Treaty of Lisbon requires a unanimity in the EU which is lacking, as Hungary's government and Prime minister Viktor Orban defend the Polish one.

--To directly pay tens of thousands of dollars for each new employee that small and medium sized companies hire (with the professed aim of bridging the pay gap with largest corporations);
--To convert temporary and contract workers into permanent employees.
--To enforce "Blind hiring" policy where large companies and government sector employers cannot mention applicants' college, arguably to level the playing field for graduates from less prestigious regional colleges.

Opposition parties during the electoral campaign charged the ruling party of "populist giveaway to voters' ahead of elections.

Appealing to voters perhaps, but such proposals may prove ineffective in the face of slower growth and budgetary constraints, such as the extreme example of Greece in the past decade has shown. Converting temporary to permanent employees also reduces hiring prospects for the newly graduated, thus increasing youth unemployment. Korea's 500 largest companies indicate decline in hiring of college graduates for 2018 [53]

Fundamentally, it was Korea's dynamic growth model supported by cultural vitality which ushered in its rapid advances in its economy. Korea in the 1950s was a war-torn, poor and largely agrarian country. Immensely patriotic and far-sighted, South Korea's first President, Syngman Rhee, instituted effective land reform, while providing compulsory education to all of its citizens in 1949. It laid the foundation for industrialization that came in the 1960s.[54] It successfully reduced illiteracy of 87 percent in 1945 (when Japanese occupation ended) to less than 13 percent by the late 1960s. The current illiteracy rate is 2.3 percent, the lowest among developed nations.

The economic successes of Korea, Taiwan, Singapore, and, most stupendously, China over the last three decades are remarkable but not a model easily replicable in other countries. These societies are homogeneous (though China is more diverse) and have deeply embedded values of education and social cohesion. Government officials, middle and upper levels, had to pass rigorous examinations dating back to 8th century. Scholar-official-gentry rule of Korea and China provided ethics and a merit-based state bureaucracy that lasted until encroachment by the western powers in the late nineteenth century.

Through the export-led growth model from the 1960s, Korea transformed labor-intensive industries in the 1960s and 1970s into companies capable of manufacturing higher-value products in the early 1990s. Semiconductors, smartphones, LCDs, refrigerators and automobiles manufactured by South Korean companies are a familiar staple in every American home today, as well as South Korean-built cars by Hyundai and Kia on American streets and roads. South Korea's largest companies, such as Samsung, LG, and Hyundai, dominate the smartphone, semiconductor, and LCD markets along with Apple and Japanese companies, with Chinese companies rapidly closing in.

The looming prospect of China's lead in artificial intelligence, alternative energy, and telecommunications underlie Trump's approach to tighten joint ventures, mergers and co-research between US and Chinese entities, threatening long running practices in technology development in Silicon Valley and other technology centers (Harvard-MIT Corridor).

---

[53] Joongang Ilbo, March 19, 2018
[54] It was during the 1960s and 1970s, under a military dictatorship, industrialization was fully launched and credited for its success

At present, legislations are in progress in US Congress and threats of executive actions to prevent private researchers and technology companies from investing, sharing knowledge or co-developing in the fields of artificial intelligence, semiconductor and autonomous vehicle technology, under the guise of national security interest.[55] Such counterproductive methods fly against the long practices which brought benefits of global partnerships and innovations resulting from collaboration and joint ventures.

Qualcomm, which pioneered CDMA based smartphone technology, had its first major market and customer base in South Korea in the early 1990s. This boosted its technology and garnered markets, over European competitors (GSM was Europe's then dominant technology). Both Qualcomm and Samsung were beneficiaries of early collaboration.

In the mid-1990s, alternative energy technology -- solar and wind power -- were not competitive to natural gas prices and their adoption stalled. With technology improvement and large-scale market adoptions in China and some European nations, technology improved, costs were reduced and demand soared throughout the world for such energy technology. Technology developers are dependent on investments and markets, which, in turn, further improve technology, costs and profits, which engender new employment opportunities.

In the real world, technology companies never give away core-differentiating technology to third entities. When they agree to share technology as part of a joint venture, distribution or co-development, legal safeguards are available for their proprietary technology or next generation developments for their exclusive or phased over-time use, under royalty and other numerous means. Demonizing some countries as "intellectual thieves" ignores a basic reality: most companies, including those in the US, imitate, lure key engineers and developers who bring built-in knowledge or cleverly redesign successful technologies. Thousands of patent or trademark litigations within the US alone testify to this phenomenon. In the early 1990s, when Samsung and Hyundai targeted semiconductors as their strategic new businesses, many senior level Japanese experts provided vital know-how and development support, many without the consent of their employers.

International lawyers and technology development experts are at the cutting edge and prosper by providing such services. For governments to politicize the issue and hamper collaborations and joint ventures is short-sighted and misguided.

The extensive role of the state in supporting certain industries was practiced by the US, Japan, Singapore and Korea, which China is also employing. Tax credits, loans and subsidies offered to certain industries, from alternative energy to biotech, to large agri-businesses, to name a few, in the United States are state interventions as well.

Stephen Roach, formerly Chief Economist at Morgan Stanley, decries Trumps' latest 301 trade action against China: "(trade) it is a win-win situation and the forced technology transfer is but a myth to justify Trump's unreasonable tariff measures against China"[56] Roach explains "that there is no such thing as an unregulated free market", and developed countries enjoyed rapid economic growth relying on subsidized industrial policy in the past. For instance, Japan's economic miracle in the 1970s and 80s should be attributed to "state-subsidized credit allocation and tariffs," which by no means is in accordance with a free market spirit. But it did protect Japan's emerging industries and give them space to develop. Other developed countries, including the US itself, also use the strategy. Influential technology breakthroughs, including the

---

[55] CNBC, April 27, 2018
[56] Stephen Roach, "America's weak case against China", on Project Syndicate, April 24, 2018

Internet, GPS, semiconductors and even nuclear power are "spin-offs" of a NASA project, which was heavily state-sponsored and taxpayer-funded in the 1960s.

Roach admits that innovation is the key to a country's future development. But, according to Roach, to assume that China is gaining it through industrial policy is "the height of hypocrisy." While it may garner political dividends to blame China, Japan, Brazil, or Mexico for trade deficits or job losses, the fundamental causes of job losses are elsewhere. Technology, automation and artificial intelligence are the lead causes of the erosion of jobs in the current and the coming decades.

Let us turn to the real underpinning of competitiveness. The Center for Economic and Business Research (CEBR), Britain's leading think tank, recently reported Britain would overtake Germany as Europe's biggest economy by 2030, second only to United States in the West. It also forecasts that China will become the world's largest economy by 2028. Other leaders in nominal GDP will be Japan, India, Britain and South Korea, in eleventh place, the latter passing France.

Professor Alexandre Muns' data indicates which are the most competitive economies in 2018, with Spain included in the top ten. It is no coincidence that these countries also lead in education rankings. The OECD's 2015 Global Rankings on student performance in mathematics, reading and science ("PISA") measure 15-year-olds in 72 countries to rank the global competitiveness of countries' educational systems. The US ranked 28th in math in the 2015 survey.

Asian countries again topped rankings across all subjects in the PISA study. Japan, Estonia, Finland and Canada were the four highest-performing OECD nations. South Korea, Denmark and Norway are in the top tier as well. Singapore performs highest with the Dominican Republic performing lowest.

Performance aside, these countries also measure well in educational equity. The report cites that socio-economic status continues to have an impact on students' opportunities to benefit from education and developing their skills. In the report, however, 29% of disadvantaged students are shown to be resilient, meaning they score among the top quarter of students in all participating countries despite the odds against them. In China and Vietnam, students facing the greatest disadvantage on an international scale outperform the most advantaged students in about 20 other PISA participating countries (China, Estonia, Finland, Vietnam, Japan, and Korea).[57]

In the United States, education is highly polarized. Educational performance is racially and socio-economically uneven. Performance and individual efforts must battle pressures for racial considerations on admissions and hiring that largely favor African-American and Hispanic members. Open critiques based on performance or individual efforts come under strong criticism by affirmative action proponents.

From the US to China, there will be pressure to open the door to more highly educated immigrants. Like Silicon Valley, innovative hubs in Bangalore, Shenzan, Hangzhou (17 national level hubs in China) Seoul, Tel Aviv, will cross-pollinate capital, talent, and market fueling innovations, high- value jobs and wealth opportunities. In these ecosystems, collaboration and breakthroughs and innovations will challenge the less developed societies where resources and governance are weak.

The US stills leads in startups. But polarizing politics undermines its ability to rationalize (economic) structural changes. Long-term structural responses need stable and far-sighted governance -- which modern electoral systems increasingly underperform. Gender, ethnic and

---

[57] See snapshot of Performance in Science, Reading and Math, figure 1.1.1, PISA 2015

special interest politics engender distrust -- and elicit a form of political tribalism – an 'us against them' mentality.[58] Some common wisdom can be distilled as to what constitutes good governance to meet challenges of the digital age, national priorities to tackle inequality and competitiveness.[59]

Openness to trade and rational immigration are vital for leading countries, as are accessible educational opportunities linked to the changing demands of their job market. Rebuilding decaying national infrastructure (US), more affordable housing, apprenticeship programs linked to specific high-skilled jobs and student debt relief are essential. Extending work benefits (sick leaves, retirement plans) for part-time contract workers, not just to permanent full-time employees, is also necessary.

In Singapore, the government has gone further in expanding lifelong opportunities. Its "Skills Future Initiative of 2015" offers education credit from all Singaporeans to return to schools if they wish, from students still in school to workers with more than a decade of experience. For instance, a mid-career Singaporean pursuing a part-time engineering undergraduate course will pay $6,800 instead of $17,000, a reduction of 60 per cent.

Skills Future has set aside over $1 billion a year from 2015 to 2020 on initiatives such as career guidance for students, enhanced internships, and subsidies for mid-career learning, among others. About $600 million a year over the last five years have already been spent on continuing education and training in Singapore. For a nation of 5.5 million, this sum is not insubstantial and demonstrates real commitment.

With respect to public expenditures on assistance and retraining for unemployed workers in developed economies, the top ten are in northern Europe and Germany. Of the 32 countries in the OECD, the US spends nearly the lowest percentage, second only to Mexico.[60] Looking at revenue draining tax cuts in American states, not to mention at the federal level, the casualties are schools, roads, bridges, hospitals and law enforcement agencies. Smaller American towns look more like those of emerging countries, not the forward-looking and admired face of the 1960s. Teachers' strikes for better pay and school funding from Arizona, Kentucky to West Virginia manifest how poorly the value of education is reflected in our society.

One third of American workers may need to change occupations and acquire new skills by 2030 according to McKinsey Global Initiative. Most vulnerable to automation in America are non-college graduates who work in manufacturing, food service, retail trade, but it also increasingly may affect financial analysts, doctors, lawyers, and journalists, to name from a growing list.

As technology disrupts industry after another, better access to skills and knowledge are needed to place more people in higher value jobs but also to create wealth without which society cannot sustain and grow. America is suited for creating wealth but it must share more fruits and returns to most Americans, including teachers, nurses, and law enforcement officers. In Germany and Japan, CEOs of large companies make a fraction of that of their American counterparts -- yet these economies are strong, stable and innovative.

As in Wordsworth's time, the late nineteenth century and in America today, discontent groups see governments in the pockets of financial and business elites, the big winners of globalization. Sirens ring loud for change. But let us recall the days of the New Deal when a humane leader,

---

[58] Yascha Mounk, People v Democracy; reviewed by Jennifer Szalza, NY Times, March 14, 2018
[59] Some of these suggestions are from Council On Foreign Relations Task Force on "The Work Ahead: Machines, Skills, and US Leadership in the Twentieth first Century", April 10, 2018
[60] OECD-2015

Franklin D. Roosevelt, embraced many of the populists' economic ideas such as a progressive income tax, regulations on big business and much wiser government control of the economy. Franklin D. Roosevelt also injected ethics into unbridled capitalism. Today, no such grand leader is in the horizon.

What compels all of us is to balance our national priorities, calibrating policies and programs to our own custom and practices, needs and aspirations, and not swayed by political winds -- disguised trade politics in the cold war mindset -- blowing toward us.

<u>**Kimio Kase**</u>

Professor, International University of Japan and Beijing Normal University.

Kimio Kase earned his doctorate in Business Administration from Manchester University and his Master's in Business Administration from IESE Business School in Spain. He also holds a degree in Business Science from ICADE and a Bachelor of Arts from the Tokyo University of Foreign Studies. Professor Kase has extensive corporate experience in the fields of global trade and management. After working for a Japanese global trading house where he specialized in industrial marketing, he was appointed to a senior position in Price Waterhouse Europe. Kase co-authored in 2005 a book published in the UK titled "Transformational CEOs: Leadership and Management Success in Japan", the Japanese version of which was published in 2006. He also co-authored the book "CEOs as Leaders and Strategy Designers: Explaining the Success of Spanish banks", which was published by Palgrave Macmillan in 2007. Kase served as president of the International University of Japan (IUJ) after being dean of its Graduate School of International Management. He remains a specially appointed professor at the International University of Japan and Ritsumeikan University, also in Japan. Kase is also a professor on leave from IESE Business School in Spain. He has drawn up many case studies on a wide range of companies and organizations, including the Imperial Army of Japan and Nissan's Carlos Ghosn.

During the past thirty years, many Japanese have had a keen interest and actually taken part in producing good animation films, costume plays and making better ramen and curry -- to name a few items -- as they perceive them to be key elements of pop culture.

In a similar way, globalization has been a buzzword in Japan in the past years. For many individual Japanese, globalization at their level entails being able to speak good English, using English in executive meetings, or for a Japanese firm to acquire a company abroad. Some Japanese positively view a purchase of a foreign company even if the Japanese company involved in the takeover *does not* have sufficient management skills to efficiently run and control the company it has taken over. At a personal level, speaking good English is an obsession among many Japanese. A typical advertisement by a long-distance language school features a Japanese person boasting about how he or she has gained proficiency in English only by listening to tape recordings in their sleep. The recordings are, of course, supplied by the language school.

But Japan needs a different kind of globalization than the aforementioned items. The globalization that Japan should strive to achieve is more complex. It requires building up a strong core of corporate competencies that are the result of efforts undertaken during many years. The globalization that Japan should promote also demands identifying and strengthening well-defined business domains. Japanese policymakers, executives and the population at large should share the consensus that foreign markets offer opportunities but also presents higher risks than the domestic market. Corporate Japan needs to do a better job of discerning between companies and sectors that can successfully expand beyond our borders and smaller firms that do not have the capability to internationalize.

Japanese society in general and corporate Japan in particular must be aware and have a deep understanding of the ways business is managed and operations are conducted. In fact, knowledge of these business management and operational elements determine which sectors Japan may excel in, or, on the contrary, fail. For example, excellent business management knowledge and that of operations have resulted in the extraordinary success of Japanese carmakers and manufacturers of machine tools at the international level. On the other hand, in the mobile telephony and chemical products sectors, for example, Japanese companies have not been successful at the global level. The key to strengthening Japan's globalization is to have companies deploy strategies based on existing resources and visible and invisible assets and capabilities.

<u>Challenges for Japanese companies going global: Takeda's case</u>

Failures by Japanese companies to internationalize occur when assets and capabilities are not accurately assessed. A recent conflict has emerged between shareholders and management in Takeda Pharmaceutical Company over its large-scale international mergers and acquisition strategy. Takeda's board announced in March 2018 that it was launching a takeover for the Irish drugmaker Shire, which specializes in treatments of rare diseases. If the acquisition is successful, the combined company would have a value of $85 billion, placing it among the ranks of the world's biggest.[61] In the past few years, Takeda, the biggest pharmaceutical company in Japan, and its domestic rivals, Astellas and Shionogi, have scooped up several small American biotechnology companies. The M&A operations so far carried out by Takeda are regarded as a failure and are destabilizing a century-old firm. We may infer that the intended globalization undertaken by the Japanese firm is aligned with its strategic design but was not designed taking into account the availability of the necessary resources required for going global. Takeda is also an outlier because, on account of the unmanageability of its foreign acquisitions, its management in higher echelons has been replaced by non-Japanese executives, a rare occurrence in corporate Japan. Takeda's boss is a Frenchman -- Christophe Weber -- as are several other members of his executive team.[62] Takeda's management is betting on the quality and quantity of the drugs that are in the late-stage pipeline of the Irish pharmaceutical company.

There are several elements that need to be taken into account as globalization transitions to a new stage. Some of the components that are a part of the so-called fourth industrial revolution are Artificial Intelligence, the widespread use of robots and the digital economy in general. An ageing population is also associated with Japan's current development. Japanese society in general and companies in particular need to analyze these trends, their impact on Japan as well as the country's globalization efforts.

<u>Japan's demographic challenge</u>

Japan's population reached an all-time high of 128,083,960 in 2008. Since then, the Japanese population has been declining. It had dropped by 285,256 by October 2011. Japan's current population (2017 figures) is 126,672,00, a reduction of almost one and a half million since 2010. It is difficult to overstate the seriousness of Japan's demographic challenge. According to data processed in 2012 by the National Institute of Population and Social Security Research, Japan's population on current trends will continue to diminish *by about one million people every year* in the coming decades. In 2012, the population had dropped for six consecutive years, the biggest fall since 1940-45, when Japan was fighting on many fronts during World War II. To put these numbers into perspective, Japan's population rose from approximately 72 million in 1945 to 128 million in 2010.

In 2014, Japan recorded a record reduction in population for one year, which reached 268,000 people. In 2013, more than 20 percent of the population was aged 65 and over. If these trends are not reversed -- and there is obviously time and ways to do so -- Japan's population would plummet to 42 million by 2110. More than 40% of Japan's population is projected to be over the age of 65 in 2060. Japan boasts one of the world's highest life expectancies. It reached 85 years in 2016, up substantially from 81.25 in 2006. But the combination of a very low fertility rate and negligible immigration have resulted in a net drop of population since 2010. In 2012, Japan

---

[61] "Takeda and Shire: Foreign Advances". The Economist. April 7th, 2018, page 57
[62] Ibidem

recorded only 1.03 million births. Many other developed countries have fertility rates which are not sufficient to prevent a fall in their population. But, in stark contrast to Japan, they have allowed significant immigration inflows which have compensated for natives' low fertility and kept their populations from declining.

In 2015, Japan was still the 11th most populated country in the world, and a stagnation of its population does relieve its high population density, which is 336 people per square kilometer. But the decline in population of almost one million between 2010 and 2015 is very concerning, especially as life expectancy continues to rise. In towns that are not more than an hour train ride from Tokyo, shops with shutters permanently lowered are everywhere and are a testament to Japan's demising and ageing population.

Japan's ageing populations presents opportunities as well as challenges for Japan's pharmaceutical and drug companies. The obvious advantage is that an ageing population will need a bigger and more varied supply of medication. The fact that people are living much longer does not negate the fact that they need medical treatment and often take several pills or other treatments permanently. On the other hand, Japanese pharmaceutical companies have come to rely on Japan's government-run health care system, which is their biggest client and is responsible for 40% of drug spending. The Japanese Health Ministry is obviously concerned about the increasing financial cost of delivering health care and medication to an ageing population. In order to contain its costs, the Health Ministry is fostering generic drugs and setting lower prices for medications, which it negotiates with the sector's companies every two years. Takeda's bid to become more global by acquiring Shire must also be understood in this context. But Takeda needs to understand its capabilities in order to pull off a successful takeover of Shire.

South Korea and China also suffer from low fertility rates and an ageing population. But Japan's demographic situation is more acute. Since Shinzo Abe became Japan's Prime Minister again in 2012 (he had earlier served as prime minister in 2006-2007), he embarked on an ambitious program to revive the country's economy, known as *Abenomics*. Abe sought to, and to some extent has achieved, a higher level of inflation and an increase in wages in a quest to spur domestic demand. Moreover, Abe has adopted some measures to foster immigration into Japan, although the results so far are modest.

During the past three decades, the yen rose in value as a reflection of Japan's post-war economic surge. As the yen appreciated vis-à-vis other currencies, part of Japan's manufacturing base had to be shifted abroad in search of cheaper labor, and to counter exports becoming more expensive as a result of the yen's appreciation. Abenomics has pursued a weaker yen, and therefore brought about a return in the manufacturing of sophisticated products to Japan. However, in the long run, it remains to be seen whether the gradual weakening of the Japanese industrial base can be halted.

<u>The impact of robotics</u>

Some fear that automation, Artificial Intelligence and the widespread use of robots may destroy millions of jobs. But the opposite may happen, at least to some extent. Japan's ageing population generates a demand in people that take care of the old. There is a growing awareness of the dearth of specialists in this area. Robotics might fill the gap between the demand and supply not only in the caretaking industry, but also in industrial production. The know-how thus gained might also help Japanese firms to go global.

Regarding Artificial Intelligence, the spread of IT and the digital economy, Japan does not seem to be at the forefront of innovations, unlike China and South Korea. One reason could be that the Japanese prefer or feel better employing analogue devices rather than in a digital environment.

In China, for example, many people no longer carry money and instead pay using their WeChat accounts. The Japanese, on the other hand, stay away from these electronic payment methods. Japanese peoples' relative unwillingness to use innovative technologies may hinder Japanese companies' ability to foster creativity and cutting-edge technologies.

In conclusion, what advise can we furnish to managers and executives at Japanese companies that seek to globalize their business? They need to deploy assessment tools that diagnose the resources available for globalization. In addition, they need to review the nature of business (integral or module type), the business domain, core competences, and an organizational routine scheme.
Globalization is becoming more turbulent and unpredictable. A process-based and emergent type of strategy may not necessarily be effective under these circumstances. The caveat is that this may sound like a self-fulfilling prophecy.

Wolfgang Knapp

International publisher and author

Wolfgang Knapp is originally from Austria but has lived and worked in Brazil for more than fifty years. His career in the publishing world has spanned many decades and included several countries, including Austria, Germany, France and Spain. His main professional achievements in the publishing world have been in Brazil. He founded the successful publishing house "Editora Pedagógica e Universitaria (EPU)", located in Sao Paolo. This publishing house specializes in Psychology, Philosophy and Education. It has made a significant contribution to the academic world in Brazil. The EPU was among the first to publish a series of books titled "Portuguese for Foreigners". Moreover, Knapp wrote a Glossary in Germany for this series. He is the author of the book "O que é editora" about the publishing world published by Editora Brasileira.

Political, economic and social developments in Brazil in the past years have to be analyzed in the context of massive corruption scandals that have tarnished the political and business class. *Lava jato* is a huge and wide-ranging criminal investigation into corruption at all political levels in Brazil. The investigations began in March of 2014 when a routine operation against money laundering at a gas station uncovered links to graft by other actors. A car wash operated next to the aforementioned gas station, as is often the case around the world. *Lava jato* means "car wash" in Brazilian Portuguese. The car wash was being employed by a currency exchanger to launder money. Pursuing this lead, investigators also found out that the exchange trader had shady connections with a politician, who in turn had business ties with Petrobras, Brazil's giant oil and gas multinational. Petrobras in turn had many ties to construction companies, including Odebrecht, Latin America's biggest construction company. Four years later, as a result of the dogged work and efforts of Brazil's judges and prosecutors, more than 500 persons have either been investigated, accused or convicted of corruption as part of the *Lava jato* probe.

From its headquarters in city of Salvador in Brazil, Odebrecht set up a worldwide network of offices that influenced political and economic events in Latin America, Asia, Africa and the United States. These offices were involved in the execution and financing of parliamentary and political lobbying. The *Operacoes Spices* department was one of the subsidiary companies of the Odebrecht conglomerate. It covered construction, the manufacture of deep-water drilling rigs, refineries, petrol stations, petrochemical and the production of oil and agribusiness. I suspect that Odebrecht was also lobbying banks and paying them bribes, but no judge has had the courage to investigate corruption in Brazil's financial sector thus far.

Brazil's endemic corruption

It is sadly a fact that corruption is endemic in Brazil. There are words in the language that are euphemisms for corruption. For example, to pay a bribe is described as giving a *jeito*, and can also be used in its diminutive form, or paying a *jeitinho* (small bribe). There is an expression in Spanish which roughly translates as, when a law is enacted, ways to get around it and not follow it are embedded in the process itself (*hecha la ley, hecha la trampa*).

Unfortunately, in Brazil laws are purposely made difficult in order for politicians and civil servants to collect favors from those who cannot or do not want to comply with them, and therefore seek an exemption. Corruption in Brazil existed long before the country achieved formal independence from Portugal in August of 1825 with the Treaty of Rio de Janeiro signed between the Kingdom of Portugal and the Empire of Brazil. The Portuguese crown, for example, routinely sold off many baronies and other nobility titles. For many decades after its independence, Brazil's population growth outpaced the expansion of its GDP. The mainstays of the economy for decades were sugar and coffee production. As a result of the Great Depression in the 1930s, demand for Brazil's agricultural exports plummeted, which in turn plunged the country into crisis. Although industrialization was undertaken and gradually attained after World War II, liberal free-trade economic policies were quickly discarded and replaced by harmful and wide-ranging import-substitution drives which sought to make Brazil self-sufficient but starved its economy of necessary foreign investment and know-how. After 1952, successive governments ramped up control of the economy by nationalizing companies, setting prices, exchange rates, subsidizing basic goods and putting up trade barriers to hamper imports. We obviously cannot chronicle in detail Brazil's economic history after World War II. But it can be summarized as a litany of plans to promote industrialization, the expansion of domestic producers and growth by import substitution through requirements for import licenses (at first for consumer goods, then for industrial products and equipment), an artificial and fixed exchange-rate, subsidies and protectionism. Although industrialization was attained, it was at the cost of developing a domestic sector which was protected from foreign competitors. This economic nationalism and protectionism actually weakened many companies that produced consumer goods and others which lacked the necessary inputs.

As a result of political upheaval and crises in the balance of payments, the military staged a coup in 1964. The military leadership pushed through a liberalization of the economy, and after the oil shocks of the 1970s Brazil posted extremely high growth rates. When the first post-military president was sworn in in 1990, Brazil had managed to industrialize and raise its income levels, but at the cost of an uncompetitive economy.

Moreover, nationalized companies became accustomed to obtaining financing from state and federal banks. The public sector could decide which tax exemptions to grant. Complicated and ambiguous laws, decrees, provisional measures, norms and rules were enacted and approved. This tangled and complex legal and regulatory framework has engendered multiple opportunities for corruption and rent-seeking. Brazil is a democracy since 1990 and obviously has NGOs and other agents of civil society. But trends tend to be passed on from the top to the bottom. It is therefore very hard to instill morality in institutions and the population. The average person may rail against corruption, but resorts to it in his or her daily transactions by paying *jeitinhos* (small bribes), evading taxes and seeking exemptions.

Brazil's corruption and inability to achieve its full economic potential is much-debated topic. Stefan Zweig was an extremely popular novelist and playwright from Austria who fled Nazi Germany in 1934 and fist moved to the UK and then to the United States. In 1940 he and his wife settled in a German-speaking colony near Rio de Janeiro. In his last book -- *Unsere Welt von Gestern* -- Zweig described Brazil as the country of the future[63]. Skeptical Brazilians complete Zweig's formulation by sarcastically asserting that Brazil *will always* be the country of the future. In the 57 years that I have lived and worked in Brazil, I have learned the hard way that skeptics are unfortunately right. Brazilians joke that when God distributed the riches of the world, there was always a good deal left over for Brazil. The other continents were overcrowded and lacked Brazil's natural resources, but God reassured them by telling them: "Wait until you see what people I am going to place there (meaning in Brazil)!"

<u>Brazil's economic evolution</u>

In 1961, Brazil had a population of 55 million inhabitants, life expectancy was 50 years and its fertility rate was 6.8. Currently, Brazil boasts a population of 210 million, its life expectancy has

---

[63] Stefan Zweig and his wife committed suicide in 1942, unable to witness the apparent descent of Europe into Hitler's hands. *Unsere Welt von Gestern* was published posthumously.

risen to 72 and its fertility rate stands at 1.8. Brazil is the world's eighth-biggest economy with a nominal GDP of 2 trillion dollars. Its per capita income measured in purchasing-power parity terms stands at $14,810 (World Bank, 2016), slightly below that of China ($15,500) and Mexico ($17,740). In 1961, the elites in Brazil still debated whether illiterates should be given the right to vote. Today, the number of formal illiterates in Brazil is fortunately very small and was sharply reduced during the period of military rule (1964-1990).

In the 57 years that I have lived and worked in Brazil, the number of formal illiterates has decreased dramatically, the number of rich increased substantially, the number of the poor has risen (but at a smaller rate), and GDP has certainly expanded. The structure of the Brazilian economy has also evolved during the past decades. The industrialization of the country was a long and difficult process, but it was ultimately achieved. There was also a transformation of colonial and family agriculture into agribusiness. The transition into a services-based economy began and gathered momentum until it was interrupted by the PT (Workers' Party)-led governments from 2003 until 2016.

Former president Luiz Inácio Lula da Silva (popularly known as "Lula") is a social and political phenomenon. I am convinced that he will not be in jail for long. He is running first in the polls to be Brazil's next president despite his conviction[64]. Marcel Odebrecht, the former CEO of Odebrecht, was convicted in March of 2016 of several counts of corruption. The former head of Latin America's largest construction conglomerate admitted paying $30 million in bribes to politicians in several countries in the region. He was sentenced to nineteen years in jail. Odebrecht did spend almost two years behind bars. As part of a plea deal that involves his payment of a $2 billion fine, his admission of guilt and providing evidence to authorities, his sentence was cut to ten years and he is allowed to serve his sentence under house arrest at his luxurious mansion since December of 2017.

Lula and his leftist intellectuals are communication geniuses. They portray the former union leader and president as a prisoner unfairly convicted of a very common crime – corruption and money laundering. There is not a day when he does not appear on the front page of the newspapers, either because his relatives or senators pay him a visit or because his football team won a game. Lula has managed to create and cultivate an international image. He is portrayed in the media as someone liked by former president Barack Obama, idolized by the largest-circulation Spanish-language newspaper El País, and hailed by left-wing media as a model of trade unionism and the democratic left, a friend of the people and a father of the poor. Yet the facts are stubborn. Brazil registered growth between 2002 and 2010 (mostly overlapping with Lula's two terms as president, 2003-2011), but was in recession or barely grew from 2011 until 2016, a period that covers the last two years of Lula's second term and all of Dilma Rousseff's first and second terms, which was ended by a vote of impeachment by Congress and her ouster in August of 2016.

There are many more rich people in 2016 than in 2002 in Brazil. There are more poor people in 2016 than in 2002. In addition, there are 14 million registered unemployed. The much-acclaimed *Bolsa familia* program implemented under the PT governments has not reduced poverty, but rather fed its beneficiaries, who have become dependent on such government hand-outs. Did the gap between rich and poor narrow after thirteen years of PT-led governments under Lula and

---

[64] Lula was sentenced to nine years and six months in prison by judge Sergio Moro but remained free pending an appeal of the sentence. In January 2018 a regional federal court unanimously upheld Moro's ruling against Lula. In April 2018, the Supreme Federal Court rejected Lula's *habeas corpus* plea and a warrant for his arrest was issued. The former president turned himself in and began serving his sentence. Lula announced he will run for the 2018 presidential elections, but he is expected to be disqualified under Brazil's law.

Dilma Rousseff? Unfortunately, it has increased. The rich have become much richer. This has happened thanks to financing from the pension funds of state-owned companies, such as the postal office, Petrobras, other energy companies, or the port workers' union. These unions are dominated by party politics and politicians exert a lot of influence. Unfortunately, the poor have not been able to lift themselves out of their condition because the PT-financed programs allow them to settle into it.

After Dilma Rousseff was impeached in August of 2016, her vice-president Michel Temer was sworn in as president. Many international observers and analysts describe Temer as a center-right politician. They overlook the fact that Lula himself hand-picked Temer to be Dilma's vice-presidential running mate. Except for semi-literate Brazilians or cynical insiders, nobody in Brazil is under any illusions about the current political landscape. Most political parties in Brazil have no clear ideology nor vision. This applies to most of the PT as well. Brazilian political parties are groups that take over the public sector's institutions at the federal, state and local level and use and influence them to look after their own interests. The only ideological parties in Brazil today are the PSOL, made up of former PT members who defected, and REDE, whose leader Marina Silva is also a former member of the PT who has ran for presidency on a pro-environment platform in 2014 and won 21% of the vote. Brazil will hold presidential and parliamentary elections at the federal and state levels in October of 2018.

The latest poll conducted by MDA in March of 2018 shows that Lula would easily win if he were allowed to run for the presidency. Brazil's law makes it extremely difficult for someone with a criminal conviction which has been upheld to run for elected office. But Lula and his supporters will litigate this matter before the courts in the coming months. If the courts definitively do bar Lula, polls indicate that populist right-wing federal congressman Jair Bolsonaro (from the Social Liberal Party, PSL) would place first and make it into the second round, where he would confront former senator and Environment Minister Marina Silva. The various center-right parties will also field their own candidates, one of which could squeak into the second round instead of Silva. With six months to go until the elections, most polls show Bolsonaro in first place. He has often incited hatred and is dubbed the "Trump of the Tropics". In the second round he is likely to face Silva or another right-wing populist. A total of twelve candidates are vying for the presidency. Other well-known candidates are the former speaker of the Chamber of Deputies, Rodrigo Maia, of the free-market DEM party and Geraldo Alckmin, who stepped down as governor of Sao Paulo to run on the Party of Brazilian Social Democracy (PSDB) ticket.

Setting aside political parties, there are many islands of excellence in the ocean of Brazilian competitiveness: the Social Service of Industry SESI, Social service of the trade SESC, National Service for Industrial Training SENAI and the National Service of Commercial Apprenticeship SENAC. The four organizations are managed by employers' organizations and financed by a compulsory contribution, which is collected together with the social contributions of the enterprises. They work very well, and in the past fifty years there have been very few reports of mismanagement at these organizations. Those who graduate from their schools and professional courses are hired and hold well-paid jobs. Lula, the former president, was trained as a mechanical turner at a SENAI school. The problem is that more than 50% of Brazilians have no formal employment. And the agricultural sector does not participate either in the financing or in the formation of new cadres.

<u>Bloated executive branch</u>

There are more causes that highlight the weakness of the three branches of government. There are more than thirty parties with parliamentary representation at the federal level. The attempt to establish a *numerus clausus* and restrict the number of parties in Parliament failed in the Supreme Court. More than 40% of the members of the federal legislature (the Chamber of

Deputies and the Senate) have been investigated, charged or convicted of corruption. In the executive branch, there are currently twenty-two ministries and five ministry-level high offices. Hundreds of high-level civil servants (ministers, deputy ministers, etc.) spend a lot of their time on matters that concern the political parties that support whichever coalition government may be in power. The total number of federal civil servants stands at 2.1 million. The United States, whose population exceeds that of Brazil by 100 million people, has a total of 2.8 million federal employees. Brazil's twenty-six states have their own swollen bureaucracies.

One of Brazil's biggest burdens is its extremely generous and unsustainable pension system. Civil servants earn a pension equivalent to 100% of their last salary after 35 years of service, regardless of their age. There are tens of thousands of retired civil servants who are fifty years old and also receive a pension which is equal to that of their full salary. Civil servants contribute 11% of their salary towards their pensions. Each year the Brazilian government earmarks a very substantial amount of money to make up the shortfall between what private-sector employees and employers pay into the pension and the high pensions that are paid out. The government also subsidizes very high pensions for one million retired civil servants. These one million retired civil servants are only 10% of the total number of retirees in Brazil. Yet the receive extremely generous pensions beginning at a young age. Most federal deputies are reluctant to pass legislation that would overhaul the pensions system, although under president Temer there has been stronger enforcement of the requirements to receive pensions, such as the age and the number of years worked. Under Temer some ridiculous pension benefits have been eliminated. For instance, dockworkers who unloaded certain cargo from ships at the port of Salvador could claim two pensions for the same period worked.

The exact number of judges at different levels and in all states is not precisely known. But the estimate is that the judiciary consumes 2% of GDP. Another example of waste and corruption is the housing subsidies paid to judges. As federal judges can be appointed to judgeships away from their normal place of residence, they are awarded a housing allowance. This grant was extended to judges at all levels regardless of whether they already own a home and whether they serve in their city of residence or not. A case in point is a federal judge and his wife -- who is also a judge -- who live in their apartment in Rio de Janeiro, where they are judges, but each of whom receives a housing allowance nonetheless. This is all perfectly legal as judges have ruled on the matter. Many analysts believe that judges have too much power in Brazil. I do not share that view. Politicians and businessmen want the judicial system to decide on matters beyond its purview. The judicial system also lacks the means to ensure that its rulings are enforced.

Brazil's Federal Supreme Court is made up of 11 judges. Of the current judges on the Supreme Court, seven were appointed by Lula or Dilma Rousseff, one was picked by former president José Sarney (1985-90), one by former president Fernando Collor de Mello (1990-92), one by Fernando Henrique Cardoso (1995-2003) and the remaining one by the current president, Michel Temer.

The method for appointing a Supreme Court justice is the following: the president proposes a candidate, the Senate vets the person and the president makes the final appointment. Supreme Court justices can serve for life, but many retire at a relatively young age to continue with their private practice and lobbying. One of Lula's current personal attorneys served in his cabinet as a minister, was also a Supreme Court judge and presided the Supreme Court. Another judge appointed by Lula to the Supreme Court (José Antonio Dias Toffoli) was an attorney for his Worker's Party (PT). Although he had never served as a judge or prosecutor, Lula named him to serve on the Supreme Court. Another judge's main qualification was to be a friend of Lula's wife. In more than fifty years in Brazil, I have only witnessed two thorough and tough hearings conducted by the Senate for potential Supreme Court judges: one who played a key role in Rousseff's campaign to prevent impeachment; another who was chosen by Temer and was subjected to tough questioning in the Senate. These two well-qualified Supreme Court judges are

Luiz Edson Fachin and Alexandre de Moraes. Fachin had a strong background as both a judge and an academic and is guided by judicial criteria when he makes a ruling. Moraes had had a stellar career as a prosecutor and minister of Justice before being appointed to the Supreme Court at the behest of president Temer.

The Brazilian constitution states that the state is responsible for the health of its citizens. A judge may therefore rule that a sick person is entitled to a remedy worth $1000. If the public hospital that is ordered to provide the free remedy does not have enough funds to pay the salaries of the nurses and doctors it employs, it may appeal the verdict. In fact, such a ruling may be appealed all of the way to the Supreme Federal Court. The patient eventually gets paid, unless he or she has passed way in the meantime. There are hundreds of thousands of such cases being litigated in the courts, and tens of thousands make their way all to Federal Supreme Court, Brazil's highest judicial body. Brazil's Supreme Court was conceived to settle disputes and rule on laws that might not be constitutional. But in practice it has become a court of last instance for criminal and commercial cases, and it lacks the personnel to deal with such a big caseload.

In the wake of the wide-ranging and long-running *Lava Jato* and Petrobras criminal investigations, some analysts argue that Brazil's judiciary has too much power. The real problem is that Brazil's two other branches of government -- the executive and the legislative -- are unable or unwilling to reconcile opposing interests in a democratic and efficient manner nor resolve disputes and they therefore wind up burdening the judicial system with the responsibility to settle them.

The ministers in charge of the economic portfolios at the federal level are efficient and competent. They were appointed by president Temer when he was sworn in to replace Dilma Rousseff in 2016 after her impeachment. The Minister of Finance, Henrique Meirelles, had an extensive professional background in private banking before he held high-level positions in the Brazilian government. Meirelles served as President and COO of BankBoston worldwide. In 1999, when BankBoston merged with Fleet Financial Group, Meirelles was appointed president of FleetBoston Financial's Global Banking.

During Lula's two terms (2003-2011), Meirelles was the president of Brazil's Central Bank (*Banco Central do Brazil*) and independent analysts give him high marks, including for his handling of the global financial crisis. Lula recognized that his left-wing background might alienate investors, so he tapped an establishment and highly-regarded banker like Meirelles to head Brazil's Central Bank and reassure markets. Dilma did not want him in her government. Meirelles stepped down from his position as Finance Minister in April of 2018 to launch his bid for the presidency of Brazil. In the first polls, his level of support is very low. The current president of Brazil's Central Bank, Ilan Goldfajn, is an economist with a PhD from MIT who was appointed to the position by Meirelles. The aforementioned officials have managed to bring down inflation from 15% (during Dilma's tenure) to the current 3%, with interest rates at 6.5%.

Brazil suffered the worst recession in its history in 2004-2016. Several sectors of the economy are showing signs of recovery, including industry, agribusiness and trade. But the service sector remains very weak. The uncertainty over the future president and the government's policies are holding back the recovery. Unemployment stands at 12% and is falling very slowly. Informal employment in the underground economy continues to rise and is still high, as is the case in many Latin American economies.

The media of course acts as a check on the power of the executive, legislative and judicial branches of government. The media landscape in Brazil is reasonably diversified. Many radio stations and television channels are awarded licenses by the state, and many have evangelical-conservative views. The increase in social media in Brazil has been remarkable. Brazil is one of the most computerized countries. The country has more than 200 million cellular telephony lines, more than one per inhabitant. Demagogues can of course spread their message with much more efficiency through social media applications like WhatsApp, Twitter, and Facebook.

There is no way to forecast what will happen in Brazil. In October of 2018 the country will hold presidential elections, and voters will also go to the polls to choose the members of the federal parliament, as well as the governors and deputies in the state assemblies. A lot is at stake. Optimists believe that Brazilian society and its institutions will withstand the surge of populism from both the extreme right and left, and possibly even a populist/nativist becoming the next president. Whoever is elected, there is no question that Brazil needs to liberalize its economy, streamline its pension system, crack down on corruption and drastically cut the public sector's involvement in the economy. It will require a true statesman/woman to carry out such profound reforms against entrenched special interest groups.

Astrid Lindström Karlsson

Adjunct professor, Central University of Catalonia

Lindström earned a Master's degree in Social Sciences with a specialization in Social Policy and Social Work from the University of Stockholm in 1972. From 1969 until 1974 she was a social worker in Sweden at St Görans sjukhus, the biggest hospital for acute-ill patients in Stockholm, and at Blackebergs sjukhus, a hospital for chronic patients in Blackeberg (Stockholm). She was a consultant to Barcelona's Institute of Social Work and Social Services (INTRESS) in drafting studies about home care policies, housing policies and spending on social services (1983-1985). Lindström was a co-founder and administrator of the Barcelona-based Consultancy for Human Resources Advisory and Selection LLC from 1985 until 1992. She was also a co-founder and consultant to the Karinter company, which imports and distributes technical assistance and resources for retirement homes between 1992 and 1993. Since 1993 she is a free-lance consultant on social policy and social services, specifically in designing and planning policies that craft and organize social services and social resources and tools. She continues to program and organize work trips for politicians, businesspeople and professionals to Nordic countries in order to examine policies for retired and handicapped persons, the design and organization of services and resources for day-care centers, assisted-care facilities for the elderly and sick, housing with services and co-housing. Lindström is also currently an adjunct professor at Catalonia's Central University.

Anybody who has lived in Sweden for forty years is entitled to a minimum income when they reach a certain age, regardless of whether they have worked or not. There may be individuals who either have never worked or who have not worked enough years to be entitled to a work-based pension. These individuals receive a minimum income when they reach a certain age. This income can also be supplemented and tops up the traditional work-based pension that retirees draw.

Sweden was one of the first countries to insert incentives into the retirement system. Those that work beyond the official retirement age are entitled to a higher pension, while those who retire early are penalized and draw a smaller amount.

In the early 1990s Sweden underwent a profound economic and financial crisis. Many of its banks had to be bailed out. The crisis prompted Swedish governments and society to examine Sweden's vaunted welfare and health care systems. In the depth of the crisis, it appeared that Sweden's famous welfare state might have to be severely downsized.

Many reforms were adopted to transform and modernize Sweden's welfare state and its social policies. One of them was to encourage and provide incentives for individuals to allocate part of their savings and invest them in pension or mutual funds. Upon retirement, an individual's pension would partly be paid by the state. But another part would be the result of the management by private institutions of the funds invested in the pension or mutual funds. This reform was implemented in the context of the appearance and application of New Public Management models.

At the same time, recognizing the ageing of its population, Sweden raised its retirement age to 67. This happened despite the fact that Sweden has mostly been ruled by the Social Democratic Party. And Sweden created a system whereby the calculation of what each individual will receive in terms of the non-work income for old people is variable. The reform sought to consider the number of people who pay into the system every year and those who draw the universal non-work-based minimum income. Therefore, the reform determined that this amount would vary.

Its quantity is determined firstly by how many people are paying into the system and how many are receiving the universal income for elderly people. The other factor that is taken into account when setting the level of the payment is how the economy is performing. If the economy is growing at a strong rate, the payments can go up, and conversely. This reform thus made Sweden's pension system more sustainable.

The elements of this reform have been adopted in other countries, such as Spain, which also reformed its pension system -- and raised the retirement age -- in order to make it more sustainable. Most countries' pension systems are based on the premise that the pensions of people who have retired are paid by taxing a part of employees' salaries. When Sweden reformed its pension system in the early 1990s it created a mechanism whereby the amount drawn from employees is invested, and therefore yields returns which ensure the sustainability of the payments of pensions. Sweden was among the first countries to add a market-based element to its pensions.

Sweden's crisis in the early 1990s was a harbinger of the banking crises that many countries and the international economy experienced beginning in 2008. Sweden had already suffered and emerged from its own financial crisis in the early 1990s and had cleaned up its banking system and restored it. In the context of its banking crisis in the early 1990s, Sweden also undertook the reforms to its welfare state that I am describing, thus making it sustainable and more innovative and advanced. This explains Sweden's strong economic performance since 2000 and the fact that it was barely affected by the global financial crisis and the Great Recession. In fact, when international institutions needed to bail out banks and weigh the pros and cons of their intervention, they looked to how Sweden had handled its financial crisis in the early 1990s.

<u>On inequality between cities and small towns and the countryside</u>

Sweden has addressed the challenge of the relative lack of economic opportunities in the countryside and smaller towns. Each of its 32 regions draws up a plan to ensure that areas with lack of economic development can harness their resources. The strengths of these underperforming areas are examined: where are their competitive advantages in terms of products they manufacture and their human capital. These plans have been rather successful in fostering the growth of regions which were not doing well.

The system adopted in Sweden seeks to encourage these regions to draw on their strengths. It stays away from furnishing subsidies, a method that is usually ineffective as it creates dependency. The Swedish system for fostering innovation and growth in underperforming regions is based on a Triple Helix, meaning cooperation between the business sector, universities and the public sector. The public sector plays a key role as a catalyst of this collaboration. In 2001, the Swedish government established the Swedish Agency for Innovation Systems (Vinnova)[65], which reports to and is a part of the Ministry of Industry, Employment and Communications. Vinnova's objective is to promote sustainable economic growth by financing needs-driven R&D and by developing innovation systems. Its focus is to strengthen research cooperation between academia, companies and politics/public sector in the Swedish innovation system.

Sweden has certainly achieved impressive results in terms of raising civilian R&D. In a ranking of leading economies performed by the OECD, Sweden in 2003 was only surpassed by Israel in terms of the combined expenditure on R&D as a percentage of GDP contributed by the private sector, universities and the public sector. Sweden's combined investment in R&D in 2003 was 4% of GDP, and three-fourths of the total was furnished by the private sector. In this ranking,

---

[65] For more information, see https://www.rieti.go.jp/en/events/bbl/06090501.pdf

Sweden surpassed the UK, Germany, Norway, Denmark, France, Canada, Japan, the Netherlands and other highly advanced developed countries.

Sweden, like many countries, has had a lack of R&D investment by small and medium-sized companies. Moreover, much of the R&D investment conducted by the public sector is in the military. In other words, a large share of R&D in Sweden is undertaken either by large multinationals or by the government in the military domain. The purpose of setting up Vinnova was precisely to boost R&D in the civilian sector and to increase the number of companies involved in R&D. Sweden has made a lot of progress in raising R&D and cooperation between businesses, universities and the public sector. Sweden's model has been adopted by other countries and the European Union.

<u>On the Impact of Technology and R&D</u>

The Swedish Ministry of Social Welfare has conducted two comprehensive studies regarding the impact of technology, robots and Artificial Intelligence. We are obviously transitioning towards a services-intensive economy. I conducted a study of my own on assisted care provided to elderly individuals. Such services are not labor-intensive and are not tangible. This means that a lot of factors are not taken into account when it comes to drawing up management models for them. The management system used for these services is often the same as that employed for companies that produce or manufacture goods. But industrial goods are tangible, whereas services are not. Therefore, mistakes are made when the systems for managing the production of tangible goods are applied to services – which are intangible.

The increased use of machines, robots, artificial intelligence and other technology will put a lot of people out of work. Millions of jobs will be destroyed. But the kinds of services I am describing -- health care, care for the elderly -- is one sector that will not be impacted my mechanization. It will be one of the areas where people will continue to find employment.

As we further shift into a services-driven economy, one-on-one on-demand services are becoming more important. The idea of an on-demand economy should be emphasized. An individual has a need for a certain service to be provided. He or she uses technology to access the provider of that service. Let us say an individual needs the services of an attorney. It is not necessary to sign a retainer with a law office. There are attorneys who will provide their expertise over the Internet on a one-to-one on-demand basis. Likewise, if an individual needs to have something repaired, he or she may already know a list of qualified technicians who can be contacted one-to-one and on-demand to do the job. Service providers will therefore have to become very specialized in order to survive and thrive in a very competitive environment. But if they do, they can adapt to and even be successful in the Digital Economy. Yes, the production of tangible goods will mostly be carried out by robots or machines in a few years. But the provision of one-on-one on-demand services will enable many professionals, technicians and others to make a good living.

I am not pessimistic about society's ability to adapt to the challenges posed by the acceleration of technology. Decades ago the Club of Rome forecast that the world would run out of oil. This prompted a wave of innovation that led to the development of new technologies. Some of these technologies are currently generating electricity in a renewable way -- whether using the wind, sun, biomass or tides. In the same manner, I think that society will learn how to cope with increased mechanization. The focus must be on stepping up innovation. And such innovation must be not just incremental but radical. We have to accept that in the next few years most tangible goods will be produced by robots. We therefore need to learn how to provide intangibles – services of many kinds. We also have to envision services that do not yet exist but which will be necessary in the future. This is the only way forward. To try and stop technological progress and somehow preserve the status quo is counterproductive and bound to fail. It makes much more sense to adapt and get ahead of the curve in terms of society's future needs than to engage in doomsday scenarios about the wholesale destruction of jobs by technology.

<u>On Sweden's policies and politics</u>

Sweden has mostly been run and governed by the Social Democratic Party since the beginning of the XXth century, and especially since the 1930s. There have been some exceptions, meaning governments headed by other parties[66]. There were three governments headed by the Freeminded People's Party and one by the General Electoral League between 1926 and 1932. Moreover, the Centre Party's Thorbjörn Fälldin was in office between 1976 and 1978 and was prime minister again under two consecutive governments between 1979 and 1982. Otherwise, in the XXth century Sweden has been governed almost exclusively by the Social Democrats. After Fälldin left office, the Social Democrats ran Sweden under prime minister Olof Palme (1982-1986) and Ingvar Carlsson (1986-1990). After a brief spell under the Moderate Party of Prime Minister Carl Bildt (1991-94), the Social Democrats were in office again for twelve years (1994-2006) in governments headed by Ingvar Carlsson (1994-96) and Göran Persson (1996-2006).

The center-right's longest period in office since the beginning of the XXth century took place between 2006 and 2014. The center-right's Moderate Party won two consecutive elections, and Fredrik Reinfeldt became the first center-right prime minister to serve two full four-year terms in office. The Social Democrats returned to power in 2014, and their latest government has been headed by Prime Minister Stefan Löfven, a former welder and head of a trade union. Unlike previous Social Democratic governments, the current one is a minority one. The Social Democrats obtained 31% of the vote in the 2014 elections. Even with the support of their ally, the Green Party, they do not have an absolute majority in the Riksdag (the lower house of Sweden's Parliament). The past four years, therefore, have featured several crises, especially in December of 2015, when Löfven was forced to negotiate with the moderate center-right parties in order to get his minority government's budget approved by Parliament.

General elections will be held in Sweden in September of 2018[67]. Therefore, there is quite a bit of coverage and analysis of how the country has evolved in the past years. During the past four years Sweden has had a minority Social Democratic-Green Party government. Previously, the center-right was in power for eight years (the two Fredrik Reinfeldt cabinets) and for three years in the early 1990s under the Moderate Party's Carl Bildt).

The aforementioned center-right governments have adopted good policies and done some good work. But they are also responsible for some of Sweden's current problems. In my view, Sweden's two most pressing problems are the shortage of housing and the way that part of the education system has been privatized. Some of the companies that manage Swedish educational institutions are ranked among the richest in the world by Forbes. Swedes have been naïve or were convinced about the virtues of the free market playing a role in education. They do not

---

[66] The Freeminded People's Party and the General Electoral League were in office from 1926 until 1932. Two of their goverments were headed by Carl Gustaf Ekman. But since 1932, governments not headed by the Social Democrats have been very short-lived and lasted between a few months and a couple of years, with the exception of those under Thorbjörn Fälldin (1976-1978, 1979-1982) and Carl Bildt (1991-94).

[67] In the elections to the Swedish parliament held on September 9, the Social Democratic Party's share of the vote dropped to 28.3% of the total, its worst performance since 1911. But together with the Swedish Green Party and Left Party, they obtained a total of 144 members of Parliament. This amount was one seat more than the Alliance coalition but short of an absolute majority. It is likely that the Social Democrats will again be the senior coalition party and govern with the support of the Swedish Green Party and the Left Party.

realize that these companies are primarily out to make a profit. Capitalism entails that smaller companies are taken over or run out of business by bigger ones.

Sweden's center-right governments allowed private companies to manage its educational system. People were attracted by the possibility of choosing which school to send their children to. Obviously, school choice can be an attractive proposition for the population. But in practice this has allowed private companies to manage Sweden's educational system from the kindergarten (which is compulsory in Sweden from age one) level all the way through elementary and high school. There are only a few private universities in Sweden. But allowing private companies to manage schools all the way from kindergarten to high school has de facto privatized Sweden's education sector.

School choice as a theoretical concept is popular. But in practice it has not worked well in Sweden. The middle and upper class are able to send their children to their schools of choice. The companies that manage the kindergartens, elementary schools and high schools exclude students from lower-class families. There have been many scandals involving cheating in exams and in issuing grades.

Another serious shortcoming in Sweden is the availability of affordable housing. Sweden urbanized relatively late in its history compared to other developed countries. Sweden experienced two baby booms in the XXth century: one in the 1940s and one in the 1960s. Another baby boom at the beginning of the XXIst century generated an even greater demand for housing. A plan to build one million housing units with public funds was drawn up and executed to deal with the lack of housing. Under the center-right governments of Fredrik Reinfeldt, authorities allowed renters who lived in these dwelling to purchase them with the support of the neighborhood association where they are located. Allowing renters to buy these publicly-funded housing units was popular. But the new owners soon were caught up by a real-estate euphoria and sold their new homes at much higher prices. This speculation has engendered a real-estate bubble that makes it impossible for young people to be able to afford housing.

On the appeal of populists

As is happening in other countries, working-class people in Sweden and those who have trouble finding and holding on to jobs or securing affordable housing become embittered. These people, who have low incomes and difficulty in adapting to the labor market, are attracted to the message from populists. Populists blame all of these people's troubles on immigrants. In Sweden, the right-wing populist Sweden Democrats Party has had electoral success by convincing lower-class native Swedes that immigrants are the source of their problems. People can be attracted by these simplistic messages, despite the fact that reality is far more complex.

The Sweden Democrats Party was founded in 1988. It has its roots in Swedish fascism and until the early 1990s espoused white supremacist policies and views. During the 1990s the party, led by Jimmie Akesson, began to distance itself from its most radical nationalist messages. It managed to surpass the 4% threshold necessary for parliamentary representation for the first time in the 2010 general election, when it garnered 5.7% of the total vote and obtained 20 seats in the Riksdag. The Sweden Democrats' share of the vote more than doubled in the 2014 general election, when it won 12.9% of the vote and obtained 49 seats in the 349-seat Riksdag. It thus became the third largest party in Sweden's Riksdag. The Sweden Democrats, however, are shunned by all of the other parties represented in the Swedish Parliament, who refuse to cooperate with them. They therefore have not been able to directly influence Sweden's policies, even when the center-right was in power. In the elections held on September 9, 2018, the Sweden Democrats increased their share of the vote to 17.5%, again coming in third place after the Social Democratic Party (28.3%) and the Moderate Party (19.8%).

In Sweden all mainstream parties refuse to cooperate with the Sweden Democrats. This is in stark contrast to what has and is happening in Austria, Denmark and recently Italy, where far-right parties have either been junior coalition parties to traditional center-right parties (Austria's Freedom Party), supported them in Parliament (Denmark) or are the biggest party in Parliament (Italy's League).

Sweden's center-left and center-right governments have allowed immigrants from outside Europe to settle in Sweden because of the country's ageing population. Sweden needs qualified immigrants because of its demographic problems. The country's population is ageing. Moreover, for center-right parties immigrants offer a source of cheap labor that undercuts the demands of Swedish trade unions. It must be noted that Sweden's fertility rate is among the highest in Europe. In 2016, Sweden was second only to France with a fertility rate of 1.85. However, Eurostat (the EU's statistical agency) emphasizes that the "2.1 replenishment level is the 'average number of live births per woman required to keep the population size constant in the absence of migration'."

In 2010, Sweden's population was projected to reach the 10 million mark in 2021. But Sweden actually reached this milestone in January of 2017. This feat can be attributed to immigration and a higher fertility rate. Between 2010 and 2015 the population grew by about 4% per year, behind only Luxembourg in the EU, and considerably above the EU's average of 1%.

"The main reason the population is increasing faster than what was thought a few years ago is because immigration was at an historic high and since then it has increased even more. Population prognoses normally expect that the immigration surplus will go down to the historic average level. That has however not happened yet," according to Tomas Johansson, population analyst at Statistics Sweden.[68]

According to Johannson, the birth surplus, or the number of newborns minus the number of deaths, has been at around 20,000-25,000 for the past couple of years. The immigration surplus has ranged from 45,000 to 78,000, mainly because of increased immigration while emigration has remained relatively stable[69].

---

[68] "Sweden's Population Reaches Historic Ten Million Milestone", The Local, 21st January 2017. https://www.thelocal.se/20170120/swedens-population-reaches-historic-ten-million-milestone
[69] Ibidem

Alberic Metivier

Senior Manager, Crisalix S.A.

Metivier, who was born in Le Mans (France), holds a Master's in Business Administration from OBS Business School. He has worked in several IT Companies such as Orange Business Group, Verizon and Interoute. At these companies, he executed account management, business development and consultancy both with small and medium businesses and large corporations. He also implemented business and technical project development and consulting, building relationship and trust with interlocutors and establishing strategic alliances with a variety of partners within innovating and fast changing environments. He is currently in strategic and executive leadership of a worldwide start-up company in the field of 3D imaging, Virtual Reality and Augmented Reality fields.

The Threat of a Digital Divide

Internet, telecommunications as well as technology in general have become a basic necessity, almost as necessary as electricity. They have become so necessary that we refer to the third industrial revolution. Do all human beings have the same access to the Internet and new technologies? What is the digital divide?

The digital divide is the inequality between people, communities or countries that use new information and communication technologies (ICT) and those who do not have access to them or who do not know how to use them. The divide involves and includes the quality of the technological infrastructure, the devices and connections, the ignorance regarding the use of the tools, but above all, the capability and knowledge to turn data and information into specific, useful and productive assets.

What are the new technologies:

There are communication network infrastructures -- such as 4G, and the race to build 5G -- that enable the transmission of data and information at extremely high speeds. These infrastructures require access points located across the network, and this obviously has a cost. These infrastructures and networks allow individuals to obtain valuable information and knowledge which can be transformed into new products, services or simply contribute to the individual's knowledge and professional capabilities and skills.

The digital divide is characterized by a lack of access to these access points, either because in some countries or places they do not exist, because individuals lack the economic means to access them, or because individuals do not have the knowledge needed to make effective and productive use of technology.

According to the World Bank, for every 10% increase in Internet connections in a country, there is a corresponding rise of 1.3% in GDP. On the flip side, according to World Bank data, more than half of the world's population -- some 4 billion people -- do not have a means of connecting to the Internet. Most of these four billion people live in developing or emerging countries. Delivering Internet access to them by traditional methods is complicated and expensive because they need the proper telecommunications systems.

However, several big technology companies are competing to try to deliver broadband access to the more remote areas of the world through other means because they could potentially reach hundreds of millions of new consumers. Are these big technology companies being altruistic? No, they are researching ways to provide internet, mobile telephony and other technology services to places and people that have trouble accessing them while still turning a profit.

<u>Some practical solutions that can narrow the Digital Divide</u>

Facebook and Google are researching and working with drones that can serve as points of access to the Internet and to routers. Microsoft, meanwhile, is looking into how it can employ the frequencies of unused television channels to provide access to the Internet in the more remote parts of the US. Some big tech companies are designing projects to increase connectivity across the world, like helium balloons that work as solar panels. Project Wing or SkyBender from Google features drones or solar planes guided by solar energy that beam 5G Internet. Facebook´s Aquila project is similar and involves wi-fi drones. It turns out that there is not a single way to connect the world. What we know is that the determination to achieve this goal is real. At Barcelona's Word Mobile Congress in February 2018, Facebook announced that it is committing to deliver Internet to 50% of the world's population by end of this year.

OneWeb, for its part, is studying how it can develop and deploy a series of satellites located at low-level orbits which would enable access to ICTs from remote terrestrial, maritime and areal parts of the planet. OneWeb appears to be teaming up with Airbus and has begun to build the first satellites.

Many people in the technology sector utter platitudes such as "access to ICT should be a universal right". But these private technology companies are really interested in gathering data about more people in order to market and sell their products and services to them for a profit. The aforementioned projects are all being carried out by private companies. But is there something wrong in the proposition that private companies invest and make profits while they seek to expand access to the Internet and other ICT networks? It is not, as long as they contribute to economic, social and cultural progress, and therefore foster growth. Moreover, schools with the necessary computers, scaled-up access networks, as well as well-trained teachers are necessary measures to enable new generations to obtain the knowledge to use ICTs.

<u>Market dynamics and regulated environments</u>

The Internet only makes sense if access to the global network is maintained. Is there a lack of initiatives by the public sector at the national and international levels to define the basis and establish rules that ensure competition, protect consumers by avoiding abuses and defend against fraud, hacking and cyberattacks? The answer is unfortunately "Yes". The Internet operates on a global level, but governments that regulate communications do so at a national or local level.

Spain enacted a new telecommunication law in 2014 (*Ley General de Telecomunicaciones*) which transposed European Union directives and recommendations. The Spanish law also sets out minimum services in terms of download speeds for users. Some prices have been fixed and are monitored. The Spanish Digital Agenda was created, and one of its aims has been to increase the percentage of citizens who communicate and interact electronically with government offices. Telecommunications have been inserted in Spain's budget. Objectives have been laid out and targets set aimed at reducing the digital divide through a digital inclusion and employability plan. The Spanish law also seeks to increase the number of people who use the Internet regularly, and particularly to raise use by the most disadvantaged groups in society. Moreover, the law aims to reduce the number of people who have never used the Internet from 30% to 15% and seeks to increase the penetration of mobile broadband among mobile phone users up to 75%.

However, if there is no clear defined and legitimate framework, big companies can game the market to their benefit and to the detriment of users. If the Internet has no regulation, those with more economic means will have better access and service, and Internet hackers and other digital criminals will continue to wreak havoc. The absence of rules and order tend to generate anarchic markets, which are unsustainable in the context of a capitalist economy.

Those who passionately defend free markets contend that competition and the laws of supply and demand will bring about the necessary adjustments to the Internet, and that governments only need to ensure the existence of a loose regulatory framework that addresses major issues. By way of analogy, financial markets are not subject to checks at borders, face customs barriers and are not subject to excessive international regulations. The financial crisis of 2008 was caused by several factors, not the least of which was the fact that regulators gave total freedom to financial agents that designed products that few really understood. Experts who had access to inside information could act on it and benefited without suffering any penalty nor prosecution.

We live in a dichotomy of global markets and national and local regulatory environments. Left to their own devices, markets tend to generate separate speeds, one for the rich and one for the poor. By their very nature, markets tend to favor the rich, and the role of democracies is to protect the poor. As John F. Kennedy put it in his inaugural address, if a society cannot help the many who are poor, it cannot protect the few who are rich. Markets, however, are usually more powerful than democratic institutions, and businessmen accrue more power than politicians.

Currently, there is no global rule of law. The rule of law is not enforced at an international level despite the existence of international institutions. There are, however, global markets and global information-sharing networks. The absence of long-term planning leads to tragic consequences. Some analysts believe that the destruction caused by hurricane Harvey in Houston could have been smaller if decisions had been made regarding CO2 emissions, which we know alter the climate, raise sea levels, increase the temperature of oceans' waters and therefore strengthen hurricanes.

Politicians work and make decisions within relatively short time periods. They need results to be achieved in time periods which coincide with their mandates, so they can run for reelection. There are initiatives on a global level which seek to come up with ideas and make decisions to deliver results in the long term. But is this enough? Are we heading towards more regulation at an international level? Or towards a retreat to the protection afforded by national borders, a certain de-globalization brought about by more nationalisms, which will result in even more inequalities?

The United States, with the policies and demands of its current president, are retreating towards protectionism. But this is not just happening in the United States. It is taking place in other leading economies. Markets have expanded, but in some cases, they are becoming smaller, as some companies realize that more expansion harms their competitive advantage and profits. Some companies retreat as they realize that more expansion lessens their competitive advantage and profits, not only because of external constraints, but also because of international tariffs and taxes.

On the other hand, there are international institutions, which are military, economic, political and enhance global governance, like NATO, the United Nations, the International Monetary Fund and the G20. And the European Union has managed to transfer sovereignty in many domains to supranational institutions. Even if this is hard, why can't this be projected and scaled up at the global level? As an obvious example, climate change is a global problem which requires international cooperation and agreements.

<u>Some data about where we are headed</u>

In order to provide solutions, it is necessary to understand where we are coming from and where we are headed. What are the most likely and known trends? Experts agree that the biggest transformations in the next fifty years will be demographic, cultural and technological, as industry will gradually wither.

In fifteen years the world is projected to have one billion more inhabitants, and 600 million of the one billion will be in Africa. The percentage of the world's population that lives in cities will rise. Moreover, there is a trend towards longer life expectancy. Analysts also project migrations that will grow exponentially and that the ranks of the middle class will swell, especially in fast-growing economies like China and India.

In the realm of technology, profound transformations will continue and even speed up, in sectors like biotechnology, nanotechnology and the neurosciences. Robots will not only be deployed in factories and assembly lines. Technology will also impact white-collar professions and jobs. Artificial intelligence as well as machines' predictive capability will affect and transform sectors like consulting, legal services and health care.

Many studies carried out, especially in the United States, project that at least half of the jobs that exist today will disappear within fifteen years. What students are learning now will almost be obsolete when they have the opportunity to employ their knowledge. A gigantic wave of job destruction will sweep our labor market due to technological progress and new technologies.

<u>Some new paradigms</u>

E-commerce has brought about a new form of payment: cryptocurrencies are a type of virtual currency, which are employed as tools that allay the shortcomings of traditional international financial markets. They charge lower interest rates than credit cards and the transactions are performed using only machines. They do not have a physical existence, as bills do. Cryptocurrencies such as bitcoin do not have a specific issuer, which means they do not operate within a centralized structure. They are protected by cryptography and their legitimacy is backed by their employment and distribution on a massive scale.

Another challenge is climate change and the increase in temperatures. Climate change is already happening and triggering more extreme weather events and a rise in ocean levels, for example. Some technologies could at least mitigate the effects of climate change. The transition to electric vehicles is a means to achieve a transportation sector with a lower carbon footprint.[70] Water is becoming scarcer. Some studies project that in fifty years approximately half of the world's population will be in "hydric stress". Although salt water is abundant, the technology needed to desalinate it on a large scale is not sufficiently developed.

On-line learning and training are becoming more popular as knowledge can be transmitted to remote locations in an efficient way, avoiding unnecessary transportation by those doing the teaching and the learning. Time is one of our most precious goods. Everything that allows us to save time is an asset, and technology plays a big role in this regard.

Self-driving cars are still in an experimental phase but making a lot of progress. Sensors, technology and the next generation of mobile broadband (5G) will enable the Internet of Things to operate, allowing billions of devices to be connected to the Internet. We can envision not just

---

[70] Electricity still has to be generated. And currently renewables only generate a small part, leaving fossil fuels and nuclear energy to produce the bulk of electricity.

smart homes, but "smart cities", urban areas focused on raising productivity, efficiency, sustainability and cutting consumption, pollution and costs.

Web 2.0 as a sharing and exchange platform linked to social media and which enables users to create and share content replaced Web 1.0, which was only informative and not interactive. Web 2.0 will be gradually replaced by Web 3.0 and the so-called semantic webs, whose contents can be processed by machines that link up different applications and systems. And Web 4.0, which features intelligent personal agents, will eventually appear.

Digital transformation goes beyond the organization of tools and technology applications and requires revising and redesigning internal communication and collaboration processes, how we relate to our environment and business models. Executives must be capable of understanding what is going on in their environment, identify practical applications and decide which digital technologies they should deploy in their processes as part of their strategies.

<u>What is really at stake</u>

Between 2012 and 2017, in less than five years, e-commerce at a global level has doubled, and it will continue to grow. Jeff Bezos, founder of Amazon, is the first person in history to amass a net worth of $100 billion.

It is in the interest of Internet service providers and operators that run the networks to reach as much of the population as possible, and that the population have the highest possible education and training level in order for it to be able to purchase products and services online. Technological giants like Facebook and Google are developing their own proprietary communications infrastructure in order not have to rely on traditional Internet service providers. Networks will reach a growing number of people as the world's population continues to rise in the short term and concentrate in cities, even though companies will be able to deliver mobile broadband to remote areas.

The stakes are enormous, as long as technology and tech companies make sure that the costs of accessing the network and the necessary gear and devices decrease so that most of the population can afford using these technologies. The educational and training level, how to employ information and the quality of technology will be the factors that determine the level of inequality in the digital age.

Many of the financial products which caused the financial crisis starting in 2007 – such as Credit Default Swaps, Collateralized Debt Obligations, Mortgage-Backed Securities, Derivatives – could be understood before the bubble burst. Although they were designed by former engineers, mathematicians and physicians who developed the most advanced weapons during the Cold War, very few people had the knowledge to fully grasp how these products were designed, how they worked and the potential negative consequences of their widespread use. And these products were premised on very strong economic and credit growth, which nobody can reliably make sure will happen in the medium to long term.

In any case, the Internet should remain open, in the sense that information and knowledge should be accessible to all. Open-source software is viewed as a guarantee for Internet neutrality and the ability of anyone to access data. But there is a threat that a few giant technological companies could try to take over the Internet, ICT infrastructure and social media.

Another dangerous development is the fraudulent use of information and its abuse to commit crimes. For example, several companies -- such as Cambridge Analytica -- used information about

Facebook users without their consent to develop misleading or false advertisements and target specific constituencies in elections in the United States, Kenya and the Brexit referendum, to name a few. Facebook's response has been slow and tone-deaf. It first admitted months ago that companies purchased millions of advertisements on Facebook. Their top executives have refused to testify before Congress or other parliaments. Their apologies are half-hearted. An executive drafted a memo with the conclusion that Facebook's purpose is to allow for the exchange of information among its users, whatever the national security implications and consequences are. Facebook has two billion users and the current backlash will not destroy it as people want to be able to share information, pictures, content, etc. with their friends.

But Facebook's stock price has diminished, and its bungled response it being compared to that of large multinationals that suffered disasters since 1980, like Johnson & Johnson, British Petroleum (Deepwater Horizon oil spill), United Airlines (assault of passenger and other incidents), ExxonMobil (Exxon Valdez oil spill), Volkswagen (Dieselgate), Valeant (price gouging and inaccurate accounts), Equifax (hack of data from 143 million users), Wells Fargo (fake accounts), Petrobras (*Lava Jato* bribing scandal) and Uber[71].

It is therefore reasonable to believe that stronger and more legitimate forms of global governance are needed, which among other tasks will ensure that freedom of access to the Internet and other technology networks and infrastructures is guaranteed. Otherwise, the Internet will be like a global market without global rules, without an international regulatory framework that ensures the rights of everybody, including needier people.

We should not lose sight of the fact that 80% of the world's wealth is in the hands of 20% of its population. The most advanced countries are those with the highest levels of technology, and which also achieve higher productivity in areas where technology comes up short or is insufficiently developed. I am not only referring to the Internet, but also to other technologies that already exist or are being developed. The Digital divide unfortunately is already a fact. We must ask ourselves whether new technologies will engender inequalities – which they are already doing – but meaningful and real opportunities for everybody. The market economy seeks opportunities for profit where it can find them. Many feel that in order to thrive in a capitalist economy, a company needs to constantly grow and generate more profits, or it will languish.

The future will depend on how access to technology and information is managed, if there are high barriers to entry and access of new knowledge and technology, or whether it will be managed by a few experts. Or if access to knowledge and ICTs will be available to everyone because a global governance structure has been put in place which creates the necessary rules to guarantee access at a reasonable cost to the maximum amount of people. The more people that access the Internet, the more buyers there will be of goods and services offered online, and these purchases will increase the profits of companies that produce or market them.

The G7 and now the G20 could play a role in the global governance of the Internet and ICTs. NGOs and Intelligent Communities or Forums are aware of the key role that Internet and ICTs play in shaping global trends and can contribute to narrowing the digital divide. Local government also has to provide the means to develop networks, foster their access at a reasonable cost and invest in training. The more people that live in countries that achieve real development and growth, the more their populations will be likely to purchase goods and services which will help narrow the digital divide.

---

[71] "Getting a handle on a scandal". *The Economist*. March 31st, page 68

<u>**Sven Oehme**</u>

President and CEO, European-American Business Organization.

Mr. Oehme is a recognized expert in European-American affairs. Until 1998, he served as Managing Director of the European-American Chamber of Commerce (EACC), with special responsibilities for the Chamber's legal department. Before joining EACC in 1991, Oehme held numerous executive positions for subsidiaries of Gruner + Jahr, the magazine and newspaper publishing division of the German media company Bertelsmann. Oehme's expertise includes European Economic and Monetary Union, the Euro and international trade. Oehme is a member of the Executive Board of the Transatlantic Business Dialogue (TABD), which is the official channel between European and American business leaders and US Cabinet Secretaries and EU Commissioners. He is the Senior Adviser for the Northeast Region of the United States for the American Chamber of Commerce in Germany. He is also a Director of the American Foreign Law Association, a member of the Advisory Committee of the European Union Studies Center of the Graduate School and University Center of the City University of New York. Oehme is also a member of the Board of Advisors of the Weissmann Center for International Business at Baruch College. Oehme earned a degree in Economics and Law from the University of Hamburg and is admitted to the bar in Hamburg. He also obtained a Masters of Law in International Business and Trade Law with a focus on European law from Fordham University's Graduate School of Law.

<u>The Demons of Globalization</u>

Globalization has become a term that sends chills down the backs of one group of people, or so it seems, and is seen by another group as a solution to many of the world's current problems. If one takes a closer look at globalization, it describes a process that has been going on for thousands of years. For most of those years people didn't know they were living on a globe. But their world kept on growing, as they encountered new places, new goods, and technologies and finally they realized the lived in a globe.

Globalization can be defined as increasing interaction between people or companies on a worldwide scale. When you hear some people talk about globalization one gets the impression it was only discovered over the last 20 or 30 years. The way many people talk about it today, it has become a scapegoat for all the evils of international trade and investment. But it hasn't always been like that.

Let's go all the way back to the time when our ancestors were living in caves. They were small groups of people living together. Over time the number of people increased and they moved out of the caves into villages and later into cities. As they were moving into the larger communities, it made sense to have people focus on specific jobs. Some continued to be hunters; others became butchers, bakers, tailors, etc. What happened on a very small scale was the fact that people divided the work that had to be done among themselves. Eventually some also became merchants who traveled from one small community to the next, took wares with them and traded them for other goods in other villages or towns.

Moving onwards, the Phoenicians ruled the Mediterranean Sea from about 1500 BC to 800 BC. They brought cloth dyed Tyrian purple with them and also spread an alphabet along the Mediterranean coastline. Ancient Greece developed parallel to the Phoenicians but the focus of the Greeks was expanding their territory in search of more land and of more goods to obtain. Their armies would move on horses and they were to enlarge their sphere of influence to Central

Asia. Wherever Phoenicians and the Greeks went, they traded goods and precious metals bringing many unknown wares back to their homelands. With the emergence of the Roman Empire, the area where merchants operated was much enlarged. Considering the expanse of the Roman Empire, it reached pretty much all the areas of the then 'developed' world. Close to the completion of the 1st millennium the Vikings emerged. They were able to eventually reach North America to the west and their ships may have gone all the way to what Istanbul is currently and perhaps even Bagdad. The Vikings did not leave major cities behind; they did not build a culture that lasted as prominently as many of the other civilizations before and after the Vikings did. But they certainly obtained goods from the people, who they reached, taking goods from those faraway places back home to the northern European countries. They were not typical traders and merchant, but rather raiders.

The Carolingian Empire was established by Charlemagne as a successor to the Roman Empire in the west. On May 7th of 1189 one of his successors, Emperor Frederik Barbarossa, issued a charter to the people of Hamburg which granted the exemption from duty for ships on the Elbe River from the city to the North Sea. This was the foundation of Hamburg as a port city. Merchants at that time were frequently attacked by gang robbers on land and pirates at the sea. The merchants in major trading cities along the Baltic Sea and the North Sea got together to protect their trading routes. This led to the establishment of what is still known as the Hanseatic League. The major trading routes of the league reached from the Novgorod region in the northwestern part of what is now Russia along the ports of the Baltic Sea to London in the West. Included were ports in Belgium and even cities along the Rhine River to Cologne. Trading routes also went up to Norway. From Norway the League was supplied with stock fish, air-dried fish. From the Eastern border of the Hanseatic League agricultural products, minerals furs and other natural products were delivered. There was also a branch connection to the Silk Road coming from China via Novgorod. Cities in the western part of the League in small manufacturing places would use materials from the East to make new products, weave clothing, and make jewelry and luxurious products that traveled to the suppliers.

The cooperation among the merchants and the Hanseatic League led to the establishment of some standards concerning quality and prices, shipbuilding and in other trade related areas. The League also had success in fighting the pirates, thus making trade across the seas safer. While it enriched the people who were merchants and the burghers of the cities that were part of the Hanseatic League over almost 500 years, eventually nation states emerged and became more focused on establishing national rules. The Hanseatic League was never officially dissolved. Some of the cooperation among port cities that were part of the Hanseatic League never ended and was restarted after wars as the merchants and the cities benefited from trading with each other. Trading with each other also meant that goods that were brought in from far away, Asia and the Americas, where sent onwards to the hinterland. Some of the old Hanseatic League cities remain wealthy. As an example, before Hamburg became part of Germany in 1860, it had consular representation in major ports all over the world: in Asia and along the coasts of North, Central and South America. They usually were the representatives of the trading companies from Hamburg that had offices abroad, and the offices would also act as a consulate.

Venice became an important trading city south of the Alps. In 1271 the Venetian Marco Polo, his father and his uncle set out for Asia on a mission that would take them far away for 24 years. When they returned from China, they brought with them many goods, objects and many items not known in the Venetian Republic at the time. Silk from China became popular and Marco Polo had opened what was later called the Silk Road from China. This trade provided a major source for the Venetian riches and allowed Venice to become a capital of trade and culture.

The products coming into Venice were not just restricted to Northern Italy, but they also went across the Alps. In Germany the Fugger family established a serious trading business in the

1450s. With the establishment of colonies by the European powers all over the world, more and more new goods came to Europe. The new raw materials delivered by boat were used for many new products that were cherished or necessary in Europe.

With the invention of the steam engine the Industrial Revolution started. Putting the steam powered engines on boats created a more reliable source of propulsion than wind. Steam locomotives pulling freight trains and passenger trains spread quickly throughout Europe and the US, giving their people greater opportunities to move around and allowing goods to be delivered in much greater numbers and much faster than in the past. The Industrial Revolution was accompanied by new means of communications. Eventually the telegraph and then the telephone were introduced and it became possible to send messages from one part of the world to another instantaneously.

All of these technologies were developed further to what we see today in our totally connected world. As far as global trade was concerned, after World War II many of the former colonies of European powers gained independence and sought to also reap the benefits of trade. Depending on how well agreements where negotiated and how successfully the transition from colony to an independent state was achieved, trade relations between the developed world and the sellers and what is still referred to as the developing world improved substantially. In a number of cases the production of machines, vehicles and other goods was also moved to other countries to be closer to the markets.

The understanding for many years was that all parties would benefit from this kind of cooperation. But there had always been the criticism that the Western countries were taking advantage of the countries in Asia and Latin America and that became a starting point for disapproval of globalization.

In the years since World War II the current trading system was established. In 1947 the GATT (General Agreement on Tariffs and Trade) was created including 23 contracting countries. Among the number of rounds of negotiations that followed, the Kennedy Round, the Tokyo Round and the Uruguay Round established today's system. For the first 20 years the reduction of tariffs between the parties to the treaties was on the agenda. The Kennedy Round added anti-dumping measures and 62 countries became part of it, a dramatic increase. The Tokyo Round concluded in 1979 reduced tariffs further, added non-tariff barriers and included 102 countries. The Uruguay Round concluded in 1994 established to a large extent the current tariffs and trading system. It included agreements on tariffs, non-tariff barriers, rules, services, intellectual property, a robust dispute settlement system, textiles, agriculture, and the creation of the WTO (World Trade Organization) with 123 member countries[72]. A further attempt was made to pursue more open markets in the Doha Round. Negotiations have dragged on for a number of years without success. This failure led to the conclusion that countries which were willing to move ahead started to negotiate regional or bilateral free trade arrangements, such as CETA (EU-Canada, Comprehensive Economic and Trade Agreement), TPP (Trans-Pacific Partnership), EU-Mexico, EU-Japan, EU-Mercosur, EU-Australia/New Zealand, EU-India (negotiations since 2007).

The North American Free Trade Agreement (NAFTA) entered into force on January 1, 1994. It was a successor to a US-Canada trade agreement. NAFTA is now being renegotiated. Over the last almost 25 years e-commerce has been created and trade flows between the three NAFTA partner countries have seen a dramatic increase and change. The U.S. has free trade agreements with Australia, Bahrain, Chile, Colombia, Israel, Jordan, South Korea, Morocco, Oman, Panama, Peru, Singapore, and CAFTA-DR (Costa Rica, Dominican Republic, El Salvador, Guatemala, Honduras, and Nicaragua).

---

[72] The World Trade Organization currently has 164 members.

One of the countries that greatly benefited from globalization is Germany. It is the third largest exporting country in the world behind China and the US. When the European Union negotiated the trade agreement with Canada (CETA) and TTIP with the United States, strong opposition emerged in some of the European countries including Germany. The free trade agreement with Canada was almost scuppered by opponents of its ratification in some EU member states. A part of the treaty still has to be approved and it seems there is new opposition to the process in some of the member states.

TTIP was being negotiated since 2013 but could not be concluded before the end of the Obama Administration. German economics minister Sigmar Gabriel in September 2016 concluded that 'TTIP is dead'. This was a surprising statement since Gabriel was not a part of the negotiations and should have probably restrained himself from making these comments. It is the European Commission that has the authority to negotiate trade agreements on behalf of EU member states. But it is a fact that more than 50% of the population in 3 or 4 European Union member states was opposed to an agreement with the United States. One has to wait and see what fate awaits the new trade agreements that the European Commission has or is negotiating with Japan, India, Mexico, Mercosur, Australia and New Zealand. It is too early to tell. But there is a good chance that the citizens of some European countries will say no and that the parliaments in those countries will not be able to ratify such agreements.

The opposition in Germany is surprising, as almost 50% of GDP is generated by exports and as such by globalization. Why do people want to 'bite the hand that feeds them'? Do they want to go back to the cave that I mentioned at the beginning? Is it the lack of information on what globalization means for Germany, Europe, and the world? Are people fearful of the future? Do they believe globalization will do more harm to the environment? It is probably all of the above and more notions that people may have. Germany has just announced it will not meet reduction goals for carbon dioxide by 2020. Is that the price it has to pay for being a champion of globalization? The US may be much closer to meeting the Paris Climate Agreement goals due to the efforts by cities and states in the US.

Without international trade, the heart of globalization, the world economy will collapse. Whether we like it or not, globalization is here to stay. There are voices from Europe that seem to indicate that the Trump administration is not interested in continuing globalization. That is a misinterpretation and wrong. President Trump has stated on many occasions that he is for free, fair and reciprocal trade. He blames the current trade system for disadvantaging the United States and the significant decrease of the number of jobs available due to the outsourcing of work. Trade imbalances are obvious, certainly with China and the European Union and within the EU, specifically Germany. There are tariff disparities in the system that the Trump administration wants to address. As such the whole system of tariff reductions and trade agreements goes back to the late forties. There have been reviews and changes over time, obviously, but the question remains whether some fundamental issues should not be reviewed and updated to reflect the current trading environment.

The US marketplace is still one of the most open and accessible in the world. Previous U.S. administrations since World War II wanted to make it easy for companies from abroad to do business in the US. It is the goal of the current administration to open foreign markets by tearing down tariff and non-tariff trade barriers for American companies. A further goal is to attract foreign companies to the US which will invest and create production facilities and jobs. With the 2017 tax reform, low labor costs, low energy costs, local and state subsidies and less restrictive labor laws, the US offers better conditions for manufacturers than most European countries. Goods produced in the US can be easily exported. Just as an example, BMW is the largest exporter of motor vehicles and many of those go to China. The focus in trade is always on goods, but all of the above applies to services too.

Globalization is here to stay, and it should, if we want future generations to enjoy a lifestyle that is somewhat similar to the one we have today. But the foundation of globalization today has to be free, fair and reciprocal trade.

Victor Pou

Professor, IESE Business School (Spain)

Victor Pou earned a B.A. in Economics and PhD in Law from the University of Barcelona. He also holds an MBA from IESE Business School and a post-graduate diploma in European Integration from the University of Amsterdam. He is a professor in the Department of Economics and founder of the IESE International Faculty Development Program. Professor Pou was the first Director of Economic Planning, the first Director of Adaption to the European Communities, and the first Director of the Catalan Trust for Europe of the Autonomous government of Catalonia (1980-87). Between 1987 and 2005, Professor Pou served at several senior positions at the European Commission, including as Head of the Enterprise and Industry Unit and Counselor for External Relations. Professor Pou has published extensively on European Integration and International Relations. He has also published books on the agreements between Andorra and the EU (2006), the Andorran economy (2006) and the effects of EU enlargement on the Catalan economy (2005).

In the XIXth century Karl Marx wrote that a ghost was haunting Europe: he was referring to Communism. There is currently another ghost that is spooking Europe and beyond -- and its name is populism. This phenomenon has grown exponentially because of the Great Recession that began in 2007, which in some regards mirrored the Great Depression of the 1930s unleashed by the stock market crash of 1929. The Great Recession aggravated the eurozone debt crisis, and to some extent they overlapped. History does not repeat itself, Mark Twain wrote, but at times it rhymes. The populisms of the 1930s caused the greatest tragedy in human history, namely World War II. Let us hope that the current wave of populism does not result in a catastrophe of similar proportions.

The year 2016 was a true *annus horribilis* for Europe due to the spread of populism on the continent: Brexit, the election of Donald Trump and the growing popularity of populist parties. In the summer of 2017, we can debate whether populism has already peaked in Europe and is waning. The defeat of populist candidates and parties in the Austrian presidential elections, the general elections in the Netherlands (March) and the regional elections in the German *Land* of Saar (March) seem to confirm that populism is in retreat. Emmanuel Macron, who staunchly believes in European integration, globalization and advocates liberal reforms for the French economy, overwhelmingly defeated the populist right-wing Marine Le Pen in France's presidential elections in April and May of 2017.

Macron's party, *la République en Marche!*, also secured an absolute majority in the French Parliament in the elections held in June. Moreover, the traditional French center-right party, the UMP, can also add to Macron's party majority in Parliament. The Socialist Party is in disarray. Macron therefore has a very strong mandate to enact his campaign promises to liberalize the French economy. Labor-market liberalization and privatization of state-owned companies are at the top of Macron's list. Let us hope the predictable opposition by French labor unions does not stop Macron, who also has the power to enact some reforms by decree. The French economy has stagnated in the past decades. Unemployment is stuck at 10%, and youth unemployment stands at 25%. No French president or prime minister has had such a strong mandate and overwhelming majority in Parliament to reform and modernize the French economy and its institutions.

The Financial Times argued in an op-ed before the elections in France that Marine Le Pen's defeat could usher in a change of the political cycle and begin to turn the tide against populism. Macron cannot squander the opportunity that French voters have given him.

Kenneth Rogoff is a former IMF economist and currently professor of Public Policy and Economics at Harvard university. He is the co-author of a brilliant book which analyzes the causes of the Great Recession. He has joined The Financial Times in arguing that the "golden age" of the current brand of populism will soon end. Rogoff is convinced that the strengthening of the economic recovery will seriously weaken populist politicians and parties. Rogoff had wondered whether the populist wave that threatened to sweep across advanced economies could stifle the growing recovery. Or, conversely, whether recovery and higher economic growth will undermine populist politicians who offer simple, unrealistic and harmful solutions to our complex reality. There are therefore many analysts who feel that the threat to globalism seems to have subsided in Europe after the aforementioned electoral defeats of the populist candidates in Austria, the Netherlands and France. German Chancellor Angela Merkel is likely to win re-election in general elections scheduled for September 24th, and the only question is whether she will form another grand coalition government with the Social Democrats or (less likely) with the liberal FDP. At any rate, the populist *Alternative für Deutschland* (AfD) also seems to have peaked. And both the CDU and the SPD have ruled out including the AfD in a coalition at the federal level. Do the stronger growth and the defeat of populists in the elections in 2017 mean that demagogues no longer pose a threat?

We must bear in mind that Italy will have to hold elections either in 2017 or early 2018. The far-left and anti-globalization Five Star Movement will probably do well. Will the left-of-center Democratic Party (PD) of Prime Minister Paolo Gentiloni be tempted to form a coalition with Bepe Grillo's Five Star Movement in order to stay in office if the center-right does not support him?

In 2018, emerging economies like Mexico will hold elections. The results of the renegotiation of NAFTA and the Trump administration's continued harsh rhetoric against Mexico is strengthening the hand of the left-wing populist Andrés Manuel López Obrador, who has twice come close to winning the presidency. Other emerging market economies have to contend with their own populists. Hungary and Poland, who joined the EU in 2004, are currently ruled by populist right-wing parties (FIDESZ and PiS, respectively) that have repeatedly undermined the independence of the judiciary, their central banks, and sought to weaken freedom of the press and NGOs. The European Commission has repeatedly warned both countries that a continuation of such illiberal and autocratic measures could lead to a suspension of their voting rights in EU institutions under article 7 of the Treaty of Lisbon. The Commission's warnings and massive demonstrations in Poland against the autocratic government's proposed measures have prompted the PiS government to backtrack in some cases. But PiS, led by the ultra-nationalist Jaroslaw Kaczinski, will not back down entirely. Surveys have consistently showed staunch support among Polish citizens for membership in the EU. Moreover, Poland is a major beneficiary of the EU's regional and structural funds. It is therefore difficult to understand why the EU Council does not summon the courage to suspend Poland's voting rights, a measure that only requires a qualified majority in the Council. This would send a strong signal to other illiberal governments.

After the failed coup last summer, President Recep Tayyip Erdogan has undertaken a crackdown against real and imagined opponents of unprecedented proportions. More than 50,000 people (including hundreds of journalists) are languishing in jail on trumped-up or false accusations, and more than 100,000 have been suspended from their jobs. In April of 2017, Erdogan called and won a referendum on a new constitution that shifts most power to the presidency (meaning himself) and can enable him to stay in office until 2029. The opposition is divided and cowed by the crackdown.

Fortunately, according to Rogoff, the Federal Reserve's patience in raising interest rates very gradually, the resilience of China's economy and the higher growth rates registered by European economies and the United States in 2016 and 2017 will help most emerging economies. In any case, global growth prospects are improving. Sensible policies should keep the current expansion on track. But it remains to be seen how populism will evolve, and a slowdown in the economy could give a new lease on life to populist parties and politicians.

How can we define populism? Many seem to know what populism is in broad terms, but it is harder to come up with an accurate and specific definition. President Obama denounced populism in a speech and remarked: "I am not sure that a good definition of populism can be found in a dictionary". He then provided his audience with a negative definition of populism when he asserted that "anyone labeling us versus them" or using rhetoric to the effect that we "will take care of you" because the elites do not is only a partial definition of populism.

There is an academic consensus that defines populism as a political ideology that believes that society is divided into two homogenous and antagonistic groups: "regular people" and a "corrupt elite". This line of thinking is based on the premise that the interests of both groups cannot be reconciled, which therefore results in an emphasis on national and popular sovereignty. The populist politician supposedly represents the voice of ordinary people against the elites. On the eve of the presidential election in the United States, Trump rhetorically asked a rally: "Who would you rather have governing America, corrupt politicians or the people?" In Europe, the Brexiteers, Marine le Pen's National Front in France, or radical left-wing parties such as Syriza in Greece or Podemos in Spain have resorted to similar rhetoric regarding a split between ordinary people and the elites. They are trying to forge a new political identity that goes beyond the traditional left-right spectrum and pits the "people" against the "oligarchies", or citizens against political castes. Therefore, all populisms share a strategy of trying to create a narrative of "us versus them". What Trump and Podemos have in common is their claim that the elites have failed people and have undermined democracy. They therefore conclude that people must "take back their country" by voting for them.

It is therefore possible to define populism in a generic way. But there are big differences between right-wing and left-wing populism. The first obvious difference lies in the policies they advocate. Podemos (radical left-wing) and the National Front (radical right-wing) both direct their attacks against a liberal elite whom they blame for citizens' problems. They differ on the kinds of issues they highlight and the policy prescriptions they advocate. A second distinction between right- and left-wing populism is how they define ordinary citizens or the "people". "The main difference between right- and left-wing populism is how they define 'the people', according to Chantal Moufle, a Belgian professor of political theory, and Ernesto Lacau, an Argentine professor of political theory, whose theories have been adopted by populists and Podemos consistently repeats. The "people" can be a civic or ethnic concept. The right tends to focus on the "ethnic" concept. Hence its rhetoric and measures against immigration. The left is more inclusive. It dilutes its definition of the people to something more ethereal.

There is another great misunderstanding about the concept of populism. Do populist measures deserve a category of their own or should they be classified as left-wing, right-wing, demagogic or stupid? Scholars have not reached a consensus. Many right-wing parties have renounced the free-market and free-trade policies they traditionally supported and now espouse interventionism and protectionism. In this regard, they resemble left-wing populists. Some scholars think that the potential success of both right- and left-wing populists fosters social division and threatens liberal democracy.

Why did populism emerge? Analysts have written that populism is grounded in the fear of an uncertain future among broad layers of society. This fear spawns xenophobia, anti-immigration stances and the need to craft easy solutions to address complex and difficult problems. Populism is good at identifying problems, but it is utterly unable to design real measures to address them. The American analyst Henry Louis Mencken famously wrote: "For every complex problem there is an answer that is clear, simple, and wrong". Populism focuses on fostering attitudes against elites, experts and international institutions. Populism is based on nationalism, identity (national, racial, religious, etc.) and a desire to rein in and undermine globalization. It advocates a return to a strong state that protects citizens and provides security. Populism has fed off a toxic cocktail consisting of various elements: an aging population, globalization, the technological changes of the fourth industrial revolution, an increase in inequality (material and in terms of dignity) and a loss of welfare. Donald Trump in his electoral campaign constantly alluded to the "forgotten", those left behind by globalization, and promised them that they would never again be ignored. This message resounded with many white middle-class Americans. Analysts compare the current bout of populism with "the revolt of the masses" that the philosopher Ortega y Gasset identified in the XXth century. They conclude that this problem can only be solved with a new social pact that brings the disaffected back into the fold.

According to the Spanish sociologist Manuel Castells, the Great Recession that began in 2007 and the eurozone crisis "have exposed the system's failures". He is referring to the banking system, European institutions, the political system in general and traditional political parties in particular. "The traditional political parties were participants in the crisis but were unable to manage it. Society, especially the young, began to mobilize outside of institutions. Now we know that there is no turning back and that what is coming is defined. Confusion, yes. But we also strive for something different, whose content is not written."

Castells believes that a real "real revolt of the masses" is taking place not only in the EU but in other parts of the world. Castells asserts that the masses feel neglected by the EU in the face of an unbridled globalization and seek to regain control of their country. *Take control* was the main theme of the successful Brexit campaign. The takeover is mainly exemplified with regards to immigration.

The nation state is making a comeback because it promises old solutions to deal with new problems. It promises to control massive flows of migration by closing borders, to meet the demands of foreign creditors by maintaining or returning to a national currency and to manage trade flows to cope with deindustrialization. Ultimately, the nation state seeks to fulfil a specific and essential objective: more control over and attention to the real problems that people on Main Street are confronting.

According to Chantal Moufle, "Europe is currently in the throes of a populist moment which is a turning point for our democracies, and whose future will depend on how this challenge is dealt with. He argues that to cope with this situation, it is foolish to dismiss populism as pure demagoguery. Instead, an analytical perspective must be adopted. To understand populism, Moufle intends to pursue Ernesto Lacau's analysis, defining populism as a way to build a political construct that establishes a border that divides society into two camps, appealing to mobilizing "those from below" against those "from above". Both Moufle and Lacau agree that populism is not in and of itself an ideology and does not translate into a specific set of policy proposals. Populism is also not a political regime and it is compatible with a variety of forms of government. Populism is thus a way of doing politics that varies according to the time and place.

Considered from this perspective, the recent rise of populist forms in Europe appears as the expression of a crisis of liberal democratic politics due to the convergence of several phenomena, which in recent years have affected how the exercise of democracy is conducted. The first is what has been called "post-politics", a reference to the blurring of the political border between right and left. A consensus between parties of the center-right and the center-left underscored that there was no alternative to globalization. In order to meet the challenge of modernization, the *diktats* of globalized financial capitalism had to be accepted, as well as the limits it imposed on what public policies the state could adopt. According to the narrative advanced by populists, the role of parliaments and institutions that allow citizens to influence political decisions was drastically reduced. The very essence of the democratic ideal -- that power lies with the people -- was under threat. It is in this context of social and political crisis that a variety of populist movements have emerged that reject 'post-democracy'." They proclaim that they will give back to people the voice and power which the elites seized from them. Some of these populist movements employ questionable means and may have dangerous goals. But part of their appeal lies in the fact that they recognize the legitimate democratic aspirations of the public.

Moufle and Lacau regard Le Pen's National Front as nationalistic and xenophobic right-wing populism. Moufle and Lacau do not advocate a return to the old leftism, but rather espouse a new populism. They want to build a new political arena by pitting two groups with apparently irreconcilable goals against one another: "those from below" against "those from above", "ordinary people against elites", and "people against the oligarchy". Those from below are not a "class" in the Marxist sense, but a variety of heterogenous political and social forces. Moufle has written that: "conceived in a progressive way, populism, far from being a perversion of democracy, constitutes the most appropriate political force to rescue it and expand it in today's Europe". This left-wing populism intends to return power to the people without any worry about breaching the law. In essence, it proposes a revolution.

Liberalism is the polar opposite of populism, as Britain's Nick Clegg explains in a recent book. Clegg is a brilliant European liberal politician, the former leader of the Liberal Democratic Party and Deputy Prime Minister of the United Kingdom in the government of Prime Minister David Cameron. Clegg chastises Cameron as the leader who called the Brexit vote, a referendum that Clegg describes as "unnecessary", "motivated by domestic political reasons" and which represents true "British self-immolation". In addition, Clegg states that Brexit could lead to "serious and unpredictable consequences for the United Kingdom, Europe and the West". In his book, titled: "Politics: Between the Extremes", he asserts that if extremism and populism are to be defeated, we need to understand why they have been embraced with such intensity and speed in our country". According to Clegg, "the referendum on Brexit was not a debate about Europe. Nor was it about what country we want to be, open or closed, committed or not, leading others, or separated from our neighbors. The Brexit campaign first and foremost was and is a debate that pits the politics of reason, imperfection and compromise against the politics of anger, utopia and complaint. The latter was victorious in the Brexit referendum. We must urgently identify a path that will lead us back to moderation and internationalism".

According to Clegg, if the right policies are to survive, if extremism and populism are to be vanquished, we need to understand why populism has gained such traction so abruptly. There are many reasons that explain the astonishing rise of right-wing populism. The growing threat from terrorism, combined with the wave of refugees who migrated to Europe, have revealed the impotence and incompetence of many European governments. In a deeper way, since the fall of the Berlin wall, away from the vaunted triumphs of the West and the "end of history", the following years witnessed a remarkable decline in the self-confidence of liberal democracies and market economies.

The onset of the Great Recession of 2007 has proven the clear and present danger of a lightly-regulated and greedy private sector, at a moment in which an authoritarian capitalism -- particularly embodied by China -- is challenging the West on the world stage. Rather than reaffirm our values in a changing world, many European politicians have rushed to praise the successes of leaders of authoritarian capitalism in China. They have thus paved the way for voters in the West to view our own authoritarian, nationalist and populist leaders in a positive light.

There are many reasons that explain the surge of left-wing populism. The damage inflicted by the Great Recession is the main one. Millions of people lost their jobs, savings and homes and they are irate at the failure of governments and regulators to protect them from banks' irresponsible practices. In a single generation, many workers have gone from expecting and enjoying lifelong job security to having to adjust to an unstable and insecure labor market. Rejection of austerity, banks and globalization have spread across society. Dissatisfaction has expanded from the left to the right of the political spectrum, along with a wave of cynicism about politics itself. Some shrewd politicians have been able to build a populist bridge that joins traditionally left-wing voters with those on the right. All share a visceral disgust against the "establishment", meaning the mainstream media and political and economic elites.

There is another, less obvious, reason that explains the rise of populism. It is what the American analyst David Brooks calls "expressive individualism". Another American analyst, Joshua Mitchell, speaks of "the age of exhaustion", a time characterized by peoples' loss of confidence in their leaders and institutions and the entrenchment of a culture of "digital individualism" and "online self-exploration". We live in an area in which "finding oneself", and "retreating to oneself" are more important than engaging with fellow human beings in order to build a better world.

Clegg calls the surge of this kind of populist policies -- on the left as well as on the right -- as "the age of unreason". And reason is precisely, in his view, at the heart of liberalism. He says that "the problem today with liberalism is that optimism, reason and commitment do not thrive in a climate that is dominated by fear".

But Clegg also believes that Europe has dealt with bouts of populism before, and reason has eventually triumphed. Clegg warns that we cannot afford to wait for the pendulum to swing away from populism out of inertia, but rather that we need to take on populism now, so the pendulum will swing back to moderation and reason as soon as possible. Clegg advocates tackling populism in three areas: the economy (a full recovery from the crisis); addressing inequality through a "new deal" between younger and older generations; and a cultural reaffirmation of a liberal patriotism in the era of globalization. The winning instruments for liberalism are public debate, facts and commitment. Clegg concludes by stating: "Reason will end up vanquishing unreason".

Clegg is an avowed Europhile and knows that at the root of European populism lies a dissatisfaction with the operational responses delivered by European institutions to manage the internal crisis and external threats. All Europeans know that there are European solutions to Europe's problems. But European member states often prevent or block European institutions from implementing policies that deal with our challenges. Three areas that require a European response are the governance of the eurozone, the refugee crisis and Islamic terrorism. We need to complete the banking union, make significant progress towards harmonization of taxes among member states and finalize a common European deposit guarantee system. We also need a common European asylum, migration and border control policy. Member states should also foster a genuine European security and defense policy that will cope with threats such as Islamic terrorism.

We cannot safely predict that populism is already on the downswing, but we can be confident that ultimately populism will be undone by the weakness of its arguments, as has occurred in the past.

Eduardo Rafael Sifontes

Professor, OBS Business School

Sifontes is a principal partner of the Latin American audit firm Sifontes, Prieto & Associates. A Public accountant who graduated from the Andrés Bello Catholic University, he has postgraduate degrees in Control Levels for Robot from England, a Master's degree in Corporate Finance in Scotland, a postgraduate degree in Public Finance and Economies in Caracas, Venezuela, as well as a master's degree in Financial Management from OBS Business School. He also pursued computer studies at Cenesco-Caracas and in Philosophy at the Center of Interdisciplinary Studies Araya in agreement with the University of Navarra. He also has fourth-level studies from the Institute of Higher Studies in Administration (IESA-Caracas). Sifontes is a university professor, international consultant and business developer. He served as president of the Opencrom Foundation and representative on several university councils in Venezuela.

Populism as the expropriation of wealth

Panem et circenses (literally "bread and circus" in Latin), in the Xth satire of the Roman poet Juvenal, 100 A.D.

Many people think that politics is the art of the possible and some people justify the means with the ends. Using Aristotelian terminology, elections are accidental. The essential thing is democracy. Populism is autocratic and allows a plutocracy to enrich itself and pretend there is still democracy by showcasing continuous elections which are neither free nor fair. That is to say, many governments use the instrument of elections to make others believe they are democratic, such as Cuba and Venezuela. In these two countries, people vote but have no choice, as the elections are a total fraud. These sham elections allow their leaders to claim they are democratic, when in fact they are dictatorships or tyrannies.

There are many meanings to the term democracy. They are highlighted in the work of Alexis de Tocqueville, and can be summarized as two that the author defines: democracy as a political system (regime), and democracy as a social condition. In the name of democracy, many cover up intentions that do not benefit citizens in the long run. The progress achieved in the past two centuries has required an effort to harmonize society. Although technological development is advanced in many countries, they are in a socially primitive condition. Identity, race, social class, nation, or any element that limits the development of democracy runs counter to the independence of public powers required for the proper functioning of society and the citizens who compose it. Understanding and living under democracy is a vaccine against populism, which makes cyclical appearances.

We have asked ourselves whether modernity is exempt from the risk of populism. For centuries populism has been present in many places. A conscious citizen is necessary, as it strengthens a virtue which will not be overwhelmed when populism resurfaces.

Causes of populism

Pay attention to emotions and sentiments, for in the long term it becomes untenable to emotionally sway citizens against populism. It involves a very high cost which someone has to pay, either in the present or in the future. When the cost accumulates, this overwhelms the future of many since the resources are exhaustible. Some assert that the costs of controlling populism will always be high and that they contribute to lower wages. The mistake is to believe that the investor is the one who pays these costs. What really occurs with a reduction in investment is that it is workers who are primarily affected. Incoherent subsidies are disastrous for societies.

The principle of subsidiarity, initially defined in the Social Doctrine of the Catholic Church and then as part of the European Union's Maastricht Treaty, provides excellent benefits when it can be applied. The problem arises when it distorts the balance between the state and the individual to the detriment of the latter. It then does not allow the individual's adequate economic, human and social development. There are documented cases that maintaining poorly implemented subsidies in order to benefit individuals produce costs and engender even more corruption.

The restrictions the state places foster the appearance of black markets, who enrich a few and whose goods and services are only available to a minority of the population anyway. You have heard the story of the Pirates of the Caribbean. They acted to evade the centralism of customs and the collection of taxes, and therefore reaped greater benefits. Human beings act accordingly when freedoms are restricted, and especially those related to free trade.

There is a correlation between the application of populism and an increase in taxes, a decrease in investment and a reduction in real wages. The result is a general impoverishment of the population. There are variables that complicate this vicious cycle, for example the ageing of the population. In order to support an ageing population, more people have to have well-paying jobs that generate tax revenue. Otherwise, older people or those who are currently working will not be guaranteed a dignified life as pension systems will lack the necessary resources.

We are witnessing the resurgence of many Pericles-like figures in societies who seek to play the role of saviors and promote magic formulae to resolve all the problems and needs of the community. These populist figures supposedly represent the people and cast themselves as the ones who will slay the "antipeople". A recent example of such grotesque populism is the so-called "Socialism of the 21st century" practiced by the late Hugo Chávez and his hand-picked successor, the current Venezuelan president Nicolás Maduro. Their regime represents populism at its purest. Chávez's and Maduro's policies have destroyed a country -- Venezuela -- which had a relatively high income and has some of the biggest reserves of oil in the world. Moreover, Chávez could hardly have picked a worse successor than Nicolás Maduro. Both Chávez and Maduro have employed an essential element of Communism disguised as populism, namely sowing the seeds of hatred between different groups in society. Both Chávez and Maduro restricted economic freedom, made it impossible to earn a reasonable return on investments, and apply strict controls to the exchange of currency, as well as controls on prices, costs and salaries. They have thus placed a straitjacket on the once dynamic Venezuelan economy, and replaced the market economy with a state-controlled economy whose failure they have attempted -- but ultimately failed -- to disguise by pursuing nationalist policies at home and in Latin America and fostering the spread of their so-called Bolivarian revolution by transferring resources to like-minded regimes.

Populism is of course not confined to the New World. It has reared its ugly head in every continent and at different times. Europe suffered a particularly egregious and ultimately devastating (for Europe and the world) bout of populism in the 1920s and 1930s with the policies adopted by Benito Mussolini in Italy, Adolf Hitler in Germany and Francisco Franco in Spain. In an alliance with Imperial Japan, Hitler and Mussolini plunged the world into its deadliest war by attacking democracies and seeking to occupy countries and territories in Europe, Africa and Asia.

Theresa May has also flirted with various elements of populism. Although she was initially opposed to Brexit, after the referendum in June of 2016 she willingly accepted the role of a Prime Minister of the United Kingdom who would lead it out of the EU. This about-face was probably a product of her ambition, as there were plenty of "pure" brexiteers – such as former Foreign Secretary and former London mayor Boris Johnson -- who sought to become Prime Minister in the wake of David Cameron's resignation. It is unlikely that Brexit will yield benefits to the United Kingdom. Before the referendum, the UK's main indicators were positive or stable and London was a great European metropolis and leading financial center which enjoyed the advantages of globalization and membership in the EU. European countries have a significant presence in all aspects and social variables in today's world. To be a part of the European Union is a privilege which benefits everyone. To choose to be excluded from the EU as a slim majority did in June of 2016 suggests that the seed of populism had been sown in the UK.

Despite the fact that many in Scotland sought independence from the UK in the past, 62% of Scots -- and 72% among the young in Scotland -- voted to remain in the EU in the Brexit referendum of June 2016. A majority of the population in Northern Ireland, in southern England and in the greater London metropolitan area also voted in favor of staying in the EU. It was the inhabitants of rural England and older people that enabled Brexit to win. Those who voted for Brexit are mostly not aware of the costs it will lead to: the United Kingdom's mandatory contribution to the pensions of EU officials; financial commitments the UK has already legally agreed to under the EU's multi-annual budget (the current financial perspectives, which run from 2014 until 2020); and payments for a range of items – from European Investment Bank loans to assistance for refugees.

Therefore, the UK will be on the hook for at least $40 billion euros in terms of its "divorce" payment to the EU, and for practical purposes the UK will remain in the EU's single market and common market until the end of 2020, so the real Brexit will not occur in March of 2018 as its supporters want and led the voters to believe was possible.

The result of the election that made Donald Trump president shows somewhat similar behavior. White voters, especially those who live in smaller towns or rural areas, blue-collar workers and the elderly overwhelmingly voted for Trump. One of the characteristics of a populist is that he establishes rules, laws and "protectionist" policies to supposedly "save the people". The populist advocates that state structures must be active and guarantee citizens' rights, while reducing free competition, fixing prices, seeking maximum profitability, and in the end may lead to the nationalization of private production capacity. Hence the populist's strong aversion to the free market, liberalism or the even more demonized neoliberalism, a label often used by left-wing candidates or politicians to discredit opponents in Europe or Latin America.

A society with economic freedoms generates wealth. We can see empiric evidence of this in modern societies: those that enjoy greater economic freedoms have a better performance and achieve tangible results for the benefit of society as a whole. When a society has attained a certain level of welfare and prosperity, it tends to learn to maintain and increase it.

The egalitarian idea does not lead to real justice and economic equality. Equality can be defined as opportunities for everyone in society according to the ability to create value for each person. Many still cling to a romantic vision of equality without realizing that it is not attainable without suppressing personal freedom. Let us review the fortunes of the populist icons of the world in order to prove that they are not really equal to their fellow citizens. The populists' hegemony, and not equality, is in all the realms, whether economic, social, legal, educational, health or cultural. It is crucial for populists to have "intellectual" allies who spin and convey false arguments to the population. These intellectual allies also use euphemisms to pretend that they are protecting the defenseless. That is why we are witnessing how a former bus driver -- Nicolás Maduro -- is the head of state of Venezuela and is responsible for the destruction of a country with so many and abundant economic resources.

The participation of intellectual allies on behalf of populists is important because the struggle over ideas continues to take place. Ideologically, it is essential for populists to maintain their status quo once they are in power. They therefore paint a rosy picture of the country's situation. Populists sweeten their discourse with words that seduce society. But populists are really not interested in the truth, but rather in imposing their vision of the world on a country regardless of the price that this implies.

Douglass North claimed that ideologies are matters of faith and not of reason and are maintained despite evidence to the contrary. Intellectuals are the creators of the arguments and theories that then permeate down to the rest of the citizens in order for populism to be effective. Societies that have had the privilege of economic progress and prosperity and benefit from being part of a free and open economic integration scheme like the European Union, as is the case of Spain, are less vulnerable to anti-establishment demagogues like Pablo Iglesias and his *Podemos* political party. *Podemos* is a neo-Communist party that preaches ideas that have failed in a resounding way every single time they have been implemented anywhere in the world. The *modus operandi* of the extreme left has not been forgotten after their interventions in Russia, Poland, Germany, China and Latin American countries in the XXth century.

The extreme left brutally intervened in the aforementioned countries in the education system, in cultural life, religion and a necessary operator: the media. A communication hegemony can be obtained in two ways: the first one, to nationalize and take over as many radio stations and television channels as possible; the second one, closing the TV and radio stations that maintain an independent editorial line with the excuse that they are owned by big businesses or another ideological enemy or scapegoat. Additionally, demagogues and dictators restrict communication services over the Internet, as is the case in China with censorship of the Internet and inability to view international television channels, hear radio stations from other countries, read posts and content from Western social media powerhouses, etc. This practice is being used frequently in totalitarian or authoritarian countries that pretend to hold elections or hold them with only one party contesting them, as is the case of China, Cuba and Venezuela.

Regardless of whether we call it left-wing populism, demagoguery or dictatorship, its practice takes place in a horizontal manner, with the messaging coming from the top and marketed cleverly. The message from populists is that they protect people, but what they really seek is to achieve and maintain power with the practices that we have described. The result is that they wreck countries. The individuals in the country ultimately pay the cost, and Venezuela is currently suffering a terrible humanitarian catastrophe, with more than four million of its citizens having emigrated to other countries in Latin America (Colombia, Peru, Ecuador, Brazil) and the rest of the world.

<u>Populists as enemies of technology and economies of scale</u>

In order to convey the message that they are protecting the "helpless", populists incur in large expenses in advertising and communications, creating unsustainable activities over time. These attempts to frame public opinion by populists are flashes of mental deformity against everything in mass production. Although populists try to use technological applications, the way they employ them contrasts directly with what globalization stands for. The inconsistency lies in that the populist uses media to spread his or her message, but in the 21st century they also need to flood social media with their messages to ensure their success.

After the industrial revolution, another significant revolution in the history of humankind is the democratization of the Internet. "If you are not on the Internet, you do not exist". The connectivity needs of the population are increasingly intense. The number of people connected in today's world is so large that they are not imaginable even for the most "intelligent" brain that exists on this planet. The presence of technology is so ubiquitous that it is easy to stoke the population's fear of the potential of robots and machines to replace humans in all jobs. Human beings are able to adapt to new environments, but this process requires time, as new challenges must be addressed. According to the European Commission's figures, the Internet grows more than 10% per year in the EU. For every two jobs lost in the digital economy, there is a significant increase in productivity.

<u>Globalization, world and segregation</u>:

Years ago, civilizations were self-sufficient, closed, needed no exchange but widespread poverty was the way of life. Today, several countries are involved in the manufacture of a Smartphone. The development takes place in one country, another one designs the marketing strategy, and the product's components are furnished by several countries. At each stage value-added is incorporated for the perfection of the good which results in benefit for the end user. In the globalization of the 21st century, the factory is China, commercial strategy is developed in the U.S., modes of production are also in Europe and there is worldwide consumption. China with huge economies of scale, very low labour protection standards, and lower costs makes it hard for other emerging countries.

Another ghost that haunts our planet is the technological threat, although it is not a new phenomenon. When the first vehicles were mass assembled, the population was frightened by the loss of their jobs. It turned out that new roles and jobs were created: mechanics, upholsterers, repairers of tires and a vast amount of new jobs. The fear of technology is due to the fact that it is now progressing exponentially.

Despite Brexit, the EU continues to have more free-trade areas than any other power in the world and is the world's biggest exporter. With these realities, let us hope that Brexit was not as bad a decision as it seems, but the variables are on the table and the future does not seem certain. Now the United Kingdom must address some technological deficiencies, since it is in charge of the managing of the processes of the transactions and customs declarations. This is a significant development and can lead to delays in the ports and other customs control areas.

We have described how all populists have a deep contempt for personal freedoms. They attack any activity inherent to free markets and they stifle competition and businesses which have risked capital to develop. Populists neuter companies with draconian laws. Societies that have suffered the disease of populism have learned that political will must be forceful above all, because the long-term results of populism are not encouraging. Everyone in the world is aware of the importance of education, although there is an inconsistency. Many scream from rooftops that education is the most important thing, and when public budgets are analyzed, the allocation for education is not the most relevant. The following is important:

. Investment in training: there are different mechanisms that have been successful, as in the German apprenticeship system, with the technical means and educated for the job, capable of solving problems.

· Allocate resources to training: adequate in terms of GDP and affording it a high priority in budgetary allocation.

· Distribute revenues: subsidiarity must be well analyzed and executed, such as individual freedom. In order to achieve proper distribution of income, everyone must produce according to their capacity. Limitation of income forces governments to execute plans with specific objectives, assigning a management system to take immediate corrective actions with deviations.

· Ensure economic stability: achieved economic and political freedom that boost production and eliminate excessive protectionism that diminishes production. Boost engines that power the economic process. The emotional part is important for economic agents to flow to prosperity, we can see how the psychological "down" after the Vietnam war paralyzed US fiscal and monetary changes.

· Attractive fiscal policy: most of the economic currents rotate in the monetarists and the tax. Regardless of the current fad, fiscal policy must have the same coherence we described in the previous point. A tax serves to stimulate or discourage a particular sector. Its aim is to boost production and tax revenues. We have examples in the United Kingdom, when the state awards benefits to certain products such as the production of films, audiovisual, TV programs, viability of VAT and double taxation conventions. With natural controls that do not open the window for the risk of corruption. If import duties are low, the importer will not try to commit corruption with the Revising Officer as the cost of the operation is minimal.

· Legal certainty must be present to prevent populism. This certainty cannot be the result of decrees, but rather stem from the certainty that the rules of the game will not be changed arbitrarily. The essence of the US Constitution has not changed since it was approved in 1787 (27 amendments have been added).

· Technology: technology is not a fad, but rather a part of the accompaniment of processes in society. Excluding technology is not an option in a world where technological progress is advancing at a very rapid pace.

· A new challenge has arisen: to establish a policy that copes with refugees and migratory movements in view of the great social changes that are taking place in the world. These public policies should be conducted with a change in management, and which includes three fundamental pillars: purpose, commitment and communication.

A communication strategy is central to including liberal factors that allow economic and social agents with tangible results to motivate others and provide continuity. These objectives can be achieved through education and training. A barrier of entry to comprehensive training is the impatience to see the fruits of the effort that has been undertaken.

Leave the area of comfort, that is not necessarily better, but do not let those phantom products of the tradition and invite a paralysis by analysis, is a heroic step that leads to the road of progress, this should activate the virtue of the will to want to choose the good that is convenient for the citizens.

It is important to confront the totalitarianism of ideas that parts of Latin America succumbed to and have been a sounding board to replicate these failed models in other parts of the world. The romanticism of such fantasies should fade when confronted with concrete facts. These facts prove that the wellbeing and prosperity for generating distributed wealth many citizens with freedom to do and bet on investment with free competition.

Eugenio Viassa Monteiro

Professor, AESE Business School

Eugenio Monteiro is originally from India. He earned a degree in Electrotechnical Engineering from the Technical University of Lisbon in 1967. He holds a PhD in Philosophy of Human Actions and Organizational Management from the University of Navarra (Spain) and took part in a Senior Managers program at Harvard University's Kennedy School of Government. He is a co-founder, former President of the Scientific Committee, and former Vice President of AESE Business School in Lisbon. He served as Dean of AESE for 17 years. He is a visiting professor at several Spanish universities: IESE, University Institute San Telmo (Sevilla) and the University Institute Bravo Murillo (Canary Islands). He is the author of numerous academic articles regarding poverty, wealth generation, the World Trade Organization's Doha Round, social initiatives and India. He has authored the book "The Rise of India" and is co-author of numerous case studies like Grameen Bank, Infosys India, Santa Casa da Misericordia of Lisbon, Aravind Eye Care System, Calouste Gulbenkian Foundation, Dr. Devi Shetty and Healthcare Revolution, and the Narayana Hrudayalaya Health City. He is the president of the Portugal-India Friendship Association.

The Organization of knowledge. The world's first university

When I ask an auditorium for the approximate date of the founding of the first Portuguese university, the audience sighs with relief and pride. As we know, the first Portuguese university was founded in 1290 at Coimbra. Then I ask the auditorium about the world's first university. People become restless in their chairs, look down to prevent eye contact lest I put the question directly to them, and wonder whether or not they have a clue. The answer is a supreme surprise: India. Yes, Takshashila University or Taxila had a hectic life between 500 BC and 400 AD in the Gandahar Kingdom where Pakistani Punjab is found today.

With a minimum admission age of 16, Taxila offered 68 different subjects which were taught to a student population that exceeded 10,000. The students came from Babylon, Greece, Syria, China and various locations on the Hindustani peninsula. Highly cultured master's taught the Vedas, languages, grammar, philosophy, medicine, surgery, archery, politics, war strategy, astronomy, accounting, commerce, documentation, music, dance, theatre, futurology, dark sciences and complex mathematic calculus. The pool of famous professors included, among others, Kautilya[73], Panini[74], Jeevak[75] and Vishnu Sharma[76]. Therefore, the concept of an all-encompassing, multi-subject and highly intellectual university was first developed in India.

Another very old university in India was located in the present-day State of Bihar: Nalanda University. It remained open for over eight centuries from 500 BC to 1300 AD before being

---

[73] Kautilya, statesman from centuries IV and III AC; Prime-Minister to Chandragupta Maurya, founder of the Maurya Empire (322-185 AC). His thoughts are collected in the Arthashastra (Cfr. Wikipédia).

[74] Panini, author of the treaty or Sanskrit grammar written in 6th and 5th centuries BC. This work launched the models for classic Sanskrit. In 4,000 *sutras* it sums up the science of phonetics and grammar (Cfr. British Encyclopaedia).

[75] Jeevak Kaumarbhritya (525-450 AC), contemporary to Buddha, he was the first doctor in India's and the world's history (prior to Hippocrates). Studied at the University of Takshila, practiced Ayurvedic medicine and surgery, cared for Buddha and commoners or VIPs alike (Ritesh Kumar Gupta, Google).

[76] Vishnu Sharma, Indian thinker and author of *Panchantra*, a collection of fables for teaching purposes. Thought to have been written in century III BC. Widely translated, in Persia in 570 AD (cfr.YouSigma).

destroyed by invaders, which unfortunately was a common occurrence throughout India's history. Over its long period of activity, Nalanda University garnered much fame. The campus had an area of 1.7 by 0.85 kilometers and 300 classrooms fitted with stone benches to sit on. It was also equipped with laboratories, an observation tower for astronomical research and a vast library named *Dharma Gunj*. The entrance exams were very difficult and only 3 out of 10 students managed to be admitted. Notwithstanding these odds, Chinese traveler Hien Tsang entered in his diary that there were 10,000 students and 200 professors at Nalanda University.

None of the two universities survived until contemporary times. But Nalanda University was re-established at its original site in 2014 having on a 190-hectare campus. Nobel prize-winner Amartya Sen was appointed as its first Dean.

There are some relevant facts that were known and practiced in India many centuries before they would be discovered and applied in the West -- Europe and other countries in its sphere of influence. Because of the high level of intellectual output that the Nalanda university spread, knowledge in the fields of astronomy, medicine, mathematics, trigonometry and human anatomy reached high standards several centuries before they did in the West.

<u>India at the forefront of Science</u>

India invented the numeric system, a system that values the position of the number. The decimal system was developed in India approximately 100 BC. Aryabhatta invented the zero. He was the first to explain the spherical form, dimension, diameter and the Earth's rotation in the year 499. Ayurveda is the oldest known medical school. Charaka, the father of medicine, consolidated Ayurveda 2,500 years ago.

At Siddhanta Siromani, Bhakkaracharya II described the Earth's gravity 400 years before Sir Isaac Newton did so. He had clear notions about differential calculus and the theory of continual fractions. Bhaskaracharya calculated the time it took for the Earth to orbit the Sun hundreds of years before the astronomer Smart. The time taken by the Earth to revolve around the sun is precisely 365.258756484 days.

The value of "pi" was first calculated by Boudhayana, who also explained the concept that we now know as the Pythagoras Theorem in the 7th century BC. This fact was validated by English academics in 1999.

Maharshi Sushruta is the father of surgery. Some 2,600 years ago, he and other health scientists performed complex surgeries like Caesareans sections, cataracts, limb prosthetics, removal of kidney stones and plastic surgery. According to the *Gemological Institute of America*, India was the world's sole source of diamonds up to 1896.

There is a wide range of fields of knowledge that India was a precursor in. The following is a partial list of scientific discoveries or inventions first developed in India. In Mathematics, the Vedic literature is filled with concepts such as the zero, techniques in algebra and algorithm, square root and the cubic root. In the field of physics, concepts on the atom and the theory of relativity were explicitly stated by an Indian philosopher, circa 600 BC. Chemical principles found practical application in the distillation of perfumes, scented liquids, in the making of paints and pigments and sugar extraction. The first compendium on medicine and surgery was compiled in ancient India approximately 800 BC.

In terms of the fine arts, the Vedas were accurately recited, leading to the study of sounds and phonetics. A natural corollary was the emergence of music and other forms of art and representation. With regards to mechanical and production technology, Greek historians identified the use of metallic alloys in India in the 4th century BC. In the domain of civil engineering and architecture, the unearthing of the cities (urbanized areas) of Mohenjodaro and Harappa points to the level of development of civil engineering and architecture. Both thrived into a civil engineering of precision and an architecture that produced many monuments of ancient India.

<u>Post-independence scientific investigation and Applied Investigation to problems of feeding</u>

The government prioritized attention for the prevention of diseases, mass vaccination and fast production of food after India's independence from the UK in 1947. Despite the appalling lack of resources it faced and the complete destruction of the economy when the British left, results would soon begin to show. Unexpected events meanwhile worsened a bad situation: religious strife stoked up by the country's division according to the dominant religion triggered the migration of millions in both directions of the border between India and Pakistan.

In hindsight and with unbiased assessment, we can state that there was something very noxious for the poor population and the country during the initial post-independence years, despite the prevailing mood of goodwill to solve existing problems: the very economic model that was adopted in a bid to end exploitation from the time of colonization and overcome abject poverty. This model implied that production means should remain in state hands. India would rely on *central planning* to organize the economy and stimulate growth. Thus was born a system of *Raj Licenses,* permits for setting up economic activity of any relevant size, which reinforced state control over the economy.

In general, only a few licenses were available. Therefore, interested parties sought to buy favors from government officials. This led to the spread of corruption across all economic sectors -- and there were very many -- that required licenses. The model of *Indian socialism* was a big failure over the forty years that it lasted. It was a period that left the country plagued by corruption and dashed every hope of improving the living standards of the population, especially the poorest.

Indian governments could and should have evaluated the national poverty situation and the dismal performance of the economic model in place -- Indian socialism -- to conclude that a transformation was necessary. As rulers do not starve or face education problems, they remained embroiled in passivity and ideology, thus wasting 43 years. It is regrettable that leaders did not draw any lessons from the failure of *Indian socialism*. On the contrary, they became convinced (such as in Indira Gandhi's case) that socialism had not been properly applied in India. She further tightened the system and nationalized the entire banking sector. A fragile situation for the poor was made even worse.

<u>Production of cereals and vegetables</u>

During the decades after independence in 1947, some worthy initiatives did come to fruition, such as the opening of many *Agronomy Colleges* featuring agronomical development centers. These Colleges offered sound scientific training to advance the practical teaching of agriculture and food production. On the other hand, R&D centers improved animal and vegetable species making available specimens for fast growth and reproduction, revealing the most adequate procedures to increase their productivity.

Further down a reference is made to cereal production that rose steadily to reach today's levels of self-sufficiency. A hefty food security *stock* is kept and there is still enough production to export 20 million tons every year. For memory, a comparison should be made with the 'shame' of 1970 when, due to a failed monsoon, India had to import 9 million tons of cereals!

The drive to produce food in bulk reached its climax when the *green revolution* initiated in Mexico by Norman Borlaug was fully implemented in India. Results soon began to show in cereal production -- rice but also wheat and maize -- whose total production increased five-fold from the paltry levels of 1960 or 1970. (See graph I).

Graph I

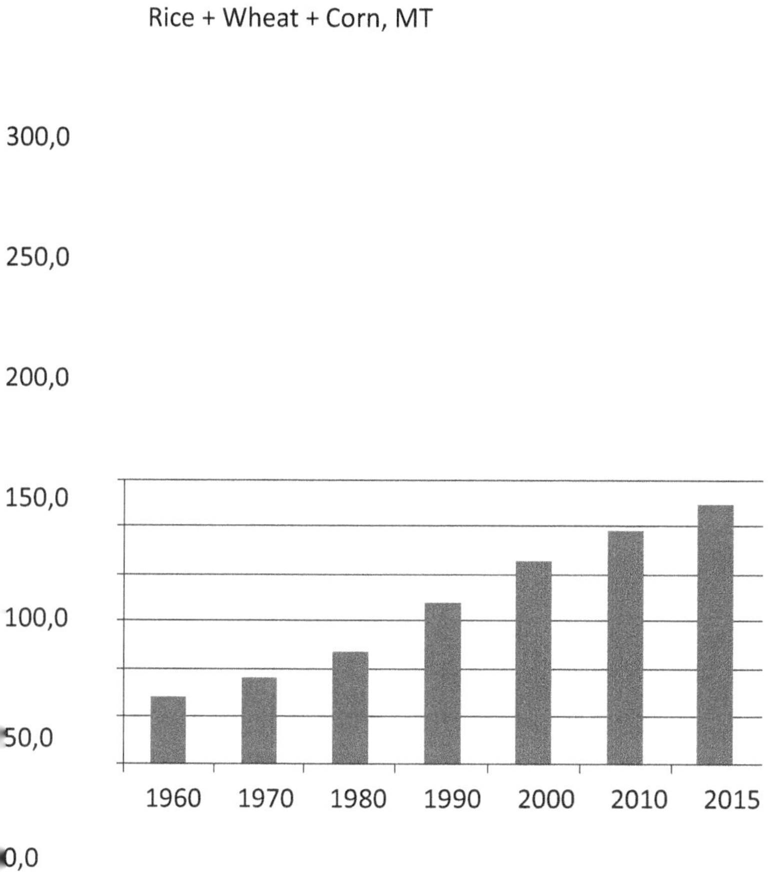

Rice + Wheat + Corn, MT

In addition, the *green revolution* and the associated *mindset* impacted other production of vegetables as well: the idea that species could be improved by making them resistant and more productive using processes adjusted to their development was expanded to the entire production of vegetables: cabbages, sugarcane, cotton, various fruits (banana, mango, citrus, grapes, cashew, etc.), tea, coffee, and spices.

During the decades of *Indian socialism* there was a lack of citizen participation and accountability. As a result, no-one was responsible for anything, and the private initiative of average citizens was replaced by an overpowering state that commanded all. State-controlled enterprises did not generate wealth, were generally poorly managed with no set objectives or accountability. In short, they wasted public money and did not benefit anyone.

There was certainly great protection given to small, mini and micro companies that had not been nationalized. As these did not have the means to invest, they stuck to doing the same as always, staying small, mini and micro. When an end to protection is not in the offing, everything stays still without any urge for modernization. The protection extended to some meant prohibition for others 'fishing' in the same waters; those who had committed themselves to doing something gave up or emigrated as they saw that the path was closed to them.

Generally, Indians are full of initiative and willing to earn their share. Many felt totally alienated living in a context of socialist processes because they were not given the chance to do anything worthwhile towards wealth creation that might serve as a model to others. The availability of private resources -- mainly intellectual resources and the major asset represented by a readiness to work hard -- could have been very useful in raising production of goods. However, the Soviet-style model or system adopted in India system did not allow it.

Large state enterprises were badly managed. When a business has a specific owner and there is no government to pay the bad debts of poor management, he is faced with one of two options: closure or turnaround to financial balance. Public investment was generally channeled to heavy industry based on metal engineering or chemicals. Few results were ever seen because the hiring of managers was based on favors and other staff was selected through political influence. To this day a stark reminder and example is the state-owned flag-carrier *Air India*. The airline is the only one losing money when other privately-run airlines must be profitable in order to survive. The socialist years caused too many bottlenecks and delayed the country's economic transformation. No attention was paid to the creativity and ability of citizens to transform the country across all sectors. Ideas had to seep through from the top, from bureaucrats working their shift.

Citizens did get a break from the government in the IT – Information Technologies and ITES – Information Technologies Enabled Services sector. They were given the green light in this domain because government did not grasp much at all; therefore it did not legislate negatively for companies in their ability to add value that would soon produce results. Several companies became competitive, achieved a boom in exports and later started competing with some of the biggest companies in the world. Jokingly it was common to hear that the Indian economy grew at night while politicians slept; during the day they would only cause undue damage.

Having run out of foreign exchange for essential imports, India had to seek foreign financial help in 1991. The IMF stepped in to provide a loan at the interest rate normally charged and the usual strings attached. The IMF mandated that the economy should open up to domestic and international competition. The outcome could not have been more robust. This proved to be a watershed moment for the country that transitioned from relative stagnation, incapacity and misery to a new beginning producing tangible wealth again, in direct competition with foreign multinationals.

Economic growth began to take hold in a sustained way due to the reforms implemented. Soon growth rates more than doubled compared to those of the socialist era. Between 2000 and 2015, India's nominal GDP multiplied by a factor of five, ballooning from $476 billion to $2,3 trillion.

<u>Milk production</u>

The setting up of the milk marketing Cooperative at Anand in Gujarat State was a memorable success led by Dr. V. Kurien. He was intelligent and dedicated, a strong personality who sought to help poor farmers achieve higher income levels.

Dr. Kurien initially knew nothing about the matter. He went to work for the Cooperative as pay-back for the scholarship he had been granted to carry on his studies in the USA. Soon V. Kurien realized the full potential to generate work and additional income for thousands of farmers in the region. He implemented a business model that was well thought-out in its details seeking to benefit the farmer while upholding the sustainability of the entire system, as follows:

– Provide maximum income to the farmer/producer as payment for his product;

– Put on sale to the general public pasteurized milk and dairy products pricing them affordably to have consumers come back to buy more;

– Collect increasing quantities of milk that farmers/producers brought to the Cooperative incentivized by the good prices they were offered;

– Make microfinance available to cooperative members to enable them to invest in new milk-producing cattle;

– Sell at the village cooperative products required by all its members, bought by the Federation in bulk at cheaper prices;

– Pay milk upfront upon delivery for quantity and fat content; this was very beneficial to poor farmers who could buy what they needed, livening up the area's rural economy with more cash going around.

– Keep tight controls over costs: logistics, pasteurization, milk packaging, fat extraction and the making of butter, cheese, mozzarella, chocolates, ice-cream, baby-foods, etc., R&D, veterinary services, communications, advertising, etc., to fulfil the main assertion of paying the best possible price to the farmer/producer ensuring the sustainability of the Cooperative.

The Federation grew in size with new village cooperatives joining in. It benefited from the comprehensive applied investigation carried out aimed at raising milk productivity and preventing diseases. Great emphasis and encouragement was placed on training cooperative members and their relatives stressing that their children should attend school.

The entire organization was structured in three tiers: local, where the village cooperative lies close enough to cooperative members; district, much broader in area where the Cooperative Union is located owning installations for the pasteurization and processing of milk; and State, where the Federation of Unions managing R&D, advertising, general growth strategy for the State of Gujarat and beyond operates.

It follows as no surprise that results were outstanding, and the concept quickly spread to other agricultural sectors across the states that make up the Indian Union. An unconfirmed figure points to 70 million families drawing a second income from producing milk. All they do is deliver the milk to their village cooperative across parts of the country where the cooperative model has taken root.

Milk production in the State of Gujarat showed impressive growth. Production in the country was energized by the example set by the Anand Cooperative. So too by operation *flood* for which Dr. Kurien's guidance was requested to replicate the model in another three States. The latter kept to the production pace and some even launched their own brand.

Higher Education institutions that support science

In the more complex domains of industry or services, especially of higher intellectual content, the Institutes created by Prime Minister Jawaharlal Nehru were of particular relevance to the country. They would later be replicated and/or expanded in their objectives. As the number of admissions was limited, they became very selective, which added to their attractiveness. From the outset the idea was very encouraging, and India is reaping the advantages to this day.

Higher education institutions were not a 100% success because while students/children from well-to-do rich families could access them, a majority of others coming from poor families were left with little or no education. The government lacked the resources to invest on all fronts simultaneously both in top quality higher education and in the effort to make basic education available to the masses. Perhaps it would have been more fruitful to first extend education to poorer people so as to extract them from ignorance and misery. Only then the rather upscale selective institutions might have been set up gradually.

Children from rich families who attended these elitist institutions (IIT- Indian Institute of Technology, IIM- Indian Institute of Management, Medical Colleges, etc.) would easily emigrate to the United States as conditions there were much better than in India. With an economy stalled by Indian socialism, professional opportunities for young graduates from good universities in India were next to non-existent.

Excluding the ones who emigrated, a majority of graduates from institutions of higher education still remained in the country doing as best they could. When the time was ripe following the opening up of the Indian economy in 1991, they set up their own companies or were hired for positions and eventually led multinational companies in IT, R&D or financial services, which were finally attracted to India by the droves. Their skills, intellectual ability and training enticed multinationals to come to India and develop large-scale operations. They found a workforce with advanced knowledge, a desire for quality work and a sense of duty at pay rates that were comparatively lower.

Role played by super-colleges in advancing Science

The following table shows a brief list of some of the more exclusive colleges or institutes that I deem as *super-Colleges*. The first two, IIM and IIT, were founded in the 1960s and later grew in number while retaining the base concept. Their trainees are highly valued in the US and many filled (or fill) top positions at many companies. A large number of them lie at the root of Silicon Valley's success, an area known for its entrepreneurship and *start-ups.* Vivek Wadva asserted that 44% of the companies created in Silicon Valley belonged to people who had immigrated to the US from India.

– *Tata Institute of Sciences* (TISC) was founded by the Tata family in 1908 in Bangalore. Its prime objective was to develop knowledge and train top scientists. Nobel-prize winner C. V. Raman worked at TISC and later became its Director. To avoid the 'paternity' of the institution getting mixed up with the British, they designated it as *Tata Institute of Science*, a name that would change to *Indian Institute of Science* after independence. By now there was no need to stress that it had nothing to do with the British. To those who may not be aware, this fact highlights the patriotism displayed by the Tatas in full synch with Mahatma Gandhi's ideals and identified with India; the ancestors of the Tata family emigrated from Persia (modern-day Iran) over 160 years ago.

– The Tata Group has made a powerful contribution to the development of various fields of knowledge among which is the investigation and treatment of cancer diseases – at the *Tata Memorial Hospital* in Mumbai. Back in the 1950s it was the only high-quality medical institution that addressed a range of diseases, extending free-of-charge treatment to all citizens. Today it is simply designated as *Cancer Research Center*. Moreover, in the fields of social science, music, and the arts in general, the Tata Group has provided extraordinary assistance, often replacing a public sector that remained under-resourced and mired in socialist poverty for too long.

AIIMSc – The All India Institute of Medical Sciences in Delhi dates back to post-independence times too and is regarded as a model for other medical schools in India and in Asia. Peter Drucker used to say that he thought AIIMSc was probably the best medical school in the world!

<u>The super-colleges</u>

• IISc - Indian Institute of Sciences, founded by the Tata family in 1908 (now Tata Institute of Science);

• IIT (15): Indian Institute of Technology, 8 were founded in the 1960s and a further 7 in 2009, and a few more will open in the future;

• IIM (13): Indian Institute of Management, 6 founded in the 1960s, the rest more recently, in 2009;

• AIIMSc, Medical Colleges (+351 MC). AIIMSC was founded soon after Independence and the other Medical Colleges were set up gradually. Many more are being created to meet current needs.

• IIIT (12): I.I. of Information Technology, 5 founded in 2010 by the government and a further 7 in the as public-private partnerships.

Partnership model. It is hoped that they will soon reach 20.

• IISER (7+1): I.I. Science Education & Research, 8, based on the Indian Institutes of Technology but catering to basic sciences.

The last two types of Institutes started more recently, in the 1990s: the IIT-Indian Institute of Information Technology following the boom in Information Technologies from 1991; the IISER with the massive inflow of multinational companies wishing to do R&D in India.

Today there are likely more than 1100 multinationals carrying out their R&D in India. There were barely 70 in 2004. The reason is not just low pay, but mainly the ingrained typically Indian attitude of *frugal innovation* that seeks to solve any problem in a quick way applying conventional wisdom as well as by focusing hard on it. This is perhaps what has drawn multinationals to doing creative jobs in India, including car *design*, advertising slogans and anything demanding ingenious imagination.

Frugal Innovation is a sound complement to the investigation *mindset*. Despite the need to follow procedures, in India a tendency is witnessed by which people seek to spot the final objective and jump directly to that end position without wasting time on bureaucratic norms. Those working in Investigation understand and appreciate such a mood, especially research managers who prioritize results over completing all the stages.

The higher education institutions mentioned above were responsible for creating an intellectual pool for scientific investigation and technology that paid off early on as a result of very demanding, creative and disciplined work outcomes. The result will likely be a flood in the near future of thousands of new patents registered annually.

ICT Investigation – Information and Communication Technologies

It should be noted that the education provided to the more hardworking students at the best colleges was not laid to waste. They became successful professionals in the US, the UK and later in India too. Furthermore, those settled in the US acted as the perfect bridge with their native India as a major upcoming IT and R&D producer to which many US companies outsourced valuable work to.

We can therefore assert that many remained illiterate in India because they were unable to study. Arguably too many resources were channeled to more expensive higher education institutions, too little for large-scale basic education. The same is true of public spending on health care, which represents a meagre 1.5% of GDP to this day, complemented by resources allocated by India's states.

Although a bit late, this skewed financing system for health care is now being corrected: rich people will always demand more for them and their offspring forgetting about the limited resources of the country. Governments must worry about the needy, offering them tools like education, professional training and access to health care, and helping them seize opportunities to move up the social ladder and earn better money.

IT - Information Technology and ITES - IT Enabled Services

Therefore, India has a part of its population in poverty and ignorance but it also boasts a well-educated large segment ready to engage in intellectual work. They have excelled in Information Technology and ITES-Information Technology Enabled Services as well as all types of BPO-Business Process Outsourcing for the interpretation of imagery reports, clinical analysis, statistical data review, financial data analysis, etc. What I state here is confirmed by the large number of multinational companies that now have a foothold in India in the fields of IT and performing all types of R&D. IT firms provided employment to 3.1 million Indians at the end of 2014 and a further 10 million in IT-related businesses or complementary, according to NASSCOM.

It would be difficult to find a single large IT multinational that does not run a vast operation in India, easily employing over a third of its intellectual staff there. For example, the rather secretive IBM has an

Indian headcount of over 150,000 employees, from a world total of 380,000; *Accenture* with a global total of 330,000, employs more than 120,000 in India. *Cap Gemini* employs 80,000 in India from a total of 160,000 worldwide. Incidentally, besides some others, these three multinationals have their Indian subsidiaries run by a woman! Nearly all the R&D in IT is done in India by very dynamic private entities in line with some of the more advanced companies in the sector. Self-explanatory is the fact that they run their R&D departments in India.

R&D Pharmaceutical Laboratories

Indian pharmaceutical companies have grown consistently. Ruined by the British, India was a poverty-stricken country with a people that lacked the resources to buy medicine unless sold at very cheap prices. The government had to instruct laboratories to learn how to make copies of existing drugs, generics that would be priced cheaply to become affordable.

That learning process enabled them to acquire the capacity to make copies of drugs at low cost. Today many Indian laboratories are preparing their medicine waiting for patents to expire for them to come forward with their generic. For the most part they have gained approval from the US Food and Drug Administration allowing them to sell into that huge market; the American seal of approval works like a passport for exports to all countries. India used to be known as the poor man's chemist shop. Now, it is also for the rich. Broadening the sale of these drugs across many countries makes for formidable economies of scale. It brings advantages to the poor who often do not have the means to buy medicine.

To get a glimpse of production cost and selling price of medicine I will bring up an old episode. In 2001, the then President of CIPLA Laboratories, Dr. Yussuf Hamied, called a press conference to announce that he would price his product for AIDS at $350 for an annual dose. Other laboratories reacted noisily and angrily claiming they had done the research and discovered the molecules of the original drug. They charged him with not having spent on R&D, and consequently having no right to produce it. At the time, laboratories working for multinationals sold their product at $10,000 the annual dose. Dr. Hamied thought he had a moral obligation to not let hope fade for those who had contracted the disease. He remained adamant that he would sell at that cheap price to make it affordable for the poor.

There are Indian laboratories doing research towards finding new molecules for certain diseases. In some cases, they are in partnerships with multinationals. Given the lower pay-scales in India, it is cheaper to do research there.

The Indian pharmaceutical market is now the third in volume and the thirteenth by value in the world. India has become the world's largest supplier of generic drugs, with a 20% share of global exports by volume. More recently consolidation has been taking place in a hitherto highly fragmented industry.

India is now in a strong position. It has a pool of scientists and engineers whose potential will take them far in terms of research and production at affordable prices. Around 80 % of anti-retroviral drugs against AIDS (Acquired Immune Deficiency Syndrome) are supplied by Indian firms. A pool of drug patents supported by the United Nations has signed six sublicenses with Aurobindo, Cipla, Desano, Emcure, Hetero Labs and Laurus Labs (pharmaceutical companies) authorizing them to make generic drugs against AIDS, like Tenofovir Alafenamide (TAF), to be sold to 112 developing countries.

India's pharmaceutical industry is expected to grow at a rate of 15% annually between 2015 and 2020. These growth rates are higher than the 5% expected for the global pharmaceutical industry over the same period. The Indian market will reach $55 billion in 2020 and will the sixth largest in the world in absolute terms. India has kept ahead of China, with exports growing at 7.55% to reach $12.54 billion in 2015, according to estimates by the Ministry for Trade and Industry.

New drugs made by Indian companies and approved by the US Food and Drug Administration (FDA) topped 201 in 2015-16 against 109 the previous year (2014-15), a rise of 84%. India's biotechnology industry encompasses bio services, bio agriculture, bioindustry and bioinformatics and is expected to grow at an average rate of 30% a year to reach $100 billion in 2025.

CSIR - Council of Scientific & Industrial Research

The *Council of Scientific & Industrial Research* (CSIR) is an R&D contemporary institution known for its cutting-edge work carried out in many areas of science and technology. Found across the whole country, it has a large network comprising 38 national laboratories, 39 diffusion centers, 3 premises dedicated to innovation and 5 units. The R&D domains of the CSIR and its experience lie with the more than 4,600 active scientists backed by 8,000 members between scientific and technical staff.

The Institution covers a broad spectrum of science and technology – from radio and space physics, oceanography, geophysics, chemistry, biotechnology and nanotechnology to mines, aeronautics, instrumentation, environmental engineering and information technology. It plays a significant technological role in areas of the environment, health, potable water, food, housing, energy and agriculture.

Having pioneered the country's intellectual property movement, CSIR is today strengthening its patents' portfolio aiming to grab global niches for India in specific technological domains. CSIR has been the recipient of 90% of patents granted by the US to publicly-financed Indian R&D entities. On average CSIR is given 200 Indian and 250 foreign patents a year. Around 13.86 % of CSIR's patents are licensed, a figure that is clearly above the global average.

The Indian central government pays the wages of staff at R&D departments of the CSIR and still helps with the annual budget. Considering the practices in place date from the days of Indian socialism, deep reform is needed in the way it operates to make CSIR more efficient while rewarding individual competence and meritocracy.

How can this be achieved? By creating incentives that will guide research work towards results. Moreover, as some research centers are already doing, by testing their newly-found autonomy venturing into private industry looking for paid work. Such output offers a sense of gainful work provided to society as well as insight into the volume and value of in-house production. In that way, research centers will compete in the market understanding what the market actually pays for the work they are able to deliver.

Highly qualified skilled people holding PhDs and masters are employed by research centers. The approach to encourage the more inventive and resourceful must be adapted to the type of work and organization; however, management must be thoughtful when it comes to setting objectives and providing fair compensation using revenue from work made for industry and that from the budget.

Some laboratories are credited with a special reference for their relevance to the country, be it economic, a matter of prestige or in the defense sector too.

ISRO - Indian Space Research Organization

Set up on August 15, 1969 by Vikram Sarabhai, ISRO is headquartered in Bangalore and its main objective is to develop space technology and related applications towards the country's needs.

It has established two important systems: INSAT for communications, television and meteorological diffusion and the Indian Remote Sensing Satellites (IRS) system to monitor resources and explore them. ISRO has developed two types of vehicles for launching satellites to their geostationary orbits: PSLV-Polar Satellite Launch Vehicle and GSLV-Geosynchronous Satellite Launch Vehicle to get the satellites INSAT and IRS to their desired orbits. The first Indian rocket RH-75 was launched on November 20, 1967.

Up to June 24, 2016 ISRO had already set in orbit 131 satellites, 74 foreign and the remaining domestic. Foreign rockets have also launched 29 Indian satellites to their orbits. Meanwhile a new agency has been created, ANTRIX, whose main goal is to market Indian capabilities, both products and space-connected services.

India today has 35 satellites in active state for signal diffusion, navigation, scientific exploration and meteorology. The last mission was carried out on June 21, 2016, used a single rocket to place 20 satellites into their respective pre-determined orbits. Also, a space probe was sent to orbit Mars (on September 24, 2014) arriving there a year later. The endeavor was successful on the first attempt (not usual with other countries) at the minimum cost of €54 million, and 10% of the cost was incurred by other countries. Future ISRO plans include the launch of heavy satellites, the use of reusable launch-vehicles and space probes for interplanetary missions.

NIO - National Institute of Oceanography

Established in 1966, it grew gradually and today boasts among its staff 170 scientists (staff strength approved is 200) of whom 120 hold PhDs. They are backed by about 210 technical and support staff and 120 administrative staff. The main campus is located at Dona Paula, Goa, where 80% of personnel is stationed. There are three regional centers in Mumbai, Kochi and Visakhapatnam that make up for the remaining 20% of NIO staff.

Understanding the oceanography of the northern Indian Ocean is important. It is a rather small tropical basin swept by strong seasonal winds: the top 200-meter layer (oceans have an average depth of 400 meters) comprises the more active section of the ocean. Currents there are driven by the winds and microscopic plants pushed by them give rise to complex interactions that far outreach current disciplines of knowledge. Thus was originated biogeochemistry of the oceans. Some of the best quoted research work carried out by the NIO refers to aspects of the ocean's top layer such as its circulation and biogeochemistry.

NIO already has about 50 registered patents (www.nio.org), 60% of which are on studies on sea biotechnology. The organisms living in sea environments contain a number of molecules that may be beneficial for the development of health products. This is one of NIO's new research areas. NIO has equally done meaningful work for Indian industry, for state-owned ONGC- Oil and Natural Gas Corporation in particular, with a view to setting down an oil pipeline from the first offshore petroleum field at Bombay High. Research work at NIO could underpin students of PhD programs working as assistants and also PhDs who supervise research works. Many universities recognize the NIO as a center for Research geared to PhDs; about 50 scientists of its staff are referenced as research supervisors by those universities.

BARC-Bhabha Atomic Research Centre

The *Bhabha Atomic Research Centre (BARC)* is the first center for nuclear research in India located in Trombay, Mumbai, Maharastra State. BARC is a multi-disciplinary research center with ample infrastructure prepared for advanced research covering a wide range of nuclear sciences, engineering and related fields.

Its prime specific objective is to take full advantage of the peaceful use of nuclear energy, especially power production. The research center encompasses all forms of power generation, from the reactor's model. The computerized model and simulation, risk analysis, development and testing of materials used in the new reactor's fuel. It also carries out research on nuclear fuel produced, its processing and safe preservation of nuclear waste. Other areas reviewed refer to the application of isotopes in industry, medicine and agriculture. BARC operates several research reactors around the country.

Conclusion

It is not only about a heritage from a past that witnessed a high level of scientific development. Since India's independence in 1947 there has been a renewed and focused thrust given to various sectors as referred to in this contribution.

There is a lot of research being done by private companies delivering positive results in terms of registered patents. Many multinational corporations paved the way and work is being directed that way: matter-of-factly speaking, it may be interesting to learn, experiment, write articles in reference publications and more. But what truly matters is to register patents for inventions made because it earns money and, in its own right, spells the creation of wealth.

A patent already is a trading value, the tangible result of targeted and witty research carried out. In the public sphere there are many laboratories doing valuable work. However, the perception is that they are not focused on results that would qualify for new patents and leading to wealth creation and the well-being of humanity. At independently-run state laboratories, managers should have a more entrepreneurial mentality to add to their scientific strand. Such entrepreneurial prowess is not hard to find in India.

In my view that should be the main priority and battleground over the coming years: the search for efficiency, quantified results and the provision of adequate incentives to those who deserve them. This can be a game-changer in scientists' mentality to incorporate result-oriented entrepreneurial acumen.

It is natural that all, including scientists, understand that the country and society as a whole need to undertake qualitative leaps forward. These alone will incorporate new products, new processes and services that will deliver benefits to society in health, food production, housing, infrastructure, education and youth training. In every domain, there is a lack of sustained progress to cut back costs while offering effective solutions to many of the existing problems.

<u>**Epilogue**</u>

As of July 29th, 2018, the consequences of the application of tariffs by the United States and the reprisals adopted by the affected countries are beginning to be felt by ordinary citizens and can be quantified. At the G20 Finance Ministers' meeting in Argentina, IMF Managing Director Christine Lagarde presented a report that concludes that protectionist measures will subtract 0.5 points from global GDP growth in 2018.

Farmers in the state of Iowa will lose $560 million in the pork sector alone in 2018. In 2017, the EU, China, Canada and Mexico imported $74.5 billion worth of agricultural products from the US, more than half of the total agricultural exports from the world's leading economy. These four U.S. trading partners (China, EU, Canada, Mexico) have already imposed tariffs on US exports of, among other products, soybeans, pork, wheat, corn, orange juice, cranberries, beans, whiskey and nuts, which will particularly affect the states of California, Louisiana, Washington, Texas, Illinois, Iowa, Kansas, Nebraska, and Florida.

The net income of the American agricultural sector has plummeted by 50% in the last five years, partly due to the decline in cereal prices. The price of soybeans has fallen to its lowest level in a decade. The solar industry association, for its part, predicts that tariffs on the import of solar panels will destroy 23,000 jobs in the US by 2018.

The main stock market indices take a beating with each new announcement or implementation of tariffs. But they have recovered substantially from the February 2018 sell-off and have factored in the initial rounds of tariffs (steel, aluminium and reprisals from China, EU, Mexico and Canada). But the aforementioned figures pale in comparison to the job losses that would occur if the Trump administration slaps exports of EU vehicles and parts with a 25% tariff and applies tariffs on $200 billion of Chinese exports. To date, the Trump administration has escalated the trade skirmishes especially with China, which at the beginning of July was hit with tariffs on $34 billion worth of exports. Beijing promptly retaliated with its own tariffs on exports of US agricultural products worth a similar amount.

The prestigious Peterson Institute for International Relations predicts that the vehicle tariff would lead to the loss of 195,000 jobs in the US automotive sector over the next three years.

If the countries slapped by US tariffs on vehicle imports were to respond with their own retaliatory tariffs, vehicle production in the US would fall by 4% and 624,000 jobs would disappear. German chambers of commerce highlight that the Mercedes, BMW and Volkswagen plants in the US employ 160,000 Americans and that 60% of the vehicles manufactured in these factories are exported.

The nonprofit Tax Foundation predicts that, if all the promised tariffs (on EU vehicles and on $200 billion of Chinese exports) come into effect, $110 billion will be subtracted from U.S. GDP and job losses will amount to 314,479.

The world's largest business association, the US Chamber of Commerce, warns that 1.8 million Americans would lose their jobs in the first year of a trade war, and another 2.6 million would be at risk. The Consumer Technology Association and the National Federation of Retail estimates that tariffs already in place with China will destroy 134,000 jobs, 67,000 of which in the agricultural sector. Such projections would make any politician's hair stand on end.

US trading partners should be aware that president Trump's threats are often not a bluff. His opposition to free trade was already part of his stump speech years before his presidential candidacy. Trump is aware of the stock market losses, as well as warnings from business associations and chambers, farmers, Republican Party leaders and experts. The President has gone on the record in one interview (with CNBC) as stating that the stock market losses might have to be a price worth paying in order to achieve the free and fair trade he covets.

Despite all of the controversial measures president Trump has announced in the last 18 months, approximately 40% of the electorate continues to support him, and over 80% of Republicans approve of his policies. The latest Quinnipiac poll, however, shows that 58% of the electorate disapproves of Trump. This number has risen since the summit meeting held between President Trump and president Vladimir Putin in Helsinki, and as the tariffs start to produce real harm to US farmers.

The president is convinced that the lowest unemployment rate in 40 years (4%), a 2.8% GDP growth forecast for 2018 and the tax cuts will allow him to win the trade wars. The agreement reached between the US and Mexico on a new trade agreement that replaces NAFTA seems to have emboldened Trump to go on offense again with regards to China. Mexico has accepted discarding NAFTA's dispute-resolution mechanism (national courts will render verdicts in investor-country warngles), increasing the requirement for regional (US or Mexican) components for vehicle manufacturing from 62% to 75% to avoid tariffs. The US also will have the right to apply tariffs if vehicle exports from Mexico to the US exceed 2.4 million yearly units, above the 1.8 million figure for 2017. Forty percent of workers assembling vehicles will have to make at least $16 per hour to avoid tariffs. The Trump administration has backtracked on a particularly disruptive demand. The new agreement will not expire after five years, but rather after sixteen.

Canada has at the time of writing not agreed to join the US-Mexico agreement. Trump has threatened to apply tariffs of 25% on vehicle exports to the US if its northern neighbor does not join the agreement. US trade negotiatiors are demanding a dismantling of the subsidies that Canada pays to its producers of dairy products. The agreement has to be ratified by each country's legislature. Incoming Mexican president Andres Manuel López Obrador has signaled that he will respect the treaty. Securing Senate approval will prove to be a harder task. If Canada does not join, 60 senators need to vote to confirm the treaty. This implies that Republicans will need some Democrats to back a trade deal negotiated by the Trump administration. If Canada does join, 51 votes will suffice.

Although the mid-terms are less than two months away, Trump probably feels that he is "winning" his trade wars, especially after Mexico accepted the aforementioned provisions and a new treaty. This is the only rational way to explain Trump's intention of slapping a 10% tariff on $200 billion of Chinese exports. This represents a major escalation, as the earlier tariffs on Chinese exports had affected only $34 billion in exports. Chinese goods subjected to the new tariff include internet technology products and other electronics, printed circuit boards and consumer goods such as furniture and lighting products, tires, chemicals, plastics, bicycles and car seats for babies. Beijing will obviously announce its own retaliatory tariffs on an equivalent amount of US exports. Donald Trump has even hinted that he is ready to subject an additional $267 billion of Chinese exports to higher tariffs. If this occurs, China's entire $506 billion in exports to the US in 2017 would be affected by tariffs. This would spark a major trade war between the world's two biggest economies. The US president is apparently unaware that China's reliance on exports to the US has diminished substantially in the past decade. Beijing can redirect its exports elsewhere, wheareas US farmers will be forced to pay tariffs regardless of their export destination, as the EU, China, Mexico and Canada have slapped tariffs on US agricultural exports. Treasury Secretary Mnuchin is attempting to maintain negotiations between Washington and Beijing from collapsing. But his boss must really believe that there will be no blue wave on November 6th and that US consumers, farmers and businesses will accept the pain inflicted by the trade wars.

It remains to be seen whether Republicans pay a big or small political price in November – loss of control of the House of Representatives – partly because of the administration's trade battles. With less than two months to go until the mid-terms, most independent and prestigious political forecasters are predicting that the Democratic Party will regain control of the House of Representatives. There are forty-two seats left open by Republicans who are either retiring or seeking another elected office. Democrats need a net gain of 23 seats to recapture the majority. Charles Cook, author of the respected Cook Political Report, has stated that there is a 70% chance the Democrats will retake control of the House in November. Professor Larry Sabato of the University of Virginia is making similar predictions. Analysts always underline that fundraising for this electoral cycle for Democratic candidates is very high, as is grass-roots enthusiasm. A record number of women are running for office, especially in the House of Representatives. But fundraising and enthusiasm must translate into participation on Election Day. Actually getting people out to vote is always the key, and younger voters (who trend Democrat) are less reliable than older ones (who trend Republican). Hence, projections of a Blue Wave must be seriously questioned. It is true that the party that occupies the presidency historically has almost always lost seats in the first mid-term of the president's first term. It happened most recently to President Barack Obama.

But Republicans in 2018 can run on a vibrant and robust economy, a tax cut, the appointment of conservative Supreme Court judge Neil Gorsuch (and the possible confirmation of another, Brett Kavanaugh), the elimination of regulations (especially environmental ones) and more arguably achievements in foreign policy (from a GOP perspective) such as a stop to North Korea's launching of missiles (and release and return of arrested and deceased Americans, respectively) and Iran's apparent inability to react to the US withdrawal from the nuclear deal.

Some headline numbers on the economy are undisputably excellent: A 40-year low unemployment rate (4%) trending downwards (4%) and near record-low unemployment for Hispanics and African-Americans; an increase in wages in many sectors of the economy; relatively low inflation, despite an uptick in energy prices; a tax cut for the middle class that has also boosted corporate investment and profits; and an acceleration of GDP growth from 2.3% in 2017 (1.6% in 2016) to a projected 2.8% in 2018.

There are however caveats in the medium term. In the next months energy prices could rise, especially if tensions with Iran ratchet up and key producers such as Venezuela, Irak and Libya continue to struggle to increase production. America's growing energy independence does not negate the fact that a concerted Russian-led campaign to achieve higher oil prices – combined with the aforementioned factors – can only be stopped with a strong Saudi hike in production.

The unemployment numbers are fantastic. But the labor participation rate is still below the historical average. Moreover, many middle and lower-class Americans will pay higher interest rates on their mortgages, credit-card and other debt, offsetting to a certain extent the one-off income gained from the tax cut and the still modest wage rises.

The Trump administration will trumpet the 4.1% GDP growth rate in the second quarter. But this figure is an outlier. Many US farmers and companies have rushed to export crops and products before the retaliatory tariffs kick in — such as Chinese tariffs on US exports of soyabeans. In addition, prices of products which use steel and aluminium are going up, making vehicles and cans (among many products) more expensive. GDP is made up of consumption, net exports, government spending and investment. The first two items will inevitable decrease in the next quarters. Companies have also increased their inventories in the second quarter to prevent having to pay for goods that will henceforth pay tariffs to be imported into the US.

The apparent pause in the Trump administration's imposition of tariffs is welcome. President Trump decided not to apply tariffs on exports of EU vehicles and parts. But I am convinced that he did so because of his recognition that American farmers are very upset at losing their export markets. His proposal to compensate farmers with $12 billion was poorly received. A deal to salvage NAFTA appears within reach, but such statements were made in the spring. It is obvious the president will not slap tariffs worth $200 billion on China before the mid-terms.

There is a common denominator in the achievements and progress of the Trump presidency. The gains are assured in the near term, but the probability of sustaining them in the medium term (even until the end of 2018) is low. Inflation will likely rise, Americans will face mounting interest payments on their debts given the Fed's decision to raise rates three times in 2018 and the pain from the tariffs will mount with every passing month, even if no new tariffs are applied. The tax cut is temporary for the middle class.

Similarly, the supposed foreign-policy achievements will be hard to build on. Kim Jong Un might not test more missiles, but he will not negotiate the elimination of his nuclear arsenal of severan dozen warheads, and even a real and verifiable freeze is unlikely. Iran will continue its harassment of shipping in the Persian Gulf. And President Putin will undoubtedly ramp up his destabilizing measures after the staging of the successful World Cup.

In sum, a Democratic majority in the House is likely. House races in suburbia will be tough for Republicans, and president Trump's desire to campaign could backfire, as his approval among independents and moderate Republicans has diminished. The picture in the Senate is different. Democrats are defending many vulnerable seats in red states that Trump carried by big margins. Incumbent democratic Senators Joe Donnelly (Indiana), Claire McCaskill (Missouri), Heidi Heitkamp (North Dakota), Joe Manchin (West Virginia), Bill Nelson (Florida), Jon Tester (Montana) are all vulnerable, and even if just three of them lose, a Democratic majority in the Senate would be unattainable. Senate races are much easier for president Trump to campaign for, as small towns and rural areas proportionally have more weight than in the House and are the pillar of his base.

After the mid-terms, with a probable Democratic majority in the House, president Trump will not be impeached, but his agenda will be stymied. If the Democratic gains are small, the Republican party establishment will remain terrified of antagonizing president Trump's base. In such a scenario, the U.S.'s trade partners and allies must be committed to maintaining all communications lines with Washington open for the sake of the international economy after the mid-terms and throughout 2019 and the beginning of 2020.

I have endured terrible hardship at my condominium in Oxon Hill, Maryland since November of 2013. Two violent squatters subjected me to multiple assaults, harassment, yelling, threats and basically made it quite unbearable for me to be able to live in my own home. I was not even safe in my own room. My fitness program, which involves jogs of 20 km every week and cold showers since 1997, enabled me to survive this ordeal. My extraordinary endurance and great health – I never get sick – are the main reason I am still well. But the destruction caused by the two individuals to my condominium has been extensive, and my economic losses very high. Four years of assaults and verbal abuse also took a toll on my usual ability to work very hard, although I continued to live a normal and quite active life.

I am especially disappointed that the only remaining member of my family was not willing to come to my aid. Evicting a violent person is a very traumatic experience. I needed somebody who cared about me to spend at least one month in the apartment so I could try to successfully evict the squatters. I did try on numerous occasions and had been successful but absurdly dropped the charges believing the person was contrite and would leave.

The heroism and sacrifice displayed by Senator John McCain during his life helped me to put my suffering in perspective. Here is my tribute to a true American hero. It is an op-ed which was published in a Spanish newspaper a few days after he was buried at the grounds of the US Naval Academy in Annapolis.

As the son and grandson of four-star admirals, John McCain III graduated in 1958 among the last of his class from the Naval Academy in Annapolis, on whose grounds he is now buried alongside his best friend, Admiral Chuck Larson. McCain was handsome and arrogant as a young Navy pilot. In October of 1967, on his 23rd bombing mission over North Vietnam, he was shot down. He incurred injuries he would have to bear the rest of his life before he even landed in a lagoon in Hanoi and was savagely bayoneted. He was tortured by the North Vietnamese in an infamous prison dubbed the "Hanoi Hilton". His captors, aware that his father was in charge of the US Navy in the Pacific, offered to release McCain hoping to pull off a propaganda coup. But McCain was faithful to the code of conduct according to which he would be freed when his turn came. The retaliation by the North Vietnamese for rejecting the offer was more than five years of brutal torture and solitary incarceration for McCain. With the end of the war in 1973 he finally came home, limping and aged, but humble and grateful to be alive. He served two terms in the House of Representatives representing his adopted state of Arizona before being elected senator in 1986. He was re-elected to the Senate five times, thus accruing 33 years of service in a chamber (the Senate) whose current Democratic leader (Senator Chuck Schumer) has proposed renaming a building in McCain's name. McCain was a multilateralist and staunch supporter of the transatlantic relationship, of the international institutions created after World War II, and a tireless fighter in upholding human rights around the world. In his three decades in the Senate he served as chairman or ranking member of the Senate Armed Services, Foreign Affairs and Commerce committees. He worked with Democratic senators to limit campaign spending (McCain-Feingold Act of 2002), confronted tobacco multinationals and ensured that war veterans receive the assistance and care they deserve. He teamed up with Democratic Senator John Kerry to pave the way for Bill Clinton to re-establish diplomatic relations with Vietnam in 1995. He angered conservatives in his Republican Party with his independence and determination to work with Democrats, also on unsuccessful projects such as immigration reform. After beating George W. Bush in the 2000 New Hampshire primary by 19 points, his opponent's campaign machinery employed dirty tactics in South Carolina, such as attributing his adopted daughter Bridget to a non-existent extramarital relationship. Defeating Barack Obama after eight years of Republican presidency in the midst of the financial crisis in 2008 was an almost impossible mission. McCain wanted his Democratic friend and senator Joe Lieberman as his vice-presidential running mate in 2008, but his advisers convinced him that such a move would severely disrupt the GOP convention. He warmly praised Obama at a public dinner three weeks before losing the 2008 election to him. He mentored numerous senators, both Republican and Democrat. Despite being treated as a statesman on his foreign trips, he never lost his sense of humor, self-effacing wit and capacity for self-criticism. He endured his wounds from Vietnam - he could not raise his arms above shoulder level - with exemplary stoicism and optimism. He fought bravely against brain cancer since 2017 and repeatedly rebuked president Donald Trump's actions. McCain delivered in dramatic fashion the negative vote that doomed President Trump's attempt to replace Obamacare. McCain always placed sense of duty and patriotism ahead of personal preferences. Although sometimes grumpy and with a strong personality, he served his country for sixty years with passion and perseverance. He always urged others to devote themselves to causes greater than personal ambitions. The world has lost a statesman and the United States a true hero.